THE POLITICAL ECONOMY
OF EAST ASIA

THE POLITICAL ECONOMY OF EAST ASIA
STRIVING FOR WEALTH AND POWER

Ming Wan
George Mason University

CQ PRESS

A Division of Congressional Quarterly Inc.
Washington, D.C.

CQ Press
1255 22nd Street, NW, Suite 400
Washington, DC 20037

Phone: 202-729-1900; toll-free, 1-866-4CQ-PRESS (1-866-427-7737)

Web: www.cqpress.com

Cover: Auburn Associates, Inc., Baltimore, Maryland
Maps: International Mapping Associates

♾ The paper used in this publication exceeds the requirements of the American National Standard for Information Sciences—Permanence of Paper for Printed Library Materials, ANSI Z39.48-1992.

Printed and bound in the United States of America

11   10   09   08   07   1   2   3   4   5

Library of Congress Cataloging-in-Publication Data

Wan, Ming
    The Political economy of East Asia : striving for wealth and power / by Ming Wan.
        p. cm.
    Includes bibliographical references and index.
    ISBN 978-1-933116-91-4 (alk. paper)
    1. East Asia—Economic policy.   2. East Asia—Commercial policy.   3. East Asia—Foreign economic relations.   I. Title.

    HC460.5.W3476 2008
    330.95—dc22   2007033250

For Maggie

CONTENTS

TABLES, FIGURES, AND MAPS

Tables

Figures

Maps

I have written this book not only because the political economy of East Asia is a fascinating subject but also because I was unable to find a textbook that matched the way I approached the subject in my teaching. There certainly are good works on East Asian political economy, but they tend to be highly specialized; most of the textbooks that exist are comparative studies of the political economy of individual countries in the region. By contrast, although I have introduced comparisons of individual countries in my teaching, I have tended to organize my lectures on East Asian political economy around issues of trade, production, finance, and money, as well as the economic miracle and the financial crisis. Students interested in East Asia need to be introduced to the political economy of these issues because East Asia has become an economic center on par with North America and Europe. To understand East Asian politics, we need to avoid studying East Asian countries in isolation. Rather, we need to understand how regional economic forces have shaped political developments and vice versa. An international political economy approach also allows the introduction of exciting theories in this vibrant subfield. The book you hold in your hands takes this approach.

I had expected this book to be difficult to write, but it turned out to be even more daunting than I had anticipated once I began serious work on it. Such a project demands far more expertise in a broader range of issues than I was prepared for, despite the fact that I've been teaching and researching in this area for more than ten years. Exploring East Asian political economy is like wandering around a massive palace: you open one door only to find several others leading to yet more rooms, each containing scholars actively debating each other. I ended up learning much about the field, particularly those subjects I had not committed much time to previously.

At times I felt discouraged about my ability to write a book that would do sufficient justice to what has happened to East Asia's political economy and to the cumulative scholarship in the field. I found that the only way I could move forward was to tell myself that this book was all along meant to be an *introduction* to East Asian political economy rather than the final word on the subject, an impossible task in any case. So, very much like a professor taking students on a field trip,

I've tried to explain a little bit of everything while highlighting the most important issues and ideas in order to give readers a strong overarching sense of the field. I've developed some common themes that run throughout the book as well—the importance of understanding how and why the region's national political economic institutions evolved the way they have, and the interplay among domestic, regional, and other foreign sources of influence—in an effort to help readers tie the material together. I'm confident that students who find a room particularly fascinating can always go back to learn more.

I know from experience that many students are unfamiliar with East Asian history, let alone its political economy. To address this, the book begins with two chapters that lay the foundation for later material: Chapter 1 outlines the political economic approach, while Chapter 2 looks at each country's national political economy and discusses how these institutions have evolved. The second part of the text then takes a look at the political economic history of the region, with particular emphasis on the effects of an earlier Chinese world order, and then under the influence of Western and Japanese imperialism. I cover recent issues as well, focusing in particular on the East Asian miracle and the region's subsequent financial crisis and reform and recovery efforts. With this theoretical and historical context in mind, the third part of the book looks in turn at issues of production, trade, and finance; lastly, it examines the regional interplay of all of those instruments.

Though the book discusses each of the fifteen countries in the region—Brunei, Cambodia, China, Indonesia, Japan, Laos, Malaysia, Myanmar, North Korea, the Philippines, Singapore, South Korea, Taiwan, Thailand, and Vietnam—readers may notice that there is, in general, more attention paid to China and Japan than to some of the others. My choices here necessarily reflect my own background as well as the relative availability of scholarship. There is simply far more material on Northeast Asia, particularly China and Japan. Throughout, I have nonetheless sought a balanced discussion in the book as well as one that is attentive to the region as a whole. In any case, I recognize and assume that instructors will choose to emphasize some countries or some issues rather than others and may wish to assign additional readings. For this purpose, I have supplied an extensive list of suggested reading materials at the end of each chapter.

ACKNOWLEDGMENTS

I want to thank Charisse Kiino of CQ Press for making this book possible. Charisse approached me several years ago with the idea of writing a textbook for CQ Press. Once I was ready to write, she supported the project and gave detailed suggestions. My thanks also go to Elise Frasier of CQ Press for helping develop the book project, to Elaine Dunn for her careful copyediting of the manuscript, and to Talia Greenberg for handling the book's production. Last but not least, I am grateful for the constructive comments from the reviewers of the book proposal and the complete manuscript, including Donald Crone, Scripps College; Joseph Fewsmith, Boston University; Kathryn Ibata-Arens, DePaul University; Timothy Lamperis, St. Louis University; Anne T. Sloan, Middle Tennessee State University; Hong Ying Wang, Syracuse University; and Ka Zeng, University of Arkansas; as well as a handful of other anonymous reviewers.

I have taught GOVT 433: East Asian Political Economy at George Mason University for the past decade. The enthusiasm of my students for the political economy of an incredibly important and complex region and their frustration at times with the reading materials were the main motivations for this book. I have class-tested some of the materials in the book over the years.

Undoubtedly, it takes a family to write a book. My wife, Anne, was as supportive of this book as she was of other research projects of mine. Her intelligence and patience have made my writing possible. The book is dedicated to our daughter Maggie, who came along while I was writing this book and has brought as much joy to our life as her big sister.

THE POLITICAL ECONOMY
OF EAST ASIA

CHAPTER 1

Introduction

East Asia is important for students of world politics. For scholars of international political economy (IPE) who study the interaction of power and wealth in the international system, East Asia is a force to reckon with in the global economy. It comprises Japan and China, two of the largest economies in the world, and dynamic economies such as South Korea, Taiwan, Singapore, and Malaysia. East Asia now engages in almost 30 percent more trade than the United States, Canada, and Mexico combined—the three countries in the North American Free Trade Agreement (NAFTA)—while trailing the twenty-five-member European Union (EU) by less than half.[1] East Asian economies have taken turns leading the world in speed of economic growth: Japan in the 1960s; Taiwan, South Korea, Hong Kong, and Singapore in the 1970s; the Association of Southeast Asian Nations (ASEAN) in the 1980s; and China since the early 1990s. Collectively, East Asia grew faster than any other region in the world prior to the Asian financial crisis in 1997–1998. Despite the financial crisis, East Asia remains a dynamic economic region paced by China's high growth. From a historical perspective, Asia's postwar rise is on par with the rise of Europe and the rise of the United States. With a recent turn of IPE toward the interaction of domestic and international politics in research focus, East Asia offers ample and diverse experience of how domestic politics helps shape the policies in production, trade, exchange rates, and development and how the global market forces and international institutions in turn affect East Asian domestic politics.

East Asia is also important for students of comparative political economy and historical sociology, who study the formation and consequences of institutions from a comparative and historical perspective. East Asia had a unique set of political and economic institutions historically. East Asian institutions of political economy have evolved, converging in some areas and diverging in others between themselves and from other regions in a global context. Thus, the East Asian experience serves as a corrective to a Eurocentric bias in how people normally understand the evolution of global political economy. To begin with, political economy—often defined as the study of interaction between the state and the market—has been informed mainly by the European experience of state formation and capitalist expansion. Recent scholarship on the origin of East Asian political economy rejects the simplistic notion that the region's modern transformation was defined by Western pressure and Asian response and suggests a more complex picture of Westerners also adapting to preexisting commercial networks and political entities in East Asia. As East Asia and Europe interacted in a wider global market, studies of East Asian IPE shed light on what was unique and universal in both regions. Moreover, studies of the Asian economic miracle and the Asian financial crisis have highlighted the central role of the state in shaping the market, for good or ill.

Students of East Asia should be familiar with the political economy approach. To understand East Asia, one needs to understand the economic driver of the region in the past and present. Current scholarship of East Asia still has a politics-in-command bias, not sufficiently taking into consideration the underlying and transformative power of economic forces, particularly in the past few decades.

East Asia is a diverse and complex region, with deep historical and cultural roots and varied political, economic, and social practices. East Asian studies are thus necessarily and rightly interdisciplinary. But this interdisciplinary nature does not mean that textbooks have to be interdisciplinary. A "little bit of everything" approach may cover much ground and provide abundant useful information, but it will not help students grasp the basic dynamic of the region. While one may enter the field of East Asian studies from any discipline, this book considers a political economy approach particularly attractive. After all, many recent students are attracted to Asian studies because of the economic dynamism of the region. Moreover, political economy offers an elegant way to deal with complex issues in a way that connects with studies of other regions, and it provides analytical tools to study the interaction of domestic and international politics and to study supranational economic interactions.

Ultimately, the book portrays the ongoing drama of East Asian states striving for wealth and power given domestic and international constraints and opportunities. Their successes or failures have been a principal force shaping modern East Asian history. The book thus adopts an evolutionary and regional perspective on East Asian political economy. East Asia has experienced profound transformations. Some countries in the region have changed far more than Western nations in a few decades, from empire to communism to state capitalism. What happens at crucial junctures affects the institutions formed, which in turn affect economic performance.

The East Asian drama plays out, often differently, in the arenas of production, trade, finance, and exchange rates. Thus, unlike most other texts on East Asian political economy, which are essentially comparisons of the political economy of major individual countries in the region, the second part of this book focuses on economic issues, using an organizing scheme typical of an IPE textbook.

WHAT IS EAST ASIA?

East Asia is defined in the book as a region that stretches from Japan to Myanmar, as shown in Map 1.1. It includes Northeast Asia and Southeast Asia. Northeast Asia can be divided into mainland (China and the two Koreas) and maritime regions (Japan and Taiwan). Similarly, Southeast Asia can be divided into mainland (Myanmar, Thailand, Laos, Vietnam, and Cambodia) and archipelago (Malaysia, Singapore, Indonesia, Brunei, and the Philippines).

From a political economy perspective, East Asia may be divided into four groups. Japan is a first-rank mature market democracy. Then there is a second group of newly industrialized economies, namely South Korea, Taiwan, Singapore, and Hong Kong. The third group includes the early ASEAN countries minus Singapore. The fourth group comprises the socialist countries in transition, namely China, Vietnam, North Korea, Cambodia, and Laos. Myanmar, which follows its own style of socialism, belongs to this group.

One cannot avoid being arbitrary in deciding which countries should be included in a region. A regional subsystem may be determined by dozens of attributes such as proximity, pattern of interaction, and recognition.[2] For East Asia, one may argue that India, Australia, or Russia should be included for historical, economic, or

MAP 1.1
East Asian Countries and Their Political Economy Classifications

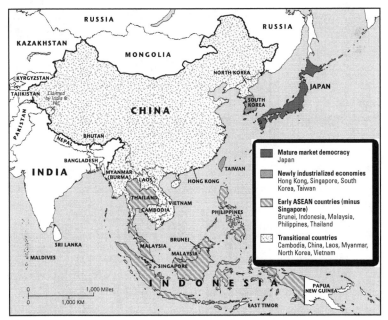

geographical reasons. Some would also argue that the United States should be included as well, given its security presence and economic significance in the region. Another major challenge to an artificial region is the boundary problem, as students of international relations have long recognized. In fact, some scholars show that the frontier is where the action is.

I consider East Asia a distinct region spanning from Japan to Myanmar for the following reasons. First, East Asia has been characterized by a high degree of interdependence and dense transactions between countries in a region over several dimensions.[3] Second, people generally recognize East Asia as a distinct region. Third, we cannot cover too many countries.

This book discusses the United States, a key player in the region. The U.S. military presence underlies the economic structure in East Asia. The United States is the largest final market for East Asian exports and is the main source of technology and investment capital. The United States remains the dominant player in international financial institutions such as the World Bank and the International Monetary Fund. But the United States is not an East Asian country. Rather, it is a North American and Pacific country that has a global presence. Conversely, even though Japan has considerable influence in Latin America, it would be absurd to call the country Latin American. In short, we will see East Asia as a distinct economic region, with the United States or other players included where and when they are relevant. It is necessary, in fact, because East Asia is part of a global political economy.

Although the book is about East Asia, we need to put it in a comparative, global perspective. East Asia is best understood in comparison with other regions, thus the book brings in other regions when it is necessary. In discussions of traditional East Asian political economy, the reference is the West. I compare East Asia with the West for the simple fact that the rise of the West was important for the evolution of East Asian political economy. At the same time, nomadic peoples bordering China were important for the nature of the Chinese system of political economy. In the imperialist stage, the East Asian response is briefly compared with that of other non-Western regions. The key is state capacities, and adaptability, to deal with the external stimuli. The chapter on the East Asian miracle contrasts East Asia with Latin America. Less discussed comparisons can also be made with South Asian nations and the Soviet Union/Russia and Eastern Europe.

THE POLITICAL ECONOMY APPROACH

The main purpose of the book is to highlight a few important issues rather than trying to cover all angles in a balanced fashion. Chapter 3 puts an emphasis on China as the principal shaping force of the traditional East Asian world order and does not give as much attention to Japan, Korea, Vietnam, and other Southeast

Asian nations or to diverse experiences within China. The chapter contrasts East Asia with the West but does not discuss other regions such as the Islamic world, South Asia, or Africa. Chapter 4 emphasizes the order-creating experience of the West and Japan but does not give detailed attention to resistance to these imperialist endeavors. Chapter 5 focuses mainly on the successful economies in East Asia but not on failed states such as Myanmar and North Korea. Chapter 6 examines the crisis states without looking more closely at the economies that escaped the crisis.

Aside from the focus on the issues discussed above, the book follows a loosely defined political economy approach as an organizing framework to expose students to some of the prevailing political economy questions set in the context of East Asia. The book will present answers to these questions to varying degrees, depending on the necessary space constraint and the depth of research in certain areas.

Defining Political Economy

Scholars define political economy differently.[4] Classical economists like Adam Smith and John Stuart Mill treated political economy as a science to increase the wealth of nations. However, Alfred Marshall removed politics from the discipline of economics in his 1890 book *Principles of Economics*. Now the term political economy has reemerged for economics and has become a mainstay for political science. For neoclassical economists, political economy means either the study of the market (failure or success) or the application of economic approach to studies of politics. Political economy basically means applying the standard economic methodology, that is, human behavior explained by individuals' rational choices under constraint and scarcity, to politics. For some other political scientists, particularly in IPE, political economy means the interaction of politics and economics, which can be studied using a wide range of methodologies.[5] That is what the term political economy means in this book.

Political economy has become important for comparative politics, international relations, and historical sociology, all of which are important for studies of East Asia. In the following section, I will illustrate the common interest in institutions and then differentiate them to clarify where this book is located in the intellectual landscape.

Institutions

For some scholars, a rationalist approach to institutions serves as a synthesis of international politics, comparative politics, and American politics, the principal subfields of political science in that they all study actor-based institutions in situations of strategic interaction. For international relations (IR) scholars, breaking the state into specific institutions and looking at international institutions mean that the findings and tools from American and comparative politics can be translated into the field of IR.[6]

Institutions help us understand human behavior. This is important for studies of political economy because the market and the state are institutions. Politics and economics are distinct areas of human activities. Politics is fundamentally about participation, justice, and authoritative distribution of resources, involving rights and duties. Economics deals with efficiency and wealth creation. But the institutions of the state and the market, which are central to the political and economic aspects, take on the dual nature of politics and economics. The market is political in that it provides freedoms to individuals in employment, residency, and consumption while also limiting choices. The market both makes things equal through the mechanism of competition and makes things less equal because of concentration of property holding. The market both contributes to societal order by satisfying individuals who have freedom of choice and making individuals more interdependent in a specialized society and disrupts societal order by eroding traditional values and structures. The state is also an economic institution in that it needs to be efficient in using resources and to promote economic growth for public interest.[7]

There are three basic ways to study institutions.[8] First, the rational choice approach focuses on the consequences of institutions and views institutions as "rules, procedures, norms, or conventions designed self-consciously to determine 'who has the power to do what when.'"[9] By contrast, historical institutionalism focuses on the origin of institutions and path dependence. Here institutions refer to "the formal or informal procedures, routines, norms and conventions embedded in the organization structure of the polity to political economy. . . . In general, historical institutionalists associate institutions with organizations and the rules or conventions promulgated by formal organizations."[10] A third approach is sociological and includes cultural practices of symbols and morality in the definition of institutions.[11]

This book uses the insight of rational choice theory to allow a coherent story of East Asian political economy. There are limits, however. Political economy takes place in time and space. Thus, it also uses historical institutionalism. By contrast, the book does not deal with cultures and traditions. This is not to deny or undermine the importance of cultures and traditions.[12] In fact, when most people think about East Asia, they often think about cultures and traditions first. That is precisely the reason why this book avoids discussion of cultures. Students of East Asia are not short on studies of symbols, cultures, and traditions from other sources.

Rational choice approach. The rational choice approach assumes that individuals are goal-oriented, rational actors who seek to maximize gains and minimize losses in a strategic environment. However, individually rational behavior may lead to a collective action problem in that everyone has incentives to exploit others, result-ing in lack of cooperation. Institutions exist because they overcome the collective action problem by creating a situation in which cooperation is self-enforcing.[13]

The rational choice approach is powerful for studies of East Asian political economy for several reasons. First, the approach is appealing in that individuals' choices matter and one cannot simply blame structural reasons for failures. What-ever policies a government adopts, individuals will rationally behave in such a way that often contradicts the original purpose of the policies. This is particularly the case when we discuss economic policies and when the market forces have expanded in East Asia. To have the intended results, the government policy has to be credi-ble. Second, the West has arisen thanks to institutions such as property rights. Countries that have effective institutions to coordinate politics and economy suc-ceed while those that do not have effective institutions perform poorly. Third, the rational choice theory explains the presence or absence of cooperation to achieve collective action for East Asian nations and East Asia as a whole. For functional areas such as trade, foreign investment, and monetary policy, the best approach is to use international regime, a standard analytical framework for studying interna-tional political economy. The focus of this literature is on how institutions help actors achieve cooperation by overcoming the collective action problem.

Historical institutionalism. The rational choice institutionalist discussion of insti-tutions emphasizes the functionality of institutions to explain why these institu-tions exist in the first place. But the rational choice approach does not offer a sufficient discussion of the historical origins of the institutions. An alternative explanation has been offered, which emphasizes that the institutions we have are profoundly historical.[14] Some economic historians have shown convincingly how timing and sequencing explain which technologies come to be selected and that the most efficient technology does not necessarily get chosen.[15] This approach focuses on path dependence, an explanation that emphasizes a logical sequence of stages of antecedent conditions, critical juncture, structural persistence, reactive sequence, and outcome. Antecedent conditions offer different options for actors; actors choose a policy option against alternatives; the choice creates institutions produced and reproduced over time; and actors react to the institutions, which lead to the final resolution.[16]

As an example of path dependence, a deteriorating economy caused by the Cul-tural Revolution (1966-1976) forced China to select a different path in a critical juncture in the late 1970s. During a highly unsettled time, Deng Xiaoping selected economic reform and opening China to the outside world without any accompa-nying democratic reform. While the dire situation demanded drastic policies, one can imagine if alternative strategies were adopted, as evidenced by fierce policy debates in China at the time. In the Soviet Union, Mikhail Gorbachev later chose a different path, of political reform first, whereas in North Korea, the government has dragged its feet in economic reform despite dire economic situations.

Deng's choice became institutionalized over time and thus became harder to reverse. Can China go back to the socialist planned economy adopted a few years after the People's Republic of China was established in 1949? Although some people wanted that in the 1980s, it is out of the question now. Chinese citizens largely reacted positively to reform, which reinforced it. At the same time, there were at least two related reactive sequences. One was when the citizens demanded political reform to resolve tensions arising from the economic reform. There was an opportunity for this type of political reform in the late 1980s, which was crushed in the 1989 Tiananmen Square incident. It is harder for another Tiananmen-like movement to occur now because rational actors have chosen to avoid politics and to concentrate instead on personal welfare and career, which has put most elites in the progovernment camp. Thus, political reform has become harder because elites now have a greater vested interest in stability.

The other reaction sequence comes from the many "losers" of the reform. Since they have few channels to vent, they have increasingly chosen to use often violent protests against corrupt officials. These protests lead to repression. The central government has interpreted these protests as a reason not to introduce political reform although they are willing to make marginal changes. At the same time, growing societal resentment means that leaders with populist tendencies like Chinese President Hu Jintao have sought to use societal sentiments as weapons against political rivals. The story of China's reform does not stop within the Chinese borders. The Chinese reform made it possible for other socialist countries to do the same, with both its promises and its limitations.

We need to look at the dynamics of East Asian political economy, where different national systems of political economies exist. Japan, for example, shares both similarities and differences with other advanced capitalist countries.[17] This raises the question of how different national institutions originated and evolved historically. While adopting a path-dependence approach, one should not ignore politics as the driver of institutional change. Institutional change does not happen automatically.[18]

Power and political institutions. The rational choice approach does not have to exclude power because the practices of rent seeking and agenda control allow power exercise, but new institutionalism, borrowed from the discipline of economics, focuses on voluntary exchanges creating institutions for cooperation.[19] However, the systems of political economy do not benefit all; some benefit whereas others do not.[20] By contrast, historical institutionalism gives a prominent role to power and asymmetrical relations. To be more specific, institutions distribute power unevenly among groups.[21]

The history of East Asian political economy illustrates the centrality of power in how the system has evolved. Institutions have often evolved to serve the purposes of the powerful, although established institutions also serve the interests of the weak. At the same time, we should not adopt a simplistic, deterministic model of power to explain everything. Power can serve as the motive for acquiring wealth (rich nation, strong army) and has served as a means for achieving wealth at crucial junctures of East Asian history. The West prevailed over East Asian nations not based on competitive prices but based on superior military power to control the trade ports and routes. Japan's rising power was integral to its rising economic power.

The modern states did not emerge from the state of nature. Rather, they evolved in an intense political environment of external threat and internal power politics. In particular, military competition was an important driver for economic and political institutions in medieval and early Europe.[22] Similarly, East Asian political economy has not been separated from security, although the book separates the two analytically and leaves a detailed discussion of East Asian security to other texts.

Comparative Political Economy and International Political Economy

The boundary between comparative and international politics has lost much meaning for many IR scholars.[23] For students of regional affairs in particular, it is difficult to differentiate international political economy (IPE), comparative political economy (CPE), and history. They deal with similar questions, namely how power and wealth relate to each other and how economic development and political development interact, and they often use similar analytical tools. One superficial difference is that a CPE book focuses more on country comparisons, whereas a typical IPE text has separate chapters on issues such as trade, exchange rates, and foreign investment.[24]

This book addresses readers of both CPE and IPE. While the book does not attempt an impossible neat division of labor, it is more consistent with CPE in the first five substantive chapters. Chapter 2 compares East Asian national systems of political economy. The next four chapters focus on how the state and the market have interacted in East Asia and how that is related to the different paths and performances of East Asian nations. But IR scholars should also be interested in the origin and evolution of the regional international system. In the last part of the book I focus on important issues of IPE, namely production, trade, finance, and exchange rates. At the same time, most chapters include a section about how politics and economics influence each other in a particular issue.

The State and the Market

The state and the market are central concepts for IPE, which explains why people often view IPE as simply the study of the interaction between the state and the market.[25] The state, as Margaret Levi defined it, is "a complex apparatus of centralized and institutionalized power that concentrates violence, establishes property rights, and regulates society within a given territory while being formally recognized as a state by international forums."[26] An important component of a state is monopoly of use of physical violence. Levi included formal recognition to differentiate states from other organizations that utilize violence. This is relevant for East Asia because Taiwan is recognized by most countries in the world as an economy rather than a state.

A central question for East Asia as well as for other regions is how to create a strong government to collect revenues to defend the country and build necessary infrastructure without preying on the society.[27] It is conceivable that a government may mobilize resources based on nondemocratic principles but offer society something in return. The question is whether that is sustainable in competition with advanced democracies. One important lesson of East Asia is that how predatory a state is makes a major difference for nondemocracies.

Well-functioning political institutions are needed for economic development, but formal institutions are not creations that come along automatically. Government officials need to have credibility in order for the population to have confidence in the state goals and behave accordingly to advance public interests.[28] East Asian governments tend to be more effective than their counterparts in the developing world. A study of the East Asian experience, both successes and failures, helps us understand this issue.

The market refers to a meeting of people at a particular time and place to buy and sell goods and services. Studies of political economy of the market tend to focus on market failures while emphasizing the positive role of the market for the economy and politics. The market failure refers to an insufficient supply of public goods caused by individuals' rational preference to free ride on others.

While people have the basic inclination to trade goods and services, a well-functioning market does not automatically spring into action. If the market is not automatic, the state has a role to play during the transition period. It would be unwise therefore for a transitional economy to simply leave everything to the market that is yet to be created. This is a major point in the debate over the Asian development model. Intellectual merit aside, we simply cannot understand East Asian economy without understanding the role of governments, for good or bad.

Economic Growth Versus Political Regime

Another important political economy question is how economic development and political regimes or institutions interact with each other. One may suggest, for example, a correspondence between agricultural advance and the Chinese empire, as Chapter 3 will show. Seymour Martin Lipset pointed out in the 1950s that a higher stage of economic development makes democracy more likely.[29] However, Samuel Huntington subsequently argued that while developed countries tend to have stable democracies, the process of economic development leads to political instability, which makes it likely and even necessary to have an authoritarian government for the transition period.[30] Fast economic development in authoritarian economies such as Taiwan and South Korea appear to support that argument. But as Taiwan and South Korea eventually democratized after they reached a more developed stage of high-tech and information, Lipset's basic thesis holds.

The source of a country's economic wealth is also believed to help shape its political development. For example, it is often suggested that there is a mostly negative relationship between mineral wealth and the quality of a political system.[31] An example is Indonesia in the 1960s and 1970s. However, we should not have an economically deterministic view. Resource-rich Malaysia did not do as badly as Indonesia. A large number of intervening variables increase and ameliorate the causal tendencies of economic factors.

Conversely, the type of political institutions of a country has different economic consequences. Douglass North and Robert Thomas argued that the rise of the Western world resulted from the development of an efficient economic organization. Economic growth needs property rights that give individuals incentives to engage in activities that allow themselves as well as the whole society to benefit. Moreover, one needs governments that protect property rights without selecting some property rights for their own political needs, which would hinder growth.[32] Mancur Olson argued that democracies make decisions to encompassing rather than narrow or predatory interests, which explains economic growth.[33]

Power of Ideas

One's ideas about the proper role of the state and the market and how to achieve political or economic objectives are important. Ideas are particularly important in modern East Asian international political economy because of these countries' historical mission to catch up with the West or with each other. Ideas are more than rationalized interests. This book shows that ideas of power and wealth, both the meaning of power and wealth and how to achieve power and wealth, are a main driver of East Asian IPE. The idea of power and wealth will be studied along three dimensions: the relationship between the state and the market, the relationship between borrowing from outside and learning from one's own experience, and national versus regional ideals.

On a more instrumental level, the concrete ideas of how to get things done are important in explaining governmental policies. Some of these ideas have been borrowed from outside or inside the region. The East Asian development model has a strong ideational dimension. Similar East Asian countries also have different ideas about how to deal with a situation. The different paths taken by Malaysia vis-à-vis Thailand, Indonesia, and South Korea during the Asian financial crisis is a case in point.

DESIGN OF THE BOOK

Besides this introduction chapter, the book includes ten chapters on national systems of political economy, traditional East Asian international relations, modern East Asian political economy, the economic miracle, the financial crisis, production, trade, finance, exchange rates, and regionalism.

The first substantive chapter compares different national systems of political economy in East Asia. Some features of East Asian political economy are converging whereas others are diverging, but the question of convergence versus divergence is not as important as the causal mechanisms driving convergence or divergence.

The next four chapters discuss the transformations of East Asian political economy to provide students, particularly those with limited background in East Asia, with a broad picture of the region and to expose them to the main debates about East Asian IPE at the outset. The chapters also put into context the specific issue areas discussed in the remaining five chapters, in a sequence of production, trade, finance, exchange rates, and regionalism.

Chapters 3 and 4 discuss three international orders established or attempted in East Asia for the past two plus millenniums: the Chinese world order, Western imperialism, and the Japanese New Order. These were dominant features that did not exhaust the rich East Asian historical experiences, and discussion of them does not imply that these international orders were justified. Rather, these terms are meant to introduce analytical schemes, based on empirical evidence, for thinking about East Asia in a regional rather than national perspective. Not meant as an introduction to East Asian history, this book offers a selective version tracing the evolution of regional political economy. My discussion focuses on the fundamental purposes embedded in it, the interaction of politics and economics, and the feasibility of these efforts to order East Asian international relations.

Chapter 3 discusses the origin of East Asian political economy. It is meant as a corrective to the Eurocentric view of the world and East Asia, and it sets the tone that this book is to follow a globally situated East Asian narrative, characterized by the Chinese world order and extensive regional trading networks. East Asia was different from the West and was advanced in agriculture, commerce, and handicrafts. Period technologies and political economies reinforced each other. Although the East Asian system made sense for their political objectives and circumstances, they could not achieve an industrial revolution similar to the one that took place in the West. At the same time, East Asian nations' previous experience with organization and achievements came in handy for the economic miracle that was to happen later. The internal justification of the political and economic institutions in the region and individual countries was important, but one should also take into consideration the historical path dependence and the social and ideational context of East Asian institutions. One important issue that I address in the chapter is how the nature of military conflict and economic competition among nations affected domestic political economy.

Chapter 4 focuses on modern East Asian political economy. Western and Japanese imperialism had an important impact on the region. Globalizing forces came to have a more powerful and faster impact on East Asia. As a result, adaptability became important, and how adaptable a country was depended on timing, institutional capacity, and private and collective interests. National systems of political economy helped to expand adaptability, which in turn affected national political economy systems.

Western imperialists were driven by commercial interests, strategic rivalries with each other, and weaknesses of the colonized. Industrialization provided both the motive and the capacity to subdue agricultural peoples. Modern organizations, ideology, and technology made the difference. Japan's effort to avoid the fate of colonization led to a successful drive to industrialization, which in turn led to an expanding empire project. As a latecomer, Japan inevitably clashed with the West. Moreover, pursuing empire-building in a different time period, Japan faced strong resistance of rising nationalism in East Asia, which imperialism both provoked and facilitated.

Wars were central for the transformation of East Asian international relations and East Asian domestic political economies. But this was a different type of warfare that was intertwined with the modern capitalist economy. East Asia did not start from far behind in terms of wealth, but the institutions that propelled the West to the top were far more developed in the West, with the effect felt only gradually. Another key story was the different paths of East Asian nations. Japan succeeded while China, Korea, and Vietnam failed. The reasons for this difference lay in timing and the institutional adaptability.

Chapters 5 and 6 examine the big stories of postwar East Asian political economy, namely the economic miracle, the financial crash, and recovery. Chapter 5 describes East Asia's rapid economic growth with relative equity and its structural transformations from an agricultural society to an industrial one and from state control to a more market-oriented economy. The economic miracle happened whether or not one questions its sustainability. The chapter then introduces opposing economic and political economy explanations of the Asian miracle. While mainstream economists view East Asia's rapid economic growth as resulting mainly from getting the fundamentals right, others maintain that the East Asian developmental state that actively intervenes in the economy has been the main reason for the growth. The chapter also discusses the regional dimension of the East Asian miracle and the American contribution to East Asian political economy. East Asian economic growth has unleashed social and political forces that create pressure for regime change.

Chapter 6 describes and explains the Asian financial crisis, which spread throughout East Asia and beyond, with a devastating effect on several East Asian economies. The crisis resulted from a combination of volatility in the global financial market, East Asian crony capitalism, and mismatched macroeconomic policies. The crisis was largely over within two years and had a major impact on the economic policies of the regional economies, such as unusually high foreign reserves to prevent another crisis. The crisis had an uneven impact on the reform efforts of different East Asian nations.

For the issue chapters from Chapters 7 to 11, production leads the discussion for the simple reason that most East Asian countries tend to be driven by production at a crucial stage of development. I have chosen to discuss production first because it is the essence of East Asian political economy. When East Asian governments talk about exports, they talk mainly about exports of manufactured goods. Production is also fundamentally regionally and globally based, with production networks. Put together, one can see the mercantilist thinking revealed in government policies. Trade follows naturally from East Asian nations' emphasis on production of manufactured goods. Trade is a crucial factor that dominates in the thinking in East Asia. There is also a major regional dynamic to trade. East Asian nations learn from each other and compete with each other. Chapter 9 discusses East Asian finance. With regard to IPE, we know that finance has become far more significant for global economy than trade even though trade is more sensitive politically than other issues. Chapter 10 covers exchange rates. The last chapter of the book analyzes East Asian regionalism in trade, finance, and exchange rates.

SUGGESTED READINGS

Borthwick, Mark. *Pacific Century: The Emergence of Modern Pacific Asia,* 3rd ed. (Boulder: Westview, 2007).

Caporaso, James A. "Across the Great Divide: Integrating Comparative and International Politics." *International Studies Quarterly* 41, no. 4 (December 1997): 563–592.

Gilpin, Robert. *Global Political Economy: Understanding the International Economic Order* (Princeton: Princeton University Press, 2001).

Hall, Peter A., and Rosemary C. R. Taylor. "Political Science and the Three Institutionalisms." *Political Studies* 44, no. 4 (December 1996): 936–957.

Islam, Iyanatul, and Anis Chowdhury. *The Political Economy of East Asia: Post-Crisis Debates* (New York: Oxford University Press, 2000).

Keefer, Philip. "What Does Political Economy Tell Us About Economic Development and Vice Versa?" *Annual Review of Political Science* 7 (May 2004): 247–272.

Kim, Samuel S., ed. *East Asia and Globalization* (Lanham, Md.: Rowman and Littlefield, 2000).

Krugman, Paul. *Pop Internationalism* (Cambridge: MIT Press, 1996).

Lipset, Seymour Martin. "Some Social Requisites of Democracy: Economic Development and Political Legitimacy." *American Political Science Review* 53, no. 1 (1959): 69–105.

Milner, Helen V. "Rationalizing Politics: The Emerging Synthesis of International, American, and Comparative Politics." *International Organization* 52, no. 4 (Autumn 1998): 759–786.

Moe, Terry M. "Power and Political Institutions." *Perspectives on Politics* 3, no. 2 (June 2005): 215–233.

North, Douglass C. *Institutions, Institutional Change, and Economic Performance* (New York: Cambridge University Press, 1990).

Olson, Mancur. *Power and Prosperity: Outgrowing Communist and Capitalist Dictatorships* (New York: Basic Books, 2000).

Pierson, Paul. *Politics in Time: History, Institutions, and Social Analysis* (Princeton: Princeton University Press, 2004).

Przeworski, Adam. *States and Markets: A Primer in Political Economy* (New York: Cambridge University Press, 2003).

Rondinelli, Dennis A., and John M. Heffron, eds. *Globalization and Change in Asia* (Boulder: Lynne Rienner, 2007).

Simone, Vera. *The Asian Pacific: Political and Economic Development in a Global Context,* 2nd ed. (New York: Longman, 2001).

Wolf, Charles, Jr. *Markets or Governments: Choosing Between Imperfect Alternatives* (Cambridge: MIT Press, 1990).

NOTES

1. East Asia, including China, Japan, South Korea, Taiwan, Hong Kong, and the ten-member Association of Southeast Asia Nations (ASEAN), had a total merchandise trade volume of $4,753 billion in 2005. The trade statistics for Hong Kong includes only domestic exports and retained imports. By contrast, NAFTA had $3,745 billion and EU had $8,136 billion. World Trade Organization, *International Trade Statistics 2006*, Table 1.6 and Table 1.10 (www.wto.org/english/res_e/statis_e/its2006_e/its06_overview_e.pdf). The trade statistics for all three regions include intraregion trade. EU now has 27 members, with Bulgaria and Romania admitted on January 1, 2007.
2. William R. Thompson, "The Regional Subsystem: A Conceptual Explication and a Propositional Inventory," *International Studies Quarterly* 17, no. 1 (March 1973): 89–117.
3. Giovanni Arrighi, Takeshi Hamashita, and Mark Selden, "Introduction," in *The Resurgence of East Asia: 500, 150, and 50 Year Perspectives,* ed. Giovanni Arrighi, Takeshi Hamashita, and Mark Selden (New York: RoutledgeCurzon, 2003), 4–7.
4. James A. Caporaso and David P. Levine, *Theories of Political Economy* (New York: Cambridge University Press, 1992); Colin Wright, "Competing Conceptions of Political Economy," in *From Political Economy to Economics—And Back?* ed. James H. Nichols Jr. and Colin Wright (San Francisco: Institute for Contemporary Studies, 1990), 57–77.
5. Robert Gilpin, *Global Political Economy: Understanding the International Economic Order* (Princeton: Princeton University Press, 2001), 25–31.
6. Helen V. Milner, "Rationalizing Politics: The Emerging Synthesis of International, American, and Comparative Politics," *International Organization* 52, no. 4 (Autumn 1998): 759–786; Barry R. Weingast, "Rational Choice Institutionalism," in *Political Science: The State of the Discipline,* ed. Ira Katznelson and Helen Milner (New York: Norton, 2002), 660–692.
7. Barry Clark, *Political Economy: A Comparative Approach,* 2nd ed. (Westport, Conn.: Praeger, 1998), 3–19. Also see David P. Levine, *Wealth and Freedom: An Introduction to Political Economy* (New York: Cambridge University Press, 1995); Charles Wolf Jr., *Markets or Governments: Choosing Between Imperfect Alternatives* (Cambridge: MIT Press, 1990).

8. Peter A. Hall and Rosemary C. R. Taylor, "Political Science and the Three Institutionalisms," *Political Studies* 44, no. 4 (December 1996): 936–957.

9. James E. Alt, "Comparative Political Economy: Credibility, Accountability, and Institutions," in *Political Science: The State of the Discipline,* ed. Ira Katznelson and Helen Milner (New York: Norton, 2002), 149.

10. Hall and Taylor, "Political Science and the Three Institutionalisms," 938.

11. For a representative work in the approach, see James G. March and Johan P. Olsen, *Rediscovering Institutions: The Organizational Basis of Politics* (New York: Free Press, 1989).

12. For useful works on the importance of cultures and traditions in East Asian development, see Ronald Dore, *Taking Japan Seriously: A Confucian Perspective on Leading Economic Issues* (Stanford: Stanford University Press, 1987); Tu Wei-Ming, ed., *Confucian Traditions in East Asian Modernity: Moral Education and Economic Culture in Japan and the Four Mini-Dragons* (Cambridge: Harvard University Press, 1996); Gilbert Rozman, *The East Asian Region: Confucian Heritage and Its Modern Adaptation* (Princeton: Princeton University Press, 1991); Francis Fukuyama, *Trust: The Social Virtues and the Creation of Prosperity* (New York: Free Press, 1995); Lawrence E. Harrison and Samuel P. Huntington, eds., *Culture Matters: How Values Shape Human Progress* (New York: Basic Books, 2000).

13. Weingast, "Rational Choice Institutionalism."

14. Paul Pierson, *Politics in Time: History, Institutions, and Social Analysis* (Princeton: Princeton University Press, 2004); James Mahoney and Dietrich Rueschemeyer, eds., *Comparative Historical Analysis in the Social Sciences* (New York: Cambridge University Press, 2003).

15. Paul A. David, "Clio and the Economics of QWERTY," *American Economic Review* 75, no. 2 (May 1985): 332–337; W. Brian Arthur, "Competing Technologies, Increasing Returns, and Lock-In by Historical Events," *Economic Journal* 99, no. 394 (March 1989): 116–131.

16. James Mahoney, *The Legacies of Liberalism: Path Dependence and Political Regimes in Central America* (Baltimore: Johns Hopkins University Press, 2001), 6. See also Ruth B. Collier and David Collier, *Shaping the Political Arena: Critical Junctures, the Labor Movement, and Regime Dynamics in Latin America* (Princeton: Princeton University Press, 1991); Douglass C. North, *Institutions, Institutional Change, and Economic Performance* (New York: Cambridge University Press, 1990); Kathleen Thelen, "Historical Institutionalism in Comparative Politics," *The Annual Review of Political Science* 2 (June 1999): 369–404.

17. Wolfgang Streeck and Kozo Yamamura, eds., *The Origins of Nonliberal Capitalism: Germany and Japan in Comparison* (Ithaca, N.Y.: Cornell University Press, 2001); Michel Albert, *Capitalism Versus Capitalism* (New York: Four Walls Eight Windows, 1993).

18. Kathleen Thelen, *How Institutions Evolve: The Political Economy of Skills in Germany, Britain, the United States, and Japan* (New York: Cambridge University Press, 2004).

19. Terry M. Moe, "Power and Political Institutions," *Perspectives on Politics* 3, no. 2 (June 2005): 215–233.

20. For some important IPE works that do emphasize power, see Margaret Levi, *Of Rule and Revenue* (Berkeley: University of California Press, 1988); Margaret Levi, "A Logic of Institutional Change," in *The Limits of Rationality*, ed. Karen Schweers Cook and Margaret Levi (Chicago: University of Chicago Press, 1990), 402–418; Jack Knight, *Institutions and Social Conflict* (New York: Cambridge University Press, 1992); Mancur Olson, *Power and Prosperity: Outgrowing Communist and Capitalist Dictatorships* (New York: Basic Books, 2000).

21. Hall and Taylor, "Political Science and the Three Institutionalisms," 940–941.

22. Thomas Ertman, *Birth of the Leviathan: Building States and Regimes in Medieval and Early Modern Europe* (Cambridge: Cambridge University Press, 1997).

23. James A. Caporaso, "Across the Great Divide: Integrating Comparative and International Politics," *International Studies Quarterly* 41, no. 4 (December 1997): 563–592.

24. For a discussion of how IPE and CPE courses are taught in the United States, see Darel E. Paul, "Teaching Political Economy in Political Science: A Review of International and Comparative Political Economy Syllabi," *Perspectives on Politics* 4, no. 4 (December 2006): 729–734.

25. Adam Przeworski, *States and Markets: A Primer in Political Economy* (New York: Cambridge University Press, 2003), 11–12.

26. Margaret Levi, "The State of the Study of the State," in *Political Science: The State of the Discipline*, ed. Ira Katznelson and Helen Milner (New York: Norton, 2002), 40.

27. Mancur Olson, "Dictatorship, Democracy and Development," *American Political Science Review* 87, no. 3 (September 1993): 567–576.

28. Philip Keefer, "What Does Political Economy Tell Us About Economic Development and Vice Versa?" *Annual Review of Political Science* 7 (May 2004): 247–272.

29. Seymour Martin Lipset, "Some Social Requisites of Democracy: Economic Development and Political Legitimacy," *American Political Science Review* 53, no. 1 (1959): 69–105.

30. Samuel P. Huntington, *Political Order in Changing Societies* (New Haven: Yale University Press, 1968).

31. Erika Weinthal and Pauline Jones Luong, "Combating the Resource Curse: An Alternative Solution to Managing Mineral Wealth," *Perspectives on Politics* 4, no. 1 (March 2006): 35–53.

32. Douglass C. North and Robert Paul Thomas, *The Rise of the Western World: A New Economic History* (London: Cambridge University Press, 1973).

33. Olson, *Power and Prosperity.* For a detailed empirical inquiry, see Adam Przeworski, Michael Alvarez, Jose Antonio Cheibub, and Frederick Limogi, *Democracy and Development: Political Institutions and Well-Being in the World, 1950–1990* (Cambridge: Cambridge University Press, 2000).

CHAPTER 2

The East Asian National Systems of Political Economy

T his chapter examines East Asian political economy from a comparative perspective, focusing on the different national systems of political economy in East Asia. One country's national system may differ from another in terms of national purpose, the role of the state in economy, and corporate governance and business practices.[1] This chapter discusses mainly national purpose and state versus economy for East Asian economies to simplify the discussion of the diverse and rich experiences of East Asian political economy.

East Asian political economy is characterized by a high degree of diversity, with regional economies ranging from advanced to the poorest in the world and with the economies often having greater similarities with nonregional countries than with each other. At the same time, East Asian economies are converging in that virtually all of them treat economic growth as a high priority and are making concerted efforts to advance that all-important goal. Viewing economic performance as a basis of political legitimacy, East Asian economies exhibit a strong tendency of "developmental state," which is reinforced by mutual learning. From a dynamic perspective, the stage of economic development corresponds roughly with that of political development in East Asia, exhibiting a tiered pattern of more advanced economy having better governance. Such a regional trend is reflected in the analysis of specific East Asian economies. The country-specific materials discussed in this chapter are also designed to prepare students for the following chapters that are organized chronologically and thematically.

THE POLITICAL ECONOMY SYSTEMS OF EAST ASIA: AN OVERVIEW

This section addresses the following two questions. First, are East Asian political economies converging, in other words, are they becoming more alike among themselves or with other regions? Second, is one particular national model of political economy superior to others?

Convergence versus divergence has been an important question for students who adopt a comparative-historical perspective.[2] National differences allow scholars to explain varying economic performance and public policy. At the same time, globalizing forces have affected all countries. Thus, whether countries are converging or not conditions our basic understanding of international political economy as well as East Asian political economy. One school of thought assumes convergence among advanced industrial democracies in the context of a homogenizing globalization.[3] Modernization theorists argue that developing nations should converge with developed nations if they want to achieve development. Neoclassical economists also believe that national economies will eventually converge as a result of market forces or harmonization through political negotiations. An opposing school sees a persistent divergence among nations.[4]

Are East Asian economies converging with each other or with the advanced nations in the world? When we look at contemporary East Asian political economy, one feature that stands out is a great diversity among regional economies, with advanced capitalist economies, major transitional countries, and small developing nations. Japan is comparable with Germany as advanced capitalist countries. China and Vietnam share some similarities with Russia as transitional economies. With large land-owning families that have had a strong hold on the state, the Philippines is more like some Latin American countries. North Korea should be compared with Cuba as laggards in market reform. Small but oil-rich Brunei is similar to a Persian Gulf state. Whereas economies such as Singapore, Taiwan, and South Korea have joined the high-income club, other states such as Myanmar, Laos, Cambodia, and North Korea have failed.[5] Last but not least, a deliberate harmonization process does not exist in East Asia, unlike in Europe.

It would be wrong to dismiss all this obvious diversity in East Asia, but we should take a more nuanced and dynamic perspective in examining East Asia. Judging by the criteria of national purpose and state versus economy, there is a certain degree of convergence among East Asian economies. To begin with, virtually all East Asian economies now desire economic growth. One should not take this collective desire for granted. Pursuit of economic development is a modern phenomenon in East Asia as well as elsewhere in the world. Economic activities have always been important because a society needs to provide for itself, but achieving sustained economic growth has only been around for several decades. Also, East Asian economies did not share this paramount goal of economic growth after the Second World War. The People's Republic of China (PRC) leadership under Mao Zedong was focused on revolutionizing Chinese society and supporting revolutionary movements worldwide, and the country did not shift to economic modernization as an overarching national objective until the late 1970s. The Kuomintang government in Taiwan was initially preoccupied with retaking the mainland and shifted to economic development of the island only in the early 1960s. The Republic of Korea government similarly aimed at reunification with the north initially and only launched a state-led industrialization plan in the early 1960s.

The national purpose of rapid economic growth has not been just convenient rhetoric. Rather, it has driven national policymaking throughout the region and has been implemented and monitored by both the state and society. Whether a government is really committed to or just gives lip service to the goal of development explains much about the difference in economic performance between East Asian economies and between East Asia and other developing regions.

We also observe an interventionist state in East Asia to the extent that we often lump East Asian economies together as practicing a "developmental state" capitalism, which is divergent from the West. Scholars of advanced democracies have generally differentiated the liberal market economies represented by the United States and Britain from the socially embedded systems of political economy found in Germany and Japan. The East Asian model should therefore not be viewed as too different from the continental European model. At the same time, much of the study from the Anglo-Saxon perspective views East Asia as significantly different from the West.

As will be discussed extensively in Chapter 5, the mainstream neoclassical view shared by the U.S. Treasury, the International Monetary Fund, and the World Bank, the so-called "Washington consensus," is that the best way to achieve economic growth is to "set the price right" and let the market work its magic. Some neoclassical thinkers have argued that East Asia's postwar economic success has resulted from market-friendly policies adopted by the successful governments. By contrast, developmental state theorists argue that the state in East Asia has only intervened in the market by "picking the winners" and that it possesses a high capacity to formulate and implement long-term economic development strategies because of its insulation from society.[6]

Not surprisingly, the developmental state model reveals flaws under scrutiny.[7] First, a strong state may lead to both economic successes and failures in East Asia as well as elsewhere.[8] To address that issue, Peter Evans proposed a notion of "embedded autonomy" that emphasizes a positive link between the state and society.[9] Second, some scholars have taken the state apart and have shown a large variation of state capacity between government agencies and between the national and local levels. The state in East Asia has been transformed by both modernizing forces and conflicts within a disaggregated state apparatus.[10] The developmental state model has also been criticized as implying a compliant society, which is often not the case in East Asia. Even in South Korea, often recognized as having the strongest developmental state in East Asia, society has often been militant against the state.[11] In fact, protest movements have taken place in all high-performing economies in East Asia.

However, few models remain intact under scrutiny. East Asian economies share a strong economic nationalism. For better or for worse, the state intervention has yielded good economic performance for these economies in the past few decades. A strong state argument also does not have to assume a weak society.

Developments in East Asian political economy are not random events. My discussion so far shows that a highly diverse East Asia looks more orderly from the perspective of political economy systems. We can see things even more clearly from a dynamic perspective. If we factor in stages of development, there is a greater degree of convergence, which may be described as a "tiered convergence."

As will be discussed in the following chapters, East Asian economies have followed similar production-oriented, export-led, state-directed credit policies, albeit not necessarily at the same time. This development is mainly due to emulation of successful national models. There was much interest in East Asia as well as elsewhere in learning the Japanese model before the early 1990s. There are also other examples, such as Taiwan's export zones and Singapore's Central Providence Fund. The Chinese government was interested in emulating the South Korean *chaebol* system before the Asian financial crisis and is now trying to learn from South Korea about building a "new countryside." All this learning helps to create a hybrid of different national models in East Asia.[12]

More broadly, a tiered convergence in political development can be observed. In an edited volume published in 1999, James Morley, Harold Crouch, and others have shown a rough correlation between levels of economic development and political regimes in the Asia Pacific region, with low levels correlating with autocratic regimes and high levels with democracies.[13] To follow up on that important research, I have created Table 2.1, which shows that one can indeed observe some large patterned economic and political developments in East Asia.

First of all, a rough correlation between level of economic development and level of political development exists. Japan led the way with the highest per capita gross national income (GNI) and the strongest democracy in East Asia. Taiwan and South Korea followed in Japan's footstep, consistent with their high-income status.[14] Hong Kong is a Special Administrative Region of the PRC. Given its strong civil society, vibrant party politics, and experience with limited elections, Hong Kong should be a functional democracy but for Beijing's opposition. Singapore also fails to have a true democracy despite its first-world level economic development. Arguably, Singapore's small urban population makes it possible for a paternalistic government to operate as long as it continues to deliver economic and social benefits and boast one of the cleanest governments in the world. Similar to Singapore, Malaysia also has an authoritarian democracy in which one party continues to dominate even though elections are held. Moving down the ladder, only China is an authoritarian country among the four East Asian lower-middle-income

TABLE 2.1
Economic Change and Political Change in East Asia

	Per Capita GNI ($ in 2004)	Population (million)	Per Capita GDP Annual Growth Rate (constant 2000 $)	Political Regime
High-income	($10,066 or more)			
Japan	37,050	128	5.3 in 1960–1990	Consolidated democracy
Hong Kong	26,660	7	5.2 in 1960–2005	Special administrative region
Singapore	24,760	4	5.6 in 1960–2005	Authoritarian democracy
Taiwan*	14,707	23	na	Consolidated democracy
South Korea	14,000	48	5.7 in 1960–2005	Consolidated democracy
Upper-middle-income	($3,256–10,065)			
Malaysia	4,520	25	4.1 in 1970–2005	Authoritarian democracy
Lower-middle-income	($826–3,255)			
Thailand	2,490	64	4.5 in 1970–2005	Formal democracy
China	1,500	1,296	8.5 in 1980–2005	Authoritarian
Philippines	1,170	82	1.2 in 1970–2005	Formal democracy
Indonesia	1,140	218	4.0 in 1970–2005	Formal democracy
Low-income	($825 or less)			
Vietnam	540	82	5.0 in 1985–2005	Authoritarian
Laos	390	6	3.2 in 1985–2005	Authoritarian
Cambodia	350	14	4.7 in 1993–2005	Authoritarian democracy
Myanmar**	na	50	na	Authoritarian

Source: World Bank, *World Development Indicators 2006*, http://mutex.gmu.edu:2416/wdi2006/contents/Usersguide.htm. Data for per capita GDP annual growth rate are calculated from World Bank, World Development Indicators Database. Data for Taiwan are from the Asian Development Bank, Key Indicators 2006. It is per capita GNP rather than GNI for Taiwan.

Note: The criteria for income categories are from World Development Indicators 2006. GNI = gross national income; na = not available.

* Taiwan's per capita information in current US$ is available but that is not comparable with constant $ statistics used in the table.

** Official information about Myanmar is exaggerated. The country is estimated to be low-income.

countries. Thailand, the Philippines, and Indonesia all have a formal democracy in which elections are held and political parties operate, although these countries face constant threats of military coup and street demonstrations. When it comes to low-income categories, three of the four East Asian countries in the table—Vietnam, Laos, and Myanmar—are authoritarian, while Cambodia allows elections but maintains single-party domination.

There is not a neat correlation between stages of industrialization and economic policies or political regimes. Political change is not predetermined in its direction and is uneven among regional economies. Facing opportunities or crises, different governments react differently, creating entrenched interests in the process. Facing the same opportunities of globalization, China and Vietnam have bravely moved forward whereas North Korea lags behind. Facing the Asian financial crisis, Thailand and South Korea chose greater liberalization whereas Malaysia opted for capital controls.

A combination of liberal democracy and market economy has proved to be the best system available, particularly when one has to compete in a world where most powerful countries are market economy democracies. At the same time, countries face tremendous challenges during the transition period, and backlash is common. It is ultimately difficult to judge the superiority of a particular system unless one adopts a teleological view of history. The purposes countries pursue can be very different. How do we determine the proper balance of economic efficiency and social harmony? Empirically, which national model is considered superior to others tends to depend on the economic performance of the country at the time. The German model was praised in the 1970s, the Japanese model in the 1980s, and the American model in the 1990s. Thus, we should not be preoccupied with which national model is "winning."

THE JAPANESE SYSTEM OF POLITICAL ECONOMY

The Japanese system of political economy has gone through two stages since the early 1950s. After World War II, Japan created a growth-oriented political system with a reinforcing dynamic of rapid economic growth, conservative politics, and social participation that became the envy of the world. By the end of the 1970s Ezra Vogel called Japan "the Number One" country in the world.[15] The catch-up, export-led Japanese model experienced severe strains with a matured economy and backlash from the West in the 1980s. But instead of introducing structural reform, Japan adapted by turning to an investment-led strategy, allowing the yen to appreciate sharply after the 1985 Plaza Accord, and adopting a loose monetary policy to limit the extent of appreciation. Such a strategy, combined with a lack of investment opportunities at home, led to a bubble in the real estate and stock markets. The burst of the bubble in 1991 ushered in the second stage of structural reforms. Much has changed, particularly on the economic front, but much remains the same. While Japan remains one of the most advanced economic and technological powers in the world, the Japanese model has lost its luster, and the country's struggles in recent years serve as a cautionary tale for many.

The Embedded Mercantilism

T. J. Pempel has used the term "embedded mercantilism" to characterize the Japanese political economy system through the 1980s.[16] One may also use the term "the 1955 system" or "the developmental state." [17] The 1955 system, which refers to the continuous rule of Japan's Liberal Democratic Party (LDP) since 1955, is more commonly used, but the embedded mercantilism and the developmental state have the advantage of highlighting the crucial economic dimension of the Japanese political system.

Japan regained sovereignty in 1952. The American Occupation authorities had created a democratic political system in the country. Through the 1980s, the primary purposes of the Japanese state were catching up with the West and ensuring social harmony. Japanese politics was divided between conservatives and progressives. In response to the unification of the Japan Socialist Party (JSP), different conservative political forces founded the LDP in 1955. Whereas the LDP shared the neo-mercantilist view that Japan should become a competitive economic power in the world, the party had to reconcile at least two different agendas. On the one hand, big business, elite bureaucrats, and bureaucrat-turned-politicians wanted to create internationally competitive large firms with industrial policy and fiscal responsibilities. On the other hand, small business and agricultural bases of the party preferred local protection and subsidies. The LDP managed to reconcile the two competing agendas by adopting an industrial policy to upgrade technologies and penetrate foreign markets while protecting the home turf from foreign competition. Japanese firms enjoyed a comparative advantage over foreign competitors because of a secure domestic base. A dual economic structure thus resulted. The Japanese state also sought to redistribute economic gains to ensure social harmony. But unlike most Western European welfare states that aim at disadvantaged individuals, the Japanese state focused on disadvantaged locations and sectors.[18]

The Japanese political system was often characterized as an "iron triangle" of conservative LDP politicians, big business, and elite bureaucrats. The LDP politicians ensured a stable business environment and adopted policies that promote the interests of big business. Big business provided financial support for the LDP. Elite bureaucrats influenced Japanese business behavior through state regulations.

The state was powerful because of heavy regulations of the economy. At the same time, the capacity or the willingness of the Japanese state to direct economy should not be exaggerated. Scholars have shown how the Japanese state adopted a market-friendly approach and the rapid Japanese economic growth was driven by market forces. Put simply, the market can be viewed as embedded in the Japanese state.[19]

The 1955 system was durable. Despite constant internal and external challenges, the LDP has ruled continuously since 1955. The reasons often cited include the advantage of incumbents, the party's ability to adapt and co-opt ideas from the opposition, and the cold war international environment that called for a conservative party trusted by the United States. The fact that the Japanese state sought societal participation and supported various social groups was an important reason for the durability of the system.[20] Put simply, since the 1955 system served Japan so well, why rock the boat?

The embedded mercantilist system came under strains in the mid-1980s. Japan's large firms had become too competitive for other developed nations, which in turn pressured Japan to open its market, which would necessarily hurt Japan's protected domestic political economy, at least in the short run. Instead of conducting structural reforms, Japan shifted to an investment-led strategy, which planted the seeds for the lost decade of the 1990s. The 1985 Plaza Accord led to a sharp appreciation of the yen meant to reduce Japan's mounting trade surpluses with the world. To prevent too much pressure on Japanese exporters and to expand the economy, the Japanese government chose a loose monetary policy, which led to a huge bubble in real estate and stock values due to limited investment opportunities.[21]

Structural Reform

The burst of the bubble in 1991 began a prolonged period of economic stagnation and made it necessary for Japan to conduct reforms.[22] Much has been said about the progress and nature of Japanese reform efforts and little has been agreed upon. Most observers do not view Japanese reforms as significant or successful, while some see substantial incremental change that may lead to a fundamental break from the past.[23] Whichever is the case, what is clear is that a stable new Japanese model of political economy is yet to emerge.[24]

Because of globalization and internal dynamic, the Japanese economic structure has changed. The Japanese government has liberalized financial flows, relaxed labor regulations, privatized special public corporations, and revised the pension system, among other measures. The government has also conducted reorganization of itself. The private sector has responded with reforms of its own.[25]

As a case in point, incremental change for the past decade has added up, making Japanese corporations different from before. The lifelong employment system has been eroded. Japanese companies have reduced new hires, hiring less than half as many new graduates in 2003 as in 1997, and now prefer to hire cheaper part-timers or temporary-contract employees. The percentage of "nonregular" workers that accounted for 18.8 percent of the labor force in 1990 reached 30 percent by early 2005.[26] Put more broadly, Japan's social protection system is unraveling.[27] Moreover, shareholders now have greater influence than before. Although 46 percent of the company stocks were held as cross-shareholdings and only 6 percent by foreign investors in 1992, foreign investors' share increased to 22 percent while cross-shareholdings accounted for 24 percent in 2004. Now institutional investors challenge the management of companies. A few high-profile hostile takeover attempts, although unsuccessful, have forced company management to pay more attention to profitability and dividends to shareholders than previously.[28]

At the same time, it is easy to understand why many Japan watchers do not see much progress in the Japanese reform. With the burst of the bubble, there was much discussion in the Japanese policy community to shift to a liberal market economy. They criticized the old system and wanted to break the iron triangle.[29] They argued that Japan can only compete better in a globalizing world by liberalizing its economy.[30] But Japan clearly is not yet a liberal market economy. It is more puzzling if we consider the fact that the Japanese public actually wants reform, as indicated in Junichiro Koizumi's astonishing victory at the September 11, 2005, snap election.

Why is it so difficult to reform, and why has there not been a significant voter revolt in Japan despite a decade of economic stagnation? As T. J. Pempel has argued, this is the central puzzle about contemporary Japanese political economy. His explanation is that the advantage of the incumbents in Japan has not been significantly weakened by the 1994 electoral system reform, particularly in the rural areas. Besides, based on the new electoral system, incumbents who lose in their swing-seat districts may still be elected on the proportional party ticket. Also, Japan's fiscal centralization means that it is difficult for opposition parties to try out new ideas and develop local power bases. Moreover, the beneficiaries of the existing system resist fiercely any structural reform efforts.[31]

Taking a middle ground between macrolevel analysis of the state and a microlevel study of the private sector, Steven Vogel has offered an institutionalist explanation of the extent and nature of Japanese reform. Structural reform is not a simple task of giving the market greater room. Because market systems are embedded in state institutions of laws, customs, and norms, reforming them requires revisions of these institutions as well. It follows then that Japan's existing institutions are transforming themselves, which explains both why there have been drastic institutional changes and why the emerging Japanese model does not look like a liberal market economy.[32] Vogel's insight will also be helpful for understanding reform efforts conducted by other East Asian economies.

THE POLITICAL ECONOMY SYSTEMS OF THE ASIAN TIGERS

The second tier of East Asian economies includes Singapore, Hong Kong, Taiwan, and South Korea, as shown in Table 2.1. These "four tigers" focused on catching up with developed countries quickly. Because they started later than Japan, they had to move up at a faster pace, which could explain why South Korea, Taiwan, and Singapore had interventionist governments. At the same time, Hong Kong has followed a free-market policy, even more so than Great Britain and the United States. Thus, the East Asian experience does not endorse state intervention in the economy as a necessary condition for rapid economic development.

The four tigers are different politically. Being Japanese colonies before 1945, Taiwan and South Korea share more similarities with Japan. By contrast, Singapore and Hong Kong had similar experiences as British colonies. Ironically, even though the British colonial governments practiced a higher degree of democracy than the Japanese counterparts and sought to leave behind a parliamentary democracy, it is Taiwan and South Korea that have become consolidated democracies. Unlike Japan, which consolidated the democratic system created by the American Occupation authorities, South Korea began with an autocratic government, experimented with democracy in 1960–1961, made an authoritarian turn in the 1960s, increased repression in the 1970s, and began democratization in the late 1980s. The Nationalist Party or the Kuomintang (KMT) government, which was authoritarian, moved to Taiwan after losing the civil war in China and began with high repression. But the KMT government began gradual reform in the 1970s and moved toward democracy around the same time as South Korea. Singapore had a stable one-party dominant system like Japan. Singapore has become one of the most affluent and well-governed countries in the world but remains largely nondemocratic. I will not discuss Hong Kong here because the island was a British colony until 1997 and has been a Special Administrative Region of the PRC since then. Hong Kong has a limited democratic system under the arrangement of "one country, two systems." Hong Kong is scheduled for full electoral democracy down the line, but it remains a question whether Beijing will allow that to happen and how a democracy may operate within the constitutional framework of the PRC.

South Korea

The Republic of Korea was founded in 1948. After the Korean War ended in 1953, the South Korean government under Rhee Syngman was initially interested mainly in unification with the North. General Park Chung Hee's coup in 1961 began almost three decades of authoritarian rule in the country. Park's declared purposes were to bring about economic and social transformations of the country and to strengthen national security.

South Korea took the Japanese model to another level. The state was more interventionist than the Japanese state and any other nonsocialist East Asian economies. It has been argued that as a later industrializer than Japan, South Korea needed a stronger government to deliberately distort relative prices to target investment for long-term economic growth.[33]

The purpose of fast industrialization and the effort to support large business were mutually reinforcing. The state tried to limit the expansion of large businesses to some extent without much success. The authoritarian state needed an alliance with big business.[34] In fact, President Park said explicitly that the country needed large modern enterprises to compete internationally, although he also saw the need for the state to control these very enterprises. With the state's power over licensing and its control of the commercial banks, the government indeed forced some large enterprises out of existence for economic or political reasons.[35] Such a cozy state-business relationship may logically lead to corruption and did in South Korea, which would come to be called crony capitalism.[36] However, until the Asian financial crisis, analysts tended to praise the South Korean model because the big South Korean companies that the government supported did become internationally competitive.

While recognizing the presence of a strong state in South Korea, South Korean society was politically active and was difficult for the state to co-opt, indicated by often militant student demonstrations and labor movements.[37] Kim Dae Jung, an opposition candidate against President Park, received 46 percent of the votes in the 1971 presidential election. In response, the Park regime increased its political repression of the opposition. However, the state could not truly subdue its opponents. The country's eventual turn to democracy had much to do with bottom-up social protests.

South Korea turned to democracy in 1987 because of societal pressure and the anticipation of the 1988 Seoul Olympics. President Chun Doo Hwan's presidential candidate Roh Tae Woo made a surprising proposal to accept the opposition demands for amending the constitution and holding direct presidential elections. With a new constitution adopted in October, the voters elected the next president by direct popular vote. With the opposition split between Kim Young Sam and Kim Dae Jung, Roh won with a plurality of 36.6 percent of the vote against the two Kims. South Korean democracy was consolidated in 1992 with the second presidential election under the new democratic constitution. Kim Young Sam defeated Kim Dae Jung for the presidency.[38]

Kim Dae Jung got his chance in the December 1997 presidential election, in the middle of the Asian financial crisis. Unlike Japan, a voter revolt put Kim Dae Jung in the seat of president. Responding to public demands, the new government under Kim Dae Jung introduced more serious reforms as the majority of voters had wanted and achieved some good results. Consequently, South Korea sustained democracy through a serious economic crisis.[39] South Korea has risen from the ashes of the crisis. Because of its young democracy, the South Korean government has also expanded social safety nets since the crisis. A similar trend is found in Taiwan.[40]

Taiwan

Similar to South Korea, Taiwan was a "frontline" economy feeling threatened by communism. Taiwan had an authoritarian regime until the late 1980s. However, unlike South Korea, which took a more authoritarian turn in the early 1970s, the KMT government began gradual reform around the same time. Also unlike South Korea, the KMT government faced a major communal divide between the minority mainlander ruling party and the Taiwanese majority society, an all-important fault line that helped shape the KMT's economic policies and the nature and progress of Taiwan's democratization.

The KMT government moved to Taiwan after losing the civil war to the Chinese Communist Party. Ironically, the KMT acquired far greater unity in Taiwan than in the mainland because Chiang Kai-shek took mainly the loyal and competent with him to the island. The KMT also imposed martial law in Taiwan from May 1949 to July 1987, with severe security measures to repress the opposition. Thus, the KMT had a strong state to implement its policies.[41] While the KMT initially hoped to retake the mainland, it increasingly accepted the fact that it should focus on Taiwan, which was particularly the case for Chiang Ching-kuo, the son of Chiang Kai-shek and the heir apparent. The KMT's survival came to depend on economic performance and inclusion of Taiwanese into the party. Concerned about the mainland, the government saw economic growth as a matter of life and death.

To accomplish the central mission of economic growth, the state largely allowed technocrats rather than politicians to handle economic decision making. Since the Taiwanese natives controlled the private sector, the state turned to state-owned enterprises for heavy industrialization.[42] It was also easier for an outsider government without local ties to conduct land reform, which would benefit the economy by turning the land to the Taiwanese tillers and benefit the KMT politically by weakening local power bases that might pose a challenge to the party. At the same time, the KMT allowed the Taiwanese businesses to prosper with few restrictions, and the government limited the scope of the state enterprises. There was thus plenty of room for social mobility and economic advancement.[43]

Although the KMT as a Leninist party is different from Japan's LDP, Taiwan was similar to Japan in that it had a one-party dominant system. Taiwan allowed limited elections as a way to mobilize political support from the Taiwanese majority and to improve its international image, particularly in the eyes of the United

States whose support was crucial for an increasingly isolated Taiwan.[44] Similar to Japan, Taiwan had a multiseat, single, and nontransferable vote electoral system that favored the incumbents. The KMT mastered electioneering.[45] Nevertheless, the one-party dominant system in Taiwan did end despite the tremendous advantage of incumbents in forging corporatist links. One main reason is that the Taiwanese majority viewed the KMT as an outsider, a handicap that proved difficult for the party to overcome even though the party adopted a "Taiwanization" strategy.

Chiang Ching-kuo began a slow process of reform after 1972, which made a dramatic turn to democratization in 1986 when the formation of the opposition party, the Democratic Progressive Party (DPP), was tolerated. Chiang subsequently announced his intention to lift martial law, which would make it much more difficult to repress freedom of speech and freedom of association. Lee Tenghui of the KMT won the first direct presidential election in March 1996. However, in a dramatic shift of the balance of power, Chen Shui-bian of the DPP won the March 2000 presidential election by a small margin in a three-way election against the KMT candidate and a candidate leading a splinter party from the KMT.[46]

Singapore

Similar to South Korea and Taiwan, Singapore had a strong sense of vulnerability. After being granted autonomy in 1959, the conservative People's Action Party (PAP) government led by Lee Kuan Yew faced a strong leftist challenge at home and in neighboring Malaysia. Like South Korea and Taiwan, Singapore experienced a separation trauma with its expulsion from Malaysia in 1965 after two years of merger. The split was a result of the Singaporean government's demand that Malaysia should belong to Malaysians as defined by citizenship rather than to Malays as defined by ethnicity.[47] Moreover, with a population of less than four million, Singapore is a small, Chinese-majority city state in the middle of a Muslim Malay world and is situated in a competitive global market. The PAP has used all these perceived vulnerabilities to justify its tough, disciplined rule in a country that has become one of the most affluent in the world.[48]

Many small countries are democratic, but economically successful small democracies are mainly found in Europe. Small countries that participate in the global economy are more exposed by definition and are therefore more vulnerable. That basic reality has political consequences for the type of political system likely to be adopted. Some small European countries use a corporatist system to manage the challenge.[49] Some small states are simply failing. Singapore offers an alternative approach.

The Singaporean government sought to control the strategic domestic markets and institutions to advance its main purpose of job creation and economic growth. The state followed a philosophy of nurturing the private enterprises to serve as an instrument of economic growth. Unlike South Korea, Singapore has actively sought foreign direct investment. The Singaporean government does not just formulate plans. Rather, it issues and enforces government directives. Utilizing the Economic Development Board offices overseas, the Singaporean government monitors closely the developments in the global market to select potential winning sectors.[50]

Similar to Taiwan and Japan, Singapore had a dominant one-party system. By 2006, the PAP had won ten straight elections since independence. As conservative as the KMT and the LDP, the PAP fought the leftists in Singapore to the extent that Lee sought integration with Malaysia to check on the power of the leftists as well as to gain access to a larger market.[51] Unlike the KMT, the PAP remains the dominant party despite new challenges. The early 1990s saw the PAP's declining electoral support and a new generation of leadership.[52] Lee Kuan Yew retired in 1990, replaced by Goh Chok Tong. But the PAP increased its electoral support in the 1997 election. Lee Kuan Yew's son, Lee Hsien Loong, became prime minister in 2004.

The PAP maintains political rule because of Lee Kuan Yew's political skills, Singapore's rapid economic growth, the party's clean image, the party's ability to field new candidates, and tough measures against opposition parties. Lee skillfully manipulated his communist and communalist opponents to his advantage.[53] Singapore's rapid growth since its independence gave the PAP an instant boost. Moreover, the PAP government introduced policy measures to improve the living standards of Singaporean citizens in addition to letting the rising tide lift all boats. In particular, the government implemented a public housing program that was the key to its continuous electoral success. Singapore has a clean government, as indicated by Transparency International's highly publicized corruption perceptions index survey. The 2006 survey ranks Singapore as the fifth cleanest government in the world, trailing only Finland, Iceland, New Zealand, and Denmark among 163 countries rated in the survey.[54] With the advantage of the incumbents, the PAP has been able to recruit competent candidates for elections. Last but not least, the PAP has employed coercive measures such as the Internal Security Act to intimidate opponents and adopted a strategy of suing opponents to bankruptcy in recent years.

THE POLITICAL ECONOMY SYSTEMS OF SOUTHEAST ASIA

Southeast Asia has ten countries, namely Singapore, Malaysia, Thailand, Indonesia, the Philippines, Brunei, Vietnam, Cambodia, Laos, and Burma/Myanmar. Singapore has been discussed in the previous section. Vietnam, North Korea, and Cambodia will be discussed in the next section. This section will not discuss Brunei, a rich, absolutist monarchy that became independent in 1983.

Analysts often lump Malaysia, Thailand, Indonesia, and the Philippines together as "the ASEAN Four." They are all third-tier countries in terms of economic development. They are not as advanced economically as the four tigers, but they have made substantial economic progress, particularly Malaysia and Thailand. Different from the second-tier tigers, the ASEAN Four are rich in resources and are major agricultural exporters. They were also largely market-oriented early on. The state in the ASEAN Four is less interventionist and developmentalist than Northeast Asian governments.[55] By contrast, Burma/Myanmar, which shares similar geographical and social features with the ASEAN Four, has chosen a semisocialist economic autarky and harsh political repression under a military junta, a lethal combination that has led to a failed state in a region that has seen much economic and political progress for the past decades.

Malaysia

Communalism defines the Malaysian system of political economy. The native Malays accounted for 50 percent of the population at the time of national independence in 1957, the Chinese community 37 percent, and the Indian community 11 percent.[56] The Malay-dominated government categorized the Malays and other indigenous people as *bumiputra* or "the son of the soil" as opposed to non-*bumiputra* like the Chinese and Indians.

The main story of Malaysia has been the interplay between Malay political power and Chinese economic power. During the British colonial period, the Malays were mainly subsistence farmers, whereas the Chinese and the Indians engaged in more lucrative rubber, mining, retail, and financial sectors. Based on their numerical advantage and traditional rule in the land, the Malays possessed political power, which they used to advance their political and economic interests.

The Malays and the Chinese struck a bargain at the time of independence: The Malays would enjoy political dominance with special rights while the Chinese could continue their dominant role in business activities. Moreover, the Chinese should help the Malays gain economically—closing the income and educational gap—while the Malays should help the Chinese gain politically—gaining more access to the public sector and greater rights such as Chinese language education. The bargain was embodied in the political structure, which was modeled after the British parliamentary system. The ruling Alliance included the dominant United Malays National Organization (UMNO), the Malaysian Chinese Association (MCA), and the Malaysian Indian Congress (MIC), and there was much deal making and compromise among them.[57] The political regime in 1957–1969 has been described as "consociational democracy" in which the elites from different ethnic groups accommodate each other to allow democracy to operate.[58]

The violent ethnic riots on May 13, 1969, undid that initial bargain. Three days earlier, the Alliance had lost seats to the opposition parties in the election. The root causes for the riots were the Chinese resentment for the special rights for the Malays and the Malay resentment that the economic gap with the Chinese had not narrowed.

After the riots, a national state of emergency was declared. The Malay political elites then created a more authoritarian regime to explicitly encourage nation-building and communal harmony on their terms, which meant less political influence for the non-Malays. UMNO created a new ruling coalition, the *Barisan Nasional* (National Front), that incorporated more parties. UMNO adopted the New Economic Policy (NEP) in 1971, which was essentially an affirmative action for the politically powerful Malay majority to enhance their economic power over the non-Malays. The NEP aimed at making employment at all occupation levels reflect the racial composition of the country and increasing the ownership of the productive wealth to 30 percent for the bumiputra by 1990. The NEP precipitated Malaysia's shift from limited state intervention in the economy to a heavily interventionist approach.

The Malaysian state became strong and developmentalist. It did not face an entrenched landowning class like in the Philippines. The dominant Chinese business community was politically vulnerable. The Malay business class grew strong but remained beholden to the state for favors and protection. Malaysia also had a strong leader in Mahathir Mohamad, who became prime minister in 1981 and ruled until October 2003.

The NEP achieved some of its objectives by 1990. The interethnic income gap narrowed, and the Chinese no longer monopolized the national economy. The fact that Malaysia has performed better in racial harmony than most other countries in similar situations means that all communities have benefited from stability. Large income gaps between ethnic communities are likely to lead to tensions and make it impossible for anybody to achieve their economic goals. Moreover, as Harold Crouch has pointed out, the Malaysian state has become more repressive and responsive at the same time.[59]

However, the goal of 30 percent Malay ownership was not achieved, and the income gap within the Malay community widened. Not surprisingly, directives from bureaucrats and politicians created economic distortions. Successful Malay businessmen owed their affluence to their connections to UMNO politicians, and few indigenous entrepreneurs had emerged. To ensure sustainable economic development, Malay politicians also tried to accommodate the non-Malays, although not as much as the Malays. Chinese businessmen basically adopted the strategy of co-opting native politicians or bumiputra business people with political connections. In short, the state used rents, which are the returns from government protection or favor, to achieve desired political and economic consequences, namely UMNO's dominance and a redistribution of wealth in favor of the Malays.[60]

When the NEP reached its twenty-year target in 1991, Mahathir announced new development strategies of Vision 2020 and the National Development Policy (NDP) to turn Malaysia into a developed nation by the year 2020. The new plans focused more on faster economic growth and liberalization than interethnic redistribution and state intervention.[61] However, interethnic considerations still drive Malaysian politics, which in turn influences its economic policy. The Asian financial crisis provided an opportunity for the society to push for greater democracy, but Mahathir survived with harsh measures against the opposition.

Thailand

Thailand has a constitutional monarchy. The absolute monarchy ended in 1932 after a military coup. King Bhumibol Adulyadel, who has reigned since 1946, enjoys high respect from the Thais and has occasionally intervened in Thai politics as a steady hand. In May 1992, the King criticized the prime minister and the opposition leader on national television for the military suppression of prodemocracy demonstrations, an action that led to the country's return to civilian rule. More recently, the King appeared to have tolerated the military coup that ousted Prime Minister Thaksin Shinawatra in September 2006.

Similar to Malaysia, Thailand also has a large ethnic Chinese community, but unlike other Southeast Asian countries, the ethnic Chinese have largely assimilated into the Thai society. This was due to the compulsory Thai language education in the Thai schools rather than a European language starting in the 1920s. Also, the Chinese immigrants found it culturally easier to accept Theravada Buddhism than Islam. Equally important, unlike most other Southeast Asian governments that adopted legislation or policy to restrict the rights of the Chinese, the Thai government removed restrictions after the Second World War.[62]

Unlike Malaysia but similar to most East Asian economies, Thai military officers were dominant in the Thai government since 1932. The military government introduced the first economic development plan in 1958, but the state had limited intervention in the marketplace. Similar to some other developing nations, the military relied on technocrats to formulate development strategies. Thai generals also became involved in business ventures, legal or illegal, for personal wealth. The military and business leaders accommodated each other. However, with the mounting social protest and insurgency and with the weakening of the military-business alliance in the early 1970s, a student movement provided the catalyst for the downfall of the military government.[63] A short period of democracy was ended by a military coup in October 1976, but the military leaders had to appear accommodating to the public.

The economic growth in the 1980s led to greater societal demands for liberalization and political participation. In particular, the business community became more powerful since the early 1970s, and they helped found political parties and supported parliamentary democracy.[64] A general election in 1988 selected Chatichai Choonhaven as prime minister, but corruption charges eroded the public support for the Chatichai government. The military launched a coup in February 1991. After the May 1992 uprising, a formal democracy was established.[65]

In the 1990s, the Democrat Party headed by Chuan Leekpai formed the ruling coalition most of the time. The party at first represented the provincial interests but became a party for the Bangkok business community and the urban middle class. The party was blamed for the country's fall during the 1997 Asian financial crisis.[66] In its place rose the *Thai Rak Thai* (Thai Love Thai) party led by Thaksin Shinawatra, who became prime minister in February 2001. Being one of the richest businessmen in Thailand, Thaksin's rise symbolized the rise of domestic capital. Tapping into postcrisis sentiment, Thaksin followed a populist policy to support the businesses hurt by the crisis and to make promises to the rural poor, which were largely delivered. Thai Rak Thai enjoyed a clear electoral majority, rare in Thai electoral politics.[67] However, Thaksin came to be viewed as corrupt. In February 2006, large street protests took place, which forced a snap election in April, which he won. The election revealed a clear class division: Thaksin was popular among the urban poor and rural population for his generous programs for them but he angered the urban middle class.

The military, which had experienced a notable decline in the 1990s, staged a bloodless coup on September 19, 2006, the first military coup since 1991. Even though Thaksin had gradually undermined the democratic institutions and created a political impasse with the opposition, the military coup was a setback for democracy.

Indonesia

After independence in 1949, the Indonesian government practiced constitutional democracy in 1950–1957. In response to regional rebellions in 1957–1958, President Sukarno created a presidential-style strong government in 1959 and ruled under the so-called "Guided Democracy" in 1958–1965. With high inflation, the economy began to decline sharply by the mid-1960s. More seriously, the Indonesian Communist Party (*Partai Komunis Indonesia*—PKI) and the army were competing for the state power, which came to a head in 1965. In a massive bloodbath, hundreds of thousands of Communists and suspected supporters were massacred throughout the country. Sukarno was forced to resign. General Suharto came to dominate in the next two years and became president in 1968. Suharto created "the New Order" in which the military that had already become part of the ruling elite came to dominate.[68]

From 1968 to 1998, the country's rapid economic growth led to more authoritarianism than democratization.[69] The Suharto government created Golkar, a type of state party in 1971, which weakened old political parties. In terms of the relationship between the state and business, the state had a clear upper hand because the dominant Chinese business community was politically vulnerable owing to their outsider status in the eyes of the largely Muslim indigenous population and was dependent on the political patronage of the government.[70]

Foreign aid from 1968 onward helped to stabilize Indonesia's economic situation. Indonesia's revenues from oil exports increased sharply in the early 1970s, which facilitated the country's political stability. Whereas the oil exports provided 29 percent of the central government's revenues in 1970, they accounted for 70 percent in 1981.[71] Windfalls often distorted the economic and political structure with long-term negative consequences.[72] The Indonesian government used the oil revenues for domestic investment rather than domestic consumption, but increased domestic investment led to higher prices of nontradable relative to tradable goods and those of imports relative to exports. The appreciation of the Indonesia currency, rupiah, due to current account surpluses reduced the competitiveness of Indonesia's exports. The oil windfalls also led to more corruption.[73]

With declining oil prices in 1982, the Indonesian government had to reduce its ambitious industrialization programs. In response, the government turned to deregulation and export-led industrialization in the mid-1980s. The Suharto government focused reforms in the areas where the politico-bureaucrats and business conglomerates could benefit or at least would not suffer.[74]

The Asian financial crisis hit Indonesia the hardest, exacting high political prices. Suharto resigned in May 1998, ending his thirty-two-year rule. The postcrisis reforms were more thorough than the liberalization measures adopted between the mid-1980s and the mid-1990s. More important, Indonesia, the world's largest Muslim country, now has a formal democracy defined as having regular and competitive elections participated in by freely associated political parties. The slowest to recover from the crisis, Indonesian economy has improved, particularly under current president Susilo Bambang Yudhoyono.

The Philippines

The Philippines became independent in July 1946, with a constitutional democracy modeled after the American system. At the same time, the country is known as the "antidevelopment state," with weaker economic performances than most of its high-flying neighbors. Thus, those skeptical of democracy often use the

Philippines as an example of why American-style democracy is inappropriate for a developing nation.

President Ferdinand Marcos introduced martial law in 1972 with the declared aim of creating a strong developmental state like South Korea. Nevertheless, the Philippine economy worsened. As Alasdair Bowie and Danny Unger observed, "whether under democratic or authoritarian regime, particular characteristics of Philippine economy and society persisted in producing poor economic results after the 1950s." The reason they gave, similar to many other analysts, is the dominance of oligarchic, landowning families that have captured the state to advance their own interests.[75] Put simply, oligarchy defines the Philippine political economy system. By contrast, the central government is weak because civil servants are beholden to their political patrons outside the bureaucracy.

The Philippines actually enjoyed healthy economic growth in the 1950s and the early 1960s, better than most Southeast Asian countries. Having a constitutional democracy with checks and balances, the country boasted one of the strongest legislatures in East Asia, which encouraged interelite competition and greater response to mass demands. At the same time, the executive branch remained strong and the state did not adopt any policies against the interests of the oligarchs. By the early 1970s, the country faced a mounting political crisis with street demonstrations and a communist insurgency. Marcos declared martial law in 1972, ushering in authoritarianism.[76]

Political scientist Samuel Huntington offered an explanation of why some democracies in the developing world had turned authoritarian in a seminal book in the late 1960s. He argued that a developing nation often experiences political disorder when it achieves rapid economic growth, which unleashes social forces and increases expectations that strain fragile political institutions.[77] His theory fit in the Philippine case. A democratic system and progress led to mass expectation that strained the political system. The ruling elite faced a choice between expanding participation in policy process, which was perceived to be against their own interest, and restricting participation. Filipino elite chose the latter.[78] The country would pay dearly for that choice.

When Marcos was elected president in 1965, he was a symbol of hope. He sought advice from technocrats for economic policy making. But his policy initiatives lost steam quickly. He won reelection in 1969 partly based on public works.[79] In 1972, while in his second term as president, Marcos declared martial law was necessary to combat civil disorder, but the real reason was to maintain his power since the constitution did not allow a third term. With martial law, the state capacity strengthened. Marcos initially talked about reform, but his regime quickly became a model of crony capitalism. Marcos used state power to enrich his family and his cronies, which led to increased social opposition.[80]

The Philippines faced a debt crisis in the early 1980s. The Marcos regime could not ensure sufficient financial resources for the central government because of the resistance of the powerful families. Marcos incurred foreign loans to finance his projects, which were largely unproductive. It was easy to borrow money from Western banks in the 1970s. The first oil shock led to a massive flow of "petrodollar" from oil exporting countries to Western banks and simultaneously decreased investment opportunities in the developed countries. As a result, Western bankers eagerly pushed large loans on governments and public enterprises in large developing countries in Latin America and elsewhere. With the second oil crisis in 1979 and rising interest rates, a major debt crisis occurred. The Latin American debt crisis that took place in the early 1980s also hit a few non-Latin American countries such as the Philippines.

The assassination of Benigno Aquino, the main opposition leader, in Manila in August 1983 led to stronger societal opposition and U.S. criticism. Aquino had just returned from political exile in the United States. In response to U.S. pressure, Marcos called an early presidential election for February 1986, in which Corazon Aquino, the widow of Benigno Aquino, claimed victory, supported by hundreds of thousands of demonstrators in the streets. Although the Filipino military had been less inclined to intervene in domestic politics than other Southeast Asian militaries, the martial law politicized the Filipino military. But the military switched side, and the Marcos family was forced to flee the country.

The Aquino "People Power" revolution did not fundamentally reform the country as triumphant street demonstrators had hoped for. Aquino's victory was not a true revolution as many had thought but a return to the dominance of the powerful provincial families.[81] Being from one of the wealthiest land-owning families herself, Aquino did not push the land reform hard. It did not help that Aquino exempted her 6,000-hectare family estate.[82] The election of Fidel Ramos as president in 1992 led to reform and modest economic growth in the early 1990s. That strategy came to be viewed as faulty when the Asian financial crisis hit. Lower-class voters put a populist former movie star Joseph Estrada into the seat of presidency. However, Estrada created his own cronies. The old elite and the middle class replaced Estrada with Gloria Macapagal Arroyo, who has focused more on supporting the United States' war on terror rather than on reforms.

Burma/Myanmar

Burma became independent from Great Britain in 1948, one of the earliest independent countries in East Asia. The current military government changed the country's name to Myanmar in 1989, a name recognized by the United Nations. I will refer to the country as Burma before 1989 and Myanmar thereafter.

Similar to other Southeast Asian countries, Burma faced a daunting task of nation-building from the beginning. The prospect for the country was promising. In fact, a contemporary observer might well have predicted that Burma would end up performing better than Thailand and South Korea, the two countries with a similar population size and comparable living standards. The reasons for such optimism came from the fact that the country was the world's largest exporter of rice before World War II, it was a producer of oil, and it had untapped natural resources, easy waterways, and a high level of literacy.[83] But as we know now, Myanmar is a failed state and one of the least developed nations in the world, sharply different from Thailand and South Korea. The best way to think about Burma's ultimate failure is to see the government making one blunder after another, leading to a vicious cycle of economic and political developments.

After independence, Burma followed parliamentary democracy in 1948–1962. Various groups contended for control of the state, resulting in a civil war and a weak government with weak financial capacity. These contestants for the state included the Anti-Fascist People's Freedom League, the Burmese Communist Party, the Karen National Union, and some other groups.[84] The civilian government allowed General Ne Win to run a caretaker government for eighteen months in 1958–1960 to avoid a possible civil war.

With a taste of political power and foreseeing continuous political chaos, Ne Win seized the state power in a military coup in March 1962 with a declared aim to restore order and to prevent a possible breakup of the country. Ne Win sought to create what he called the "Burmese Way to Socialism," which mixed elements of Buddhism, humanism, and Marxism. The government launched a nationalization campaign in 1963 and adopted economic autarky in its foreign economic policy, the opposite of the more open orientation of the ASEAN Four even though Indonesia and Thailand also had military governments. Ne Win's development strategy had a devastating effect on Burmese political economy. More seriously, since the government had little control over the border regions, illicit trade boomed. It was estimated that the black market operation accounted for 40 percent of the nation's GDP by 1987, which explained why some insurgent groups ended up better financed and better armed than government troops.[85] Ironically, the strengthened quasi-states and insurgent groups in the border regions were also used to justify a military government in Rangoon.[86]

With mounting social unrest, Ne Win was forced to resign in 1988. A military junta, the State Peace and Development Council, has ruled in the country since 1988. In 1988, the military government announced a shift of development strategy to a market-oriented economy and to attract foreign investment, including in its prized oil and natural gas sector. However, with the crackdown after the electoral victory by the National League for Democracy led by Aung San Suu Kyi in

May 1990, the West imposed sanctions on Myanmar. With political repression and mismanagement by the military government, the prospect for the country remains bleak.

THE TRANSITIONAL POLITICAL ECONOMIES

East Asia has had a number of socialist countries, namely China, North Korea, Vietnam, Cambodia, and Laos. Myanmar, discussed above, also follows a unique socialist path by the military. I discuss China, North Korea, Vietnam, and Cambodia in this section. North Korea was more industrialized and urbanized than China and Vietnam. The Chinese Communist Party and the Vietnamese Communist Party won the state power even though they both received substantial external assistance. The communist victory in North Korea had much to do with the Soviet occupation, which made the country similar to Eastern Europe. Similarly, the Cambodian People's Party (CPP), the current ruling party in Cambodia, traced its origin to the Vietnamese invasion in 1978. But the CPP did not have as much time to consolidate its power as its counterpart in North Korea. Unlike China and North Korea, Vietnam experienced a prolonged period of war after the Second World War, which affected its economic system.

The socialist system includes political rule by a communist party and a command economy, in which the government dictates economic activities. The socialist countries all sought to achieve rapid economic development through multiple-year plans based on high accumulation. The national purpose of rapid economic growth is embedded in the communist ideology. The communist system is supposed to represent the highest level of material production. The socialist countries also competed with advanced capitalist countries. So for both security and propaganda purposes, they needed to catch up with the West or their capitalist rivals in their regions.

China

The People's Republic of China (PRC) was founded in 1949. The Chinese Communist Party (CCP) government transformed the Chinese economic system into a Soviet-style command economy by 1957. Beijing introduced the first five-year plan in 1953.[87] Mao Zedong decided to develop China's own unique path to socialism and launched the "Great Leap Forward" campaign in 1958, which essentially involved mass mobilization to achieve rapid industrialization and collectivization of the agriculture. The ensuing three-year Great Famine was the worst man-made disaster in postwar East Asian history. Mao retreated to some extent and allowed Liu Shaoqi and Deng Xiaoping to restore economic order by implementing moderate policy. China's economic recovery in the early 1960s served as the backdrop for a rivalry between two lines within the party leadership. For Mao, China's main purpose should be to create a revolutionary society and to engage in a continuous revolution to educate the young. Liu and his supporters did not oppose that objective, but they did not endorse Mao's radical positions. Mao launched the Cultural Revolution in 1966 to purge Liu and his supporters, resulting in ten years of political chaos and economic stagnation.

Deng launched reform in 1978, leading to a major shift in China's national purposes. The Chinese government and society now share the same goal of making the country stronger and its people richer. At the same time, there were early challenges from hardliners who argued that Deng's reform was leading China astray. There were also social protests and intellectual demands for political reform. The Deng line has held after several rounds of ideological and policy debates within the government.

We can ask three major questions about the contemporary Chinese political economy. First, why did the Chinese leadership decide to adopt economic reform and opening policy in the late 1970s? Second, why did China succeed in economic reform compared with economic reforms in some other transition economies? Third, why did the Chinese leadership adopt economic reform without political reform, and will economic reform lead to political opening in the foreseeable future?

Why did the CCP decide on reform? One simple explanation is that they had little choice since the country was on the brink of bankruptcy. However, when a country is facing crises, it is possible to imagine other policy choices such as retrenchment or muddling-through. An analysis of the Chinese institutions offers a good explanation. It is both the strengths and the weaknesses of the state that explained the choice of the CCP. The fact that China was not as institutionalized in the communist political economy system as the Soviet Union meant that it was easier for the CCP to try something new.[88] China's administrative decentralization also meant that local officials could experiment with new policies that might become models for other localities.

The Chinese state could sustain the reform because the Chinese reform was done in such a way that it turned party officials into entrepreneurs who benefit from the new political economy system emerging in the country. Take China's countryside, for instance. Fiscal decentralization and decollectivization have allowed local officials to become winners in the reform era.[89]

The CCP wants to maintain its dominance, which it believes is important for social stability. To some extent, it is easy to understand why a ruling party does not want to let go of political power. However, in the late 1980s, the Soviet Union and Eastern Europe did have political reform, which led to the demise of communism in Europe. Why not China? A simple way to look at this is that Mikhail Gorbachev wanted to reform the Soviet Union rather than ending the communist rule, but his choice to start with political reform unleashed forces that led to the demise of the communist system. By choosing to start with economic reform and doing so very gradually, the CCP had a greater capacity to manage the change, and China managed to grow out of its planned economy.[90]

Over time, the Chinese economic reform has transformed China. As far as the political economy system is concerned, the direct state role in economy has diminished. By the 2000s, the percentage of national economy directly controlled by the state sector declined to about one-third. It is inevitable that China's rapid economic development and transformation for the past three decades should impact its political system, but the CCP continues to adapt. For one thing, the party is co-opting the new and powerful private business interests by absorbing them into the party system. Private entrepreneurs are the products of economic reform and will naturally support economic reform, but they are unlikely to become agents of political change in China because of their behavior and beliefs and their close ties with the state.[91] In fact, Minxin Pei argued that China's economic reform has stalled and a gradualist approach has led to a trapped transition, in which an emerging predatory state prevents democratization. The reasons he cited include weak institutions, lack of government accountability, and corruption.[92] Similarly, Mary Gallagher suggested that Chinese reform has so far strengthened the Chinese state, which will delay democratization.[93] Conversely, Bruce Gilley maintained that economic reform has transformed the Chinese elite, who will lead China down the path of democracy.[94]

It has often been noted that if Taiwan could democratize, China could too. The KMT is a Leninist party, just like the CCP. However, despite considerable similarities between the two parties, they are different in important ways, particularly leadership's willingness to listen to the society and the parties' adaptation to the changed domestic and external environments. Thus, the KMT's evolution may not be a good indicator of what's to come for the CCP.[95] The KMT also allowed limited elections, which gave a valuable training experience to the opposition and allowed better feedback from society to the ruling party.

A combination of political and economic power is emerging in China that share interest in repressing the societal discontent from the "losers." Government officials can easily gain personal wealth based on their political power and policy influence, which is of course the essence of crony capitalism. There has been much discussion about social justice in China. In a populist appeal, the government now talks about creating a "harmonious society." However, without a genuine political reform that leads to competitive elections, an independent judiciary, and freedom of press, there is little hope that the CCP party state will be able to discipline itself.

Vietnam

Under the 1954 Geneva Accord, Vietnam was divided into the communist north and capitalist south. The Democratic Republic of Vietnam in the north adopted the Soviet model in 1955 and nationalized most of its industrial and transportation enterprises by the end of 1960. The communist government also collectivized agriculture. Hanoi introduced the first five-year plan for 1961–1965 at the end of the 1950s. Once North Vietnam unified the country in 1975 and established the Socialist Republic of Vietnam in 1976, it introduced the socialist planned economy in the south as well.[96]

The Soviet approach of planned economy led to economic crises in 1978–1979. In 1981, the Vietnamese government adopted reform measures within the central planning framework. Vietnam could not adopt more drastic reform until Le Duan, the head of the wartime leadership, died in 1986.[97] Political leadership at a crucial junction is important. The Sixth Party Congress held in December 1986, under new leadership, adopted a policy of economic reform, or *doi moi*. Vietnam's reform shares similarities with China's. Both reforms were gradual and cautious, ending with more drastic transformation of economy. Both countries have experienced a virtuous cycle of early successes encouraging later reform initiatives.[98]

Vietnam also adjusted its foreign policy. Vietnam invaded Cambodia in 1978 and did not withdraw until 1989. Because of the invasion, Vietnam isolated itself from everyone in Southeast Asia except Laos, as well as from China, Japan, and the United States. A few years after the launch of doi moi, Vietnam withdrew from Cambodia and eventually joined ASEAN in 1995.

Significantly, the Tenth National Congress of the Vietnamese Communist Party held in April 2006 demonstrated greater political openness than the Chinese Communist Party. Before the congress, the Vietnamese citizens were encouraged to submit comments, which were discussed in the media. At the congress, delegates were allowed for the first time to recommend candidates for the position of general secretary. An intriguing political economy question is whether Vietnam's greater political openness, assuming that it will continue and deepen, will give the country a comparative advantage in democratization over China in attracting foreign investment given the presence of a more transparent government or gaining easier access to the Western markets given the partial removal of human rights as a reason for protectionism.

North Korea

The Democratic People's Republic of Korea (DPRK) has diverged from Vietnam drastically. Whereas Vietnam has enjoyed strong economic growth thanks to economic reforms, North Korea has become a failed state. North Korea began with hesitant reform measures in July 2002, but the country remains repressive, unreformed, and confrontational. By the end of 2006, the difference between the two countries could not be greater. North Korea tested a nuclear bomb on October 9, 2006, which was condemned by the international community, and a UN Security Council resolution authorized economic sanctions on Pyongyang. By contrast, Vietnam joined the World Trade Organization on November 7, 2006, and hosted the Asia-Pacific Economic Cooperation summit on November 12–19.

The DPRK nationalized most industrial enterprises in 1946 and introduced economic planning in 1947. The state launched land reform after the Korean War and collectivized agriculture by 1958. Pyongyang introduced the first five-year plan in 1957. North Korea focused on heavy industrialization, but the collapse of the Soviet Union deprived North Korea of aid, cheap fuel, and export markets, triggering a serious economic crisis.[99]

Kim Il Sung, the founder of the DPRK, died in July 1994. His son Kim Jong Il has been ruling the country since then. Kim Jong Il wanted to modernize the country and sought to normalize diplomatic relations with the United States and Japan. Upon formally assuming the official title after mourning the death of his father for over three years, Kim decided to have a new development strategy of "building *kangsong taeguk*" (strong and prosperous great state), which essentially means "enrich the nation and strengthen the army," similar to the Japanese objective before the Second World War and the declared objectives of South Korea leader Park Chung-hee in the 1970s. But Kim resorted mainly to nuclear weapon blackmail, which led to increased economic pressure on his country. In 1994–1998, two or three million people reportedly starved to death and the country increasingly turned to the international community for aid. Instead of reforms, however, Kim chose a "military-first" strategy in the late 1990s.[100]

Kim's confrontational foreign policy creates a serious problem for North Korean reform. By contrast, China improved relations with the United States and Japan before its reform. Vietnam began relaxing economic policy in the late 1970s and then conducted a more drastic reform in the mid-1980s while it was still isolated internationally. Vietnam's invasion of Cambodia is similar to North Korea's current situation with its nuclear program. But Hanoi adjusted its foreign policy shortly after doi moi began, as discussed above, which helped to create a favorable international environment for its economic reform and development.

Cambodia

The Cambodian case is highly unusual in that the country adopted a formal democracy in the early 1990s, which made it part of the democratization wave sweeping the world at the time. It is unusual also in that Cambodia is one of the poorest countries in East Asia but now has a multiparty electoral system that more advanced economic powers like China have failed to embrace.

Cambodia suffered from an extreme collectivization campaign under the Pol Pot regime in the late 1970s. Vietnam invaded in 1978, overthrew the Pol Pot regime, and created a puppet regime in the People's Republic of Kampuchea, which was later named the State of Cambodia (SOC). The new regime allowed private plots for farmers in the early 1980s and conducted market reform in the late 1980s. Simultaneously, Cambodia went through two other transformations, namely from war to peace and from authoritarianism to democracy. The two transformations were closely related. With the end of the cold war and the withdrawal of the Vietnamese troops, the United Nations brokered a peace agreement among the warring parties in 1991 and created a democratic system that began with an UN-sponsored election in 1993.[101]

Prime Minister Hun Sen's Cambodian People's Party (CPP) lost the election but maneuvered into a joint government with the winning royalist United National Front for an Independent, Neutral, Peaceful, and Cooperative Cambodia (Front Uni National pour un Cambodge Independent, Neutre, Pacifique et Cooperatif—FUNCINPEC). The CPP then forced FUNCINPEC leaders to flee after a gun battle near Phnom Penh in July 1997. A fair election was held in 1998 and the CPP formed a coalition party with FUNCINPEC, which was now a junior partner. Hun Sen has won reelections based on personal patronage and power. The prospect of a true democratic Cambodia thus remains questionable. International democracy promotion has its limitations as the CPP continues to hold sway over the rural villages by controlling the flow of resources to them.[102]

CONCLUSION

The discussion of the East Asian economies in the chapter shows a rich diversity of the national systems of political economy in the region. This diversity is an important reason why East Asia has experienced far greater difficulties in achieving regional integration than Europe, which has far less divergence than Asia. At the same time, East Asian postwar developments have exhibited a rough pattern of a higher stage of economic development corresponding to better governance and ultimately to democracy. To be sure, economic development is not a sufficient condition for political development. As the country-specific discussions in the chapter show, how a government chooses to respond to internal and external challenges explains much about different public policy, economic performance, and social well-being for its citizens. From a regional perspective, the countries that have made better choices have outdone the countries that have adopted terrible policies. Economic development does not necessarily have a linear relationship with political development. Those countries that are catching up and that are experiencing fast socioeconomic transformations and rising social expectations can and have often experienced more heavy-handed political rule. One should note, however, that some of those early authoritarian governments have turned democratic in recent years.

My discussion of the East Asian economies in this chapter is focused on postwar developments. To have a better understanding of contemporary East Asian political economy, we need to look at it first from a historical lens from ancient time to the present, a task for the next four chapters.

SUGGESTED READINGS

Bello, Walden F., Herbert Docena, Marissa de Guzman, and Mary Lou Malig. *The Anti-Development State: The Political Economy of Permanent Crisis in the Philippines* (New York: Palgrave, 2005).

Bowie, Alasdair, and Danny Unger. *The Politics of Open Economies: Indonesia, Malaysia, the Philippines, and Thailand* (New York: Cambridge University Press, 1997).

Brødsgaard, Kjeld Erik, and Susan Young, eds. *State Capacity in East Asia: China, Taiwan, Vietnam, and Japan* (New York: Oxford University Press, 2000).

Crouch, Harold. *Government and Society in Malaysia* (Ithaca, N.Y.: Cornell University Press, 1996).

Dickson, Bruce J. *Red Capitalists in China: The Party, Private Entrepreneurs, and Prospects for Political Change* (New York: Cambridge University Press, 2003).

Fforde, Adam, and Stefan de Vylder. *From Plan to Market: The Economic Transition in Vietnam* (Boulder: Westview Press, 1996).

Gallagher, Mary Elizabeth. *Contagious Capitalism: Globalization and the Politics of Labor in China* (Princeton: Princeton University Press, 2005).

Gold, Thomas B. *State and Society in the Taiwan Miracle* (Armonk, N.Y.: M. E. Sharpe, 1986).

Gomez, Edmund Terence, and K. S. Jomo. *Malaysia's Political Economy: Politics, Patronage, and Profits,* 2nd ed. (Cambridge: Cambridge University Press, 1999).

Haggard, Stephan, and Marcus Noland. *Famine in North Korea: Markets, Aid, and Reform* (New York: Columbia University Press, 2007).

Hughes, Caroline. *The Political Economy of Cambodia's Transition, 1991–2001* (London: RoutledgeCurzon, 2003).

Katz, Richard. *Japan: The System that Soured—The Rise and Fall of the Japanese Economic Miracle* (Armonk, N.Y.: M. E. Sharpe, 1998).

Kihl, Young Whan, and Hong Nack Kim, eds. *North Korea: The Politics of Regime Survival* (Armonk, N.Y.: M. E. Sharpe, 2006).

Lee, Kuan Yew. *The Singapore Story: Memoirs of Lee Kuan Yew* (Singapore: Prentice Hall, 1998).

Lieberthal, Kenneth. *Governing China: From Revolution Through Reform* (New York: Norton, 1995).

Lin, Justin Yifu, Fang Cai, and Zhou Li. *The China Miracle: Development Strategy and Economic Reform* (Hong Kong: Chinese University Press, 1996).

Masina, Pietro P. *Vietnam's Development Strategies* (New York: Routledge, 2006).

Morley, James M., ed. *Driven by Growth: Political Change in the Asia-Pacific Region*, rev. ed. (Armonk, N.Y.: M. E. Sharpe, 1999).

Naughton, Barry. *Growing out of the Plan: Chinese Economic Reform, 1978–1993* (New York: Cambridge University Press, 1995).

Oi, Jean C. *Rural China Takes Off: Institutional Foundations of Economic Reform* (Berkeley: University of California Press, 1999).

Pei, Minxin. *China's Trapped Transition: The Limits of Developmental Autocracy* (Cambridge: Harvard University Press, 2006).

Pempel, T. J. *Regime Shift: Comparative Dynamics of the Japanese Political Economy* (Ithaca, N.Y.: Cornell University Press, 1998).

Phongpaichit, Pasuk, and Chris Baker. *Thailand: Economy and Politics,* 2nd ed. (New York: Oxford University Press, 2002).

Radius, Prawiro. *Indonesia's Struggle for Economic Development: Pragmatism in Action* (Kuala Lumpur: Oxford University Press, 1998).

Rigger, Shelley. *Politics in Taiwan: Voting for Democracy* (New York: Routledge, 1999).

Rodan, Garry, ed. *Singapore Changes Guard: Social, Political, and Economic Directions in the 1990s* (New York: St. Martin's, 1993).

Rosser, Andrew. *The Politics of Economic Liberalization in Indonesia: State, Market, and Power* (Richmond, Surrey: Curzon Press, 2002).

Schoppa, Leonard J. *Race for the Exits: The Unraveling of Japan's System of Social Protection* (Ithaca: Cornell University Press, 2006).

Shirk, Susan L. *The Political Logic of Economic Reform in China* (Berkeley: University of California Press, 1993).

Taylor, Robert H., ed. *Burma: Political Economy Under Military Rule* (New York: Palgrave, 2000).

Vogel, Steven K. *Japan Remodeled: How Government and Industry Are Reforming Japanese Capitalism* (Ithaca, N.Y.: Cornell University Press, 2006).

Woo, Jung-en (Meredith Woo-Cummings). *Race to the Swift: State and Finance in Korean Industrialization* (New York: Columbia University Press, 1991).

Wurfel, David. *Filipino Politics: Development and Decay* (Ithaca, N.Y.: Cornell University Press, 1988).

NOTES

1. Robert Gilpin, *Global Political Economy: Understanding the International Economic Order* (Princeton: Princeton University Press, 2001), 149.
2. Colin Crouch and Wolfgang Streeck, eds., *Political Economy of Modern Capitalism: Mapping Convergence and Divergence* (London: Sage, 1997).
3. Ethan B. Kapstein, "Workers and the World Economy," *Foreign Affairs* 75, no. 3 (May/June 1996): 16–37; Paulette Kurzer, *Business and Banking: Political Change and Economic Integration in Western Europe* (Ithaca, N.Y.: Cornell University Press, 1993).
4. Suzanne Berger and Ronald Dore, eds., *National Diversity and Global Capitalism* (Ithaca, N.Y.: Cornell University Press, 1996); Eisuke Sakakibara, *Beyond Capitalism: The Japanese Model of Market Economics* (Lanham, Md.: University Press of America, 1993); Peter A. Hall and David Soskice, eds., *Varieties of Capitalism: The Institutional Foundations of Comparative Advantages* (New York: Oxford University Press, 2001); Torben Iversen, Jonas Pontusson, and David Soskice, eds., *Unions, Employers, and Central Banks: Macroeconomic Coordination and Institutional Change in Social Market Economies* (New York: Cambridge University Press, 2000); Michel Albert, *Capitalism Versus Capitalism* (New York: Four Walls Eight Windows, 1993); Herbert Kitschelt, Peter Lange, Gary Marks, and John D. Stephens, eds., *Continuity and Change in Contemporary Capitalism* (New York: Cambridge University Press, 1999).
5. The World Bank created a list of seventeen failing nations in 2003, which included Myanmar and Laos. An updated list of twenty-six issued in September 2006 includes also Cambodia and East Timor. Karen DeYoung, "World Bank Lists Failing Nations that Can Breed Global Terrorism," *The Washington Post*, September 15, 2006, A13.
6. Chalmers Johnson, *MITI and the Japanese Economic Miracle: The Growth of Industrial Policy, 1925–1975* (Stanford: Stanford University Press, 1982); Robert Wade, *Governing the Market: Economic Theory and the Role of Government in East Asian Industrialization* (Princeton: Princeton University Press, 1990).
7. Kjeld Erik Brødsgaard and Susan Young, "Introduction: State Capacity in East Asia," in *State Capacity in East Asia: China, Taiwan, Vietnam, and Japan*, ed. Kjeld Erik Brødsgaard and Susan Young (New York: Oxford University Press, 2000), 1–16.
8. After the Asian financial crisis, the strong state was associated with crony capitalism in many people's minds. David C. Kang, *Crony Capitalism: Corruption and Development in South Korea and the Philippines* (New York: Cambridge University Press, 2002).

9. Peter Evans, *Embedded Autonomy: States and Industrial Transformation* (Princeton: Princeton University Press, 1995).

10. Thomas B. Gold, "The Waning of the Kuomintang State on Taiwan," in *State Capacity in East Asia* (see note 7), 84–113; Jürgen Domes, "State Capacity in an Asian Democracy: The Example of Taiwan," in *State Capacity in East Asia* (see note 7), 114–130.

11. Hagen Koo, ed., *State and Society in Contemporary Korea* (Ithaca, N.Y.: Cornell University Press, 1993).

12. Peter J. Katzenstein, "East Asia—Beyond Japan," in *Beyond Japan: The Dynamics of East Asian Regionalism,* ed. Peter J. Katzenstein (Ithaca, N.Y.: Cornell University Press, 2006), 4–14.

13. James M. Morley, ed., *Driven by Growth: Political Change in the Asia-Pacific Region,* rev. ed. (Armonk, N.Y.: M. E. Sharpe, 1999).

14. According to studies by the Economist Intelligence Unit of *The Economist,* of 165 countries and 2 territories, only Japan belongs to the 28 "full democracies" (20); South Korea (31) and Taiwan (32) are termed "flawed democracies," but they have a higher ranking than Italy and India. Economist Intelligence Unit, www.economist.com/theworldin/international/display Story.cfm?story_id=8166790&d=2007. Also see Laza Kekic, "A Pause in Democracy's March," *The Economist: The World in 2007:* 59–60.

15. Ezra F. Vogel, *Japan as Number One: Lessons for America* (Cambridge: Harvard University Press, 1979).

16. T. J. Pempel, "A Decade of Political Torpor: When Political Logic Trumps Economic Rationality," in *Beyond Japan* (see note 12), 37–62.

17. Johnson, *MITI and the Japanese Economic Miracle.*

18. Pempel, "Decade of Political Torpor," 41–45.

19. Ikuo Kume, "Institutionalizing Post-War Japanese Political Economy: Industrial Policy Revisited," in *State Capacity in East Asia* (see note 7), 61–83.

20. Ikuo Kabashima and Terry MacDoughall, "Japan: Democracy with Growth and Equity," in *Driven by Growth* (see note 13), 307–309.

21. T. J. Pempel, *Regime Shift: Comparative Dynamics of the Japanese Political Economy* (Ithaca, N.Y.: Cornell University Press, 1998), 200–201.

22. Richard Katz, *Japan: The System that Soured—The Rise and Fall of the Japanese Economic Miracle* (Armonk, N.Y.: M. E. Sharpe, 1998).

23. Richard Katz, *Japanese Phoenix: The Long Road to Economic Revival* (Armonk, N.Y.: M. E. Sharpe, 2002).

24. As a case in point, Japan has yet to create a new social protection system to provide both production and protection. Leonard J. Schoppa, *Race for the Exits: The Unraveling of Japan's System of Social Protection* (Ithaca, N.Y.: Cornell University Press, 2006).

25. Steven K. Vogel, *Japan Remodeled: How Government and Industry Are Reforming Japanese Capitalism* (Ithaca, N.Y.: Cornell University Press, 2006).

26. "The Sun Also Rises," *The Economist,* October 8, 2005, 4.

27. Schoppa, *Race for the Exits.*

28. "Capitalism with Japanese Characteristics," *The Economist,* October 8, 2005, 6–7.

29. See for example Eisuke Sakakibara, *Structural Reform in Japan: Breaking the Iron Triangle* (Washington, D.C.: Brookings Institution Press, 2003).

30. Derek Hall, "Japanese Spirit, Western Economics: The Continuing Salience of Economic Nationalism in Japan," in *Economic Nationalism in a Globalizing World,* ed. Eric Helleiner and Andreas Pickel (Ithaca, N.Y.: Cornell University Press, 2005), 91–138.

31. Pempel, "Decade of Political Torpor." See also Ethan Scheiner, *Democracy Without Competition in Japan: Opposition Failure in a One-Party Dominant State* (New York: Cambridge University Press, 2006).

32. Vogel, *Japan Remodeled,* 3–4.

33. Alice H. Amsden, *Asia's New Giant: South Korea and Late Industrialization* (Oxford: Oxford University Press, 1989), 8–11; Meredith Jung-En Woo (Cummings), *Race to the Swift: State and Finance in Korean Industrialization* (New York: Columbia University Press, 1991).

34. Jong-Chan Rhee, *The State and Industry in South Korea: The Limits of the Authoritarian State* (London: Routledge, 1994).

35. Amsden, *Asia's New Giant,* 11–18.

36. Kang, *Crony Capitalism.*

37. Koo, *State and Society in Contemporary Korea.*

38. Sung-Joo Han and Oknim Chung, "South Korea: Economic Management and Democratization," in *Driven by Growth* (see note 13), 210–223.

39. Young Whan Kihl, *Transforming Korean Politics: Democracy, Reform, and Culture* (Armonk, N.Y.: M. E. Sharpe, 2005), 149–182.

40. Joseph Wong, *Healthy Democracies: Welfare Politics in Taiwan and South Korea* (Ithaca, N.Y.: Cornell University Press, 2004).

41. Thomas B. Gold, *State and Society in the Taiwan Miracle* (Armonk, N.Y.: M. E. Sharpe, 1986), 123.

42. Li-Min Hsueh, Chen-kuo Hsu, and Dwight H. Perkins, *Industrialization and the State: The Changing Role of the Taiwan Government in the Economy, 1945–1998* (Cambridge: Harvard University Press, 2001), 4–6.

43. Gold, *State and Society in the Taiwan Miracle,* 125–126.

44. Shelley Rigger, *Politics in Taiwan: Voting for Democracy* (New York: Routledge, 1999).

45. Rigger, *Politics in Taiwan,* 39–54.

46. Shelley Rigger, *From Opposition to Power: Taiwan's Democratic Progressive Party* (Boulder: Lynne Rienner, 2001).

47. For Lee Kuan Yew's own account of the early years of Singapore, see Lee Kuan Yew, *The Singapore Story: Memoirs of Lee Kuan Yew* (Singapore: Prentice Hall, 1998).

48. Lam Peng Er, "Singapore: Rich State, Illiberal Regime," in *Driven by Growth* (see note 13), 260–261.

49. Peter J. Katzenstein, *Small States in World Markets: Industrial Policy in Europe* (Ithaca, N.Y.: Cornell University Press, 1985).

50. W. G. Huff, *Economic Growth of Singapore: Trade and Development in the Twentieth Century* (Cambridge: Cambridge University Press, 1994).

51. Lam, "Singapore," 265.

52. Garry Rodan, ed., *Singapore Changes Guard: Social, Political, and Economic Directions in the 1990s* (New York: St. Martin's, 1993).

53. Lee, *The Singapore Story*.

54. Transparency International, "Transparency International Corruption Perceptions Index 2006," www.transparency.org. Hong Kong ranked 15th, Japan 17th, Taiwan 34th, South Korea 42nd, Malaysia 44th, Thailand 63rd, China 70th, Laos and Vietnam 111st, the Philippines 121st, Indonesia 130th, Cambodia 151st, and Myanmar 160th.

55. Alasdair Bowie and Danny Unger, *The Politics of Open Economies: Indonesia, Malaysia, the Philippines, and Thailand* (New York: Cambridge University Press, 1997), 14–15.

56. James P. Ongkili, *Nation-Building in Malaysia 1946–1974* (Singapore: Oxford University Press, 1985), 153.

57. Ongkili, *Nation-Building in Malaysia 1946–1974*, 126–131.

58. Zakaria Haji Ahmad and Sharifah Munirah Alatas, "Malaysia: In an Uncertain Mode," in *Driven by Growth* (see note 13), 180–183.

59. Harold Crouch, *Government and Society in Malaysia* (Ithaca, N.Y.: Cornell University Press, 1996).

60. Edmund Terence Gomez and K. S. Jomo, *Malaysia's Political Economy: Politics, Patronage, and Profits*, 2nd ed. (Cambridge: Cambridge University Press, 1999).

61. Gomez and Jomo, *Malaysia's Political Economy*, 166–176.

62. Charles F. Keyes, *Thailand: Buddhist Kingdom as a Modern Nation-State* (Boulder: Westview Press, 1987), 133–134.

63. Pasuk Phongpaichit and Chris Baker, *Thailand: Economy and Politics*, 2nd ed. (New York: Oxford University Press, 2002), 296–317.

64. Bowie and Unger, *Politics of Open Economies*, 133–134; Phongpaichit and Baker, *Thailand*, 341.

65. Suchit Bunbongkarn, "Thailand: Democracy Under Siege," in *Driven by Growth* (see note 13), 161–175.

66. Phongpaichit and Baker, *Thailand,* 447.

67. Chris Baker, "Pluto-Populism: Thaksin and Popular Politics," in *Thailand Beyond the Crisis,* ed. Peter Warr (New York: RoutledgeCurzon, 2005), 107–137.

68. Harold Crouch, *The Army and Politics in Indonesia,* rev. ed. (Ithaca, N.Y.: Cornell University Press, 1978).

69. Jamie Mackie, "Indonesia: Economic Growth and Depoliticization," in *Driven by Growth* (see note 13), 123–141.

70. Bowie and Unger, *Politics of Open Economies,* 47–48.

71. Radius Prawiro, *Indonesia's Struggle for Economic Development: Pragmatism in Action* (Kuala Lumpur: Oxford University Press, 1998), 101.

72. See Erika Weinthal and Pauline Jones Luong, "Combating the Resource Curse: An Alternative Solution to Managing Mineral Wealth," *Perspectives on Politics* 4, no. 1 (March 2006): 35–53.

73. Bowie and Unger, *Politics of Open Economies,* 51–52.

74. Andrew Rosser, *The Politics of Economic Liberalization in Indonesia: State, Market, and Power* (Richmond, Surrey: Curzon Press, 2002).

75. Bowie and Unger, *Politics of Open Economies,* 99–100.

76. David Wurfel, *Filipino Politics: Development and Decay* (Ithaca, N.Y.: Cornell University Press, 1988), 325–329.

77. Samuel P. Huntington, *Political Order in Changing Societies* (New Haven: Yale University Press, 1968).

78. Wurfel, *Filipino Politics,* 328–329.

79. Lela Garner Noble, "Politics in the Marcos Era," in *Crisis in the Philippines: The Marcos Era and Beyond,* ed. John Bresnan (Princeton: Princeton University Press, 1986), 72–84.

80. Wurfel, *Filipino Politics,* 329–338.

81. David Joel Steinberg, *The Philippines: A Singular and a Plural Place,* 2nd ed. (Boulder: Westview Press, 1990), 147–148.

82. Walden F. Bello, Herbert Docena, Marissa de Guzman, and Mary Lou Malig, *The Anti-Development State: The Political Economy of Permanent Crisis in the Philippines* (New York: Palgrave, 2005), 33.

83. David I. Steinberg, "Burma/Myanmar: Under the Military," in *Driven by Growth* (see note 13), 35–36.

84. Robert H. Taylor, ed., *Burma: Political Economy Under Military Rule* (New York: Palgrave, 2000), 229–290.

85. Martin Smith, "The Paradox of Burma: Conflict and Illegality as a Way of Life," *IIAS Newsletter* 42 (Autumn 2006): 20–21.

86. Mary P. Callahan, *Making Enemies: War and State Building in Burma* (Ithaca, N.Y.: Cornell University Press, 2003), 2–20.

87. A. Doak Barnett, *Cadres, Bureaucracy, and Political Power in Communist China* (New York: Columbia University Press, 1967); Kenneth Lieberthal, *Governing China: From Revolution Through Reform* (New York: Norton, 1995).

88. Susan L. Shirk, *The Political Logic of Economic Reform in China* (Berkeley: University of California Press, 1993) and *How China Opened Its Door: The Political Success of the PRC's Foreign Trade and Investment Reforms* (Washington, D.C.: Brookings Institute, 1994).

89. Jean C. Oi, *Rural China Takes Off: Institutional Foundations of Economic Reform* (Berkeley: University of California Press, 1999).

90. Minxin Pei, *From Reform to Revolution: The Demise of Communism in China and the Soviet Union* (Cambridge: Harvard University Press, 1994); Barry Naughton, *Growing Out of the Plan: Chinese Economic Reform, 1978–1993* (New York: Cambridge University Press, 1995); Justin Yifu Lin, Fang Cai, and Zhou Li, *The China Miracle: Development Strategy and Economic Reform* (Hong Kong: Chinese University Press, 1996).

91. Bruce J. Dickson, *Red Capitalists in China: The Party, Private Entrepreneurs, and Prospects for Political Change* (New York: Cambridge University Press, 2003); Margaret M. Pearson, *China's New Business Elite: The Political Consequences of Economic Reform* (Berkeley: University of California Press, 1997).

92. Minxin Pei, *China's Trapped Transition: The Limits of Developmental Autocracy* (Cambridge: Harvard University Press, 2006).

93. Mary Elizabeth Gallagher, *Contagious Capitalism: Globalization and the Politics of Labor in China* (Princeton: Princeton University Press, 2005), 10.

94. Bruce Gilley, *China's Democratic Future: How It Will Happen and Where It Will Lead* (New York: Columbia University Press, 2004).

95. Bruce J. Dickson, *Democratization in China and Taiwan: The Adaptability of Leninist Parties* (New York: Oxford University Press, 1997).

96. Thaveeporn Vasavakul, "Vietnam; Sectors, Classes, and the Transformation of a Leninist State," in *Driven by Growth* (see note 13), 60–68.

97. Adam Fforde and Stefan de Vylder, *From Plan to Market: The Economic Transition in Vietnam* (Boulder: Westview Press, 1996).

98. Barry Naughton, "Distinctive Features of Economic Reform in China and Vietnam," in *Reforming Asian Socialism*, ed. John McMillan and Barry Naughton (Ann Arbor: University of Michigan Press, 1996), 273–296.

99. Dick K. Nanto, "North Korea's Economic Crisis, Reforms, and Policy Implications," in *North Korea: The Politics of Regime Survival*, ed. Young Whan Kihl and Hong Nack Kim (Armonk, N.Y.: M. E. Sharpe, 2006), 118–142.

100. Young Whan Kihl, "Staying Power of the Socialist 'Hermit Kingdom,'" in *North Korea: The Politics of Regime Survival* (see note 99), 3–33.
101. Caroline Hughes, *The Political Economy of Cambodia's Transition, 1991–2001* (London: RoutledgeCurzon, 2003), 1–3.
102. Hughes, *The Political Economy*, 3–17 and 214–221.

CHAPTER 3

The Chinese World Order

This chapter examines the traditional East Asian international political economy (IPE). It addresses two questions. First, what was the state of East Asian IPE before the European arrival in the early sixteenth century? I answer this question by first focusing on the regional structure of political economy. Discussing the Chinese world order in the context of world orders, I show that East Asia had a system of political economy distinct from the modern Westphalian international system. The Westphalian system is composed of sovereign states equal legally if not in power. By contrast, the Chinese world order was constructed as a hierarchical, moral, international arrangement, which was in reality incomplete, sometimes in name only, often challenged, and involving frequent use of violence. An extensive regional trade network existed in East Asia, responding to both political and market forces. East Asian nations did not evolve in isolation. The political economy approach helps us understand a regional economic impact on politics, a process we are only beginning to comprehend.

Next, I compare the political economy of key East Asian countries, focusing on the origins and evolution of their political and economic institutions, thus connecting to the previous chapter. The institutions created in these countries reflected their goals and circumstances, which partly explained the variations among them. Power was a principal driving force for East Asian political economy. Interplay between the ideas of power and wealth were particularly important in guiding choices. Locations and timing also mattered.

The second question addressed in the chapter is why Western Europe rather than East Asia achieved the Industrial Revolution and subsequently surged ahead of the rest of the world. I first compare East Asia and Western Europe prior to the latter's rise. East Asia shared much in common with Western Europe in agriculture, commerce, level of wealth, and population control as late as the mid-eighteenth century. The next section explains that Western Europe achieved an industrial breakthrough largely because of a highly competitive interstate system that encouraged innovation and its forcible possession of rich resources in the Americas. Power based on the modern state and the market economy allowed the

West to dominate the world and triggered a process of adaptation and reform in East Asia and other developing regions.

WORLD ORDERS

International Order

The notion of order helps us understand how states in a region are organized. Order in international relations is often viewed as a normative goal for those who seek stability in relations between nations. Order is preferable to disorder, which means chaos, violence, and insecurity. By *international order*, I mean a predictable international arrangement in which states act in accordance with the purposes embedded in the system. Although international order is often associated with stability, I stress predictability in my definition. What makes order different from disorder is that members in the system are aware of the norms and rules and expect rewards and sanctions from certain behavior. In other words, order is associated with a set of institutions, although these institutions may not necessarily lead to peace. It is important to keep this caveat in mind when we discuss the East Asian international system in the context of the Chinese world order. No international order is complete, unchallenged, or necessarily just for all. Rome in the ancient times and Pax Americana, an international political authority created and maintained by the United States, in the contemporary world are cases in point.

International order is a systemic variable. It includes not only distribution of power, which is the structure of the international order, but also purposes, which are crucial elements of the normative basis of the order.[1] Although order is an actual state of affairs, it is not divorced from goals embedded in the order. Hedley Bull defined order in social life as "not *any* pattern or regularity in the relations of human individuals or groups, but a pattern that leads to a particular result, an arrangement of social life such that it promotes certain goals or values."[2] International order is therefore broader than international system or structure.[3] Two similar situations of power balance between states may create different international orders if their dominant purposes are different. Unless we know the accepted purposes embedded in the international order, the balance of power cannot fully indicate how states will act.

The argument above that power alone does not explain the exact nature of an international order does not negate its centrality in international affairs. Violence or threat of violence occupies a central place in creating and reproducing institutions. Shifting power balance explains partly why the international orders by the Chinese, Westerners, and Japanese in East Asia were created, expanded, maintained, ignored, challenged, or destroyed.

The Chinese World Order

For two thousand years until the mid-nineteenth century, the East Asian international system could be best described as the Chinese world order.[4] Labels are often loaded ideologically and emotionally. Using the term *Chinese world order* does not imply that China was always at the center of East Asian international relations or should be. Rather, the term is a useful way to summarize the nature of the ancient East Asian international system in contrast to the contemporary international system. The term has more substance than alternatives such as "the East Asian international relations of the past two millenniums." Equally important, the Chinese world order draws attention to an analytical framework based on both power and legitimacy, consistent with the theory of international order, for studying traditional East Asian international relations in contrast to later projects to create order in East Asia, namely Western and Japanese imperialism, and regionalism.

China was not at the center of the world. Even if we view the world narrowly as the Eurasian continent, the steppe peoples were the true world players who treated East Asia as an important but not the only sedentary region to trade with or to raid; there were rich and developed states in South Asia, West Asia, and Europe.[5] China was not always at the center of East Asian international relations either. Frequent and often successful incursions of non-Chinese into what is called China today created a dynamic process in which the definition of who is Chinese has been highly contingent historically. Although early China historians tended to emphasize the theme of Sinicization, a process for non-Chinese to assimilate into Chinese culture, more recent studies often point at hybrid origins of the Chinese civilization.[6]

At the same time, however, we define who Chinese really were at a given moment; China was at the center of East Asia more consistently than any other powers in the past millenniums. Moreover, the Chinese articulated a universal system and sought to practice it in the political and economic arenas. Once the Chinese system was formulated, non-Chinese rulers often emulated it to create their own "Chinese" world orders. Although the term Middle Kingdom might glorify China unnecessarily, the country was indeed located geographically and strategically in one of the most developed regions of the time. Furthermore, China accounted for 26.1 percent of world gross domestic product (GDP) in AD 1 and 32.9 percent in 1820. Only India was in the same league.[7]

The Chinese world order did not overlap neatly with what we call East Asia today. It was composed of a complex set of concentric circles centered on China. The Chinese culture zone included China, Korea, Japan, Annam (Vietnam), and Ryukyu (Okinawa), which shared the Chinese writing system, the Confucian ideology, and certain lifestyles such as use of chopsticks. Emperors in China conducted military campaigns against Korea, Vietnam, and Japan and at times had direct administrative control over Vietnam (111 BC–AD 938, 1407–1428) and Korea (108 BC–AD 313, 668–676). Vietnam regained independence in 938 after a millennium of Chinese rule. The country fought hard to maintain its independence while accepting a tributary state status for much of its history until the nineteenth century. After Koguryo ended the Chinese administration in the Korean peninsula in the early fourth century, the Korean states were active participants in East Asian international relations. Silla, which unified the Korean peninsula in 671, was modeled after the Chinese Tang Dynasty political system. For much of the following centuries, Korea remained largely an independent state but also a tributary to the Chinese court.

Japan was in a unique position in the Chinese world order. Japan borrowed heavily from China but was never ruled by China. In fact, Japan challenged China politically. Japan had an emperor, a title forbidden in the hierarchical Chinese world order. Geography facilitated Japan's independence from China. The main Japanese islands are separate from Korea by more than 100 miles and from China by about 450 miles. Thus, Japan was close enough to borrow culturally from the continental civilization but too distant to be invaded easily.

Japanese shogun Ashikaga Yoshimitsu accepted the tributary state status to engage in trade with China. Japan sent eleven tribute missions to China from 1433 to 1549 but stopped the practice after the mid-sixteenth century. Japan did not resume official relations with China after the Qing Dynasty was established. Tokugawa Japan engaged in active foreign relations in Asia and sought to structure a new East Asian international order around Japan based on the divinity of the Japanese emperor and the notion that Japan was on par with or superior to China given its high virtue and China's conquests by barbarians.[8] In fact, Japan's General Hideyoshi tried to conquer Korea and China in the late sixteenth century, but a joint force of Ming China and Korea stopped the Japanese invasion.

The Chinese world order went beyond the Chinese culture zone. It included an Inner Asian Zone of nomadic peoples culturally different from the Chinese. More than any other external players, continuous interaction with steppe peoples profoundly shaped Chinese history in terms of culture, territoriality, and ethnic stock. The Chinese emperors were sometimes forced to take an equal or even inferior position vis-à-vis steppe peoples during periods of military weakness. Various nomadic peoples became rulers in China although they largely adopted the Chinese way to rule the settled Chinese territories, sometimes out of admiration and sometimes out of political pragmatism. Nomadic empires typically adopted "dual administration" to rule the nomads and sedentary states. In particular, the Mongols conquered China and established the Yuan Dynasty (1206–1368) and the Manchus founded the Qing Dynasty (1644–1911).

Extending further out still, the Chinese world order included Southeast Asian states that sent tributes to China. In mainland Southeast Asia, Chinese troops destroyed Champa's (now South Vietnam) political center at Hue in 446. The Mongols tried unsuccessfully to conquer Champa in the 1280s. The Qing army conducted inconclusive military campaigns against Burma in the 1760s. By contrast, Chinese power rarely reached maritime Southeast Asia. As exceptions, Chinese military power was projected in the region in the Yuan period (1206–1368) when Kubilai Khan waged unsuccessful military campaigns against Java in 1293, and Ming Admiral Zheng He's seven expeditions in the early fifteenth century (1405–1433) increased Chinese influence in the region and brought more states into the Chinese tributary system.[9]

The Chinese saw their world order in universal terms, though they themselves did not use the term world order. From as early as two millenniums ago, they used the word *tianxia* or "all under heaven" to characterize a zone of high culture, and they saw what was beyond as "barbarian." At the core of the Chinese world order was a strong sense of universal kinship. The emperor, the Son of Heaven, possessed universal authority on a religious and cosmic basis. Such universal Chinese claims were similar to other great civilizations of the ancient times. What made the Chinese worldview unique was the association of Confucianism with high civilization after the Han Dynasty (206 BC–AD 220).[10] In the Chinese mind, Chinese superiority was proven with a powerful, enduring empire.

The Chinese world order was hierarchical. The emperor was at the apex of the universe. Smaller countries paid tributes to the rulers of China, known as the Middle Kingdom. This view was consistent with status-conscious Chinese society, in which a desirable sociopolitical order was based on obedience of son to father, wife to husband, and official to emperor. By contrast, the contemporary world order based on the Westphalian principles considers all countries equal legally despite inequities in power.

The Chinese world order was also supposed to be moral, explicitly based on Confucian criteria of moral leaders and moral behavior. The Confucian ideal stipulates that a leader should be benevolent and exemplary in moral conduct. Based on correct ceremonies and principles, virtuous conduct by rulers would influence subjects through attraction and awe. Order is maintained if the ruler remains benevolent and subordinates play their roles accordingly. With a virtuous emperor, non-Chinese would come from all corners of the world to pay their respects (*weide*). Thus, Chinese emperors treated proper ceremonies as central to relations with other peoples and considered studies of Chinese classics to be an indication of degree of civilization.

A gap existed between myth and reality, however. It was not always moral examples based on Confucianism that guided China's foreign policy. There was a strong school of militant thinking based on Legalism that emphasized discipline and punishment.[11] The Chinese emperors mainly used military force rather than moral persuasion to expand the Chinese empire. In fact, war and coercion shaped the formation of state in ancient China, similar to early modern Europe.[12] Chinese territorial expansion often provoked hostile reactions. The Xiongnu empire, the first serious threat from steppe peoples to the Chinese empire, was formed as the first known Inner Asian empire in reaction to Qin Emperor Shihuangdi's decision to send a large army to conquer the territory in the great bend of the Yellow River, which had been the best grazing land for the Xiongnu.[13]

At the same time, Confucianism still mattered in that it limited the Chinese expansion. Confucianist criticism of the expansionist policy of Han Emperor Wudi (140–87 BC) played an important role in reversing that policy after his death. Like any political ideals such as democracy and human rights, Confucianist ideals for virtuous leaders and social stability mattered because they helped frame policy choices for a government and because choices made out of political necessities inconsistent with the ideals were recognized as such by proponents of those ideals, who sought to return to "the way" when circumstances permitted.

The Chinese world order was operationalized in the tribute system, which was the sum of the ceremonies that guided relations with non-Chinese peoples. In the tribute system, the emperor provided an official title to a non-Chinese ruler and an official seal for communications. Tributary states had to use the Chinese reign titles as the calendar to date correspondence, present a symbolic tribute (*gong*) of local products, and perform the *kowtow* (prostrating and touching the head on the ground) in front of the emperor. In return, the emperor offered imperial gifts and allowed the tribute missions to exchange goods in the capital and at the border.

Chinese rulers began to record all foreign missions as tribute missions in the Later Han Dynasty (25–220), viewing tribute relations as the norm in their dealings with non-Chinese.[14] The Ming (1368–1644) and the Qing dynasties (1644–1911) institutionalized the tribute system, with detailed regulations for all parties involved. The Qing court decreed as of 1818 that Korea could send tributes four times a year, Ryukyu once in two years, Annam (Vietnam) two tributes combined into one for every four years, Laos once every ten years, Siam (Thailand) once every three years, Sulu (now southern part of the Philippines) once every five years, and Burma once every ten years.[15]

Mutual deception often existed in tribute relations. What the Chinese recorded as tributes was often not intended as such. Chinese officials did so to maintain the appearance of Chinese superiority and to avoid the emperor's wrath. Symbolic submission was often the chief objective of the Chinese court in any case. Sometimes, foreign rulers did not know that their missions to China were recorded as tributes in Chinese archives. Other times, they knowingly played along to engage in lucrative trade with China.[16] Inner Asia, which was culturally distinct from China, simply did not accept China's supremacy, but that did not prevent principalities and merchants from playing the game just to preserve court-subsidized goods exchanges; the leadership of a tribute mission could be purchased for a price.[17]

While China dominated in East Asia, smaller tribute systems evolved around other states. Ryukyu paid tributes to both the Chinese emperor and Satsuma *daimyo* (feudal lord) of Japan. After invading Ryukyu in 1609, Satsuma effectively controlled the kingdom while concealing the fact from Chinese envoys in order to maintain lucrative tribute trade with China.[18] Laos was a tributary state to Vietnam. Korea maintained its own version of tribute system when dealing with Japanese and Ryukyuans who did not represent their governments.[19]

POLITICAL ECONOMY OF EAST ASIAN TRADE

The Chinese tribute system was essentially a managed trade system. As such, the system reflected China's political calculations. Tributes from "all corners of the earth" confirmed the emperor's central place in the world. That was why the Chinese court was often willing to offer expensive gifts for symbolic submission. Chinese imperial gifts for the tributary Hsiung-nu increased from 6,000 catties (a traditional Chinese measurement of weight; 1 catty = 244 grams) of silk floss and 8,000 pieces of silk fabric in 51 BC to 30,000 catties and 30,000 pieces in 1 BC.[20] Politics dominated in Chinese official thinking because the Chinese government was convinced that domestic order should be based on agriculture. Confucianists had little trust in merchants. Equally important, the Chinese government did not encourage trade with steppe peoples in part because they did not want frontier people to gravitate toward "the barbarians," a process that might destabilize the border area and even the core areas of the country. By contrast, foreign dynasties, particularly the Mongol empire, valued trade as an important source of revenues and protected traveling caravans.[21]

Considering trade to be a favor to foreigners, the Chinese government often intended to use permission for tribute missions as a control mechanism over non-Chinese peoples by making them dependent on China, which was of course difficult to accomplish in practice then as now. Conversely, the Han Dynasty rulers often bribed nomadic peoples with luxury goods to maintain frontier stability because it was far more costly, dangerous, and often futile to seek out highly mobile enemies deep in the steppe. Trade was thus seen as an unpleasant but necessary cost for security, which would become a dominant frontier strategy for native Chinese dynasties.[22]

China could see itself running a tributary system not only because of its cultural sense of self-importance. Chinese agriculture and manufacturing were highly developed. Grains such as millet and rice and iron tools were desired by the steppe peoples. There was a major silk textile industry in Han China, particularly in what is now Shandong Province and Sichuan Province. Lacquer work and bronze mirrors were also important for export in the Han Dynasty. China remained a major economic center until the mid-nineteenth century. The Chinese court generally considered China to be self-sufficient and trade with non-Chinese to be a favor. In a famous letter to King George III of Great Britain dated October 3, 1793, Emperor Qianlong announced, "We have never valued ingenious articles nor do we have the slightest need of your country's manufactures."[23]

At the same time, economic interests mattered to China. The Chinese government was not always restrictive on the merchant class. Ying-shih Yu termed the commercial policy of the Later Han Dynasty (25–220) "laissez-faire."[24] The Chinese government was interested in trading for horses and products such as jade from nomads. As another example, China had a sustained high demand for foreign silver and was the world's largest silver importer from Japan and Spanish Mexico for over a century (1550–1650). Also, "foreign" dynasties in China were less controlling regarding trade. Given their cultural roots and familiarity with the steppe, these dynasties were more successful in keeping steppe peoples divided and weak.

The importance of trade for China was reflected in widespread legal or contraband trade by Chinese merchants. Chinese history recorded as early as the third century AD that China imported a variety of valuable forest products from the Malay kingdoms (Java, Sumatra, the Malay Peninsula, and Borneo).[25] Chinese traders traveled to Southeast Asia in the Song and Yuan dynasties for various local products. Ming/Qing China periodically forbade private overseas trade, which led to a problem of "pirates," who were really armed traders with bases overseas. The tighter the government control on private trade, the more serious the piracy problem was. When the Ming government lifted the sea ban in 1567, 50 junks were licensed to travel to Southeast Asia each year. That number increased to 117 by 1597.[26]

The flag followed the trade. The activities of Chinese merchants along the border led to China's imperial expansion. In the Han Dynasty, Chinese merchants from Sichuan often illegally entered the territories of non-Chinese peoples, and their trading activities drew in Chinese political and military expansion, resulting in the creation of several new Chinese provinces.[27]

Politics played a role in the calculations of non-Chinese nations as well. Nomadic peoples needed to trade with sedentary states like China for grain, iron tools, and other commodities. But starting from the Xiongnu, nomadic empires often needed to exhort tributes or subsidies from the Chinese court to ensure their political power. They did this by sharing luxury goods such as silk with political elites whose political loyalty was fluid in their imperial confederacies and then demanding open border markets to allow commoners to benefit in trade.[28] Steppe empires arose when China was unified because they depended on subsidies and tributes from the country. A close economic interaction with the Chinese empire put a steppe leader in an advantageous position vis-à-vis his competitors. In the case of Korea, Hae-jong Chun suggested that Korea, the model tributary state, received less than it gave in its regular tributary relationship with China; nevertheless, Korean rulers found it politically advantageous to maintain a tribute relationship with China to boost their legitimacy.[29]

At the same time, economic considerations mattered for tribute states. Many states sent tribute missions for commercial rather than for political reasons. Some foreign merchants were allowed to accompany tributary missions and to sell a certain quantity of goods in the Chinese capital. Because of profits to be made, some foreign merchants would pretend to be tribute missions to carry out trade. As the largest economy in the region, China was an attractive market, and the Chinese court had to regulate the frequency of such missions. The market principle was at work here, with the amount and composition of tributes determined by supply and demand and price differential within and outside China. In fact, Takashi Hamashita maintained that the Chinese tribute system ended not just because of Western pressure but because it became less profitable for tributary states in the nineteenth century as a result of Qing currency inflation, a situation that encouraged private trade at the expense of official relationships.[30] With currency inflation in China, the Chinese currency became cheaper, which meant that foreigners would receive less for their goods when the official price remained the same. Foreigners then naturally had incentives to engage in often "illegal" private trade based on the true market value of their goods.

East Asian regional trade was broader than China-centered tribute trade. East Asian trade patterns reflected complex economic conditions and domestic order of political economy in different countries. For example, the Ryukyu sent missions to Southeast Asia to purchase pepper and sappanwood to present to Beijing as part of its tribute trade.[31] Tokugawa Japan, which did not have official relations with China, traded with Chinese merchants who came to Nagasaki.

There was long-distance trade involving many states. As shown in Map 3.1, the Silk Road was one of the most important trade networks in the world at the time, linking markets in East Asia, Central Asia, the Middle East, and Europe, starting around the late second century BC.[32] The Silk Road started in the city of Xian in China, to Samarkand and Bukhara in Central Asia, around the Caspian Sea to Turkey, and finally to Europe. There were also other routes through Mongolia, Kazakhstan, Russia, and to Europe. Other routes and branches reached Afghanistan, India, Iran, and the Middle East. Because silk was a major product, there was a good reason that people called the East-West trade route the Silk Road. But other products were also traded, such as porcelain, tea, and lacquer

MAP 3.1
Eurasia and the Silk Road, 100 BC

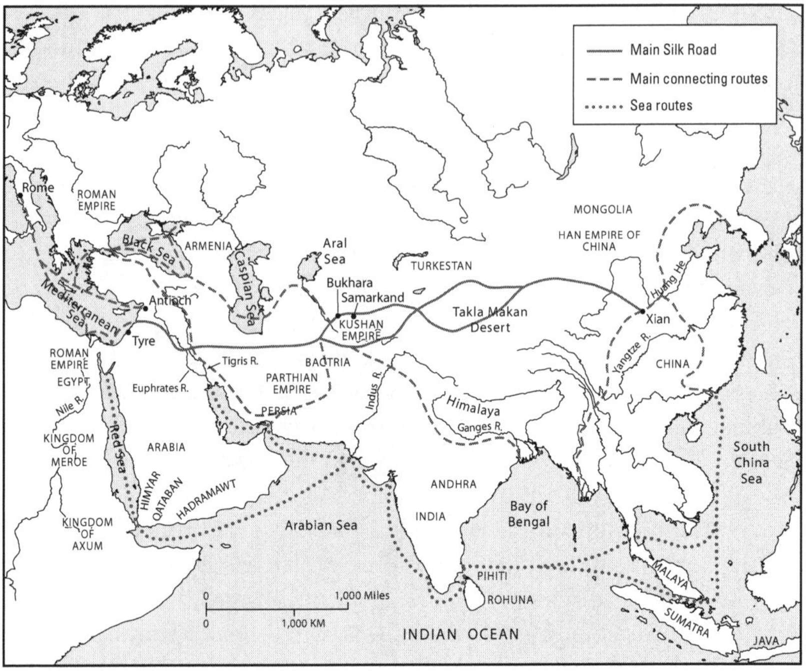

ware from East Asia; furs from Siberia; horses from Central Asia; dyes, glassware, and incense from the Middle East; pepper, cotton, and sandalwood from India; and ambers, silver, and gold from Europe. The Silk Road also allowed new technologies, ideas, and religions to spread between East and West. The wealth generated from the access to the Silk Road helped shape international politics of the time. The Silk Road decayed when the Ming court decided to close the Chinese border in 1426.

An equally important Spice Route operated for two millenniums, originating from the Spice Islands (now part of Indonesia) in Southeast Asia and linking East Asia, India, the Middle East, and Europe. The trade in spices that were light in weight but high in value was highly lucrative, which provided an important motivation for Columbus to cross the Atlantic Ocean seeking a new route to the source of spices. When the over-land Silk Road declined, the ocean-going ships along the Spice Route also carried Chinese silk and porcelain to the extent that the Spice Route came to be known as the Maritime Silk Road.[33]

Japanese traders and pirates traveled throughout Northeast and Southeast Asia and set up trade outposts in the Philippines, Vietnam, and Thailand. When the Ming court lifted the ban on trade with Nanyang (the Chinese expression for

Southeast Asia) but not with Japan in 1567, Chinese and Japanese traders used Southeast Asian ports as entrepôts, with Japanese exporting silver for Chinese silk and Southeast Asian sugar, spices, and deer hides. In the period of 1604–1635, 355 Japanese ships went to Southeast Asia.[34] Even though the Tokugawa government forbade Japanese from traveling overseas in 1635, that ban did not stop Japanese trade with the outside world. It is commonly assumed that the Tokugawa government "closed the country" (*sakoku*) after 1640. The Dutch were the only Europeans allowed to trade in a small island in Nagasaki. However, from an East Asian regional perspective, Japan maintained significant trade with Korea and China, and its trade volume did not decrease significantly.[35] Thus, Hamashita Takeshi called the Tokugawa policy "selective opening."[36] In fact, some Japanese scholars have pointed out that the word *sakoku* did not appear until 1801 when a Japanese scholar coined the word when translating a German book.[37]

Southeast Asians always depended on commerce. The region is accessible to waterways, and most political centers are right on the water. Native traders as well as those from India, the Arab world, China, and Japan were active players before the arrival of Europeans. Southeast Asia, which entered the age of commerce in 1450, was part of a global trade expansion. Chinese imported most pepper and spices from Southeast Asia until 1500. In the next century, exports of pepper and spices to Europe and the Middle East grew rapidly, amounting to half of the region's exports by 1600. In fact, the export of spices was one reason Westerners came to East Asia in the first place.[38] The Westerners did not create but participated in the formation of the modern Asian market that had already been regionally linked when they arrived in the region.[39] East Asian trade networks developed because of technology in production, transportation, and financial institutions.

Trade links in ancient East Asia also had an impact on exchange rates and finance, which would affect domestic political economy in a way not well understood by the contemporaries. China developed a paper currency system as early as the eleventh century. The Ming government's financing of military expeditions and the move of the capital to Beijing from the south with paper money led to hyperinflation and the collapse of the paper money system by the mid-fifteenth century. In response, Chinese merchants turned to silver as their preferred currency, followed first by local governments and then the central government. China now had a silver standard, which meant that merchants used silver as the medium of transaction and governments accepted only silver for taxes and for tributes. As the world's largest economy at the time, China's turn to silver shaped the global economy. China's tremendous demand for silver was met by Spanish America and Japan, the world's two largest silver producers at the time. Spanish America produced 150,000 tons of silver between 1500 and 1800, accounting for about 80 percent of global production. Japan was the major supplier of silver to China in the late sixteenth and early seventeenth century, exporting about 200 tons a year mainly through European and Chinese middlemen. Spaniards and Japanese exported silver to China in exchange for gold for high profit. China's gold-to-silver price was 1:6 when Spanish silver arrived, compared to 1:11 or 1:12 in Europe. It took one century to level the relative price of silver in China with the rest of the world. But even after arbitrage profits diminished, China continued to attract silver inflows because the country had more buyers at the same price. China's silverization, with imports of silver, essentially created a silver zone in East Asia because the Chinese court demanded silver from tribute states as the medium of exchange.[40] This inflow of silver led to inflation of prices, which put a tremendous financial strain on local governments. Corruption became worse when local officials sought to compensate losses through levies.

COMPARATIVE POLITICAL ECONOMY

Comparative political economy studies state formation and the interplay of the state and the market. The conception and practice of the nation state emerged in Europe and became the norm for contemporary international relations. Thus, whatever political form a non-Western nation possessed prior to its entry into the West-dominated international system came to be called a state even if it did not meet all the essential requirements of a modern state. The universal, hierarchical Chinese world order would disqualify East Asian countries as modern states, which are supposed to be sovereign and equal in a legal sense. At the same time, East Asian political entities met the key domestic requirement for a nation state, namely monopoly of violence over a population within a territory. Scholars of the European state formation emphasized war making and domestic political authority in defining the modern state.[41] East Asia nations had highly developed political and social institutions to ensure what they considered to be valuable goals, namely stability and moral life. Most Northeast Asian and mainland Southeast Asian political entities that exist today were formed centuries or millenniums ago. The way the state interacted with the market varied from country to country in East Asia. Although I spent considerable time earlier discussing the interaction between nomadic empires and China, I will not discuss nomadic political systems in this comparative political economy section.[42]

China

The first state in East Asia emerged in northern China in the Shang Dynasty (1450–1122 BC), although some scholars date it as early as the Xia Dynasty (2000–1450 BC). The Chinese civilization took shape in the Xia, Shang, and Zhou (1122–221 BC) dynasties. The Chinese nation expanded in all directions, conquering and absorbing other peoples in the process. The main Chinese traditions such as Confucianism, Legalism, and Taoism as well as the notion of the Middle Kingdom were fully articulated in the Zhou period. Confucianism refers to a system of teachings by Confucius (551–479 BC) and his followers that emphasize the practice and cultivation of virtues of benevolence, righteousness, filial piety, and loyalty as the basis of personal ethic and politics. Legalism refers to a system of teachings that originated around the same time as Confucianism that emphasize rewards and punishment for an orderly society. Taoism refers to a system of teachings by Laozi (believed to be Confucius's elder) that emphasize inactivity, search for immortality, and retreat from the world.

A centralized Chinese empire was established in 221 BC. Judging by duration, China had the most successful empire in human history, lasting for two millennia (from 221 BC to 1911) despite periodic breakdowns. What stands out about China's political history is that the Chinese empire endured while the Roman Empire (27 BC–AD 312) and the Byzantine Empire (330–1453) disintegrated. The Chinese empire, established in the Qin Dynasty in 221 BC and degenerating into warring entities after AD 311, was reconstituted with the establishment of the Sui Dynasty in 589. While China and Europe evolved similarly for a thousand years, China began to diverge from Europe with the establishment of the Song Dynasty in 960. While semifeudal landed aristocracies had considerable strength, the central government prevailed eventually after the Ming Dynasty (1368–1643) was established. The Chinese empire used civil service examinations to select officials, a practice firmly established in the Song Dynasty. By contrast, feudal lords in Europe controlled their fiefdoms in return for military service, and the Roman Catholic Church and cities were centers of power that challenged the monarch for resources and influence.[43]

The Chinese political tradition that emphasized autocratic rule is a well-known story. The Chinese emperor was the absolute, omnipotent ruler as well as a religious leader. The only check on the emperor was the Confucian obligation to be a benevolent leader and the danger that an emperor's misbehavior might lead to loss of the Mandate of Heaven, that is, the collapse of the dynasty.

At the same time, the Chinese state was weak, as measured by its limited ability to raise revenues for state projects.[44] China's principal source of government revenue was land tax. The Ming government (1368–1643) collected around 10 percent of the nation's total grain output, and the Qing government (1644–1911) collected roughly 5–6 percent of the total in the mid-eighteenth century. Other sources of revenues, namely salt tax and native customs, accounted for one quarter of the land tax prior to the mid-nineteenth century. In fact, the economic power of the central government declined during the six centuries of the Ming and Qing dynasties.[45]

Chinese rulers chose to limit revenue collections from peasants, motivated by their overarching concern to maintain political control over a vast empire and ensure social stability. With an agrarian empire, the emperor's major concern was to prevent emergence of power centers from challenging central authority and to maintain social order. Facing no corporate challengers, the Chinese court learned that the secret of a stable political rule lies in a low tax burden on peasants. The court was prudent fiscally. During the Qianlong reign (1736–1795), government revenues amounted to 43–44 million taels (Chinese ounce = 1.208 English ounces of pure silver) a year, mostly from land tax, while its annual expenditure was around 35 million taels.[46] By 1500, the Chinese state promoted agricultural production as the foundation of the state economy, complemented by commerce and crafts production. The Chinese state saw the market as useful but distrusted concentration of wealth through commerce, although in practice the government was often more sophisticated than official rhetoric suggested.[47] Moreover, the court was concerned that people might leave the land to engage in commerce, a situation considered detrimental to social stability.

By contrast, European states emerged after centuries of fighting by the monarchy to mobilize resources to expand their political power over nobility and towns and to compete with other states. As corporate entities, the nobility, towns, and the church were accommodated politically in measures such as representation in exchange for tax and an impartial legal system. Thus, a successful European state could raise revenues. Beginning around 1500, the European monarch, who was constantly at war and broke financially, actively sought tax revenues from all sources, including foreign commerce.

The Chinese institutions created to advance the objectives of maintaining social order and preventing domestic challengers came with costs. The central government's inability to raise revenues as the economy expanded was one reason for its difficulty in achieving modernization compared with Japan.[48] After the An Lushan Rebellion in the Tang Dynasty, the Chinese rulers carefully avoided creating strong military commanders and often diverted revenues from defense to other purposes, which led to military weakness vis-à-vis nomads. Chinese military weakness became a serious problem in the nineteenth century when the Chinese government needed resources to fend off pressure, first from Western nations and then from Japan.

The high premium China placed on stability also prevented institutional and technological innovations. In fact, the Ming financial administration was inferior to the previous dynasties, which had learned to formulate tax policy based on an expanding economy. Ming practice retarded the growth of public services and government-owned industries and led to insufficient investment in infrastructure such as transportation. The Manchu conquerors essentially adopted the Ming financial administration.[49] By contrast, security necessities forced European monarchs to adopt costly new military technologies, which led to the urgent need to raise revenues, which in turn led to creation of new institutions such as standing armies, tax-collecting bureaucracies, and mints to raise money and to fight wars—two purposes at the core of the modern nation states.[50]

The fact that China struggled to achieve a modern economy led to arguments that the state in the Qing period blocked China's economic advance with ineffective management, exploitation of the private sector, and structural corruption. Recent research shows, however, that the Qing government was rational in that its administrative institutions and practices were consistent with what it wanted to achieve: social stability, security, and control of its vast empire by emphasizing the empire's agricultural base, and economic stability. The government cooperated with the private sector, promoted agricultural development by encouraging farms and experimenting with new seeds, and combined ritual, custom, and law to promote family-based agriculture and craft production to ensure self-sufficiency and stability.[51] The main problem for China, however, was that the government's limited financial resources did not allow it to promote new technologies or capital formation. As Dwight Perkins noted, "China's retarded industrialization was more a result of sins of omission than of commission."[52]

Moreover, a fiscally sound Chinese government did not need overseas trade expansion as a source of income. Ming rulers initially forbade foreign trade. Although private traders remained active, China's overseas trade could have developed much further but for government restrictions. Without government support, Chinese private traders were at a distinct disadvantage against Western armed traders fully supported by their home governments. In fact, both Ming and Qing courts saw armed Chinese traders as a threat to their authority and sought to destroy them.[53]

Korea

Korean nationalists believe that Dangun, the god-king, founded the Korean nation in 2333 BC, but there was no written history at the time. The Koreans came under strong Chinese cultural influence in the third century BC. Chinese emigrants founded the state of Choson in Korea in the third century BC. The Chinese Han Dynasty troops conquered Korea by 109 BC and set up an administrative structure, part of which lasted until AD 313. The kingdom of Koguryo rose in the early fourth century and destroyed the Chinese commanderies in northwest Korea. In 313–668, Koguryo, the state of Paekche, and the state of Silla participated actively in the East Asian international system. The Tang army defeated Koguryo in 668, which allowed Silla to unite Korea in 671 for the first time in Korean history.

After the Silla unification, Korea modeled its political system after China. Silla sent thousands of students to China to learn Confucianism, Buddhism, bureaucratic organization, and science. Korea followed Confucianist principles faithfully and accepted the basic notion of the Chinese world order. Still, Koreans saw themselves as occupying a high place in the civilized world and came to view their country as the last fortress of civilization when "barbarian" Manchus conquered China and established the Qing Dynasty.[54]

Underneath the appearance of similarities, Korea's political system differed from China's in that the Korean government's main purpose was to protect the interests of the *yangban,* the aristocracy who inherited status and land. While Korea had a civil service examination system to select bureaucrats, mainly aristocrats could apply.[55] The yangban also rigidly maintained the purity of their bloodlines. The Korean society was divided into three classes: commoners, serfs or slaves, and the yangban class. During the Yi Dynasty (1392–1910), the size of the slave class declined and most of the land in the country was privately owned and could be bought and sold. The disappearance of slaves resulted in part from the country's growing population density: Labor abundance made slaves less necessary. Korea experienced centuries of relative peace during the Yi Dynasty, which led to population growth and an extremely limited per capita land endowment (0.12 hectares of arable land per capita in 1918). Similar to China and Japan, Korean cities emerged as political centers where elites and their servants resided. The growth of cities in Korea, though not as large as in China and Japan, led to more developed commerce in the eighteenth and the nineteenth centuries.[56] Unlike more self-reliant villagers, urban residents require supplies of food and goods from other regions.

Similar to China but different from Japan, the Korean state was financially weak, taking in about the same percentage (2 percent) of GDP for government use as China. Much of the wealth was in the hands of the ruling yangban class.[57] The Korean king and his aristocrats needed each other to maintain a stable hierarchical political and social structure, but the landlords who had the power to tax peasants provided an insufficient share of revenues to the court.[58] This of course meant limited government capacity to deal with external challenges.

Koreans participated culturally in the Chinese world order. Economically, Korea participated in Northeast Asian trade networks with China, Japan, and the nomadic peoples to the north. During the Silla Dynasty, Koreans founded trading settlements in China's Shandong and Jiangsu provinces. They also traded with Arab merchants who came to the region.[59]

Japan

The state of Yamato unified Japan in the second half of the third century. After the Taika Reform in 645, the Japanese rulers made systemwide efforts to introduce the Chinese political and legal system, ideology, and language. Japan sent study emissaries to China. This process lasted for almost two centuries. Japanese called this period their country's "first opening." However, the Japanese political system diverged from the Chinese model. By the twelfth century, Japan had developed a feudalist system, which was drastically different from China but similar to the feudalist experiences in Western Europe. Unlike China where Confucian scholars were eminent, the warrior class (*samurai*) was dominant in Japan. Diverging from European feudalism, Japan achieved political unification by the end of the sixteenth century and formed a centralized feudal political system.[60]

In the Tokugawa shogunate (1603-1868), the Japanese emperor was a figurehead while the *shogun* (general) ruled over subordinate *daimyo* (feudal lords) who had their own armies, administrative system, and tax collection systems in their autonomous fiefs. The shogun controlled about a quarter of the land while assigning the rest to allegiant daimyos. The shogun controlled daimyos by assigning loyal ones nearby and potential rivals far from the political centers. He also controlled them by threat of force, by keeping hostages, and by requiring an annual residence in Edo (now Tokyo), the seat of the *bakufu* (shogun's office), for each daimyo. The Tokugawa administration in Edo developed a large bureaucracy to run the country, but unlike China, which depended on civil service examinations to staff the government, the Japanese government turned to hereditary daimyos and the shogun's retainers. The dominant warrior class during the Tokugawa period was different from the European aristocracy in two important ways: Japanese warriors did not own land and they were largely bureaucrats.[61] Also, samurai culture was heavily influenced by Zen, a meditative form of Buddhism introduced from China. In a major difference from China, the Tokugawa government had greater financial resources as measured by percentage of the country's national income, estimated at 25-27 percent in the 1860s.[62]

Peace and stability in the Tokugawa period led to an improved economy. Population control mechanisms helped to slow the population growth, thus leading to higher per capita wealth. Also, the political control mechanism for feudal lords to reside alternatively in Edo helped to promote urban commerce. The shogun and daimyo became heavily indebted to urban merchants. The Japanese society was divided by class and status with samurai, merchants, and artisans living in cities and peasants living in villages. At the same time, Tokugawa merchants participated actively in conceptualizing politics from an economic perspective and in advising the government on economic affairs.[63]

Since the 1970s, scholars came to view the economy of Tokugawa Japan as highly sophisticated. Japanese scholars argue that Japan became an "economic society" in the Tokugawa period in that the market guided economic activities and people behaved rationally. In fact, it is argued that Japan had an "industrious revolution," in which peasants worked hard and acquired a good work ethic.[64] It is also suggested that Japan entered a proto-industrialization—growing domestic industry that aims at nonlocal markets—during the Tokugawa period.[65] The Tokugawa government experimented successfully with an import-substitution strategy to produce domestically imported goods such as raw silk and sugar after silver and copper mines were exhausted. Tokugawa's success with import substitution was one reason that some Japanese scholars saw Japan diverging from the rest of Asia even in the preindustrial period to stand alone among non-Western nations as having a rational national economy similar to that in Western Europe.[66] However, studies of China's economic history have shown similar developments in China.[67] (Table 3.3, to be found later in the chapter, shows that Japan and China had a similar level of GDP per capita.)

With political unification, the Tokugawa government proceeded to eliminate all possible sources of challenge. Continuing a campaign by General Hideyoshi to root out Christian influence, the Tokugawa prohibited Japanese who left the country from returning to Japan after 1636 and forbade construction of boats suitable for ocean voyages. Japan still engaged in foreign trade, particularly with its Asian neighbors, but Japan ceased to venture out to engage directly in East Asian trade.

Southeast Asia

The history of Southeast Asia is not as well documented as Northeast Asia's.[68] The dominant features of Southeast Asia are easily accessible waterways and dense forests, which allowed the people in the region to interact closely with each other and to maintain distinctiveness from outsiders such as China and India that projected cultural influence in the region. Surrounded by the Pacific and the Indian oceans, Southeast Asia was accessible mainly by sea for travelers from China, India, or elsewhere. On the northern border of Southeast Asia, Vietnam blocked any possible Chinese expansion into Southeast Asia by land routes. Unique among Southeast Asian nations, Vietnam was politically and intellectually modeled after China.[69] Ironically, Vietnam's success in copying Chinese military and bureaucratic practices helped the nation to maintain independence from China.

The dominant religious and political forms in Southeast Asia prior to colonial times were Hindu, Buddhist, and Islamic. With the exception of northern Vietnam, Southeast Asia was thus drastically different from Confucianist Northeast Asia.

Buddhism and Hinduism spread along trade routes from India to Southeast Asia. Unlike Confucian rulers in Northeast Asia, Southeast Asian rulers were god-kings. In precolonial times, a dominant form of state formation was modeled after India, in which an exemplary monarch resided at the center of a state whose authority radiates outward from a central core. Political power is centralized through personal connections and patronages. Southeast Asian rulers were supposed to have absolute power, but their actual influence was compromised by weak legal and bureaucratic structures.[70] The states in Southeast Asia tended not to have a clear sense of frontiers. With a sparse population, the Southeast Asian states cared more about whom (allegiance) rather than what (territories) they controlled.[71] Thailand and Burma (now Myanmar) remain Buddhist states and Hinduism has survived in Bali, Indonesia, to the present day.

Muslims came to the archipelago via trade between India and the Arab world on the one end and China on the other end as early as the eighth century. With the expansion of Islam in the twelfth and thirteenth centuries, Islam spread through trading ports in the region from the thirteenth to the seventeenth century.[72] Islam is now the dominant religion in Indonesia, Malaysia, and southern regions of the Philippines and Thailand.

On mainland Southeast Asia, Vietnam, Cambodia, Thailand, and Burma existed as recognizable political entities long before Western colonialism, although their modern boundaries were mostly colonial artifacts. By contrast, the archipelago states of Indonesia, Malaysia, Singapore, and the Philippines were largely colonial creations, although coherent polities influenced by Indian culture began to develop in the seventh century, and the Melaka sultanate that converted to Islam became the dominant political center in the Malay Peninsula in the fourteenth century.

The states in precolonial Southeast Asia were highly dependent on maritime trade. They were essentially urban centers around seaports. They imported rice and other essentials from the international market and paid with profits from reexporting goods and from producing goods in the cities.[73] Unlike Northeast Asia, the Southeast Asian states depended on commerce as their principal source of government revenue. Wealth derived from control of trade routes and markets as well as technical innovations explained the rise and fall of the states in the region.[74] As a case in point, the Burmese state received increased taxes from trade as a result of its increased participation in the Indian Ocean trade from the late sixteenth century. The state's decreased dependence on agricultural taxes enhanced its consolidation.[75]

Southeast Asian commerce expanded after 1400 and included intense intraregional commerce. Anthony Reid called the period of the fifteenth to the seventeenth century "the age of commerce" for the region.[76] Increased trade enlarged cosmopolitan coastal cities, which became political, economic, and cultural centers, and the state evolved around them. Buddhism, Islam, and Christianity all entered the region via cities. In addition, China's trade policy, whether to send expeditions to the region or to ban trade, had a major impact on the development of Southeast Asia. The rise of port states in Southeast Asia beginning in 1400 had much to do with the Ming Dynasty's heightened interest in the region. Trade with China brought wealth to some states.

Unlike China and Japan, which severely restricted foreign traders' freedom of action inside their countries, Southeast Asia was open to foreign people, goods, and religions. In Southeast Asian states, foreign merchants from within or outside the region played an active role in the city life and even served as court officials. In fact, foreigners had considerable bargaining leverage vis-à-vis local governments because they could always move to another port city.[77]

BEYOND EUROPEAN MODELS OF WORLD HISTORY

Why Western Europe grew rich and consequently surpassed the rest of the world by the mid-nineteenth century is an intriguing question for students of world history. Attempts to answer this question have also shaped the views of the contemporary international political economy of East Asia. Here I will discuss two related questions. First, what was the level of development in East Asia compared with Western Europe? Second, why did the West end up outranking the rest of the world? This section discusses the first question and the next section the second.

We compare East Asia with Western Europe because of the dominance of the West in modern times. If we look at world history millenniums ago, it would be more appropriate to compare East Asia with Egypt, Mesopotamia, and India, the three other ancient civilizations that preceded China by 500–1,500 years. As Jared Diamond showed, with easy access to domesticated high-yield plants and large animals, these four civilizations enjoyed a head start in global competition for wealth and power.[78] However, this book focuses on contemporary East Asian political economy, which has experienced an overwhelming impact from the West. In fact, all four ancient civilizations faced similar challenges to adapt to the modern world.

Eurocentric Models of World History

Early research maintains that Western Europe possessed unique features that explain its success in the Industrial Revolution. First, some suggest that Europeans became wealthier than Asians, which allowed a more capital-intensive path of development. Europeans had more livestock compared with Asians, which translated into greater transportation capacity and healthier people. More important, Europeans became wealthier than East Asians because they managed to lower their fertility rate from the sixteenth to eighteenth century owing to a high rate of celibacy and late marriages. Such family planning behavior allowed Europe to escape the trap of population growth keeping down per capita growth.[79]

Second, other scholars see economic institutions such as property rights as the secret of Europe's dramatic rise. Douglass North and Robert Thomas argued that "the development of an efficient economic organization in Western Europe accounts for the rise of the West" because "the establishment of institutional arrangements and property rights . . . creates an incentive to channel individual economic effort into activities that bring the private rate of return close to the social rate of return."[80] More broadly, Fernand Braudel viewed the profits of the wealthy as laying the foundation for capitalism.[81]

A third school of thought emphasizes unique European cultural factors. Max Weber famously talked about the "Protestant ethic" and "worldly ascetic" capitalism, which motivates efforts to create wealth in this world.[82] Others talked about the attitudes of the European elite and then middle class toward luxury consumption, which led to a unique European materialism that turned aristocratic luxuries such as sugar into modern daily necessities and stimulated the market economy. Consumers had to work harder to obtain these luxury goods, which were available principally from the market.[83]

For Eurocentric scholars, the modern world political economy based on the state and the market economy originated from Western Europe and spread to the rest of the world. It follows then that what matters is how successfully or unsuccessfully East Asians have adapted to the dominant Western political economy. By contrast, the East Asian version of political economy before the West matters little since it was at best a tributary to the Western mainstream or was simply a dead end for historical development.

New Scholarship on World History

Some recent studies show that East Asia was similar to Western Europe in living standards, agriculture, commerce, and proto-industrialization (handicraft manufacturing for the market) as late as 1750.[84] While Europe had more livestock per capita than East Asia, East Asia had sufficient farm animals to sustain a living standard similar to Western Europe.[85] In addition, East Asia had a high level of transportation capacity. China transported 30 million *shi* (a shi is about 160 pounds) of grain over long distances to feed about 14 million people in the eighteenth century, about five times Europe's long-distance grain transportation in the same period.[86] The fact that Asia had more large cities than Europe (22 percent urban in Japan and 15 percent in the Malay Archipelago compared with 10–15 percent in Western Europe) in the eighteenth century also indicated East Asia's ability to transport bulk goods.[87] Chinese and Japanese arguably had similar if not higher life expectancy than West Europeans.[88] Life expectancy for Southeast Asians is harder to measure, but as an indication of nutrition level, Southeast Asians appeared to have similar heights as Europeans in the sixteenth and seventeenth centuries.[89]

East Asians also had their mechanisms to keep population growth under control in order to improve living standards, using practices such as long breast-feeding periods, infanticide, and abortion.[90] Japan's population, for instance, increased less than Europe's population from 1730 to 1870.[91]

Recent studies also show that Chinese agriculture was more market-driven than European agriculture. The majority of land in China could be legally sold or rented.[92] By contrast, it was far more difficult to buy or rent land in Western Europe because of hereditary tenures. Thus, Western Europe's property land rights were not as efficient as in China. The labor market situation in China was similar to that in Western Europe. The practice of labor being bound to the landlords became unimportant in the Yangzi Valley by the eighteenth century, and agricultural laborers had become unbound to the land in North China even earlier.[93] China also experienced far greater long-distance labor migrations than Western Europe did. Ten million Chinese made long-distance migrations from the Middle Yangzi region to the Upper Yangzi in the late seventeenth and eighteenth centuries. Most migrants were free farmers while the rest were mostly free tenants.[94] By contrast, European migration to the Americas did not reach 1.5 million before 1800, and two-thirds of English emigrants were indentured servants.[95] Chinese peasants could sell their farm products to more buyers in the marketplace and had an easier time engaging in commercial handicraft production than their English and French counterparts.[96]

In terms of culture and values, China and Japan had a comparable level of consumption of durable luxury goods in furniture and clothing to Europe. China also enjoyed higher per capita consumption of daily luxury goods such as sugar and tobacco as late as 1800.[97] Merchants in Osaka, Japan, elevated their position in the Confucian order. In fact, scholars began to argue in the 1980s based on East Asia's economic success that Confucianism, which emphasizes education and organizational identity, was conducive to modernization.[98] Some even suggest that neo-Confucian cultures are better at supporting industrialization or modernization than Western cultures.[99]

East Asia was a shaping force for global political economy. Europe did not evolve in isolation but in a dynamic relationship with the rest of the world. Silver trade, discussed earlier, was often cited as the primary example of how East Asia helped to expand Europe's success. Ming China's need for silver helped to maintain the Spanish Empire until around 1640, and declining profits from the silver trade led to a financial crisis for the Spaniards.[100] More directly, Europe benefited from the transfer of technology such as guns, printing, textiles, and metallurgy from China at the outset of the Industrial Revolution.[101]

The best available estimates of international comparisons of wealth show East Asia ahead of Europe as late as 1820. Tables 3.1 and 3.2 show that China (32.9

TABLE 3.1

Economic Development, Asia and the West, 1–2001 (1990 international Geary-Khamis dollars, in millions)

	1	1000	1500	1600	1700	1820	1870	1913	1950	1973	2001
Western Europe	11,115	10,165	44,162	65,640	81,302	160,145	367,591	902,341	1,396,188	4,096,456	7,550,272
France			10,912	15,559	19,539	35,468	72,100	144,489	220,492	683,965	1,258,297
Germany			8,256	12,656	13,650	26,819	72,149	237,332	265,354	944,755	1,536,743
Italy			11,550	14,410	14,630	22,535	41,814	95,487	164,957	582,713	1,101,366
Britain			2,815	6,007	10,709	36,232	100,180	224,618	347,850	675,941	1,202,074
Western offshoots	468	784	1,120	920	833	13,499	111,493	582,941	1,635,490	4,058,289	9,156,267
United States			800	600	527	12,548	98,374	517,383	1,455,916	3,536,622	7,965,795
Japan	1,200	3,188	7,700	9,620	15,390	20,739	25,393	71,653	160,966	1,242,932	2,624,523
Asia (excluding Japan)	77,040	78,930	153,601	206,975	214,117	392,194	401,616	608,695	822,771	2,623,004	11,481,201
China	26,820	26,550	61,800	96,000	82,800	228,600	189,740	241,344	239,903	740,048	4,569,790
India	33,750	33,750	60,500	74,250	90,750	111,417	134,882	204,242	222,222	494,832	2,003,193
World total	102,619	116,787	248,308	330,982	371,269	695,346	1,112,655	2,732,131	5,329,719	16,023,529	37,193,868

Source: Angus Maddison, The World Economy: Historical Statistics (Paris: Development Center, OECD, 2003), 259.

Note: The twelve Western nations include Austria, Belgium, Denmark, Finland, France, Germany, Italy, the Netherlands, Norway, Sweden, Switzerland, and the United Kingdom. The Geary-Khamis method: R. S. Geary and S. H. Khamis developed the method, based on purchasing power parity and international average prices of commodities to allow international comparisons.

TABLE 3.2
Shares of World GDP, 1–2001

	1	1000	1500	1600	1700	1820	1870	1913	1950	1973	2001
Western Europe	10.8	8.7	17.8	19.8	21.9	23.0	33.0	33.0	26.2	25.6	20.3
France			4.4	4.7	5.3	5.1	6.5	5.3	4.1	4.3	3.4
Germany			3.3	3.8	3.7	3.9	6.5	8.7	5.0	5.9	4.1
Italy			4.7	4.4	3.9	3.2	3.8	3.5	3.1	3.6	3.0
Britain			1.1	1.8	2.9	5.2	9.0	8.2	6.5	4.2	3.2
Western offshoots	0.5	0.7	0.5	0.3	0.2	1.9	10.0	21.3	30.7	25.3	24.6
United States			0.3	0.2	0.1	1.8	8.8	18.9	27.3	22.1	21.4
Japan	1.2	2.7	3.1	2.9	4.1	3.0	2.3	2.6	3.0	7.8	7.1
Asia (excluding Japan)	75.1	67.6	61.9	62.5	57.7	56.4	36.1	22.3	15.4	16.4	30.9
China	26.1	22.7	24.9	29.0	22.3	32.9	17.1	8.8	4.5	4.6	12.3
India	32.9	28.9	24.4	22.4	24.4	16.0	12.1	7.5	4.2	3.1	5.4
World total	100.0	100.0	100.0	100.0	100.0	100.0	100.0	100.0	100.0	100.0	100.0

Source: Angus Maddison, *The World Economy: Historical Statistics* (Paris: Development Center, OECD, 2003), 261.

percent of the global total) alone had a GDP 32 percent larger than the combined GDP of Western Europe and Western offshoots (25.0 percent) in 1820. Moreover, as Table 3.3 shows, China and Japan were not far behind Europe in per capita GDP as late as 1820.

While recognizing East Asian economic progress, one still needs to explain the basic fact that the Industrial Revolution took place in Western Europe rather than in East Asia. The three tables in the chapter show a dramatic rise of the West beginning in the early nineteenth century. If level of wealth, economic institutions, and cultures did not explain Western Europe's rise sufficiently, what would be the reason then? A related question, as shown in the three tables, is why Japan, unlike China, never trailed far behind the West. A principal reason for the rise of the West and Japan's catching up lies in the international system and domestic political economy of East Asia versus Europe.

WHY DID THE WEST RISE?

The Industrial Revolution resulted from technological progress. It took place in Great Britain because the country succeeded in developing a capital- and technology-intensive modern sector of the economy, which grew at the expense of the traditional sector and eventually penetrated the traditional sector as well. A modern scientific revolution preceded the Industrial Revolution. While East Asia made great achievements in applied science, modern science developed mainly in Western Europe.[102] Modern market economy grew from extended application of science to production.[103] Without a technological breakthrough, China was caught in a "high-level equilibrium trap" in which once a country reaches the limit of resources due to expanding population it reverses to stagnation and decline.[104] Technology and science did not just happen, however. Technological advance required a suitable environment.

Politics made a major difference. On the domestic level, the nature of the relationship between the state and merchants was different between China and Western Europe. The Chinese government did not interfere with commerce as much as the European governments did, but it also provided fewer opportunities for merchants.[105] The European state had to compete with aristocracies, church clergy, and urban residents. By contrast, the Chinese emperor ran a centralized bureaucracy and faced few institutionalized power centers outside the state.[106] Political pluralism and diversity in organizations and technology allowed Europeans to experiment with new ways of doing business and politics.[107] Different political experiences in Europe and China provided different scenarios for future leaders.

However, the difference between political systems is not a sufficient condition to explain Europe's rise and Asia's decline. For one thing, Japan, which had

TABLE 3.3
International Comparison of GDP per Capita, 1–2001 (1990 international Geary-Khamis dollars)

	1	1000	1500	1600	1700	1820	1870	1913	1950	1973	2001
Western Europe	450	400	771	890	998	1,204	1,960	3,458	4,579	11,416	19,256
France			727	841	910	1,135	1,876	3,485	5,271	13,114	21,092
Germany			688	791	910	1,077	1,839	3,648	3,881	11,966	18,677
Italy			1,100	1,100	1,100	1,117	1,499	2,564	3,502	10,634	19,040
Britain			714	974	1,250	1,706	3,190	4,921	6,939	12,025	20,127
Western offshoots	400	400	400	400	476	1,202	2,419	5,233	9,268	16,179	26,943
United States			400	400	527	1,257	2,445	5,301	9,561	16,689	27,948
Japan	400	425	500	520	570	669	737	1,387	1,921	11,434	20,683
Asia (excluding Japan)	450	450	572	575	571	577	550	658	634	1,226	3,256
China	450	450	600	600	600	600	530	552	439	839	3,583
India	450	450	550	550	550	533	533	673	619	853	1,957
World average	445	436	566	595	615	667	875	1,525	2,111	4,091	6,049

Source: Angus Maddison, *The World Economy: Historical Statistics* (Paris: Development Center, OECD, 2003), 262.

a feudal aristocracy, resembled Western Europe more than China in terms of political structure. Nevertheless, whether Japan's structure allowed the country to be better prepared to emulate the West than China, it did not result in the Industrial Revolution. It was also not clear that political pluralization in Europe by itself would naturally lead to modernity.

To understand how domestic political economy affected the performance gap between Western Europe and East Asia, one has to move up to the international level for better explanations. Some scholars have argued that the West rose by exploiting the periphery in a process of "primitive accumulation," which was central to the Industrial Revolution.[108] James Blaut argued that Europe was not superior to the rest of the world prior to 1492, but European colonialism led to the rise of the West and underdevelopment of the rest of the world.[109] Similarly, Immanuel Wallerstein saw a world system in which Western Europe prospered by exploiting the periphery.[110] Critics have challenged this line of argument based on empirical evidence showing that non-European trade was small compared with domestic capital accumulation.[111] At the same time, the opening of the new world was important for the West. As Pomeranz argued, trade with the Americas was an important if not sufficient reason for Europe's great divergence from the rest of the world after 1750; metal ore found overseas and coal in Europe allowed Europe to avoid a labor-intensive path found in East Asia.[112]

Moreover, an intensely competitive interstate system in Western Europe was more conducive to technological and organizational innovation than the hierarchical Chinese world order in East Asia. The West prevailed over the East largely by using military force. The West had superior military weapons and organizations because of intense competition among equals in Europe, a system that emerged after 1500. Sustained warfare had a profound impact on state building in Europe.[113] War called on the state to figure out ways to collect revenues.[114] A related development is that the European state considered profit from trade as central to its ability to compete with other states. Thus, a competitive international system contributed to the emergence of capitalism and militarism.[115] By contrast, firearms, which had been developed and widely used previously in China, enjoyed little progress once Ming rulers (1368–1644) stabilized the country. In Japan, Tokugawa Ieyasu, who ended the civil war and established a stable shogunate government in 1603, forbade feudal lords to own firearms and banned information about guns.[116]

It is historically incorrect to picture a stark contrast between a progressive, competitive, balance-of-power system in Europe and a repressive, coercive, unified China. Both Europe and China had periods of empires and of balance-of-power systems.[117] And both regions have experienced progress and decay. The point here is simply that a truly competitive international system in Europe at a critical juncture accelerated the pace of technological, economic, social, and political transformations, which gave Europeans significant advantages over non-European peoples.

CONCLUSION

East Asia had a sophisticated and regionally connected economy prior to the European arrival in the region. East Asia was on par economically with Western Europe in many areas by the mid-eighteenth century. East Asia's post–World War II economic growth is thus a resurgence to its ancient status as a vibrant economic center.

East Asia had readily identifiable political entities, with sustained and extensive experience in organizing political, military, economic, and cultural affairs. Thus, the developmental state, to be discussed in Chapter 5, emerged naturally from this political tradition. Unlike some other developing regions, it was relatively easy for East Asian states to devote themselves to development based on their strong nation state traditions. One needs to have a nation to begin with in order to have national development.

East Asia failed and the West succeeded in making the industrial breakthrough because of the different nature of the regional orders that had evolved on opposite ends of the Eurasian continent. The Chinese world order was highly successful judging by its duration. It was different from the European international order because of different purposes and related practices, which resulted from different circumstances. The Chinese emperor, who did not face corporate power centers at home, rationally sought to perpetuate imperial rule through fiscally responsible policy of limiting the tax burden on peasants and of keeping government expenditure under control. By contrast, Western monarchs needed to generate new resources to compete in an anarchical regional system. Necessity was the mother of institutional and technological innovations. Armed trade and monopoly played an important role in explaining Europe's success.

The history of East Asian international political economy matters because East Asians bring their historical experience into analysis of current affairs and into their policy prescriptions. The cultural and economic connections among East Asians for centuries in the past make it possible for them to imagine an Asian community.

The Chinese world order provides China with both a longing to revive its past glory and a sense of confidence in being a natural leader in East Asia. The memory of the ancient Chinese world order is a source of fear and respect for other East Asian nations. Having had to deal with strong outside powers from a weak position in the past, Southeast Asia can live with a strong China while seeking also to form strong relations with other greater powers as a check on the Middle Kingdom. By contrast, Japan, which was mostly outside China's political order historically, does not accept Chinese regional leadership and views China's alleged Middle Kingdom mentality with grave concern.

SUGGESTED READINGS

Arrighi, Giovanni, Takeshi Hamashita, and Mark Selden, eds. *The Resurgence of East Asia: 500, 150, and 50 Year Perspectives* (New York: RoutledgeCurzon, 2003).

Barfield, Thomas. *The Perilous Frontier: Nomadic Empires and China* (Cambridge: Blackwell, 1989).

Cohen, Warren I. *East Asia at the Center: Four Thousand Years of Engagement with the World* (New York: Columbia University Press, 2000).

Elvin, Mark. *The Pattern of the Chinese Past* (Stanford: Stanford University Press, 1973).

Fairbank, John King, ed. *The Chinese World Order: Traditional China's Foreign Relations* (Cambridge: Harvard University Press, 1968).

Flynn, Dennis O., and Arturo Giraldez. "China and the Spanish Empire." *Revista de Historia Economica* 14, no. 2 (Spring 1996): 309–338.

Goldman, Merle, and Andrew Gordon, eds. *Historical Perspectives on Contemporary East Asia* (Cambridge: Harvard University Press, 2000).

Hamashita, Takashi. "The Intra-Regional System in East Asia in Modern Times," in *Network Power: Japan and Asia,* ed. Peter J. Katzenstein and Takashi Shiraishi (Ithaca, N.Y.: Cornell University Press, 1997), 113–135.

Ho, Ping-Ti. "In Defense of Sinicization: A Rebuttal of Evelyn Rawski's 'Reenvisioning the Qing.'" *The Journal of Asian Studies* 57, no. 1 (February 1998): 123–155.

Huang, Philip C. C. *The Peasant Economy and Social Change in North China* (Stanford: Stanford University Press, 1985).

Hui, Victoria Tin-Bor. *War and State Formation in Ancient China and Early Modern Europe* (New York: Cambridge University Press, 2005).

Kazui, Tashiro. "Foreign Relations During the Edo Period: Sakoku Reexamined." *Journal of Japanese Studies* 8, no. 2 (Summer 1982): 283–306.

Lawton, John. *Silk, Scents, and Spice: Retracing the World's Great Trade Routes* (Paris: UNESCO, 2004).

Lee, John. "Trade and Economy in Preindustrial East Asia, c. 1500–c. 1800: East Asia in the Age of Global Integration." *The Journal of Asian Studies* 58, no. 1 (February 1999): 2–26.

Leonard, Jane Kate, and John R. Watt, eds. *To Achieve Security and Wealth: The Qing State and the Economy, 1644–1911* (Ithaca, N.Y.: Cornell University Press, 1992).

Maddison, Angus. *The World Economy: Historical Statistics* (Paris: Development Center, OECD, 2003).

Palais, James B. *Politics and Policy in Traditional Korea* (Cambridge: Harvard University Press, 1975).

Perkins, Dwight H. "Government as an Obstacle to Industrialization: The Case of Nineteenth-Century China." *The Journal of Economic History* 27, no. 4 (December 1967): 478–492.

Pomeranz, Kenneth. *The Great Divergence: China, Europe, and the Making of Modern World Economy* (Princeton: Princeton University Press, 2000).

Rawski, Evelyn S. "Reenvisioning the Qing: The Significance of the Qing Period in Chinese History." *The Journal of Asian Studies* 55, no. 4 (November 1996): 829–850.

Reid, Anthony. *Southeast Asia in the Age of Commerce 1450–1680.* Vol. 1, *The Lands Below the Winds* (New Haven: Yale University Press, 1988).

Reid, Anthony. *Southeast Asia in the Age of Commerce 1450–1680.* Vol. 2, *Expansion and Crisis* (New Haven: Yale University Press, 1993).

Reischauer, Edwin O., and Marius B. Jansen. *The Japanese Today: Change and Continuity,* enlarged ed. (Cambridge: Harvard University Press, 1995).

Rosenberg, Nathan, and L. E. Birdzell Jr. *How the West Grew Rich: The Economic Transformation of the Industrial World* (New York: Basic Books, 1986).

Rowe, William T. *Hankow: Commerce and Society in a Chinese City, 1796–1889* (Stanford: Stanford University Press, 1984).

Rozman, Gilbert, ed. *The East Asian Region: Confucian Heritage and Its Modern Adaptation* (Princeton: Princeton University Press, 1991).

Smith, Thomas C. *Native Sources of Japanese Industrialization, 1750–1920* (Berkeley: University of California Press, 1988).

Tarling, Nicholas. *Nations and States in Southeast Asia* (Cambridge: Cambridge University Press, 1998).

Toby, Ronald P. *State and Diplomacy in Early Modern Japan: Asia in the Development of the Tokugawa Bakufu* (Stanford: Stanford University Press, 1984).

Wang, Gungwu. *The Nanhai Trade: The Early History of Chinese Trade in the Southeast China Sea* (Singapore: Times Academic Press, 1998).

Wong, R. Bin. *China Transformed: Historical Change and the Limits of European Experience* (Ithaca, N.Y.: Cornell University Press, 1997).

Woodside, Alexander Barton. *Vietnam and the Chinese Model* (Cambridge: Harvard University Press, 1988).

Yu, Ying-shih. *Trade and Expansion in Han China: A Study in the Structure of Sino-Barbarian Economic Relations* (Berkeley: University of California Press, 1967).

NOTES

1. See Hedley Bull, *The Anarchical Society: A Study of Order in World Politics* (New York: Columbia University Press, 1977); John G. Ruggie, "International Regimes, Transactions, and Change: Embedded Liberalism in the Postwar Economic Order," in *International Regimes*, ed. Stephen D. Krasner (Ithaca, N.Y.: Cornell University Press, 1983), 195–231; Judith Goldstein and Robert O. Keohane, "Ideas and Foreign Policy: An Analytical Framework," in *Ideas and Beliefs, Institutions, and Political Change*, ed. Judith Goldstein and Robert O. Keohane (Ithaca, N.Y.: Cornell University Press, 1993), 3–30.

2. Bull, *Anarchical Society*, 4.

3. For literature on international system and structure, see Morton A. Kaplan, *System and Process in International Politics* (New York: Wiley, 1957); Stanley Hoffmann, *The State of War* (New York: Praeger, 1965); Kenneth Waltz, *Theory of International Politics* (Reading, Mass.: Addison-Wesley, 1979).

4. For a classic on the topic, see John King Fairbank, ed., *The Chinese World Order: Traditional China's Foreign Relations* (Cambridge: Harvard University Press, 1968).

5. Thomas Barfield, *The Perilous Frontier: Nomadic Empires and China* (Cambridge: Blackwell, 1989); Carter Vaughn Findley, *The Turks in World History* (Oxford: Oxford University Press, 2005); Anatoly M. Khazanov and André Wink, eds., *Nomads in the Sedentary World* (Richmond, Surrey: Curzon Press, 2001).

6. Evelyn S. Rawski, "Reenvisioning the Qing: The Significance of the Qing Period in Chinese History," *The Journal of Asian Studies* 55, no. 4 (November 1996): 842. For a rebuttal, see Ping-Ti Ho, "In Defense of Sinicization: A Rebuttal of Evelyn Rawski's 'Reenvisioning the Qing,'" *The Journal of Asian Studies* 57, no. 1 (February 1998): 123–155.

7. Angus Maddison, *The World Economy: Historical Statistics* (Paris: Development Center, OECD, 2003), 261.

8. Ronald P. Toby, *State and Diplomacy in Early Modern Japan: Asia in the Development of the Tokugawa Bakufu* (Stanford: Stanford University Press, 1984).

9. Wang Gungwu, "Without Southeast Asia: A Background Essay," in *The Chinese World Order* (see note 4), 52–60. Also see Louise Levathes, *When China Ruled the Sea: The Treasure Fleet of the Dragon Throne 1403–1433* (New York: Simon and Schuster, 1994).

10. Benjamin I. Schwartz, "The Chinese Perception of World Order, Past and Present," in *The Chinese World Order* (see note 4), 277. See also Charles Patrick Fitzgerald, *The Chinese View of Their Place in the World* (New York: Oxford University Press, 1964).

11. Alastair I. Johnston, *Cultural Realism: Strategic Culture and Grand Strategy in Chinese History* (Princeton: Princeton University Press, 1995).

12. Victoria Tin-Bor Hui, *War and State Formation in Ancient China and Early Modern Europe* (New York: Cambridge University Press, 2005).

13. Findley, *Turks in World History*, 28–29.

14. Wang, "Without Southeast Asia," 41.

15. John King Fairbank, "Framework," in *The Chinese World Order* (see note 4), 11.

16. For examples, see Sarasin Viraphol, *Tribute and Profit: Sino-Siamese Trade, 1652–1853* (Cambridge: Harvard University Press, 1977).

17. Joseph F. Fletcher, "China and Central Asia," in *The Chinese World Order* (see note 4), 206–224.

18. Robert K. Sakai, "(Liu-Chiu) Islands as a Fief of Satsuma," in *The Chinese World Order* (see note 4), 112–134; Ta-tuan Chen, "Chiu Kings in the Ching Period," in *The Chinese World Order* (see note 4), 135–164.

19. Kenneth R. Robinson, "Centering the King of Choson: Aspects of Korean Maritime Diplomacy, 1392–1592," *The Journal of Asian Studies* 59, no. 1 (February 2000): 109–125.

20. Ying-shih Yu, *Trade and Expansion in Han China: A Study in the Structure of Sino-Barbarian Economic Relations* (Berkeley: University of California Press, 1967), 47.

21. Barfield, *Perilous Frontier*.

22. Yu, *Trade and Expansion in Han China*, 36–64.

23. Cited in Jonathan D. Spence, *The Search for Modern China*, 2nd ed. (New York: Norton, 1999), 122.

24. Yu, *Trade and Expansion in Han China*, 18–19.

25. Wang Gungwu, *The Nanhai Trade: The Early History of Chinese Trade in the Southeast China Sea* (Singapore: Times Academic Press, 1998), 29–35.

26. Anthony Reid, "An 'Age of Commerce' in Southeast Asia," *Modern Asian Studies* 24, no. 1 (1990): 9.

27. Yu, *Trade and Expansion in Han China*, 93.

28. Barfield, *Perilous Frontier*.

29. Hae-jong Chun, "Relations in the Ch'ing Period," in *The Chinese World Order* (see note 4), 90–111.

30. Takashi Hamashita, "The Intra-Regional System in East Asia in Modern Times," in Peter J. Katzenstein and Takashi Shiraishi, eds., *Network Power: Japan and Asia* (Ithaca, N.Y.: Cornell University Press, 1997), 117.

31. Takeshi Hamashita, "Tribute and Treaties: Maritime Asia and Treaty Port Networks in the Era of Negotiation, 1800–1900," in *The Resurgence of East Asia: 500, 150, and 50 Year Perspectives*, ed. Giovanni Arrighi, Takeshi Hamashita, and Mark Selden (New York: RoutledgeCurzon, 2003), 21–22.

32. John Lawton, *Silk, Scents, and Spice: Retracing the World's Great Trade Routes* (Paris: UNESCO, 2004), 11–73.

33. Lawton, *Silk, Scents, and Spice,* 75–113.

34. Reid, "An 'Age of Commerce' in Southeast Asia," 9–10.

35. Toby, *State and Diplomacy in Early Modern Japan*; Tessa Morrison-Suzuki, *The Technological Transformation of Japan: From the Seventeenth to the Twenty-First Century* (Cambridge: Cambridge University Press, 1994); Tashiro Kazui, "Foreign Relations During the Edo Period: Sakoku Reexamined," *Journal of Japanese Studies* 8, no. 2 (Summer 1982): 283–306.

36. Hamashita Takeshi, *Kindai chūgoku no kokusaiteki keiki: chōko bōeki shisutemu to kindai ajia* [Modern China's international opportunity: The tributary trade system and modern Asia] (Tokyo: Tokyo daigaku shuppankai, 1990), 44.

37. Tashiro, "Foreign Relations During the Edo Period," 283–284.

38. Anthony Reid, *Southeast Asia in the Age of Commerce, 1450–1680,* vol. 1, *The Lands Below the Winds* (New Haven: Yale University Press, 1988) and *Southeast Asia in the Age of Commerce, 1450–1680,* vol. 2, *Expansion and Crisis* (New Haven: Yale University Press, 1993).

39. John Lee, "Trade and Economy in Preindustrial East Asia, c. 1500–c. 1800: East Asia in the Age of Global Integration," *The Journal of Asian Studies* 58, no. 1 (February 1999): 2–26.

40. Dennis O. Flynn and Arturo Giraldez, "China and the Spanish Empire," *Revista de historia economica* 14, no. 2 (Spring 1996): 309–338; "China and the Manila Galleons," in *Japanese Industrialization and the Asian Economy,* ed. A. J. H. Latham and Heita Kawakatsu (London: Routledge, 1994), 71–90.

41. Charles Tilly, *Coercion, Capital, and European States,* A.D. *990–1990* (Cambridge: Blackwell, 1990).

42. For useful readings of pastoral nomadic political organizations, see Anatoly Khazanov, *Nomads and the Outside World,* 2nd ed., trans. Julia Crook-enden (Madison: University of Wisconsin Press, 1994); Barfield, *Perilous Frontier.*

43. Mark Elvin, *The Pattern of the Chinese Past* (Stanford: Stanford University Press, 1973), 69–83.

44. For a general study of rule and revenue, see Margaret Levi, *Of Rule and Revenue* (Berkeley: University of California Press, 1988). She argued that rulers maximize revenues to the state, which relates to their ability to rule, but they are constrained by their bargaining power and transaction costs, including the cost of inviting revolts.

45. Dwight H. Perkins, *Agricultural Development in China, 1368–1968* (Chicago: Aldine, 1969), 176–182; Ray Huang, *Taxation and Government Finance in 16th Century Ming China* (Cambridge: Cambridge University Press, 1974); Yeh-chien

Wang, *Land Taxation in Imperial China, 1750–1911* (Cambridge: Harvard University Press, 1973).

46. Immanuel C. Y. Hsu, *The Rise of Modern China* (New York: Oxford University Press, 1970), 75–82.

47. See, for example, William T. Rowe, *Hankow: Commerce and Society in a Chinese City, 1796–1889* (Stanford: Stanford University Press, 1984).

48. Gilbert Rozman, ed., *The Modernization of China* (New York: Free Press, 1981), 75–77.

49. Huang, *Taxation and Government Finance in 16th Century Ming China*, 316–323.

50. Charles Tilly, *Big Structures, Large Processes, Huge Comparisons* (New York: Russell Sage Foundation, 1984), 142.

51. Jane Kate Leonard and John R. Watt, eds., *To Achieve Security and Wealth: The Qing State and the Economy, 1644–1911* (Ithaca, N.Y.: Cornell University Press, 1992).

52. Dwight H. Perkins, "Government as an Obstacle to Industrialization: The Case of Nineteenth-Century China," *The Journal of Economic History* 27, no. 4 (December 1967): 478.

53. Wang Gungwu, *Anglo-Chinese Encounters Since 1800: War, Trade, Science, and Governance* (New York: Cambridge University Press, 2003), 55.

54. JaHyun Kim Haboush, "The Confucianization of Korean Society," in *The East Asian Region: Confucian Heritage and Its Modern Adaptation*, ed. Gilbert Rozman (Princeton: Princeton University Press, 1991), 85–86; Carter J. Eckert, "Korea's Transition to Modernity: A Will to Greatness," in *Historical Perspectives on Contemporary East Asia*, ed. Merle Goldman and Andrew Gordon (Cambridge: Harvard University Press, 2000), 122–126; Chai-Sik Chung, *A Korean Confucian Encounter with the Modern World: Yi Hang-no and the West* (Berkeley: Institute of East Asian Studies, University of California, 1995), 13–16.

55. Takashi Hatada, *A History of Korea*, trans. and ed. Warren W. Smith Jr. and Benjamin H. Hazard (Santa Barbara, Calif.: ABC-Clio, 1969).

56. Dwight H. Perkins, "The Historical Foundations of Modern Economic Growth," in *The Economic and Social Modernization of the Republic of Korea*, ed. Edward S. Mason et al. (Cambridge: Harvard University Press, 1980), 62–70.

57. Perkins, "Historical Foundations of Modern Economic Growth," 66.

58. James B. Palais, *Politics and Policy in Traditional Korea* (Cambridge: Harvard University Press, 1975), 12–18, 61–67.

59. Warren I. Cohen, *East Asia at the Center: Four Thousand Years of Engagement with the World* (New York: Columbia University Press, 2000), 98.

60. Edwin O. Reischauer and Marius B. Jansen, *The Japanese Today: Change and Continuity*, enlarged ed. (Cambridge: Harvard University Press, 1995), 52–77.

61. Thomas C. Smith, *Native Sources of Japanese Industrialization, 1750–1920* (Berkeley: University of California Press, 1988), 133–147. This explains why some samurais were willing to destroy the aristocracy after the Meiji Restoration.

62. E. Sydney Crawcour, "The Tokugawa Heritage," in *The State and Economic Enterprise in Japan,* ed. William Wirt Lockwood (Princeton: Princeton University Press, 1965), 31.

63. Tetsuo Najita, *Visions of Virtue in Tokugawa Japan: The Kaitokudo Merchant Academy of Osaka* (Chicago: University of Chicago Press, 1987), 8–10.

64. Hayami Akira and Miyamoto Matao, eds., *Nihon keizai shi, ichi; keizai shakai no seiritsu, jushichi juhachi seiki* [A history of Japanese economy, vol. 1, The coming of economic society, the seventeenth and the eighteenth centuries] (Tokyo: Iwanami shoten, 1988).

65. David L. Howell, *Capitalism from Within: Economy, Society, and the State in a Japanese Fishery* (Berkeley: University of California Press, 1995); Kären Wigen, "The Geographic Imagination in Early Modern Japanese History: Retrospect and Prospect," *The Journal of Asian Studies* 51, no. 1 (February 1992): 3–29.

66. Lee, "Trade and Economy in Preindustrial East Asia."

67. Eric Jones considered Tokugawa Japan, Song China, and Western Europe the only three areas where intensive economic growth, which refers to increased per capita income, took place before industrialization. Eric Jones, *Growth Recurring: Economic Change in World History* (Oxford: Clarendon Press, 1988).

68. Few written documents survived after 1500 and the Europeans kept more detailed records of Southeast Asia than Chinese and Arabs before them. Reid, "An 'Age of Commerce' in Southeast Asia," 1–30.

69. Vietnam was also part of Southeast Asia culturally. This is particularly the case for the "Indianized" southern peoples such as Cambodians and Malayo-Polynesian Chams, whom the northern Vietnamese conquered relatively late. Alexander Barton Woodside, *Vietnam and the Chinese Model* (Cambridge: Harvard University Press, 1988), 22–25.

70. O. W. Wolters, *History, Culture, and Region in Southeast Asian Perspectives* (Singapore: Institute of Southeast Asian Studies, 1982); George M. Kahin, ed., *Government and Politics in Southeast Asia,* 2nd ed. (Ithaca, N.Y.: Cornell University Press, 1964).

71. Nicholas Tarling, *Nations and States in Southeast Asia* (Cambridge: Cambridge University Press, 1998), 47–48.

72. Robert W. Hefner, *Civil Islam: Muslims and Democratization in Indonesia* (Princeton: Princeton University Press, 2000), 26–31.

73. Anthony Reid, "The Organization of Production in Southeast Asian Port Cities," in *Brides of the Sea: Port Cities of Asia from the 16th to 20th Centuries,* ed. Frank Broeze (Honolulu: University of Hawaii Press, 1989), 55–74.

74. Reid, *Southeast Asia in the Age of Commerce, 1450–1680,* vol. 2, 203–266.

75. Robert H. Taylor, *The State in Burma* (Honolulu: University of Hawaii Press, 1987), 45.

76. Reid, *Southeast Asia in the Age of Commerce, 1450–1680,* vol. 1.

77. Reid, "An 'Age of Commerce' in Southeast Asia," 4.

78. Jared Diamond, *Guns, Germs, and Steel: The Fates of Human Societies* (New York: Norton, 1999).

79. David Landes, *The Unbound Prometheus: Technological Change and Industrial Development in Western Europe from 1750 to the Present* (Cambridge: Cambridge University Press, 1969); Eric L. Jones, *The European Miracle: Environments, Economies, and Geopolitics in the History of Europe and Asia* (Cambridge: Cambridge University Press, 1981); John Hajnal, "Two Kinds of Preindustrial Household Formation Systems," *Population and Development Review* 8, no. 3 (September 1982): 449–494; Jan DeVries, *The Economy of Europe in an Age of Crisis, 1600–1750* (New York: Cambridge University Press, 1976), 9–12.

80. Douglass C. North and Robert Paul Thomas, *The Rise of the Western World: A New Economic History* (Cambridge: Cambridge University Press, 1973), 1.

81. Fernand Braudel, *Afterthoughts on Material Civilization and Capitalism,* trans. Patricia M. Ranum (Baltimore: Johns Hopkins University Press, 1977).

82. Max Weber, *The Protestant Ethic and the Spirit of Capitalism,* trans. Talcott Parsons (New York: Scribner's, 1958).

83. Chandra Mukerji, *From Graven Images: Patterns of Modern Materialism* (New York: Columbia University Press, 1983); Sidney W. Mintz, *Sweetness and Power: The Place of Sugar in Modern History* (New York: Penguin, 1985).

84. R. Bin Wong, *China Transformed: Historical Change and the Limits of European Experience* (Ithaca, N.Y.: Cornell University Press, 1997); Kenneth Pomeranz, *The Great Divergence: China, Europe, and the Making of Modern World Economy* (Princeton: Princeton University Press, 2000).

85. Philip C. C. Huang, *The Peasant Economy and Social Change in North China* (Stanford: Stanford University Press, 1985), 145–151.

86. Wu Chengming, *Zhongguo zibenzhuyi yu guonei shichang* [Chinese capitalism and the national market] (Beijing: Zhongguo shehui kexue chubanshe, 1985), 254– 258; Perkins, *Agricultural Development in China,* 297–307; Pomeranz, *Great Divergence,* 34.

87. Thomas C. Smith, *The Agrarian Origins of Modern Japan* (Stanford: Stanford University Press, 1958), 67–68; Reid, "Organization of Production in Southeast Asian Port Cities," 57; Gilbert Rozman, *Urban Networks in Ching China and Tokugawa Japan* (Princeton: Princeton University Press, 1973).

88. Susan B. Hanley and Kozo Yamamura, *Economic and Demographic Change in Preindustrial Japan, 1600–1868* (Princeton: Princeton University Press, 1977),

221–222; William Lavely and R. Bin Wong, "Revising the Malthusian Narrative: The Comparative Study of Population Dynamics in Late Imperial China," *The Journal of Asian Studies* 57, no. 3 (August 1998): 714–748.

89. Reid, *Southeast Asia in the Age of Commerce, 1450–1680*, vol. 1, 45–50.

90. George Barclay, Ansley J. Coale, Michael A. Stoto, and T. James Trussell, "A Reassessment of the Demography of Traditional China," *Population Index* 42, no. 4 (October 1976): 606–635; James Z. Lee and Wang Feng, *One Quarter of Humanity: Malthusian Mythology and Chinese Realities, 1700–2000* (Cambridge: Harvard University Press, 1999).

91. Laurel L. Cornell, "Infanticide in Early Modern Japan? Demography, Culture, and Population Growth," *The Journal of Asian Studies* 55, no. 1 (February 1996): 22–50.

92. Huang, *Taxation and Government Finance in 16th Century Ming China*; Huang, *Peasant Economy and Social Change in North China*; Kenneth Pomeranz, *The Making of a Hinterland: State, Society, and Economy in Inland North China, 1853–1937* (Berkeley: University of California Press, 1993).

93. Elvin, *Pattern of the Chinese Past*, 235–267; Luo Lun and Jing Su, *Qingdai shandong jingying dizhu jingji yanjiu* [Economic research on managerial landlords in Shandong during the Qing Dynasty] (Jinan: Qilu shushe, 1984).

94. James Lee and Bin Wong, "Population Movements in Qing China and Their Linguistic Legacy," in *Languages and Dialects of China*, ed. William S.-Y. Wang (Berkeley: Journal of Chinese Linguistics Monograph Series, 1991), 52–77. In addition, 3 million migrants moved from the Middle Yangzi and the Upper Yangzi to southwest China in the late eighteenth and the early nineteenth century. Twelve million people moved from north China to settle in northeast China in the late nineteenth century and the early twentieth century.

95. Pomeranz, *Great Divergence*, 83.

96. Ming-Te Pan, "Rural Credit in Ming-Qing Jiangnan and the Concept of Peasant Petty Commodity Production," *The Journal of Asian Studies* 55, no. 1 (February 1996): 94–117; Hanchao Lu, "Arrested Development: Cotton and Cotton Markets in Shanghai, 1350–1843," *Modern China* 18, no. 4 (October 1992): 468–499.

97. Pomeranz, *Great Divergence*, 114–165.

98. Yu Ying-shih, *Zhongguo jinshi zongjiao lunli yu shangren jingshen* [Modern Chinese religious ethics and merchant spirit] (Taipei: Lianjing chubanshe, 1987); Najita, *Visions of Virtue in Tokugawa Japan*; Michio Morishima, *Why Has Japan Succeeded?: Western Technology and the Japanese Ethos* (New York: Cambridge University Press, 1982); Peter L. Berger and Hsin-Huang Michael Hsiao, eds., *In Search of an East Asian Development Model* (New Brunswick, N.J.: Transaction Books, 1988).

99. Herman Kahn, *World Economic Development: 1979 and Beyond* (Boulder: Westview Press, 1979), 117–126. For a study of neo-Confucianism, see William Theodore de Bary and Irene Bloom, eds., *Principle and Practicality: Essays in Neo-Confucianism and Practical Learning* (New York: Columbia University Press, 1979).

100. Flynn and Giraldez, "China and the Spanish Empire"; Richard Von Glahn, *Fountain of Fortune: Money and Monetary Policy in China, 1000–1700* (Berkeley: University of California Press, 1996); Ward Barrett, "World Bullion Flows, 1450–1800," in *The Rise of Merchant Empires,* ed. James Tracy (New York: Cambridge University Press, 1990), 224–254; Andre Gunder Frank, *Reorient: Global Economy in the Asian Age* (Berkeley: University of California Press, 1998).

101. Frank, *Reorient,* 185–204.

102. Joseph Needham, *Science in Traditional China: A Comparative Perspective* (Cambridge: Harvard University Press, 1981); Joseph Needham, *The Great Titration: Science and Society in East and West* (London: Allen and Unwin, 1969).

103. Karl Polanyi, *The Great Transformation: The Political and Economic Origins of Our Time* (Boston: Beacon Press, 1957); Simon Kuznets, *Modern Economic Growth Rate, Structure, and Spread* (New Haven: Yale University Press, 1966), 8–16.

104. Mark Elvin, "The High-Level Equilibrium Trap: The Causes of the Decline of Invention in the Traditional Chinese Textile Industries," in *Economic Organization in Chinese Society,* ed. William E. Willmott (Stanford: Stanford University Press, 1972), 137–172.

105. Pomeranz, *Great Divergence,* 173.

106. Wong, *China Transformed,* 101–102.

107. Nathan Rosenberg and L. E. Birdzell Jr., *How the West Grew Rich: The Economic Transformation of the Industrial World* (New York: Basic Books, 1986).

108. Andre Gunder Frank, *Capitalism and Underdevelopment in Latin America: Historical Studies of Chile and Brazil* (New York: Monthly Review Press, 1969); Eric Williams, *Capitalism and Slavery* (London: Andre Deutsch, 1964); Samir Amin, *Accumulation on a World Scale: A Critique of the Theory of Underdevelopment,* trans. Brian Pearce (New York: Monthly Press, 1974).

109. James M. Blaut, *The Colonizer's Model of the World: Geographical Diffusionism and Eurocentric History* (New York: Guilford Press, 1993).

110. Immanuel Wallerstein, *Capitalist Agriculture and the Origins of the European World System* (New York: Academic Press, 1974) and *The Modern World-System III: 1730–1840s* (New York: Academic Press, 1989).

111. Jan DeVries, *The Economy of Europe in an Age of Crisis, 1600–1750* (New York: Cambridge University Press, 1976), 139–146. See also Patrick O'Brien, "European Economic Development: The Contribution of the Periphery," *Economic History Review* 35, no. 1 (February 1982): 1–18.

112. Pomeranz, *Great Divergence.*
113. Thomas Ertman, *Birth of the Leviathan: Building States and Regimes in Medieval and Early Modern Europe* (Cambridge: Cambridge University Press, 1997).
114. Tilly, *Coercion, Capital, and European States.*
115. Giovanni Arrighi, Po-Keung Hui, Ho-Fung Hung, and Mark Selden, "Historical Capitalism, East and West," in *The Resurgence of East Asia* (see note 31), 317–318.
116. Elvin, *Pattern of the Chinese Past,* 89–97.
117. Hui, *War and State Formation in Ancient China and Early Modern Europe.*

CHAPTER **4**

Modern Imperialism

This chapter examines the modern transformation of East Asian international political economy (IPE) with the European arrival in East Asia. It answers two major questions. First, how did the European arrival in Asia influence the evolution of East Asian IPE? What was the nature of the Western impact, and how did East Asians respond? The chapter shows that East Asia's modern transformation, partly defined by Western pressure and Asian response, presents a complex picture of Westerners also adapting to the preexisting commercial networks and political realities in East Asia. As East Asia and Europe interacted in a global market, studies of East Asian IPE shed light on what was unique and universal in both regions. The strategies and purposes pursued by various East Asian nations, including Japanese imperialism, nationalism, and communism, helped to shape the region's modern international political economy.

The Western imperialist order in Asia went through two stages. The first stage lasted from the early sixteenth century to the mid-nineteenth century. Europeans gained a strategic position in maritime Southeast Asia. Around the same period, China and several other Asian states were also expanding dramatically. Europeans came to dominate in East Asia after the mid-nineteenth century and maintained that dominance for only a century, a short period in the long history of East Asia. However, the impact of the West was profound. To begin with, Europeans forged new states in maritime Southeast Asia, such as Indonesia, Malaysia, and the Philippines. They also helped to define the current borders of continental Southeast Asia and Northeast Asia. The European impact was also reflected in the profound transformation of the state, economy, and culture throughout East Asia.

The second question the chapter addresses is how Japanese imperialism influenced East Asian IPE. Japan's expansion constituted an Asian comeback at the expense not only of the West but also of the rest of East Asia. Japanese elites saw building a modern economy as essential for building a strong army to defend against encroaching Western powers. The Japanese expansion was initially driven by a desire to control the "lines of advantage" but came to incorporate an economic rationale for strategic materials and markets as its industrialization progressed and as the Great Depression led to protectionist blocs controlled by

Western powers. Japanese imperialism left statist legacies in places like Korea and Taiwan that it had administered for a lengthy period of time. Japan helped destroy the Western imperialist order in the early years of the Pacific War, which could not be restored easily afterward. Japan's loss of the war facilitated the emergence of a cold war structure in East Asia, with Japan itself becoming a market democracy while creating conditions for the eventual triumph of communism in China, Vietnam, and North Korea.

WESTERN IMPERIALISM

Imperialism

Much has been studied about imperialism. For some scholars, imperialism and empires describe the same political situation in which one nation imposes its political control on others.[1] Imperialism is a type of international order.

East Asia was not unfamiliar with empires and subjugation of one people by another. But Western imperialism was different from the Asian empires in that it was based on the nation state and market economy.[2] Thus, some scholars see modern imperialism as distinct from empires. Imperialism refers to the expansion of the sovereignty of the European state beyond its border; by contrast, empires do not have fixed boundaries.[3] The notion of sovereignty introduced by the West would reshape East Asian international relations.

Students of political economy should know economics-based studies of imperialism. To scholars using this approach, capitalist overproduction drives imperialism, and bankers and financiers support imperialism.[4] Critics argue that capitalism is unrelated to imperialism.[5] Financial investments did not always go to the new colonies; capital-poor Russia and Italy also engaged in imperialist expansion.[6] Nevertheless, economic motives were clearly important for imperialist powers, certainly when it came to East Asia.

History of Western Domination in East Asia

Westerners arrived in East Asia in the early sixteenth century and succeeded by the late nineteenth century in creating a new imperialist order in East Asia driven by economic interests but based on military power and military organization, which reflected and contributed to the emergence of the modern state and to the Industrial Revolution in Europe.[7] Although individual Europeans had reached East Asia centuries before the sixteenth century, they were not state-sanctioned operations.

The Europeans first acquired a strong strategic position in archipelago Southeast Asia for the wealth of the region and for access to the markets in China and Japan. The Portuguese were the first Europeans to arrive in East Asia. Vasco da Gama reached India in 1498 following a voyage around Africa's Cape of Good

Hope. Alfonso d'Albuquerque captured Melaka (Malacca) in 1511. The Portuguese monarch sent the first European mission to China in 1517. The Portuguese bribed Chinese officials to allow them access to dry goods in Macau in 1535 and appointed officials to the territory in 1557. The Portuguese based in Macau monopolized the China trade and excluded other Europeans. From Macau, the Portuguese also served as middlemen between Chinese and Japanese merchants since the Chinese Ming court banned trade with Japan for not paying tribute.

The Spaniards were next in line. A Spanish fleet led by Ferdinand Magellan arrived in Luzon (the Philippines) in 1521 from South America. The Spanish king ordered that the Philippines be colonized in 1532. The Spaniards established the first permanent settlement in the Philippines in 1565 and took control of Manila in 1571. Two Spanish delegates visited China's Fujian Province in 1575, the first official China-Spain contact. Trade, particularly in silver, flourished between Spanish Mexico and China via Manila.

Dutch merchants made the first trip to Sumatra and Java in 1596. With state support, Dutch merchants formed the Dutch East India Company (VOC) in 1602. The Dutch government authorized the company to possess troops, colonize territories, declare war, and enter into treaties with Asian nations. The VOC sought to establish trade with China in Canton (now Guangzhou) but was blocked by the Portuguese in Macau. However, the company seized Sumatra, Java, and the Moluccas from the Portuguese and obtained trading rights from Japan's Tokugawa government. The Dutch founded the city of Batavia in Java in 1618 and the Batavian government the following year. The VOC established a trading post in Taiwan in 1624 after driving out the Spaniards there. They defeated the rulers in Aceh and Mataram in 1629. By 1639, the Dutch monopolized the European access to Japan. They secured Melaka from the Portuguese in 1641 and conquered part of Maluku, which was rich in clove and nutmeg. Successfully exploiting divisions among indigenous rulers, the Dutch now controlled the supply of pepper. The Dutch sent the first mission to China in 1656.

The Europeans, particularly the Dutch, used force rather than competitive pricing or better services to turn Southeast Asian commerce to their advantages. As Reid argued, the only advantages Europeans had at the time were military weapons and organizations, which Europeans did not hesitate to use.[8] One wonders what would have happened if China and Japan had adopted a proactive and expansionist foreign policy in Southeast Asia and used military force to back up their commercial operations in the region.

It was fortunate for early European adventurers in East Asia that China and Japan were turning inward. The Chinese state did not support its citizens' activities overseas and actually punished them. Emperor Jiaqing of the Ming Dynasty (1522–1566) forbade foreign traders to land in China and Chinese citizens to take ocean voyages. The market forces were such that private Chinese citizens settled in Japan and Southeast Asia to smuggle and trade. Many turned into pirates, who were often really armed traders. Fujianese were particularly engaged, which explained why it was the Fujianese governor who persuaded the court to end the trade ban in 1567. Without state support, Chinese residents in Southeast Asia were often victims of Europeans.

As shown in Hideyoshi's attempts to conquer Korea and China in 1592 and 1597, Japan was a country to contend with in East Asia. Tokugawa Ieyasu chose to concentrate on internal affairs. The Tokugawa government banned Portuguese shipping in Japan. Only the Dutch were allowed in 1640 to reside in Nagasaki. As discussed in the previous chapter, the Japanese government did not close the country in the early seventeenth century since it maintained active trade with the Chinese and the Koreans. However, Japan did not allow its citizens to travel overseas, let alone engage in state-supported adventures in East Asia.

Other Westerners followed the Portuguese, Spanish, and Dutch pioneers. English explorer Francis Drake crossed the Pacific in 1579. In 1600, the English monarch granted a charter to some London merchants to conduct business in the Far East, which led to the creation of the British East India Company. The company quickly established posts in India and East Asia. In the early seventeenth century, however, the English could not compete with the Dutch in East Asia in terms of naval power and the marketability of commodities. The English wanted to sell English cloth, which was not as attractive as Indian cloth and Chinese silk. The French began their move to East Asia in 1604 but remained a minor player through the eighteenth century. The Russians expanded to Asia by land in the north, beginning aggressively in the mid-sixteenth century and reaching the Bering Strait in 1648. The first Russians arrived in Beijing in 1567. The Americans were latecomers. The *Empress of China,* the first American ship to China, arrived in 1784.

Western powers dominated in East Asia after the mid-nineteenth century. As Table 3.2 in the previous chapter shows, East Asia and the West traded places in economic power around the mid-nineteenth century; the share of the Western nations in the global gross domestic product increased from 24.9 percent in 1820 to 43.0 percent in 1870 while the share of the Asian nations decreased from 59.4 percent to 38.4 percent. Western domination was also based on superior military power and organization that originated from modern nationalism and the industrial and technological revolution in Europe.

The power struggle in Europe spread to the rest of the world. Like other non-Western regions, East Asia became an arena for Western power competition. Britain defeated China in the Opium War and imposed an unequal treaty on China, opening five Chinese ports for trade and seizing the island of Hong Kong. Britain thus introduced China into a treaty port system. In a separate commercial agreement signed in October 1843, Britain fixed the import and export duties at 5 percent, won the right to establish consular courts to try civil and criminal cases involving British citizens (extraterritoriality), and included a most-favored-nation (MFN) clause that would automatically give Britain any privileges given to other nations. These agreements were unequal because China did not enjoy the same rights in Britain. France and the United States followed the British lead with treaties signed in 1844. Russia (1858), Prussia (1861), Portugal (1862), Denmark and Holland (1863), Spain (1864), Belgium (1865), and Italy (1866) joined the group. They also cooperated to pressure China for more privileges.

Commodore Matthew C. Perry of the United States forced Japan to open for trade in 1853. Britain signed a treaty with Japan in October 1854 and Russia in February 1855. Under pressure from the Western business community for terms similar to the China arrangement, the U.S. government signed an unequal treaty with Japan in July 1858, which imposed a 5 percent tariff and extraterritoriality on Japan. Similar to the case of China, other Western nations followed the American lead with similar unequal treaties imposed on Japan. Holland and Russia signed their treaties in August. Britain signed a treaty shortly afterward, with the MFN clause. France took its turn in October.

Around the same time, Europeans shifted from control of strategic ports and trade routes based on indirect rule and protection of native states to direct colonial administration in Southeast Asia. After indirect rule for almost two centuries, the Dutch began to construct a state called Netherlands India in the early nineteenth century and succeeded in depriving most Indonesian states of their independence by 1848. Great Britain secured a settlement in Singapore in 1819. Britain extended influence over the Malay kingdoms on the Malay Peninsula and created the Federated Malay States in 1895. In the meantime, the Spaniards engaged in state-building in the Philippines. The Philippines was passed from Spain to the United States as a result of the Spanish-American War of 1898. Britain and France managed to sever the Chinese suzerainty in mainland Southeast Asia. Siam King Chulalongkorn ended his kingdom's recognition of China's suzerainty and accepted the Western system of international relations in 1882.[9] France forced Vietnam into a protectorate in 1883 and fought a war with China to maintain that claim and ended the special relationship between China and Vietnam. After three wars, Britain destroyed the Burmese kingdom in 1886 and then negotiated with China over the border of British Burma.

By the late nineteenth century, the Western powers had destroyed the Chinese world order and forced most East Asia countries open for Western goods and ideas in an imperialist order. In contrast to the tribute system, the *treaty system* was an operational feature of the Western-dominated imperialist order in which a series of unequal treaties were forced upon East Asian nations. In most cases, unequal treaties

MAP 4.1
Western Imperialism in East Asia to 1910

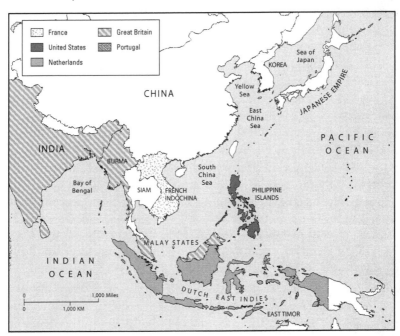

led to direct administrative control. While Europeans viewed each other as equal sovereign states, they treated non-Western peoples differently. East Asian nations also began to conclude treaties among themselves, including the 1876 Japan-Korea Treaty of Kangwha, the 1882 Regulations for Maritime and Overland Trade between Chinese and Korean subjects, and the 1885 China-Japan Tianjin Treaty.

East Asia was incorporated into the global capitalist system by force, ending up as a peripheral region exporting primary products while importing manufactured goods from the West. East Asian nations could not resist because they lost the control of tariffs and foreigners effectively administered treaty ports through which foreign goods and ideas poured into East Asia. The situation began to change toward the end of the nineteenth century when national capitalists in Japan and China began to compete more effectively with Western countries.

By the outbreak of the First World War, as shown in Map 4.1, East Asia was divided among Western nations: the East Indies (what is now Indonesia) by Netherlands, the Philippines by the United States, Malaya and Burma by Britain, and Indochina (what is now Vietnam, Laos, and Cambodia) by France. The only independent countries were Japan, Thailand, and China, although the Chinese considered their country to be semicolonized given Western extraterritorial rights. Japan became an imperialist power and colonized Korea.

East Asian Responses to Western Domination

To say that the dynamic between the Western impact and the Asian responses defined modern East Asia is overly simplistic. We need to examine the internal dynamic for transformation within the region. Westerners in the early stage of the East-West interaction also participated in the existing regional trading networks.[10] Although the Europeans had controlled important Southeast Asian ports and commodities by 1650, they did not yet have enough strength to impose direct rule on the native peoples.[11] Before the mid-nineteenth century, Westerners engaged East Asia essentially on East Asian governments' terms, particularly in Northeast Asia.[12] The Dutch East India Company, for example, was frustrated in their effort to establish trade with China in the late seventeenth century but did not take any actions to change the terms of the contact with the Chinese. In 1661 Zheng Chenggong (known as Koxinga to Westerners), who was a Ming rebel against the Qing court, destroyed the Dutch rule in Taiwan. In fact, the Dutch envoys to Beijing in 1656 accepted the role of tributary envoys and performed kowtow to the Chinese emperor.[13] The Qing government severely restricted the Westerners' access to the China market. In 1757 Beijing designated Canton (now Guangzhou) as the only port open to foreign commerce. The Qing government authorized only thirteen Chinese commercial firms to handle foreign trade and imposed strict regulations on foreign traders, restricting foreigners' contact with the Chinese and imposing arbitrary fees. The system collapsed only after the Opium War of 1839-1842.[14] Japan's Tokugawa government allowed only the Dutch to trade in Japan, and they could reside only in a restricted area in Nagasaki. Korea went even further and allowed only an indirect foreign contact via China and "emerged" only in the 1870s.

Furthermore, some East Asian countries were expanding their own empires during this period.[15] China paid far more attention to its northern border, as it had done for most of the past two millenniums. The Ming court engaged in major military campaigns against the Mongols, who were perceived to be the principal threat to China. At the same time, Nurhaci (1559-1626) and Hongtaiji (1592-1643) in Manchuria built a strong state and conquered Ming China. As shown in Map 4.2, the Manchus built an empire twice as large as Ming China. It was largely the Qing territories that modern China lays claim to. While Chinese nationalists can refer to earlier times in the Han and Tang dynasties when the emperor had large territories as well, Qing China's expansion was on the same scale as America's move to the west and Russia's move to the east. Qing scholars generally consider the Qing the most successful conquest dynasty in Chinese

MAP 4.2
China in the Qing Dynasty, 1644–1911

history.[16] Japan's Hideyoshi Toyotomi tried in vain to conquer Korea and then China in the late sixteenth century. Japanese territories expanded in the seventeenth and eighteenth centuries with the conquest of the Ainu lands, which are now Hokkaido, Sakhalin, and the Kuriles.[17] Burma expanded in all directions in the 1750s. From the early sixteenth century, Vietnamese were moving south and incorporated central Vietnam and southern Vietnam. In short, the East Asians were as willing and capable of building empires as the Europeans.

With Northeast Asia forced into free trade by Western powers after the mid-nineteenth century, East Asians could also penetrate neighboring markets. Chinese merchants took advantage of the free trade environment maintained by the Western powers and built an extensive and competitive network in East Asia through intra-Asian trade, migration, and capital flows. Indian and Japanese merchants were also active. Thus, East Asians had to respond to East Asian commercial challenges as well as to the Western challenge. As some Japanese scholars have argued, the Japanese industrialization had much to do with a desire to end the Chinese commercial domination.[18]

The European military domination after the mid-nineteenth century forced East Asian states to respond. If East Asians had been blind to the power of the

West in the early stage of the East-West contact, contemporary officials and thinkers throughout East Asia had come to recognize the severity of the Western challenge by now. After all, resistance to Western conquest in East Asia in the nineteenth century was fierce and largely futile. Throughout East Asia, elites talked about reform. There were two main schools of reformist thought about how best to respond to the West: one was to *revitalize* traditional values and the other was to *borrow* from Western powers. To some extent, the two schools of thought continue to this day.

East Asian governments mixed revitalization and borrowing differently. When assessing the different responses, it is easy to adopt a post hoc explanation and conclude that those countries that avoided Western domination such as Japan must have adopted better strategies and those that failed to do so such as China must have adopted faulty ones. This was true to some extent. At the same time, there are two inherent dangers in post hoc reasoning. First, whether a country was successful or not was not always contingent on its strategies. We need to examine the internal and external conditions to determine what was possible and what was not possible for East Asian nations. It was conceivable for Northeast Asia and mainland Southeast Asia to survive or thrive in the new international system. They had a long history of political unity prior to the Western arrival and possessed considerable institutional capacities. This explains why Western powers penetrated and controlled archipelago Southeast Asia relatively easily while accepting the terms of Northeast Asian and mainland Southeast Asian governments until they built up sufficient power to break down the resistance. Second, when a state failed in responding to the West, it did not necessarily mean that all elements of its response failed and a radical alternative would always be preferable.

In Northeast Asia, Japan successfully adapted to the new Western imperialist order and joined the Western powers on an equal footing by the end of the nineteenth century. Japan will be discussed in detail in the next section. By contrast, China and Korea could not reform themselves thoroughly and fast enough to avoid becoming victims of imperialism. China ended up as a so-called semicolony with foreign powers creating spheres of influence in the country. Korea became Japan's colony.

As the center of the Chinese world order, China the Middle Kingdom was resistant to fundamental change. The Opium War shattered China's position in East Asia but did not immediately change China's conduct of foreign policy and domestic policy. Rather, it took another twenty years for China to use treaties as a basis for dealing with the West and another twenty years for China to join the Westphalian system diplomatically. During the forty years of adjustment, the Manchu court used treaties to manage Westerners in terms of Chinese traditions.[19] It took more military defeats for the Chinese government to introduce more drastic reforms to strengthen its dynasty, first after the British and French troops seized Beijing and burned the Summer Palace in 1860 and then after a humiliating loss to Japan in the Sino-Japanese War of 1894–1895. In the 1890s Chinese reformist thinkers such as Yan Fu, Liang Qichao, and Kang Youwei broke from the Confucianist world order and endorsed the Western international system by seeking to transform China from a universal empire to a strong state. The Qing reform movement afterward essentially accepted China's position as a state in a multistate system.[20] The Chinese court's reform failed to save it. The dynasty collapsed in 1911, and China sank into a chaotic period of warlords.

China did not fail on all fronts, however. China was being transformed on the societal level. Native Chinese capital grew competitive. Chinese traders came to defeat foreign rivals in controlling China's domestic market and foreign trade.[21] After the 1895 Shimonoseki Treaty allowed foreign firms to invest in industrial operations in China, native Chinese industrial firms proved competitive vis-à-vis foreign firms.[22] With the collapse of the Qing dynasty, Chinese capitalism entered a "golden age" with Chinese enterprises and banks emerging, particularly in 1910–1920.[23] Chinese merchants were actually dominant in an intra-Asia trade network, beating both Western and Asian competitors in the second half of the nineteenth century.

Ultimately, China failed because the Chinese state failed. As discussed in the previous chapter, the Chinese empire operated on a political system suitable for an agrarian society facing no competing civilizations. Seeing limited tax burden on peasants as central to social order and political stability, the Chinese empire traditionally did not have sufficient resources. The Qing court continued to follow the traditional logic of political and social stability even after the Opium War. Put simply, the Chinese government did not have enough resources to build a modern military force and modern infrastructures. Rampant corruption, typical of the end of the Chinese dynasty, further diverted resources away from modernization. On top of that, unlike in Japan where the elite and society could rally behind the emperor as a direct descendent of the sun god, it was difficult for the majority Han Chinese to place hope on Manchu emperors they still considered to be foreigners. In such an environment, reform measures by local governments created local power centers that came to challenge the central government.

The removal of the oppressive Chinese state helped the Chinese bourgeoisie to grow in 1915–1927, but the weak Chinese state, specifically weak policy initiatives and public investment, explained why China could not sustain this development. In a stage of late development and weak power position in the world, China needed a strong state to achieve sustainable economic development: Society could substitute for state initiatives to some extent but not replace them completely.[24]

Korea came into contact with the West later than China and Japan. Korea was even more resistant to borrowing from the West.[25] After opening China and Japan for trade, Westerners also pressured Korea for the rights to trade, to conduct missionary activities, and to establish diplomatic relations. The Koreans saw their country as occupying a high place in the Confucianist Chinese world order. Korea's sense of cultural superiority affected its attitudes toward the West and Japan. Considering Westerners and reforming Japanese as inferior barbarians, the dominant conservative forces in the Korean government refused to take any reform measures in a changing time. In fact, Korean elites also viewed China's decision to open to the West with disdain.[26] At the same time, there were disgruntled elements within the ruling *yangban* elite and second-tier elite who wanted to change the status quo. Based on their historical experience, Korean reformers saw the Western order as a hierarchical one based on culture and in which Korea could learn to excel. But their emphasis was on culture and education in an imperialist age based on military and economic power.[27] Smaller than China and adopting reforms later than China, Korea's fate was sealed in an imperialist age. Japan established control over Korea after its victories against China in the 1894–1895 War. Japan became a protector of Korea after defeating Russia in the 1904–1905 War and annexed Korea in 1910.

In Southeast Asia, there were also revitalizers and borrowers. Revitalizers called on people to resist the West in a just and righteous cause. They blamed the failure of their states on deviation from traditional values and wanted to resist the West by going back to their traditions. By contrast, borrowers viewed the technical superiority of the West as the key to Western power and therefore saw the solution in borrowing Western technologies to beat the West. Southeast Asian monarchs tried to obtain steamships, the symbol of Western power. Vietnam had steamships and built a factory to reproduce steam engines in the 1830s. Siam and Burma acquired steamships in the 1850s. However, borrowers came to realize that they needed to copy more than just steamships and gradually expanded borrowing to include government and education.[28] Ultimately, reforms did not succeed in most cases. Southeast Asia, except Thailand, was colonized.

The Jesuits arrived in Vietnam in 1615. Vietnam adopted an approach similar to those of China and Korea. Once a civil war ended and Nguyen Anh became the emperor in 1802, the Vietnamese government reasserted Confucian principles and sought to stamp out Western influence, particularly the French missionaries. The French who had become involved in the civil war seized the opportunity and established colonial control in Vietnam. The French naval ships attacked Vietnamese ports in the 1840s to demand release of imprisoned missionaries. A joint French-Spanish force sacked Saigon in 1859 and created a colony of Cochin-China in the south. The 1862 treaty between France and Vietnam gave France an indemnity of $4 million, trading rights, rights to spread Christianity, and direct control of three provinces in the south. In 1883, the French established a protectorate over Annam and Tonkin after attacking the north and fighting a war with China.

Burma asserted itself against the British with a tragic ending. Burma's expansion came into conflict with Britain, which jealously guarded its interests in India. The British and Burmese fought a two-year war. Britain scored military victories, and the Treaty of Yandabo was signed in 1826. The Burmese court did not reform its military or adjust its foreign policy toward Britain after that war. When British troops fought another war in Burma in 1852 and seized lower Burma, Burma tried to reform and to accommodate British interests. However, the French arrival in Southeast Asia in the 1870s and 1880s prompted Britain to seize full control of Burma. In 1885 Britain waged the third war against Burma and annexed the remainder of Burma in January 1886.

Thailand succeeded in defending its independence. The Thai kingdom was at its peak of power when Western pressures began, which allowed the Thais to make concessions to Western powers in Laos, Cambodia, and the south while keeping the core Thai territories. The Thai government avoided confrontation and signed unequal treaties with the West. In 1826 the Thai Kingdom concluded the Burney Treaty with the British East India Company. In 1855 Thailand and Britain agreed to allow extraterritoriality and limits to Thai tariffs on British products. Thailand also began reforms. Thailand's flexible diplomacy clearly contributed to its survival, but the country also benefited from its position as a buffer zone between British Burma and French Indochina. After all, Burma had tried to reform and to accommodate Britain after the 1852 War, to no avail. Thailand secured an equal status by joining the British and French during the First World War and participating in the Paris Peace Conference.

Legacies of Western Colonialism

East Asia had traditional empires and states with distinct identities lasting for hundreds or thousands of years and had a vibrant economy linked regionally. At the same time, Western imperialism had a profound impact on East Asian IPE. The interaction with the West served as an external catalyst for domestic transformation in East Asia.

East Asian international political economy. The Western arrival had a profound, direct impact on East Asian IPE. First, Western imperialism destroyed the Chinese world order, created an imperialist order, and colonized virtually all East Asian states. Thus, most East Asian peoples fought to win independence as an equal sovereign state in the West-dominated international system. Sovereignty, once achieved, is a jealously guarded national treasure. East Asians are fully embracing the Westphalian system, particularly the notion of noninterference in domestic affairs, while Europe is moving away from that conception. As will be discussed in Chapter 11, East Asia's emphasis on sovereignty and Europe's abandonment of nation state sovereignty is one reason why Europe has been far more successful than East Asia in institutionalizing regional integration.

A specific legacy from the colonial days is a widely held belief that a strong and supportive state is needed to ensure national security and national capacity to compete internationally, thus the root of economic nationalism. The Chinese businessmen, for instance, found trading conditions worsened by the 1880s and felt strongly that without a strong state they could not compete against Western firms that enjoyed advantages in the treaty ports and strong backing from home governments.[29]

Second, Western powers created some states in East Asia. Indonesia, Malaysia, the Philippines, and Singapore were colonial creations. While Burma, Thailand, Cambodia, and Vietnam had had political identities before the Western arrival, Western powers determined their current borders. Western colonialism had a varied impact on the domestic political institutions and practices of East Asian nations. The United States, for example, decentralized the Philippines' political system based on the assumption that the Philippines was historically overly centralized.[30]

Third, Western imperialism integrated East Asia more closely into the global market. While controlling footholds in Melaka, Macao, Nagasaki, and Manila, Europeans facilitated trade expansion between East Asia and the rest of the world. Manila, for instance, was a center for the galleon trade in which Chinese traded silks, ceramics, and cottons for silver shipped from the new world.

Fourth, European and American treaties with East Asians allowed the treaty ports to be connected, forming an intra-Asia network for East Asians as well as Westerners.[31] Western powers also left a legacy of institutions, education, technologies, and cultures. Colonial legacies were part of the reason for the later successes of Hong Kong and Singapore. A familiarity with Western culture and practice and with the English language gave the two cities advantages over the rest of East Asia in international commerce.[32] As a testament to colonial legacies, the most vibrant commercial cities such as Singapore, Hong Kong, Manila, and Shanghai traced their origins to the Western imperial period. It is no coincidence China's economic reform began with coastal cities.

Fifth, a mass migration in the Western imperialist period explains why Chinese networks strengthened in Southeast Asia, which would become a major shaping force for East Asian IPE in later years. Chinese had been moving southward for centuries, but large migrations did not take place until Western powers came to control Southeast Asia.[33] Because of the Ming court's ban on Chinese returning home, Chinese settlers married local women and became assimilated in the sixteenth century. The Western colonial rule in Southeast Asia meant greater commercial opportunities for the Chinese. Chinese population in Thailand, Malaya, Singapore, and Indonesia increased from about 700,000 in 1860 to 3.8 million in 1931.[34] One estimate put the influx of Chinese to Southeast Asia at over 16 million between 1891 and 1939. While most returned to China after a short stay, around 6.2 million Chinese resided in the region in the 1930s. The Chinese migration networks greatly facilitated an intra-Asia network.[35]

Nationalism and communism. Western imperialism also had a profound impact on East Asian nations' underlying ideologies. East Asians had to make sense of the drastic changes they were observing and to create a new system to view the world and to act accordingly. Two of the ideologies in response to colonialism were nationalism and communism.[36] Both nationalism and communism had a profound impact on East Asian political economy then and now, shaping the basic geography of political economy in East Asia after 1945. One camp comprised firmly nationalist, capitalist countries and the other communist countries.

Nationalism as a modern ideology originated in Europe. It refers to an emotional attachment to one's nation and the idea that members of a nation should be able to determine their own destiny and create a state of their own.[37] The rise of East Asian nationalism was in part a direct response to Western imperialism. Unequal treaties were an immediate reason for resistance. Japanese, Chinese, and other East Asians were eager to restore rights such as tariff autonomy. The nationalist ideology borrowed from Europe by East Asians would later be used against colonial powers. Europeans trained some local elites but did not offer them opportunities. These elites were resentful and came to realize that there was equality in the colonial powers' home countries.[38] In fact, the nationalists from the Dutch East Indies who were studying in Netherlands began to use the term Indonesia in the 1920s. Nationalism arose in the Philippines in the late nineteenth century. Similar to what happened in Latin America, the Creoles (island-born Spaniards) and Mestizos (mixed race) tried to forge a separate identity because the Spanish colonial government excluded them from decision making.[39]

Although nationalism as a modern ideology came from Europe, nationalism evolved naturally from a strong sense of nationhood and communities that already existed in East Asia. For Korean nationalists, for example, Korea "regained" political independence from Japan in 1945 because Korea had been independent practically for centuries already.[40] A similar sense of nationhood existed in Vietnam.[41] The challenge of nationalism in archipelago Southeast Asia was to forge new nations within the boundaries artificially created by colonial governments.

One school of nationalism came early. The early modernization drive in East Asia had a clear nationalist basis. Chinese, Japanese, and Koreans recognized the technological superiority of the West, and all sought to borrow Western technologies while maintaining traditional values. The Chinese differentiated *ti*, which is essence or Confucian values, from *yong*, which is the practical or the Western technologies. Japan's nationalism after encountering the West in the nineteenth century traced its origin to the Japanese spirit. The myth of the land of gods and the emperor descended from Gods created a religious, nationalist fervor about Japan's superiority over other peoples. Japanese talked about *wakon yōsai*, which means Japanese spirit, Western technology. The early version of East Asian nationalism was reflected in the slogan "enrich the nation, strengthen the army" (*fukoku kyohei* in Japanese and *fuguoqiangbing* in Chinese). Such a nationalist origin of modernization effort explains the state's active support and paternalist attitudes toward the private sector.[42] With Western thoughts largely filtered through Japan and China, Korean intellectuals also sought to understand the secret of Western power and wealth.[43] The tradition of economic nationalism runs deep in East Asia. Economic nationalism remains potent in an era of globalization, particularly in Northeast Asia.[44]

Although response to the West was a principal reason for East Asian nationalism, it was not the only one. For some nations, anti-Chinese sentiment was a major source of nationalism. Vietnamese defined their national identity partly by their millennium struggle to maintain independence from China.[45] Indigenous Indonesian nationalists targeted the Chinese who enjoyed economic success and influence under the Dutch rule.[46] In Malaya, ethnic Malays were more interested in working with the British to maintain their privileges as sons of the soil (*bumiputras*), so the Malay nationalism was aimed at the immigrant communities, particularly the Chinese. By contrast, ethnic Chinese were more willing to challenge the British colonial governments. For China and Korea, nationalism was heavily anti-Japanese as well as anti-Western. Burma faced a problem of competing nationalisms by ethnic minorities such as the Karens.

Communism refers to the Marxist ideology, which sees a structural exploitation in the capitalist systems and advocates creation of a political system in which properties are commonly owned. Though a European creation, communism resonated with some East Asians. Communism promised a universal system with universal kinship, which was similar to Confucianism in that regard. It also promised an alternative to what they viewed as a predatory Western capitalist system. The Bolshevik Revolution in Russia inspired many Asian revolutionaries, and the Soviet government explicitly appealed to East Asians in a common struggle against imperialism.

Communism was a potent political force in East Asia, prevailing in China, North Korea, and Indochina. Communist parties were also active in other countries including Japan. In particular, the Indonesian Communist Party was the largest communist party in the noncommunist world until it was crushed in a bloody massacre in 1965.

In East Asia, nationalism and communism were related. Communists were also nationalists, the only difference being that they wanted a more drastic approach toward political and societal change. Nationalists and communists often came from similar educated backgrounds. Communists often cooperated with nationalists in coalitions while maintaining their own organizational identity in China, Vietnam, Indonesia, Korea, and elsewhere in East Asia. Communist states tried to sever economic ties with the West while connecting to the socialist camp. As soon as communism faded in countries like China and Vietnam, nationalism seamlessly stepped into the void.

JAPANESE IMPERIALISM

Japanese Response to Western Imperialism

Japan's contact with Westerners began in the sixteenth century. The Portuguese came to Japan in 1542 and converted half a million Japanese, more than the percentage of Christians in Japan today. They also introduced firearms to Japan. In 1603 Tokugawa Ieyasu established the Tokugawa shogunate in Edo, now called Tokyo. The Tokugawa shogunate stamped out Catholicism by 1638. As a result of this anti-Christian sentiment, Japan banned trade with Western nations except Holland. The Tokugawa government dictated the terms by which it would engage the outside world.

Like China, Japan became a victim of Western imperialism after the mid-nineteenth century. In 1853, Commodore Matthew Perry forced the Japanese to allow port access to American ships. The United States signed a treaty in 1854, with limited success, and then a full treaty in 1858. Other European powers followed suit. These treaties were unequal, similar to those imposed on China. They allowed Western powers to provide military protection of foreign merchants at open ports and to enjoy extraterritorial privileges, and they ended Japan's autonomy in determining tariffs.

Unlike China, Japan responded quickly to the new challenge. The unequal treaties imposed on Japan led to a fundamental shift in Japan's worldview, which in turn led to fundamental transformations of Japanese politics, economy, and society.[47] A coalition of outer *daimyos* seized Kyoto and restored direct imperial rule on January 3, 1868. The imperial forces then occupied Edo and ended the Tokugawa rule. The 1868 Meiji Restoration started with a slogan of "honor the emperor and expel the barbarians." But Japanese elites came to realize that while the slogan was convenient for overthrowing the shogunate, a confrontation with the West would be disastrous. Japan's strategic goal was seen as building up national strength by learning the advanced military and economic technologies from the West.

Some Japanese strategic thinkers had proposed such a program before the Meiji Restoration. Hotta Masayoshi wrote in a memorandum in 1857 that "military power always springs from national wealth" and that wealth is "principally to be found in trade and commerce." A related school of thought was that the best defense was offense. Yoshida Shōin (1830–1859) reasoned that Japan should seize Manchuria, Korea, and the islands to the south to keep watch on Russia and China. An opposing view represented by Aizawa Seishisai (1782–1863), who was guarded against "corrupt" foreign ways, urged preservation of traditions.[48]

Japan now followed the slogan of wakon yōsai (Japanese spirit, Western ability), namely to acquire modern institutions and technologies while sticking to Japanese traditions. Japan conducted more thorough reforms than did China, introducing a whole range of institutions, ideologies, and technologies from the West. The Japanese reformers centralized military and political power and mobilized limited resources to build a strong military and improve infrastructure to fend off Western pressure. The Meiji Restoration was an impressive accomplishment. Few nations have been able to transform their societies in such a short period.

Japan also emphasized the Japanese spirit to an extent unmatched in China. A reinforced Japanese spirit based on the myth of the "land of gods" and of the Japanese emperor as a direct descendant of the sun god justified Japanese superiority to other peoples. Later Japanese leaders used such a myth to become a grave threat to other nations. Moreover, Japanese elites at the time felt that Japan should emulate the West in an imperialist age, namely to create its own colonial empire for security from the West and an equal status with Western powers.[49] An emulation of the West meant that Japan should behave like Western powers in dealing with other Asian nations.[50]

A key purpose of Japan's Meiji reformers was to modernize Japanese economy to provide the base for a strong military. Japan also responded to both the opportunities and competition from other Asian countries, particularly China. Japanese merchants utilized the Chinese commercial network in Asia to promote exports. The presence of Chinese competition also spurred Japanese efforts to upgrade technologies and organizations. Put simply, Japan's industrialization also resulted from an intra-Asia dynamic.[51]

From the Meiji Restoration to 1914, Japan's economy went through three stages. In the first stage from 1868 to 1880, the Japanese government sought to protect Japan's domestic market and use government investment in strategic sectors such as munitions, shipyards, transport, and communications and to support import-substituting industries such as textile, cement, and glass. In the next stage from 1880 to 1894, Japan achieved progress in silk and cotton industries. In the third stage from 1894 to 1914, an industrial sector emerged in Japan, and the Japanese government began to facilitate heavy industrial development in shipbuilding, iron and steel, and electric power.[52] Japan achieved impressive economic growth. While not yet an economic power on a par with Western nations by 1914, Japan was on its way to becoming an industrial power.

History of Japanese Imperialism

Japan first sought to reestablish relations with Asia on Western terms. In 1870 the Meiji government sought to establish official relations with China by concluding a formal treaty. The Manchu court concluded a treaty with Japan despite opposition from conservative officials who treated Japan as a former tributary state. Some Japanese leaders wanted to attack other Asian nations immediately after the Meiji Restoration, partly to divert the aggressiveness of the samurai class that had been deprived of privileges and fringe benefits. The government rejected an appeal to attack Korea but approved an expedition to Taiwan in 1874. The Meiji government also contacted the Korean government to adjust the traditional relationship between Korea and the Japanese feudal lord of the Tsushima Islands. The Korean government refused to acknowledge the Japanese emperor on the ground that only the Chinese emperor could use such a title. As a tributary state to China, Japan that becomes an equal of China would necessarily be higher in status than Korea. Japan sent gunboats to Korea in 1875 and forced Korea to conclude the Treaty of Kangwha in 1876. Korea opened three ports for Japan, exchanged diplomatic envoys, and allowed Japanese consular jurisdiction in the three ports.

As shown in Map 4.3, Japan began expansion toward the end of the nineteenth century.[53] Japan seized Bonin Islands in 1876 and annexed Ryukyu Islands in 1879. In 1894–1895, Japan defeated China, acquired its first colony, Taiwan, and increased its influence in Korea. After defeating Russia in the Russo-Japanese War of 1904–1905, Japan received a long-term lease on China's Liaodong Peninsula, renaming it as the Kwantung Leased Territory, and Southern Sakhalin from Russia, renaming it Karafuto. Japan also turned Korea into a protectorate in 1905 and annexed the country in 1910.[54] Japan joined the First World War on the side of Great Britain and the United States and was awarded mandatory control over the German islands in Micronesia, namely the Marshalls, the Carolines, and the Marianas (not including Guam), which Japan renamed Nanyō guntō. Thus Japan established its formal colonial empire by 1922, including Taiwan, Korea, the Kwantung Leased Territory, Karafuto, and Nanyō guntō. Japan also formed an informal empire in China after 1895, based on trade, investment, treaty port settlements, and cultural activities.[55]

While Japan's slogan was "enrich the nation, strengthen the army," it did not wait to strengthen the army until after enriching the nation. The two goals went hand in hand. Japan's early success against China and Korea showed that power

MAP 4.3
Japanese Expansion in Asia, 1895–1941

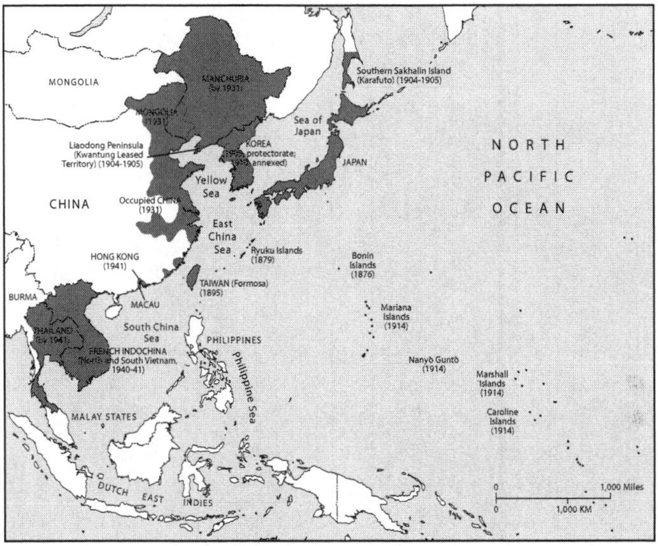

can also enhance wealth. In the Sino-Japanese War of 1894–1895, Japan did not have a stronger economy than China or better weapons than China. Rather, the strength and the effort of the Japanese state made the difference. Japan mobilized resources for national defense. The war cost the Japanese government about ¥200 million, but Japan received an indemnity of ¥366 million, which was 4.6 times Japan's annual public expenditure or 4.3 times its annual ordinary revenues before the war, and Japan expanded territories by seizing Taiwan.[56] By contrast, the war cost China dearly and weakened the state further.

The Meiji government was basically bankrupt by 1880 owing to expenditures to buy off the samurai class, to pay for the expedition to Taiwan and a civil war, and to repress several peasant uprisings. To fight off high inflation, the Meiji government sold off state enterprises at low prices to "political merchants" with close ties with the government or former high government officials. The *zaibatsu* who traced their origin to this period would cooperate closely with the government. The old zaibatsu came to have political influence on the government by financing political parties. The military, which distrusted the old zaibatsu and politicians, promoted new zaibatsu to meet the needs of the military. Both old and new zaibatsu kept Japan's perceived national interest in mind. The Japanese state and the military used state capitalism to finance and support frequent foreign wars and acquisition of colonies. The government favored certain enterprises deemed capable of competing with Western firms. A dual economic structure of large competitive firms versus small enterprises emerged. The Japanese enterprises were forced to adapt to a war economy in the 1930s. From that experience, the Japanese government, companies, and workers learned how to adapt to achieve industrial change, which would be useful for Japan's postwar development.[57]

Japan's initial push in Korea, Taiwan, and Manchuria was driven mainly by strategic interests and prestige. Economic reasoning was present but not dominant. After all, the concern was mainly economic costs rather than economic necessities. This would change when Japan became a more industrialized country by the end of the First World War. Japan was now more concerned about securing supplies of raw materials and markets overseas. Japan's greater economic ability also meant that Japan used economic power, backed by military power, vis-à-vis its Asian neighbors the same way as Western powers. This is particularly the case in China. Japan invested heavily in strategic sectors such as railways and mining. The Japanese government also participated in consortium loans to the Chinese government to support pro-Japanese Chinese leaders and secure more advantages. In the case of China, Japan participated with Western powers to lend to the Chinese government within the treaty port system in 1895–1930. This form of "cooperative imperialism" did not last long because of Japan's continuous rise and its far greater needs for raw materials from China than the Western powers. By the 1920s, Japan increasingly relied on imports of coal for its heavy industry. Once the Great Depression took place, Japan turned unilateralist.

In the late 1920s, Japan faced difficulties abroad because of the protectionist policies adopted by major powers in the aftermath of the Great Depression. The Japanese armed forces increasingly agitated against party politicians and businessmen, whom some young officers considered to have been corrupted by Western capitalism. The pressure on Japan to expand its trade and send its people to other regions was a driver for a more aggressive foreign policy since Japan was a latecomer in the imperialist game.

Japan turned to China as a target for expansion. The Japanese army took action in Manchuria in anticipation of a weaker Japanese position due to China's rising nationalism. On September 18, 1931, the Japanese army seized China's three northeastern provinces. Japan's aggression threatened the status quo in East Asia and started a second round of imperial expansion. On July 7, 1937, war broke out between China and Japan. After Germany occupied France in June 1940, Japanese troops seized North Vietnam in the summer of 1940 and South Vietnam the next summer. The United States resorted to embargo of oil supplies to Japan after Japan occupied South Vietnam. On December 7, 1941, Japan attacked Pearl Harbor. Simultaneously, Japan conquered Southeast Asia. By the end of 1942, Japan came to control 340–350 million people in East Asia, with a territory larger than that indicated in Map 4.3.

Japanese imperialism had a clear economic dimension. A strong economic basis was seen as the source of national wealth, and industry and trade were viewed as central elements of acquiring wealth. Military force would provide protection and create commercial opportunities. This does not mean that economic rationale drove every single Japanese move. In the early days, security concerns about Japan in a competitive international environment were dominant, but Japan's military expansion created opportunities for Japanese trade and industry. Economic weaknesses sometimes also served as a check on Japan's ambition in policy debates. The Great Depression decreased Japan's trade with China and Manchuria while Japan's trade with Taiwan and Korea increased, which made Japan believe that it would be more advantageous for Japanese commercial interests where it enjoys direct administrative control.[58] Japan became more integrated with Korea, Taiwan, Manchuria, and China proper. However, Japan became increasingly dependent on Southeast Asia for strategic materials such as oil, iron, rubber, and tin. Economic self-sufficiency now required a much larger formal or informal colony than before.

In short, Japan was creating an imperialist order in East Asia. Similar to other imperialist powers, there was hesitancy and pullback at times. Japan's expansion was based on brute force, but Japan also wanted to legitimize its empire by creating a rationale behind it. In the early days, Japan justified its empire-building based on security (line of advantages) and international prestige (an advanced country has to have colonies). This line of argument would make Japan a major player in the existing imperialist order dominated by the West. In later years when Japan wanted to dominate the region and engaged in direct competition with the West, Japan increasingly espoused a race-based co-prosperity notion to sugarcoat its imperialist order. The notion had been discussed in the early days of Meiji but was now pushed with greater urgency. By the end of 1937 Prime Minister Konoe Fumimaro talked about creating a new order in Northeast Asia. Some intellectuals working for Konoe argued that unlike individualistic Western imperialism, Japan was seeking to lead a true partnership with Asia, based on an Asian conception of justice and Japanese ethic.[59] Foreign Minister Matsuoka Yosuke announced the goal of the Greater East Asia Co-Prosperity Sphere in a press conference in August 1940, using the slogan of freeing fellow Asians from Western powers.[60] In practice, the Japanese colonial empire shares much in common with all empires in that the colonizers use brute force to subdue the colonized.

Ultimately, Japan's imperialist agenda failed. Japan could not match the United States in material wealth. The pattern of trade between Japan and the United States shows a high percentage of silk in exports to the United States while cotton, oil, machinery, and automobiles came from the United States. Japan had become an exporter of manufactured products to Asia but was still a backward supplier of raw materials to the United States. Equally important, rising nationalism in Asia made Japan's project impossible to implement.

Legacies of Japanese Imperialism

What is striking about Japanese imperialism is the speed by which Japan built a massive colonial empire within a mere fifty years (1895–1945). By contrast, it took European colonial powers more than three centuries to exercise direct colonial administrations in East Asia. Japanese colonialism also had a varied impact on East Asia, fifty years in Taiwan, thirty-five years in Korea, and three or four years in Southeast Asia. Short though it was, Japanese imperialism as a historical force had a strong impact on the future developments of East Asian IPE. To say that Western imperialism or Japanese imperialism left some positive legacies in no way justifies imperialism in the first place.

East Asian international political economy. First, similar to what Western imperialism did to the Chinese world order, Japanese imperialism helped to destroy the Western imperialist order in East Asia. Despite a pan-Asian rhetoric, Japan invaded Southeast Asia for its own strategic interests and to replace Western powers as the master in the region. But its short stay in the region contributed to the end of Western colonialism in Southeast Asia. The Japanese destroyed the prestige of Westerners in Southeast Asia by defeating them soundly in the early stage of the war. They also elevated local people into the colonial administration, which would make return of former colonial rulers difficult. The Japanese created puppet states in Burma and the Philippines in 1943 and proposed a future independent Indonesia in 1944. In Indonesia, Japanese trained and equipped local troops, which gave Indonesians modern military experience. By 1945, the Java auxiliary army had 35,000 men.[61] This armed group would fight the returning Dutch troops. The Japanese military government in Java granted independence to the East Indies four days before Japan surrendered. Japan also granted nominal independence to Burma on August 1, 1943. Aung San, the father of Burmese independence, led the Burmese Independence Army trained by the Japanese.

Second, Japan's colonialism had a long-term impact on East Asia's later developments in political economy.[62] Japan introduced a highly centralized political system and heavy state intervention in the economy. While Japan's colonial policy was meant to benefit itself and was brutal in implementation, it improved the infrastructure and public education. The Japanese reinvested much of the surplus in the economic development of Korea and Taiwan. Unlike Western powers, Japan created heavy industry in the colonies.[63] Thus, Japanese colonial rule laid the foundations for Taiwan and Korea to enjoy a head start against the rest of East Asia in postwar economic development.

East Asian nationalism and communism. Nationalism and communism predated Japan's attempt to create its international order in East Asia, but Japan's imperialist expansion had an unintended consequence of strengthening the nationalist and communist movements throughout East Asia.

Japan served as a model for many reformers throughout East Asia. In Korea, some young progressive reformers sought reform modeled after Meiji Japan. Japan's defeat of Russia in 1904–1905 left a deep impression on East Asians. A major wave of Chinese students went to Japan to learn the secret of modernization. Similar admiration for Japan's accomplishments developed in other parts of East Asia. Vietnamese anticolonialists, for example, sent a delegation to Japan in 1905 to seek Japanese intervention in Southeast Asia and Japanese help to liberate Vietnam.[64]

Japan's rapid military victory in Southeast Asia encouraged nationalists in the region by destroying the mystique of European superiority, but Southeast Asian nationalists would later turn against Japanese invaders.[65] Japan's surrender in August 1945 also created a temporary power vacuum in countries like Indonesia and Vietnam where nationalists seized the opportunity to establish governments, which would make it difficult for the Dutch and French to reestablish their respective colonial rule in these countries.[66] The Japanese occupation of Indochina also provided opportunities for Lao nationalism and Lao independence.[67]

The Japanese occupation also helped explain the communist success in China and North Korea. Japan's invasion weakened the Chinese Nationalist government's control over large parts of the country, particularly in the north, and gave the Chinese Communist Party a golden opportunity to mobilize peasants by appealing to their nationalism and establishing political dominance in the countryside.[68] Mao Zedong himself famously thanked the Japanese for invading much of China, which made it possible for the Chinese people to unite and for the Chinese Communist Party to seize power.[69] Korean nationalists and communists were motivated by their resistance to Japan's colonial rule.[70] Ironically, the Korean students who studied in Japanese universities and colleges, often under liberal-minded Japanese intellectuals, became critics of Japanese colonial policy in Korea with enhanced nationalist awareness.[71]

Japan's imperialist past on Japan. Japan's imperialist endeavor has also profoundly affected Japan itself.[72] Its failure discredited that strategy, which channeled Japan to a drastically different path after World War II. Also Japan possessed a rich pool of economic professionals, businessmen, and officials with intimate knowledge of using the state to achieve economic growth and of East Asia. Their expertise acquired during the war in the 1940s would be important for postwar

Japanese economic development and for Japanese thinking toward development in Asia in general.

CONCLUSION

Imperialism, Western or Japanese, was a powerful shaping force for East Asian IPE. Western imperialism ended the Chinese world order and ushered in a new era of a modern international system. The West prevailed over East Asia not because of commercial superiority. Rather, use of force and violence was central to the European success in seizing the market in Asia. Equally important, it was not merely Western merchants or Western companies but the Western states that served as the agents of Western expansion in East Asia. This experience taught East Asian nations a major lesson about the reality of modern international relations: Nation states compete with each other for wealth and power. That recognition explains why the slogan of "enrich the nation, strengthen the army" has been a common theme for key nations such as Japan and China. Having an effective state or not partly explained Japan's subsequent successes and China's continuous decline and disintegration.

A new international order triggers responses. States that imitate the successful ones tend to survive and thrive. Emulating the West and drawing from its own traditions, Japan established a formal colonial empire by 1922 and sought to monopolize East Asia in the late 1930s and early 1940s. Japanese imperialism helped to bring an end to Western colonialism in East Asia by destroying the mystique of Western invincibility, encouraging Asian nationalists, and creating opportunities for Asian nationalists and communists to assert themselves during and immediately after the Second World War.

Both Western powers and Japan had a direct impact on the developments of East Asian IPE. The Westerners forcibly shaped the state system in East Asia by creating new states in maritime Southeast Asia and settling the borders in mainland Southeast Asia. They also brought modern education, institutions, technologies, and cultural products to East Asia and integrated the region more closely to the global market. Japan brought a state-led development strategy to its colonies and created the foundations for modern economy in Taiwan and Korea by emphasizing public education and infrastructure and by creating a labor force experienced with modern agricultural and industrial activities.

Furthermore, Western and Japanese imperialism helped to bring new ideologies such as nationalism and communism to East Asia. Both ideologies, as powerfully and violently demonstrated in the region, have had a profound impact on the nature of East Asian IPE.

While recognizing the importance of Western and Japanese imperialism, one should recognize that modern East Asian political economy was not simply a story of Western impact and Asian response. Westerners initially played the Asian game on Asian terms. China, Japan, Vietnam, and Burma, among others, were engaged in their own empire-building projects. Even when the West came to dominate after the mid-nineteenth century, the new international order also created opportunities for Asian entrepreneurs to enter markets of their neighbors, particularly Chinese and Indians who wove an extensive intra-Asia network. Put simply, East Asians were responding to each other as well as to the Western challenge.

SUGGESTED READINGS

Adas, Michael. "Imperialism and Colonialism in Comparative Perspective." *The International History Review* 20, no. 2 (June 1998): 371–388.

Allen, George C. *A Short Economic History of Modern Japan, 1867–1937,* 4th ed. (New York: St. Martin's Press, 1981).

Austin, Michael R. *Negotiating with Imperialism: The Unequal Treaties and the Culture of Japanese Diplomacy* (Cambridge: Harvard University Press, 2004).

Beasley, W. G. *Japanese Imperialism 1894–1945* (Oxford: Oxford University Press, 1987).

Bergère, Marie-Claire. *The Golden Age of the Chinese Bourgeoisie 1911–1937,* trans. Janet Lloyd (Cambridge: Cambridge University Press, 1989).

Christie, Clive J. *Ideology and Revolution in Southeast Asia, 1900–1980: Political Ideas of the Anti-Colonial Era* (Richmond, Surrey: Curzon, 2001).

Cochran, Sherman. *Big Business in China: Sino-Foreign Rivalry in the Cigarette Industry, 1890–1930* (Cambridge: Harvard University Press, 1980).

Cumings, Bruce. "The Origins and Development of the Northeast Asian Political Economy: Industrial Sectors, Product Cycles, and Political Consequences." *International Organization* 38, no. 1 (Winter 1984): 1–40.

Deuchler, Marina. *Confucian Gentlemen and Barbarian Envoys: The Opening of Korea, 1875–1885* (Seattle: University of Washington Press, 1977).

Duiker, William J. *The Rise of Nationalism in Vietnam 1900–1941* (Ithaca: Cornell University Press, 1976).

Duus, Peter, Ramon H. Myers, and Mark R. Peattie, eds. *The Japanese Wartime Empire, 1931–1945* (Princeton: Princeton University Press, 1996).

Duus, Peter, Ramon H. Myers, and Mark R. Peattie, eds. *The Japanese Informal Empire in China, 1895–1937* (Princeton: Princeton University Press, 1989).

Gao, Bai. *Economic Ideology and Industrial Policy in Japan: Developmentalism from 1931 to 1965* (New York: Cambridge University Press, 1997).

Gelber, Harry G. *Nations Out of Empires: European Nationalism and the Transformation of Asia* (New York: Palgrave, 2001).

Hutchcroft, Paul D. "Colonial Masters, National Politicos, and Provincial Lords: Central Authority and Local Autonomy in the American Philippines, 1900–1913." *The Journal of Asian Studies* 59, no. 2 (May 2000): 277–306.

Jones, Francis C. *Japan's New Order in East Asia: Its Rise and Fall 1937–45* (New York: Oxford University Press, 1954).

Kahin, George McTurnan. *Nationalism and Revolution in Indonesia* (Ithaca: Cornell University Press, 1970).

Lee, Chong-Sik. *The Politics of Korean Nationalism* (Berkeley: University of California Press, 1965).

Leifer, Michael, ed. *Asian Nationalism* (London: Routledge, 2000).

Mungello, David E. *The Great Encounter of China and the West, 1500–1800* (Lanham, Md.: Rowman and Littlefield, 1999).

Myers, Ramon H. and Mark R. Peattie, eds. *The Japanese Colonial Empire, 1895–1945* (Princeton: Princeton University Press, 1984).

Ohkawa, Kazushi, and Miyohei Shinohara, with Larry Meissner, *Patterns of Japanese Economic Development: A Quantitative Appraisal* (New Haven: Yale University Press, 1979).

Reid, Anthony. *Southeast Asia in the Age of Commerce, 1450–1680. Vol. 2, Expansion and Crisis* (New Haven: Yale University Press, 1993).

Schwartz, Benjamin. *In Search of Wealth and Power: Yen Fu and the West* (Cambridge: Harvard University Press, 1974).

Sugihara, Kaoru, ed. *Japan, China, and the Growth of the Asian International Political Economy, 1850–1949* (New York: Oxford University Press, 2005).

Viraphol, Sarasin. *Tribute and Profit: Sino-Siamese Trade, 1652–1853* (Cambridge: Harvard University Press, 1984).

Young, Louise. *Japan's Total Empire: Manchuria and the Culture of Wartime Imperialism* (Berkeley: University of California Press, 1998).

NOTES

1. As Michael Doyle put it simply, "imperialism is the process of establishing and maintaining an empire." Michael W. Doyle, *Empires* (Ithaca, N.Y.: Cornell University Press, 1986), 19.

2. As Leonard Woolf noted, "Europe has almost universally accepted the principle of policy that the power of the State should be used upon the world outside the State for the economic purposes of the world within the State." Leonard Woolf, "Empire and Commerce," in *The New Imperialism: Analysis of Late Nineteenth-Century Expansion*, ed. Harrison M. Wright (Boston: D. C. Heath, 1961), 39.

3. Michael Hardt and Antonio Negri, *Empire* (Cambridge: Harvard University Press, 2000), xii.

4. John A. Hobson, *Imperialism: A Study* (Ann Arbor: University of Michigan, 1902); Vladimir I. Lenin, *Imperialism: The Highest State of Capitalism* (New York: International Publishers, 1939).

5. Joseph A. Schumpeter, *Imperialism and Social Classes,* trans. Heinz Norden (New York: Augustus M. Kelley, 1951).

6. Eugene Staley, "Foreign Investment and Foreign Expansion," in *The New Imperialism* (see note 2), 77–80.

7. Harry G. Gelber, *Nations out of Empires: European Nationalism and the Transformation of Asia* (New York: Palgrave, 2001).

8. Reid, *Southeast Asia in the Age of Commerce, 1450–1680,* vol. 2.

9. Viraphol, *Tribute and Profit,* 236–277.

10. Giovanni Arrighi, Takeshi Hamashita, and Mark Selden, eds., *The Resurgence of East Asia: 500, 150, and 50 Year Perspectives* (New York: RoutledgeCurzon, 2003).

11. This period is often referred to as an informal colonial empire or "free trade imperialism." See John Gallagher and Ronald Robinson, "The Imperialism of Free Trade," *Economic History Review* 2nd ser., 6, no. 1 (1953): 1–15.

12. Warren I. Cohen, "The Foreign Impact on East Asia," in *Historical Perspectives on Contemporary East Asia,* ed. Merle Goldman and Andrew Gordon (Cambridge: Harvard University Press, 2000), 1.

13. Hsu, *Rise of Modern China,* 127.

14. Hsu, *Rise of Modern China,* 183–213.

15. Michael Adas, "Imperialism and Colonialism in Comparative Perspective," *The International History Review* 20, no. 2 (June 1998): 371–388.

16. Evelyn S. Rawski, "Reenvisioning the Qing: The Significance of the Qing Period in Chinese History," *The Journal of Asian Studies* 55, no. 4 (November 1996): 829–850.

17. Brett L. Walker, *The Conquest of Ainu Lands: Ecology and Culture in Japanese Expansion, 1590–1800* (Berkeley: University of California Press, 2001).

18. Kaoru Sugihara, ed., *Japan, China, and the Growth of the Asian International Political Economy, 1850–1949* (New York: Oxford University Press, 2005); A. J. H. Latham and Heita Kawakatsu, eds., *Japanese Industrialization and the Asian Economy* (London: Routledge, 1994).

19. John K. Fairbank, "The Early Treaty System in the Chinese World Order," in *The Chinese World Order: Traditional China's Foreign Relations,* ed. John King Fairbank (Cambridge: Harvard University Press, 1968), 257–275.

20. Benjamin I. Schwartz, "The Chinese Perception of World Order, Past and Present," in *The Chinese World Order* (see note 19), 285.

21. Edward Le Fevour, *Western Enterprise in Late Ch'ing China* (Cambridge: Harvard University Press, 1968); Kwang-ching Liu, "British-Chinese Steamship Rivalry in China, 1873–85," in *The Economic Development of China and Japan: Studies in Economic History and Political Economy,* ed. Charles D. Cowan (New York: Praeger, 1964), 49–78; Yen-ping Hao, *The Comprador in Nineteenth Century China: Bridge Between East and West* (Cambridge: Harvard University Press, 1970).

22. Sherman Cochran, *Big Business in China: Sino-Foreign Rivalry in the Cigarette Industry, 1890–1930* (Cambridge: Harvard University Press, 1980).

23. Marie-Claire Bergère, *The Golden Age of the Chinese Bourgeoisie 1911–1937,* trans. Janet Lloyd (Cambridge: Cambridge University Press, 1989). China's industrial growth was an impressive 13.8 percent between 1912 and 1929 (p. 70).

24. Bergère, *Golden Age of the Chinese Bourgeoisie 1911–1937,* 7–8.

25. Martina Deuchler, *Confucian Gentlemen and Barbarian Envoys: The Opening of Korea, 1875–1885* (Seattle: University of Washington Press, 1977).

26. Chung, *A Korean Confucian Encounter with the Modern World: Yi Hang-no and the West* (Berkeley: Institute of East Asian Studies, University of California, 1995).

27. Eckert, "Korea's Transition to Modernity: A Will to Greatness," in *Historical Perspectives on Contemporary East Asia,* ed. Merle Goldman and Andrew Gordon (Cambridge: Harvard University Press, 2000), 126–132.

28. Anthony Reid, *Charting the Shape of Early Modern Southeast Asia* (Chiang Mai, Thailand: Silkworm Books, 1999), 246–271.

29. Wang Gunwu, *Anglo-Chinese Encounters Since 1800: War, Trade, Science, and Governance,* (New York: Cambridge University Press, 2003), 61.

30. Paul D. Hutchcroft, "Colonial Masters, National Politicos, and Provincial Lords: Central Authority and Local Autonomy in the American Philippines, 1900–1913," *The Journal of Asian Studies* 59, no. 2 (May 2000): 277–306.

31. A. J. H. Latham, "The Dynamics of Intra-Asian Trade, 1868–1913: The Great Entrepôts of Singapore and Hong Kong," in *Japanese Industrialization and the Asian Economy,* ed. A. J. H. Latham and Heita Kawakatsu (London: Routledge, 1994), 145–193; W. G. Huff, *The Economic Growth of Singapore: Trade and Development in the Twentieth Century* (Cambridge: Cambridge University Press, 1994).

32. Ezra F. Vogel, *The Four Little Dragons: The Spread of Industrialization in East Asia* (Cambridge: Harvard University Press, 1991), 66–68.

33. Wang Gungwu, *The Chinese Overseas: From Earthbound China to the Quest for Autonomy* (Cambridge: Harvard University Press, 2000).

34. J. A. C. Mackie, "Introduction," in *Sojourners and Settlers: Histories of Southeast China and the Chinese,* ed. Anthony Reid, with Kristine Alilunas Rodgers (St. Leonards, Australia: Allen and Unwin, 1996), xxiv.

35. Kaoru Sugihara, "Patterns of Chinese Emigration to Southeast Asia, 1869–1939," in *Japan, China, and the Growth of the Asian International Political*

Economy, 1850–1949, ed. Kaoru Sugihara (New York: Oxford University Press, 2005), 244–274.

36. Clive J. Christie, *Ideology and Revolution in Southeast Asia, 1900–1980: Political Ideas in the Anti-Colonial Era* (Richmond, Surrey: Curzon, 2001); Michael Leifer, ed., *Asian Nationalism* (London: Routledge, 2000).

37. Anthony D. Smith, "Theories of Nationalism: Alternative Models of Nation Formation," in *Asian Nationalism* (see note 36), 1–20; Ernest Gellner, *Nations and Nationalism* (Ithaca: Cornell University Press, 1983) and *Nationalism* (New York: New York University Press, 1997).

38. Nicholas Tarling, *Nations and States in Southeast Asia* (Cambridge: Cambridge University Press, 1998), 75–78.

39. James Putzel, "Social Capital and the Imagined Community: Democracy and Nationalism in the Philippines," in *Asian Nationalism* (see note 36), 170–186.

40. Chong-Sik Lee, *The Politics of Korean Nationalism* (Berkeley: University of California Press, 1965).

41. William J. Duiker, *The Rise of Nationalism in Vietnam 1900–1941* (Ithaca: Cornell University Press, 1976).

42. Lucian W. Pye, "The New Asian Capitalism: A Political Portrait," in *In Search of an East Asian Development Model,* ed. Peter L. Berger and Michael Hsin-Huang Hsiao (New Brunswick, N.J.: Transaction Publishers, 1988), 87–89. See also Benjamin Schwartz, *In Search of Wealth and Power: Yen Fu and the West* (Cambridge: Harvard University Press, 1974).

43. Michael Edson Robinson, *Cultural Nationalism in Colonial Korea, 1920–1925* (Seattle: University of Washington Press, 1988), 28–33.

44. Meredith Woo-Cumings, "Back to Basics: Ideology, Nationalism, and Asian Values in East Asia," in *Economic Nationalism in a Globalizing World,* ed. Eric Helleiner and Andreas Pickel (Ithaca, N.Y.: Cornell University Press, 2005), 91–117.

45. Duiker, *Rise of Nationalism in Vietnam 1900–1941.*

46. George McTurnan Kahin, *Nationalism and Revolution in Indonesia* (Ithaca, N.Y.: Cornell University Press, 1970).

47. Michael R. Austin, *Negotiating with Imperialism: The Unequal Treaties and the Culture of Japanese Diplomacy* (Cambridge: Harvard University Press, 2004).

48. W. G. Beasley, *Japanese Imperialism 1894–1945* (Oxford: Oxford University Press, 1987), 28–29.

49. Marius B. Jansen, "Japanese Imperialism: Late Meiji Perspectives," in *The Japanese Colonial Empire, 1895–1945,* ed. Ramon H. Myers and Mark R. Peattie (Princeton: Princeton University Press, 1984), 61–79; Mark R. Peattie, "Japanese Attitudes Toward Colonialism, 1895–1945," in *The Japanese Colonial Empire* (Princeton: Princeton University Press, 1984), 80–127.

50. Bunsō Hashikawa, "Japanese Perspectives on Asia: From Dissociation to Coprosperity," in *The Chinese and the Japanese: Essays in Political and Cultural Interactions,* ed. Akira Iriye (Princeton: Princeton University Press, 1980), 328–355.

51. Kaoru Sugihara, ed., *Japan, China, and the Growth of the Asian International Political Economy, 1850–1949* (New York: Oxford University Press, 2005); A. J. H. Latham and H. Kawakatsu, eds., *Japanese Industrialization and the Asian Economy* (London: Routledge, 1994); Shinya Sugiyama and Linda Grove, eds., *Commercial Networks in Modern Asia* (Richmond, Surrey: Curzon, 2001).

52. George C. Allen, *A Short Economic History of Modern Japan, 1867–1937,* 4th ed. (New York: St. Martin's Press, 1981); William W. Lockwood, *The Economic Development of Japan: Growth and Structural Change, 1868–1938* (Princeton: Princeton University Press, 1954); Kazushi Ohkawa and Miyohei Shinohara, with Larry Meissner, *Patterns of Japanese Economic Development: A Quantitative Appraisal* (New Haven: Yale University Press, 1979).

53. Peter Duus, *The Abacus and the Sword: The Japanese Penetration of Korea, 1895–1910* (Berkeley: University of California Press, 1995); Ramon H. Myers and Mark R. Peattie, eds., *The Japanese Colonial Empire, 1895–1945* (Princeton: Princeton University Press, 1984); Peter Duus, Ramon H. Myers, and Mark R. Peattie, eds., *The Japanese Wartime Empire, 1931–1945* (Princeton: Princeton University Press, 1996); Morinosuke Kajima, *The Emergence of Japan as a World Power, 1895–1925* (Rutland, Vt.: Charles E. Tuttle, 1968).

54. Hilary Conroy, *The Japanese Seizure of Korea, 1868–1910: A Study of Realism and Idealism in International Relations* (Philadelphia: University of Pennsylvania Press, 1960).

55. Peter Duus, Ramon H. Myers, and Mark R. Peattie, eds. *The Japanese Informal Empire in China, 1895–1937* (Princeton: Princeton University Press, 1989).

56. Allen, *Short Economic History of Modern Japan,* 42–44.

57. Morishima, *Why Has Japan 'Succeeded'?* 93–132; Allen, *Short Economic History of Modern Japan,* 42–55.

58. Beasley, *Japanese Imperialism 1894–1945,* 188–192.

59. Beasley, *Japanese Imperialism 1894–1945,* 198–219.

60. Francis C. Jones, *Japan's New Order in East Asia: Its Rise and Fall 1937–45* (New York: Oxford University Press, 1954).

61. Herbert Feith, "Indonesia," in *Government and Politics in Southeast Asia,* ed. George M. Kahin, 2nd ed. (Ithaca, N.Y.: Cornell University Press, 1964), 198.

62. Bruce Cumings, "The Origins and Development of the Northeast Asian Political Economy: Industrial Sectors, Product Cycles, and Political Consequences," *International Organization* 38, no. 1 (Winter 1984): 1–40.

63. Sang-Chul Suh, *Growth and Structural Changes in the Korean Economy, 1910–1940* (Cambridge: Harvard University Press, 1978); Ramon H. Myers and Mark R.

Peattie, eds., *The Japanese Colonial Empire, 1895–1945* (Princeton: Princeton University Press, 1984).

64. Duiker, *Rise of Nationalism in Vietnam 1900–1941*, 38–41. The Vietnamese delegates were disappointed as the Japanese dignitaries they had met showed reluctance to offer any military assistance.

65. As a good example, Singapore's senior leader Lee Kuan Yew made such an observation. Lee Kuan Yew, *The Singapore Story: Memoirs of Lee Kuan Yew* (Singapore: Prentice Hall, 1998), 52–53.

66. Stein Tonnesson, "Filling the Power Vacuum: 1945 in French Indochina, the Netherlands, East Indies, and British Malaya," in *Imperial Policy and South East Asian Nationalism*, ed. Hans Antlov and Stein Tonnesson (London: Curzon, 1995), 110–143.

67. MacAlister Brown and Joseph J. Zasloff, *Apprentice Revolutionaries: The Communist Movement in Laos, 1930–1985* (Stanford: Hoover Institution Press, 1986), 269.

68. Chalmers A. Johnson, *Peasant Nationalism and Communist Power: The Emergence of Revolutionary China, 1937–1945* (Stanford: Stanford University Press, 1962); Tetsuya Kataoka, *Resistance and Revolution in China: The Communists and the Second United Front* (Berkeley: University of California Press, 1974).

69. As Mao put it, "Japanese say to me that they are very sorry for attacking us. I say, Friends, you did a good thing. They really became confused [at this]. I say, if you had not attacked, had not occupied so much land, [then] the Chinese people wouldn't have been educated. You were our teachers, motivating all the Chinese people to oppose you, this is your contribution." Mao, "On the Correct Handling of Contradictions Among the People [Speaking Notes], February 27, 1957, in *The Secret Speeches of Chairman Mao: From the Hundred Flowers to the Great Leap Forward*, ed. Roderick MacFarquhar, Timothy Cheek, and Eugene Wu (Cambridge: Harvard University Press, 1989), 182.

70. Robert A. Scalapino and Chong-sik Lee, *Communism in Korea. Part I, The Movement* (Berkeley: University of California Press, 1972); Robinson, *Cultural Nationalism in Colonial Korea, 1920–1925*.

71. Lee, *Politics of Korean Nationalism*, 276–277.

72. For studies of how empire-building affected the Japanese state and society, see Louise Young, *Japan's Total Empire: Manchuria and the Culture of Wartime Imperialism* (Berkeley: University of California Press, 1998); Bai Gao, *Economic Ideology and Industrial Policy in Japan: Developmentalism from 1931 to 1965* (New York: Cambridge University Press, 1997).

CHAPTER 5

The East Asian Miracle

T his chapter discusses the East Asian miracle, which is a striking feature of contemporary East Asian political economy. Although one may view East Asia as returning to its historical glory, its recent success has taken on distinct modern features of industrialization, the nation state, and the market economy in a globalizing international system. It is important to discuss the miracle story upfront because economic development is a complex process involving all the functional areas such as production, trade, and exchange rates. Thus, the chapter provides a context for linking different issues to be discussed later in the book.

The first question the chapter addresses is whether there has been an economic miracle and what kind of miracle. The chapter shows that there has been an economic miracle—one that can be explained—in East Asia's rapid economic development with relative income equity, even though one may question the sustainability of rapid growth. The fact that the Asian financial crisis took place in 1997 does not negate East Asia's postwar achievements. The second question is why the East Asian miracle has taken place. Rejecting single-cause explanations, the chapter argues that East Asia's miracle has resulted from a strong commitment of governments to development, basically sound macroeconomic policies, a controlled integration into the global market, positive externalities of regional growth, and the region's close security and economic ties to the United States.

POSTWAR TRANSFORMATION OF EAST ASIAN POLITICAL ECONOMY

East Asian political economy has experienced a dramatic transformation since the 1960s. The first long-term trend in East Asia is rapid, shared economic growth that allows the region to catch up with the West. I discuss this and then address the question, was there an economic miracle? The second trend is the fundamental change in East Asia's economic structure from agriculture and primary commodities to manufacturing and service. The third trend is a march toward capitalism throughout the region. The three trends have been mutually reinforcing.

Rapid Economic Growth with Equity

The East Asian miracle refers to East Asia's rapid postwar economic development accompanied with decreased income inequalities. East Asia has led the world in speed of economic growth—Japan in the 1960s, the four tigers of Hong Kong, Singapore, Taiwan, and South Korea in the 1970s, the newly industrializing Association of Southeast Asian Nations (ASEAN) countries in the 1980s, and China in the 1990s. In an influential 1993 study on the East Asian miracle, the World Bank called Japan, the four tigers, and newly industrializing Indonesia, Malaysia, and Thailand "high-performing Asian economies" (HPAEs). Since 1960, HPAEs had grown three times as fast as Latin America and South Asia, twenty-five times faster than sub-Sahara Africa, and much faster than developed nations and oil-producing regions of the Middle East and North Africa. From 1960 to 1990, real income per capita more than quadrupled in Japan and the four tigers and more than doubled in the three ASEAN nations.[1] As Table 5.1 shows, East Asia outperformed other regions from 1965 to 1990. The data in the table came from another influential study on the East Asian miracle published by the Asian Development Bank (ADB) in 1997.

While Japan began a decade of economic slowdown, the rest of East Asia continued to excel in the 1990s and since the Asian financial crisis in 1997–1998, as shown in Table 5.2. In particular, we see a dramatic rise in China's economy since the early 1990s. According to World Bank projections, while Japan will continue low economic growth, developing East Asia and Pacific will enjoy a 5.3 percent annual growth rate in real GDP per capita in 2006–2015, faster than the rest of the world.[2]

To highlight East Asia's economic growth, I have included Figure 5.1, which tracks GDP annual growth rates of Japan, South Korea, Malaysia, China, and Vietnam, compared to the world average. The figure shows clearly that as a trendsetter, Japan outperformed the world in the 1960s, but its growth rates slowed down in the 1970s and actually grew more slowly than the world average in the 1990s. In the second wave, South Korea took off after the mid-1960s and has maintained a high speed of economic development, followed not far behind by Malaysia of the third-tier achievers. China suffered a major economic setback during the Great Famine of 1959–1961 and experienced high volatility until the late 1970s when it began economic reform. China became the trendsetter after the early 1990s. Starting belatedly in the mid-1980s, Vietnam's economic growth rates are now second only to China's. Figure 5.2 tracks East Asia's GDP per capita annual growth rates, which measures real economic growth by taking into consideration offsetting population growth, and shows similar trends.

The HPAEs have managed to grow with relative equity as measured by the Gini coefficient. The Gini coefficient is a number between 0 and 1, where 0 indicates perfect equality (everyone has the same income) and 1 indicates perfect inequality

TABLE 5.1
Growth in the Global Economy, 1965–1990

Region/Economy	Average Annual GDP Growth per Capita (PPP adjusted)
East Asia	6.7
Hong Kong	5.8
Korea, Republic of	7.4
People's Republic of China	5.1
Singapore	7.4
Taipei, China	6.3
Southeast Asia	3.8
Indonesia	4.7
Malaysia	4.5
Philippines	1.4
Thailand	4.6
South Asia	1.7
Bangladesh	0.8
India	2.0
Pakistan	1.8
Sri Lanka	2.3
Pacific Islands	
Papua New Guinea	–0.7
OECD	2.7
Middle East	2.5
Sub-Saharan Africa	0.7
Latin America	0.8

Source: Asian Development Bank, *Emerging Asia: Changes and Challenges* (Manila: Asian Development Bank, 1997), 2.

Note: OECD = Organization for Economic Cooperation and Development; PPP = purchasing power parity.

(one person has all the income and everyone else has none). Income equality is an important indicator of the quality of economic growth. In fact, the very definition of economic development often includes an equitable distribution as a criterion. As the 1993 World Bank miracle report points out, "The HPAEs are the only economies that have high growth *and* declining inequality. Moreover, the fastest growing East Asian economies, Japan and the Four Tigers, are the most equal."[3] Case studies of some East Asian achievers support the argument. A relatively equitable income distribution, for example, was a striking feature in Taiwanese and South Korean economic development.[4]

East Asia's experience in income distribution varies. The 1993 World Bank miracle report did not cover China, which sees greater inequality while its economy

TABLE 5.2
East Asia's GDP Annual Growth Rates, 1990–2005

Region/Economy	1990	1991	1992	1993	1994	1995	1996	1997	1998	1999	2000	2001	2002	2003	2004	2005
China	3.8	9.2	14.2	14.0	13.1	10.9	10.0	9.3	7.8	7.6	8.4	8.3	9.1	10.0	10.1	9.9
Japan	5.2	3.4	1.0	0.2	1.1	2.0	3.4	1.8	-1.0	-0.1	2.4	0.2	-0.3	1.3	2.7	2.7
Hong Kong	1.9	5.6	6.6	6.3	5.5	3.9	4.3	5.1	-5.0	3.4	10.2	0.6	1.8	3.2	8.6	7.3
South Korea	9.2	9.4	5.9	6.1	8.5	9.2	7.0	4.7	-6.9	9.5	8.5	3.8	7.0	3.1	4.7	4.0
Singapore	9.2	6.6	6.3	11.7	11.6	8.1	7.8	8.3	-1.4	7.2	10.0	-2.3	4.0	2.9	8.7	6.4
Taiwan*	5.4	7.6	6.8	6.3	6.5	6.4	6.1	6.4	4.3	5.3	5.8	-2.2	3.9	3.3	5.7	3.7
Indonesia	9.0	8.9	7.2	7.3	7.5	8.4	7.6	4.7	-13.1	0.8	4.9	3.8	4.4	4.7	5.1	5.6
Malaysia	9.0	9.5	8.9	9.9	9.2	9.8	10.0	7.3	-7.4	6.1	8.9	0.3	4.4	5.4	7.1	5.3
Thailand	11.2	8.6	8.1	8.3	9.0	9.2	5.9	-1.4	-10.5	4.4	4.8	2.2	5.3	7.0	6.2	4.5
Philippines	3.0	-0.6	0.3	2.1	4.4	4.7	5.8	5.2	-0.6	3.4	6.0	1.8	4.4	4.5	6.0	5.1
Vietnam	5.1	6.0	8.6	8.1	8.8	9.5	9.3	8.2	5.8	4.8	6.8	6.9	7.1	7.3	7.7	8.4
East Asia and Pacific (developing only)**	5.5	8.3	11.1	11.3	11.1	9.9	9.0	7.3	2.3	6.3	7.6	6.6	7.9	8.8	9.0	8.7
South Asia	5.6	1.8	5.6	4.4	6.6	7.0	6.7	4.2	5.4	6.4	4.2	4.7	3.6	7.6	8.0	8.1
Middle East	6.4	5.7	4.7	2.0	3.3	3.1	5.5	3.3	5.9	4.0	3.2	3.3	3.9	2.9	5.8	4.6
Sub-Saharan Africa	1.1	0.6	-1.2	0.5	1.9	3.8	5.1	3.5	2.3	2.7	3.3	3.5	3.4	4.1	5.1	5.3
Latin America	0.4	4.7	3.9	3.7	4.9	0.4	3.8	5.5	2.5	0.4	4.0	0.3	-0.8	2.0	5.9	4.4
OECD	3.0	1.4	2.0	1.2	3.1	2.6	3.0	3.3	2.5	3.1	3.6	1.2	1.4	2.0	3.2	2.7
World	2.9	1.6	2.2	1.8	3.4	2.9	3.5	3.8	2.5	3.1	4.0	1.5	1.8	2.8	4.1	3.6

Source: World Bank, World Development Indicators Database.

* Data for Taiwan's economic growth in 1990–1994 are from Council for Economic Planning and Development, Taiwan Statistical Data Book, 1996 (Taiwan: June 1996), 1, and data for the period of 1995–2005 are from the official Taiwanese statistics network, www.stat.gov.tw/public/Attachment/5105143757711.XLS.

** Does not include high-income economies of Japan, South Korea, Hong Kong, Singapore, and Taiwan.

FIGURE 5.1
East Asia's GDP Annual Growth Rates, 1961–2005

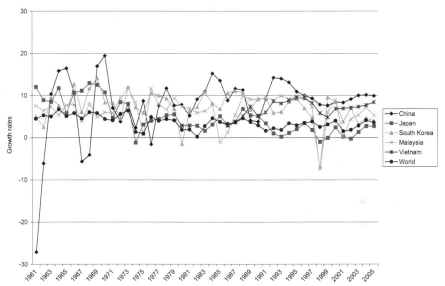

Source: World Bank, World Development Indicators Database.

FIGURE 5.2
East Asia's GDP per Capita Annual Growth Rates, 1961–2005

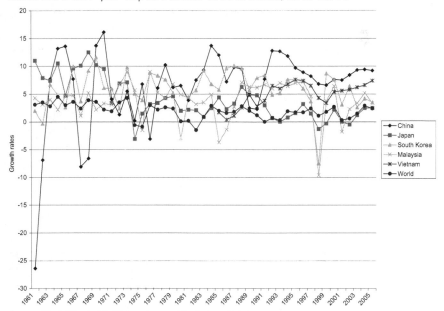

Source: World Bank, World Development Indicators Database.

grows rapidly, particularly sharpening regional disparities.[5] United Nations Development Program (UNDP) statistics show a clear decline in the Gini coefficients for China. China's Gini coefficient was 0.403 in 1998, the poorest 20 percent of the population accounts for only 5.9 percent of the total income or consumption whereas the richest 20 percent account for 46.6 percent.[6] The inequality measure increased to 0.447 in 2001.[7]

At the same time, East Asia has been successful and will probably continue to be successful if one looks at the poverty reduction. The number of people living under $1 a day in developing East Asia and Pacific (excluding Japan and the newly industrializing economies [NIEs]) was reduced by 55 percent between 1990 and 2002 while the rest of developing countries experienced an increase of 7 percent.[8]

East Asia's rapid economic development seemed miraculous. From a historical perspective, wealth did not increase until the rise of the West. But even then, the West rose only gradually. Western Europe shifted from poverty to wealth in the nineteenth and twentieth centuries at a steady pace.[9] Western Europe grew by an annual average growth rate of 0.40 percent in 1500–1820, 1.68 percent in 1820–1870, 2.11 percent in 1870–1913, and 1.19 percent in 1913–1950.[10] In addition, East Asia's economic growth had not been anticipated. In an influential three-volume, 2,284-page book *The Asian Drama* (1968), Gunnar Myrdal was pessimistic about Asia's prospect.[11] Also, the HPAEs' *shared* economic growth was miraculous because the prevalent conventional wisdom in the 1950s was that there exists a tradeoff between rapid growth and equity. Simon Kuznets and others argued that developing nations had a less equal income distribution than developed nations and that income distribution tended to worsen when developing nations begin to grow.[12]

As a result of rapid economic growth, East Asia as a whole is closing the gap with the West. In fact, some East Asian nations have caught up. One may describe Japan's accomplishment as unsurprising, because the country was already a major economic power before the Second World War. But South Korea joined the Organization for Economic Cooperation and Development (OECD), the rich countries' club, in December 1996. While not members of OECD, Taiwan, Hong Kong, and Singapore have even higher GNP per capita than South Korea. In fact, Hong Kong ($22,310) and Singapore ($20,987) had higher GDP per capita, measured in purchasing power parity (PPP), than their former colonial master Great Britain ($18,620) in 1994.[13]

Quality of life is another measure of economic development. The UNDP uses the human development index that includes life expectancy at birth, adult literacy rate, school enrollment, and GDP per capita. Of the 177 countries and economies listed (Taiwan and North Korea not included), Norway ranked the highest at 0.965 in 2004. East Asia had 6 of the 63 countries with high human development: Japan 7th at 0.949, Hong Kong 22nd at 0.927, Singapore 25th at 0.916, South Korea 26th at 0.912, Brunei 34th at 0.871, and Malaysia 61st at 0.805. Thailand (74), China (81), the Philippines (84), Indonesia (108), Vietnam (109), Cambodia (129), Myanmar (130), and Laos (133) were in the next tier of 83 countries with medium human development, and none of the countries in East Asia were among the 31 countries with low human development.[14] All of these countries, except Japan, saw major improvements in their ranking since the late 1980s.

Was There a Miracle?

The East Asian miracle has attracted naysayers as well as admirers. In a widely read paper published in *Foreign Affairs* in 1994 prior to the Asian financial crisis, Paul Krugman called the Asian miracle a myth.[15] He compared the Asian miracle to the touted economic miracle achieved by the Soviet Union and its satellite states in Eastern Europe in the 1950s in that both are based on a sharp increase in economic input rather than productivity gains and that neither is therefore sustainable. His argument is based on the theory of *total factor productivity* (TFP). According to the TFP theory, economic growth depends on increased input in labor and capital, such as a better educated labor force and increased stock of physical capital. Economists estimate TFP by creating an index that includes all the measurable input and then the rate of economic growth of national income relative to that index. The residual or what cannot be accounted for by input is assumed to be productivity gains. The key for sustainable growth is efficiency gains, namely increased output per unit of input. Without productivity improvement, additional increase in input will have diminishing returns. Krugman argued that the four East Asian tigers had achieved no real technology gains, that while Japan had closed the technology gap with the West its economic growth had slowed, and that China's economic development statistics are questionable although it is possible that the country has achieved some technological gains. Thus, Krugman noted that it is wrong to see a shift of the world economic power center from the West to Asia.

Krugman's argument was based on the empirical research conducted by Alwyn Young, Jong-il Kim, and Lawrence Lau. Young had showed that the East Asian NIEs have not performed exceptionally well in productivity growth, with Singapore having virtually no TFP gains in nonagricultural economy and slightly negative growth in manufacturing.[16] Kim and Lau also concluded that the most important source of economic growth for Hong Kong, Singapore, South Korea, and Taiwan is capital accumulation, which accounts for 48–78 percent of their economic growth. By contrast, technical progress accounted for 46–71 percent of growth for France, Germany, Japan, Britain, and the United States.[17]

However, whether sustainable or not, East Asia's rapid economic growth has given the region an opportunity to gain ground with early developers. Other developing regions would be more than happy to be in that position. Moreover, some analysts dispute Krugman's conclusion. Stephan Haggard and Euysung Kim argued that there were productivity gains in East Asia although not as impressive as previously assumed and that an increase in inputs was also the main source of Western economic growth. Therefore, the real question is why East Asia has been able to make heavy investments over a long period of time.[18] The 1993 World Bank miracle report concluded, based on calculations of TFP, that two-thirds of East Asia's growth results from accumulation in physical and human capital and the remaining third is attributable to increased efficiency. East Asia's productivity gain has been larger than other developing regions.[19] Seiji Naya of the ADB pointed out that unlike the former Soviet Union and its Eastern European allies during the cold war, East Asian economies are integrated with the global market. Moreover, diminishing return may not be appropriate for studying a national economy undergoing structural shift; new investment is used to produce new products rather than adding to the capacity in existing sectors. He also pointed to some recent studies that suggest TFP growth.[20] Specifically addressing Singapore's low TFP gain, Chang-Tai Hsieh showed in his empirical analysis that Singapore's national account has overstated investment spending and the country has gained as much in TFP as Hong Kong, Taiwan, and South Korea.[21]

Some scholars have questioned the accuracy of Chinese economic growth statistics. In a 2001 article, Thomas Rawski argued that China's GDP statistics after 1998 contained serious exaggerations due to widespread falsification at the local level. He calculated that China's real GDP growth was only one-third of the official claims.[22] Because of similar concerns, the Chinese State Statistics Bureau announced in December 2004 that the central government would announce GDP statistics starting in 2005 and the statistics announced by local governments would no longer have legal force. At the same time, Chinese citizens and companies also have incentives to understate their earnings to reduce taxes. This was confirmed in a national survey on China's service industry conducted by the National Statistics Bureau, which showed a serious underreporting in the service sector (a high 32.8 percent). As a result, the bureau added 2.3 trillion yuan ($285 billion) to the 2004 figure, almost doubling the 2004 growth rate to 16.8 percent.[23] The government also revised growth statistics back to 1993, based on which China's annual GDP growth rates were adjusted up by 0.2 percent to 9.6 percent in 1979–2004.[24]

The Asian financial crisis does not prove that the Asian miracle was merely a mirage. One crisis may have ended the miracle, but it does not negate the existence of the miracle in the first place. All major market economies have experienced economic crises. Moreover, East Asia, with the exception of Indonesia, recovered within two years and is experiencing growth again. In particular, largely unaffected by the Asian financial crisis, China has continued a fast pace of economic growth. Because of its size, China's growth has pulled East Asia and the world along with it. Measured by PPP, China accounts for between 20 and 30 percent of world GDP growth since the Asian financial crisis.[25]

Structural Change

When one examines contemporary East Asian political economy, it is not enough just to look at growth statistics. East Asian nations have become industrialized, judging by a sharply rising share of industry in GDP, as shown in Table 5.3. This structural change is important. After all, the goal of economic development is to create a more industrialized and modern economy. East Asia is also rapidly moving up the technological ladder. East Asian nations have built some high-value-added industries and built brand names in the global market. Many patents are awarded to Asia. Asian students tend to study science and technologies more. As an indicator of Asia's technological edge, South Korea leads the United States and Europe in broadband penetration, and Japan leads in speed and price even though they do not dominate in the global information and communication industry.[26] Also, the fact that East Asia has a greater share of manufacturing means intangible technological gains. As Ronald I. McKinnon pointed out, "Manufacturing—and manufacturing-associated education, in the form of learning-by-doing—are most likely powerful sources of external benefits that accelerate economy-wide productivity growth."[27] Moreover, Dwight Perkins argued that East Asian governments' promotion of exports has been important for productivity gains and imports of technologies because exporters have to become competitive internationally by introducing advanced technologies and best practices.[28]

As an indicator of East Asia's overall competitiveness, leading East Asian economies rank among the best along with North American and European countries in the global competitiveness reports by the World Economic Forum. The 2005–2006 country rankings put Taiwan as No. 5, Singapore as No. 6, and Japan as No. 12. The 2004–2005 rankings had Taiwan as No. 4, Singapore as No. 7, and Japan as No. 9.[29]

March to Capitalism

Another major structural shift is a march to capitalism. Existing capitalist countries are reducing government control over market activities. Socialist countries are also making the transition from planned to market economy.[30] If one looks at East Asia today, it is clear that there is no longer a viable socialist alternative in the region. The debates are over what type of capitalist system to have, with the fault line between an "American system" and some milder alternatives of capitalism.

China's transition to the market is well known.[31] Working with the Chinese National Bureau of Statistics, the OECD in a major survey of Chinese economy

TABLE 5.3
Structural Change of East Asian Economy (percent of sectors in GDP)

	Agriculture							Industry							Services						
	1960	1970	1980	1990	2000	2004	2005	1960	1970	1980	1990	2000	2004	2005	1960	1970	1980	1990	2000	2004	2005
Hong Kong	–	–	0.8	0.2	0.1	0.1	–	–	–	30.9	24.4	13.3	9.9	–	–	–	68.3	75.4	86.6	90.0	–
Korea	38.5	29.2	16.2	8.9	4.9	3.7	–	17.7	26.0	36.6	41.6	40.7	40.8	–	52.8	44.7	47.3	49.5	54.4	55.5	–
China	22.3	35.2	30.1	27.0	14.8	13.1	–	44.9	40.5	48.5	41.6	45.9	46.2	–	33.0	24.3	21.4	31.3	39.3	40.7	–
Singapore	–	–	1.6	0.4	0.1	0.1	0.1	–	–	37.8	34.7	37.0	33.7	33.8	–	–	60.5	64.9	62.8	66.1	66.1
Indonesia	51.5	44.9	24.0	19.4	15.6	16.0	14.0	15.0	18.7	41.7	39.1	45.9	44.3	40.7	33.5	36.4	34.3	41.5	38.5	41.4	45.3
Thailand	36.4	25.9	23.2	12.5	9.0	10.1	9.6	18.5	25.3	28.7	37.2	42.0	43.5	46.9	45.0	48.8	48.1	50.3	49.0	46.4	43.5
Malaysia	34.3	29.4	22.6	15.2	8.8	9.5	–	19.4	27.4	41.0	42.2	50.7	50.4	–	45.7	43.2	36.3	42.6	40.5	40.1	–
Philippines	25.7	29.5	25.1	21.9	15.8	15.2	14.4	27.6	31.7	38.8	34.5	32.3	31.9	32.6	46.7	38.8	36.1	43.6	52.0	52.9	53.0
Vietnam	–	–	–	38.7	24.5	21.8	–	–	–	–	22.7	36.7	40.1	–	–	–	–	38.6	38.7	38.2	–
East Asia*	26.7	34.6	28.5	24.9	14.9	13.2	–	37.7	36.0	45.0	40.0	44.5	45.1	–	35.6	29.3	26.5	35.1	40.6	41.8	–
South Asia	46.0	44.7	37.1	30.7	24.2	20.1	19.2	19.0	20.9	24.2	26.7	25.8	26.9	27.3	35.4	34.8	38.6	42.6	50.0	53.0	53.5
Latin America	–	13.0	10.2	9.0	6.7	8.5	8.1	–	36.0	39.0	35.8	29.8	34.0	32.1	–	51.0	50.9	55.4	63.5	57.5	59.8
Middle East	–	–	14.5	18.6	12.0	12.1	11.4	–	–	41.3	32.6	43.6	39.2	40.5	–	–	44.2	48.8	44.4	48.7	48.1
OECD	–	–	4.0	2.8	1.8	–	–	–	–	36.8	32.3	27.8	–	–	–	–	59.2	64.9	70.4	–	–
World	–	–	6.7	5.5	3.7	–	–	–	–	37.5	33.4	29.3	–	–	–	–	55.9	61.1	67.0	–	–

Source: World Bank, World Development Indicators Database.

* Does not include high-income economies of Japan, South Korea, Hong Kong, Singapore, and Taiwan.

issued on September 16, 2005, pointed out that in 2003 private companies accounted for 59.2 percent of China's GDP. The private sector share increased to 66.3 percent if one includes so-called collective enterprises that typically operate as private enterprises, an increase of 63.1 percent in 1998. The report also showed that the private sector is more efficient. The TFP growth for private firms is twice that for directly owned state enterprises while controlling for company size, location, and industry.[32]

Vietnam has tried to emulate the Chinese experience, and its ASEAN membership has also facilitated its transition to a market economy.[33] Vietnam's preparation to join the World Trade Organization (WTO) furthered its economic and political reform. Vietnam joined the WTO in November 2006. Other communist countries such as Laos and Cambodia have also adopted economic reform measures.[34] Even North Korea is experimenting with some economic reform measures, half-hearted and piecemeal as they may be.[35]

EXPLAINING THE EAST ASIAN MIRACLE

It is more difficult to explain than to describe East Asia's fast economic growth. The development experience in East Asia varies greatly. The eight high-performing East Asian economies include three models of development: the manufactured export-led, state interventionist model of Japan, South Korea, and Taiwan; the free port, commercial center model of Singapore and Hong Kong; and the natural resource-rich model of Indonesia, Malaysia, and Thailand.[36] In addition, East Asia's recent performers include the transitional models of China and Vietnam. It is thus difficult to generalize the true cause of the East Asian miracle. Analysts also view the East Asian miracle from different angles. The neoclassical school of thought, mainly by economists, argues that East Asia's economic miracle has resulted from market forces and the right incentives provided by the government. A developmental state approach, mainly by political scientists and area specialists, suggests that the East Asian governments have played a constructive, central role in guiding economy to success. In yet another approach, some scholars resort to a cultural explanation for the East Asian miracle.[37] A fourth argument focuses on the regional contagion of economic successes.[38] I will discuss the first and the second arguments in this section and the regional dynamic explanation in the next section. I do not include the cultural approach in the book because an adequate discussion of cultures and traditions goes beyond the scope of this political economy text.

Neoclassical Economics

Neoclassical economists believe that the East Asian NIEs have done well because they have "got the fundamentals right." The governments in the East Asian miracle economies provided a stable macroeconomic environment and right incentives for saving and investment, adopted an export-oriented trade strategy, invested heavily in human capital, and maintained competitive markets for factors of production.[39] As the 1993 World Bank study concluded,

> What caused East Asia's success? In large measure the HPAEs achieved high growth by getting the basics right. Private domestic investment and rapidly growing human capital were the principal engines of growth. High levels of domestic financial savings sustained the HPAEs' high investment levels. Agriculture, while declining in relative importance, experienced rapid growth and productivity improvement. Population growth rates declined more rapidly in the HPAEs than in other parts of the developing world. And some of these economies also got a head start because they had a better-educated labor force and a more effective system of public administration. In this sense there is little that is "miraculous" about the HPAEs' superior record of growth; it is largely due to superior accumulation of physical and human capital.[40]

Neoclassical economics has been the dominant school of economics. The term *neoclassical* came from the 1955 edition of Paul Samuelson's influential textbook, *Economics*. He used a neoclassical synthesis to characterize the theoretical consensus among economists to integrate microeconomics and macroeconomics. The consensus broke down in the 1970s, but people still refer to mainstream economics as neoclassical. Neoclassical economists view economics as the study of choice under conditions of scarcity and maintain that one can provide a comprehensive explanation of human behavior based on markets and prices.[41]

The neoclassical approach criticized the popular state-led development strategy in the 1950s and 1960s.[42] The first generation of development economists provided the intellectual foundation for the state-led development doctrine.[43] Leading scholars like Gunnar Myrdal and Raul Prebisch were pessimistic about the ability of developing nations to export because of their dependence on primary products: Since the share of primary product in the global trade will shrink as a result of structural change from agriculture to manufacturing and service, developing nations will suffer. Since developing nations also had other profound problems, including what Myrdal called a "culture of poverty," developing nations needed the state to give development a big push.[44] Operationally, the state-led development strategy advocated import substitution industrialization (ISI) to protect domestic industry, state control of banks, policy credits, some protection of labor and unions, state enterprises, and planning.

Neoclassical economists challenged the state-led development doctrine on two grounds. On a theoretical ground, using standard economic tools they showed that the state-led doctrine lacks a strong analytical foundation. In the 1950s, Robert Solow and Trevor Swan developed a neoclassical theory of growth, namely the TFP theory. They argued that economic growth is a function of capital input, labor input, and technological progress. The theory is based on several assumptions. One assumption is constant return to scale: If we double the capital and labor input, the economic output will also double. Another assumption is diminishing return: Additional investment in one factor while the size of the other factor remains unchanged leads to diminishing returns. But technological progress may offset diminishing returns and thus sustain long-term economic growth.[45] The main implication of the neoclassical growth theory is that government policy to promote investment will have no real impact on long-term economic growth.

On an empirical ground, Ian M. D. Little, Tibor Scitovksy, and Maurice Scott conducted a comprehensive study of ISI in seven developing economies: Argentina, Brazil, Mexico, India, Pakistan, the Philippines, and Taiwan. In a major blow to the intellectual basis of the ISI strategy, the authors concluded that the seven cases under study had reached a stage in which continuous ISI had become harmful to further economic growth. Protection has created high-cost enterprises, which produce expensive goods for a small middle class. Costly and ineffective industrialization has created a high burden for agriculture. Moreover, ISI hurts exports of agriculture and nonprotected industry. Inputs needed for export products are expensive with import restrictions, and import restrictions tend to keep the exchange rate higher than it would be under free trade. On top of all that, ISI does not save foreign exchange because one still needs to import input and capital goods. Little, Scitovksy, and Scott argued that developing nations should encourage exports and that the postwar experience had shown the effectiveness of policy favoring exports.[46] Indeed, Taiwan and Korea liberalized trade and depreciated exchange rates to promote exports. The export-led strategy has a favorable effect on the economy because of economies of scale and foreign competition. The strategy also forces one to recognize and correct mistakes often disguised in the import-substitution strategy.[47]

Based on evidence from Southeast Asia, a 1971 ADB report also listed ISI's high costs. Because the region had exhausted the relatively easy opportunities for import substitution and because fast growth in Northeast Asia and the Western Pacific would create favorable demands in the 1970s, Southeast Asia now should adopt an export-oriented strategy.[48] In a separate study, Ronald McKinnon showed that if the state manipulates the financial market by directing credit to desirable sectors and by controlling interest rates, it would create distortion in saving and investments, which would serve as a drag on economic growth. He argued that a successful liberalization of the domestic capital market would allow liberalization of trade and rationalization of domestic fiscal policy. He cited South Korea, Indonesia, and Taiwan as successful examples.[49] In addition, Gary Fields maintained that a flexible and competitive labor market is important for economic growth for East Asian economies. By contrast, some developing nations outside East Asia had higher-than-market-clearing wages because of the institutional forces of trade unions, minimum wages, government pay policies, and multinational corporations.[50]

By the late 1980s, neoclassical economics came to dominate in the Washington policy circle. John Williamson coined the term "the Washington consensus" to refer to the neoclassical notions shared by the U.S. Treasury, the International Monetary Fund (IMF), and the World Bank as universal truths. Specifically, he saw the Washington policy community sharing consensus on the following policy instruments: fiscal discipline, reduction of public expenditure rather than increase in tax revenues, broad tax base and moderate marginal tax rates, market-determined interest rates, competitive real exchange rates to promote exports, import liberalization, removal of restriction on foreign direct investment, privatization of state enterprises, deregulation, and protection of property rights.[51] The policy prescription based on the Washington consensus was "structural adjustment lending" by the World Bank and conditionality by the IMF. Put simply, countries that wanted financing from the IMF and the World Bank needed to make structural reform, which involved removing government intervention in economic activities.

Modifying neoclassical economic theory of growth, some economists have suggested possibilities for the government to make a difference in long-term economic development. The new growth theory proposed in the mid-1980s incorporates technological innovation and knowledge advancement into the growth model. Technology and knowledge are considered endogenous to the growth model in that firms make investment in technology for the same reason that they invest in capital and labor. As a separate factor, technology and knowledge result from conscious decisions. The capital investment and technology may form a virtuous cycle. As a result, there may be a long-term economic growth as a result of increasing returns. The new growth theory thus explains why some firms, with a head start in technology, may maintain a lead and why some regions and countries do better than others.[52] Some other economists suggested in the early 1990s that private investment in research and development increases the knowledge level of the whole society, thus reducing costs for future innovations.[53]

Moreover, some economists employ insights from industrial organizations to show how the state in East Asia may overcome the market failure. According to the theory of the firm, firms emerge to overcome the problem of transaction costs, that is, the costs of performing tasks such as negotiation and implementation. While firms reduce transaction costs, they often encounter organization failure, such as bureaucratic inertia. Thus, a firm generally has a headquarters and functional divisions, and the headquarters strategize and monitor the performance of different divisions. A successful firm distributes resources effectively to where they yield best results. In this sense, there is an internal capital market that ensures effi-ciency. Chung H. Lee and Seiji Naya argued that the East Asian state acts as such an internal capital market by channeling credits to targeted firms or sectors deemed crucial for national economic development and by monitoring perform-ances of different firms and sectors. Wrong policies are avoided in East Asia thanks to their outward-oriented development strategy in which prices are deter-mined by the global economy and cannot be changed to cover up policy mistakes, which is often the case for inward-oriented governments.[54]

Mancur Olson's theory of encompassing organizations offers another eco-nomic explanation. Olson argued that narrowly based, rent-seeking distributional coalitions are obstacles to economic growth. A larger organization that does not see a zero-sum game is needed to overcome such a problem.[55] Following this logic, the East Asian state serves as an encompassing organization. As a concrete exam-ple, one key for development is to spread advanced technologies throughout industry and sectors quickly. But technology diffusion is difficult when compa-nies try to undermine each other. What Japan and other East Asian governments did was to form public-private consortium, which allows technology sharing. The government also used its power to pressure foreign companies to give up advanced technologies in exchange for access to their markets.

The economic theories discussed above modify the neoclassical growth theory but do not challenge the basic assumption that the market is the best solution to long-term growth. By contrast, the developmental state argument constitutes a bigger challenge to the neoclassical orthodoxy.

The Developmental State Approach

The developmental state approach did not begin as an intellectual project aimed at unseating the dominant neoclassical thought on development. Rather, it was a collection of East Asian development practice. As such, it was not a coherent body of concepts and theories. In addition, there was a variation in how the develop-mental state actually operated in different East Asian countries.

Western specialists provided the earlier studies of the developmental state. Chalmers Johnson was among the first scholars to use the term *developmental state*, defined as a state that is focused on economic development and takes necessary policy measures to accomplish that objective. He argued that Japan's economic miracle had much to do with far-sighted intervention by bureaucrats, particularly those in the Ministry of International Trade and Industry (MITI). Japanese bureaucrats picked the winners and channeled resources into targeted sectors to achieve rapid economic growth.[56] Chapter 7 will provide a more detailed discus-sion of how the Japanese government picked winners and created losers in the process. Johnson then argued that South Korea and Taiwan adopted the Japanese model. He explicitly challenged the neoclassical economists' dismissal of state intervention.[57]

Alice Amsden, Robert Wade, and Stephan Haggard further developed the developmental state argument.[58] While Johnson emphasized the competent bureaucracy, some later studies examined the broader political institutions. The core argument for the developmental state theorists is that the state can be a powerful engine for economic development, as shown in the East Asian experience. Although these scholars vary in what they emphasize, they share some common themes: The state improves infrastructure (roads, energy, telecommunication, and education) for business; the state finds capable bureaucrats who select winning sectors; policy tools include export zones, institutional encouragement for saving and strategic credit giving, control over foreign investment, government-private sector consortium to spread technology, and administrative guidance. Although neoclassical economists recognize some of the same state activities as important for economic development, developmental state theorists go much further than infrastructure and market failure.

Developmental state theorists also pay more attention to history, culture, and politics in economic development. For example, Johnson pointed out that Japan's developmental state resulted from its modern history. The U.S. Occupation left economic bureaucracy intact and strengthened as other pillars of prewar power were destroyed.

To intervene effectively in economic activities and to adjust development strategies in a timely fashion and facilitate public interests, the state has to be "strong," measured by insulation from society. By contrast, interest groups compete for and dominate state policy in a weak state. Among the four tigers in East Asia, only Hong Kong adopted a free market approach. In Taiwan and South Korea, the governments were authoritarian. General Park Chung Hee seized power in a military coup in South Korea in 1961. In Taiwan, the Nationalist government knew that the native Taiwanese majority saw them as an outsider government. So both the Taiwanese and South Korean governments turned to economic performance as the basis for legitimizing their political rule and gave techno-bureaucrats much autonomy in formulating economic policy. The Singaporean government engaged in selective intervention in the city state's economy after 1959, with much success.[59] In Indonesia General Suharto established a New Order in 1965, the year that separated the economic stagnation of the previous two decades and the subsequent economic growth. The Suharto government maintained macroeconomic stability, thanks largely to competent technocrats allowed to run the show. But the Indonesian government did not engage in the type of industrial policy seen in South Korea.[60] Some scholars also attribute the success of Indonesia's economic reform in the 1980s to the effective rule of the Suharto government.[61] .

A strong state can mobilize resources for public goods. This is particularly important for late-industrializing countries. Moreover, a strong state is supposed to be able to make painful policy adjustments while weak states cannot because of entrenched domestic interests. In particular, strong state scholars point out East Asia's shift to export-led strategies in the early 1960s and Latin America's inability to do so even though people in that region also came to realize that import-substitution strategies no longer worked. The East Asian state encouraged high savings and used regulations to channel savings into strategic sectors to best position the country in the global market.[62]

The development state has to be credible in its development strategy. Virtually all governments say that they want economic development and may even have documents to show for it, but few are committed to the development goal or are credible to citizens who need to invest in the economy for the government plan to work. Without a private sector believing in the state by betting their money for future gains, the developmental state will not work. To convince the private sector, the government needs to create an external check on its credibility. For example, Taiwan and South Korea's shift to an export-oriented strategy, in which export performance may be viewed objectively, convinced private investors that the state was indeed creating a sound investment environment. Once a country's economy grows, the state will acquire greater credibility among private businessmen.[63]

It is ultimately difficult to prove how effective state intervention has been. To prove that state intervention has worked, one has to prove that state intervention worked as well as a free market would. In fact, state intervention should work even better than the market. However, what would be a good approach in a real world where distortions already exist? The 1993 World Bank miracle study did not provide such a criterion, and there are simply no rigorous studies to prove definitely that government intervention really works.[64] Equally important, we can point out case after case in which an insulated state adopts disastrous policies for the country.

The East Asian experience does not endorse the view that the strong state necessarily promotes economic growth. It is true that the strong state coincided with rapid expansion in Japan, South Korea, Taiwan, and Singapore. But Hong Kong, which is not even a state, has done fabulously well. It is also important to note that the strong state does not necessarily do the right things. A case in point, Marcos justified his 1972 martial law as necessary to centralize decision-making power in the president's hand to promote reforms modeled after the four tigers. However, after some initial attempts, the Marcos administration quickly degenerated into crony capitalism. Rather than promoting industrialization to benefit as large a proportion of population as possible, the Marcos administration rewarded public and private monopolies to politically favored individuals or companies. Unlike South Korea, Taiwan, or Singapore, the Marcos administration lacked coherence or discipline in its economic planning. The socialist states in East Asia monopolized all power in their countries but yielded miserable economic results. The strong state could also make huge mistakes, such as China's Great Leap Forward campaign in the late 1950s.

It is important, however, to study the role of the state in East Asian political economy. Whether or not the state is the source of rapid economic growth, it has been actively involved in economic activities. As such, we need to study the state as a central issue rather than assuming it away.

The East Asian Challenge

Beginning in the early 1980s, some political scientists and regional specialists began challenging the neoclassical interpretations of East Asian economic growth. The developmental state argument was a serious challenge to neoclassical economists. If, as Chalmers Johnson suggested, government is not always inefficient and East Asia has succeeded with active government intervention, what does that say about neoclassical economics?

What made the challenge interesting was the involvement of East Asian bureaucrats and politicians in the 1980s. Japan became a major source of capital for structural adjustment loans through cofinancing arrangements with the World Bank but became frustrated with what the Japanese considered to be a rigid policy prescription based on neoclassical economics. They also began thinking about the Japanese approach to development, which they considered to be insufficiently appreciated by the international aid community. In 1989–1990, when the World Bank asked Japan to terminate a loan to the Philippines because it was inconsistent with the World Bank principle, Japanese officials refused and subsequently raised a broader issue about Japan's positive experience in economic development. They pushed for studies of East Asian experience and helped fund the World Bank's 1993 East Asian economic miracle report.[65]

The report gave a nod to some developmental state arguments by acknowledging that some state interventions may have helped larger East Asian economies like Japan, South Korea, and Taiwan, but it emphasizes that selective intervention was not really effective in general and should not be emulated. Put simply, the East Asian miracle came about mainly because of economic fundamentals and because the East Asian governments were disciplined to avoid rent-seeking behavior by making sure that there is competition for state support. The result of the World Bank's study should not be surprising. After all, the World Bank itself had been providing neoclassical advice to developing nations. It would be a slap in its own face to recognize the importance of state intervention.

The World Bank report generated immediate critiques. While praising the contribution of the report to studies of East Asian development experience, Toru

Yanagihara noted that the study essentially reaffirmed "the World Bank's official system of belief" and believed that selective intervention and industrial policy should have received a more positive assessment.[66] Sanjaya Lall called the report a "flawed work." After all, no one is opposed to getting the fundamentals right or to the importance of exports. Rather, the debate is really about the role of states versus markets in promoting industries and exports. Thus, Lall viewed the World Bank report as lacking an adequate theoretical framework for studying the effects of industrial policy and as having only incomplete evidence.[67] The Japanese wanted to push further the developmental state arguments. They argued that to follow market principles one has to have a market to begin with. In developing nations, one often does not have a real market. The state can play a useful role. Since every country is different, it is wrong to apply one-size-fits-all solutions for all countries.[68]

The ADB published a report titled *Emerging Asia: Changes and Challenges* in May 1997, right before the Asian financial crisis.[69] The report concluded that economic growth results from institutions and policies, and East Asia had done better than other regions because of the differences in institutions and policies. The report showed that export promotion is a good policy while industrial policy is suspect. Some East Asian economies such as Taiwan and South Korea could adopt an industrial policy because they had disciplined bureaucrats and because they operated in an international environment where their action was not noticed that much. By contrast, it is a lot harder now to use those kinds of protectionist measures to promote a particular industrial sector.

The 1997 Asian financial crisis took some steam out of the developmental state arguments. While people had warmed up to the developmental state idea, they now saw crony capitalism. At the same time, along with underperformance by transitional economies in the former communist countries, Latin America, and sub-Saharan Africa, the Asian financial crisis has also been viewed as discrediting the policy prescriptions based on the Washington consensus and leading to a revival of interest in the industrial policies adopted by East Asian economies such as Japan, South Korea, and Taiwan. In response, Marcus Noland and Howard Pack argued in 2003 that evidence does not support the claim that the three East Asian countries' selective industrial policy has been the principal source of their economic performance and that developing nations today cannot hope to emulate East Asia's industrial policy because of changes in the international economic system and differences between contemporary developing nations and the three East Asian economies.[70] The state-versus-the-market debate continues.

What Exactly Explains the East Asian Miracle?

After discussing all these debates, one may ask what would be the best explanation of the East Asian economic development. While debates sharpen our understanding of the miracle and particularly the relative saliency of a particular factor, economic development clearly is a complex process involving a combination of factors. The fact that the East Asian economic miracle has been accomplished by countries of different political regimes shows that there is simply not one single path to economic success. Different economic policies in areas of trade, finance, and exchange rates at different historical moments experienced by East Asian nations reinforce this observation. Thus, we need to discuss a laundry list of "must-dos" for achieving economic growth. We do so because we have no choice. We do so also because this is a textbook that introduces various explanations rather than privileging a particular one. More important, this laundry list points at different issue areas to be discussed later in the book.

For Seiji Naya of the ADB, high-growth Asia includes the following common factors. Macroeconomic stability includes low and stable inflation, stable exchange rates, and stable growth rates. Political stability means stable direction from successive leaders who share the same goals. Good governance is defined as transparent, accountable, and participatory rule under law.[71]

(i) Macroeconomic stability (relative to developing countries in other regions).

(ii) Political stability, policy consistency, and good governance (compared with other developing regions).

(iii) Universal primary education and literacy, and more generally, health and education policies appropriate to the economy's level of development.

(iv) Import-substituting industrialization that was short in duration, limited in scope, and targeted at sectors of emerging comparative advantage. Because Asian policymakers were in general not ideologically committed to a particular trade strategy, they could combine elements of each, often pursuing import-substituting industrialization in one sector and export promotion simultaneously in another.

(v) Openness, not just to trade but to investment and news ideas.

(vi) Following (iv) and (v) above, limited bias against traditional exports, particularly labor-intensive agricultural exports. Thus, agriculture was not neglected or heavily taxed, and agricultural workers (the majority of the labor force and the poor in most economies in the early stages of development) were not impoverished.

(vii) Policies that encouraged savings and investment.

(viii) Infrastructure expansion, financed by governments, donors, and borrowing, augmenting natural geographic advantages.

(ix) A strong "social infrastructure" of community, family, and institutions, sometimes extending across national boundaries (most notably in the case of the Chinese diaspora).

(x) Positive feedback effects from growth in world trade, growth among regional trading partners, expansion of international financial markets/private capital flows to developing countries, and the U.S. security umbrella/cold war aid.

(xi) Geographic advantages based on access to shipping lanes, proximity to one another, and other factors.

This list includes market forces, state intervention, social conditions, and foreign policy. Not much is really left out. However, economic development is not like a perfect storm where everything has to be present and lined up in the right proportion. After all, when one looks at economic successes, not all identified factors are present. In fact, there has been a huge variation among East Asian developmental states in terms of degrees of intervention, the size of economy, and timing of integration with the global market.

A REGIONAL PERSPECTIVE OF EAST ASIAN POLITICAL ECONOMY

Bruce Cumings, one of the leading scholars on East Asian political economy, observed that it is important to adopt a regional perspective and to go beyond single-country studies to understand how these countries have grown economically.[72] As Peter Petri put it, "East Asian economic growth may have been partly induced by regional contacts—including flows of goods, investments, technologies, aspirations and ideas about governance."[73] Mutual learning and regional competition have served to push the whole region forward. Those who adopt a regional perspective also tend to adopt a historical perspective by placing the Asian economic miracle in a historical context. Put simply, we should emphasize the sequence of economic development in the region. Factually, some empirical studies on the impact of initial conditions have shown that being part of Asia contributes to faster economic growth while controlling for other factors.[74]

Flying Geese Formation

Two main regional perspective theories are the product cycle theory and flying geese formation theory. The flying geese formation theory is distinctly Japanese. This theory predated the product cycle theory to be discussed later. Akamatsu Kaname came up with the analogy of the flying geese formation (*ganko keitai*) in the late 1930s. Akamatsu studied the textile industry and concluded that there was a flying geese formation of import, domestic production, and export for less developed countries. The cycle starts with introduction of new products and technologies into a less developed country. That country achieves "homogeneous industries" over time and also acquires the related capital goods industries. The country then enters the third stage of exports. Such a process resembles an inverse V formation of wild geese for developing nations.[75]

Raymond Vernon introduced the product cycle theory in the 1960s.[76] Unlike Akamatsu who studied industrial sectors, Vernon focused on individual firms. Vernon studied how the life cycle of a product affects the competitiveness of a firm and the location of production in developed nations. In the first stage, innovative products come out of developed countries and are exported to other countries. In the second stage, foreign producers start imitating the technologies. Exports begin to slow and the innovating company launches foreign direct investment to secure foreign markets. In the last stage, as production techniques for the product mature, production and labor costs become important. The innovating country now imports the product from abroad. Vernon's theory is used to explain why foreign direct investment takes place.

Some scholars have combined the flying geese formation, the product cycle theory, and comparative advantage to chart East Asia's regional development.[77] The flying geese formation now refers mainly to a catch-up product cycle pattern whereby industries pass from Japan to the four tigers, to ASEAN countries, and to China. Japan is the head goose, and the followers benefit from Japan in terms of industrial technologies and receive industries it sheds due to a loss of comparative advantage in these industries. The followers will become more sophisticated in an orderly fashion. In a widely cited paper, Bruce Cumings argued that the product cycle theory explains East Asia's rapid industrialization and traced that process to Japan's success in modernization and Japanese colonialism.[78]

The flying geese formation is different from both dependency and liberal arguments. The flying geese formation is different from the dependency school in that it allows less developed countries to become industrialized. It also incorporates the notion of comparative advantages. On the other hand, there is an implicit hierarchy, with Japan as the lead goose. The defenders suggest that the formation could be flattened or even have the head goose replaced.

Some scholars have challenged the flying geese formation theory. Mitchell Bernard and John Ravenhill argued that the theory does not describe accurately what is happening in East Asian political economy.[79] Homogenization of industry has not taken place. Japan remains the center of innovation in the same sector or industry. Taiwan and South Korea remain dependent on Japanese technologies. The product cycle theory assumes a "steady state" of product, an assumption that scholars now question. Innovation on the product and production process often continues because there are different generations of the same product. With new process technologies, it is possible to provide nonstandardized products for specialist markets on a short run. Complexity and rapid pace of technological progress mean that it is difficult to use reverse engineering as a way to catch up. Facing current account deficits, debt problems, and declining official flows in the mid-1980s, Southeast Asian nations embraced Japanese and NIE investments. Unlike in Taiwan and South Korea, Japanese firms had a higher degree of control over their technologies. As a result, they were comfortable in bringing their more advanced technologies to the region. Japanese suppliers followed, recreating the Japanese networks in Southeast Asia. Moreover, as Andrew MacIntyre and Barry Naughton argued, a Japan-led regional economy lasted for only a short period of time and can no longer explain East Asian regional economy after the mid-1990s.[80]

Regional Integration and Learning

Regional integration, as will be discussed in greater detail in the following chapters, has provided incentives for countries to emulate each other and reform their economies. A main feature of East Asian political economy since the late 1970s was the transition of socialist economies to market economies. Regional integration provided explicit incentives for Vietnam, Cambodia, and Laos.[81] In fact, ASEAN used regional integration as an incentive to integrate Indochina into its structure.

A regional effect is also reflected in countries learning from each other. South Korea and Taiwan tried to emulate Japan selectively while paying attention to the lessons of Japanese development experience.[82] Southeast Asia also looked to Japan for inspiration and experiences. In fact, Singapore's Lee Kuan Yew started a "Learn-from-Japan Campaign" in 1981, and Malaysia's Mahathir launched his "Look East Policy" later in December. Both leaders sought to emulate Japan's success, while Mahathir took a stronger anti-West tone in his campaign. Both policies met public criticism that Japan's experiences and institutions were too different to be transplanted to Southeast Asia, with Lee toning down his policy and Mahathir charging forward.[83] One does not need a serious national campaign for learning to take place. The Taiwanese and South Korean governments never launched any national campaigns to learn from Japan. The four tigers also became role models for other East Asian countries. Malaysia, for instance, launched a heavy industrialization drive in the early 1980s modeled after South Korea's heavy industrialization success in the 1970s.[84]

China launched reforms in the late 1970s partly due to awareness of the economic successes of Japan and other East Asian economies. For example, Mainland China had GDP per capita of $537 (in 1990 dollars) compared with Hong Kong's $2,499 in 1952, but the gap widened to $979 to $9,246 in 1978.[85] We know that Vietnam tried to emulate China's economic reform. North Korea adopted a Foreign Joint Venture Law in 1984 to attract foreign investment, which was modeled after China's 1979 joint venture law.[86] North Korea adopted reform measures to decentralize administration in 1998 and economic reform measures in July 2002.[87] North Korea has lost economic competition with South Korea. While North Korea began with a stronger manufacturing base than South Korea before the end of the Second World War, it has become a backwater economically while South Korea has become a first-world economic power.

THE UNITED STATES AND EAST ASIAN POLITICAL ECONOMY

The East Asian economic miracle cannot be viewed as solely an economic phenomenon. Rather, it has taken place in the larger international political and security environment. Economic affairs and national security affairs are reciprocal in the long run. It is thus important to understand the U.S. factor in East Asian political economy.[88] The U.S. role in East Asian political economy has gone through three stages: maintaining hegemony over half of East Asia through the early 1970s, acting as a coleader with Japan in the 1980s and early 1990s and managing China's rise since the early 1990s, and watching the development of East Asian regional integration with a certain wariness since the late 1990s.

The U.S. Hegemony

The U.S. hegemony is not a sufficient condition for the East Asian miracle. Not all countries allied with the United States have achieved economic success. The real question is whether the U.S. hegemony has been a necessary condition. One way to think about the positive effect of the United States on the East Asian miracle is that the early successful economies were all allies of the United States and were thus provided with military protection, financial assistance, access to the U.S. market, and supplies of crude oil and other natural resources. The economic success of the "free Asia" versus the failure of the socialist camp was a piece of the puzzle of why communism failed and the cold war ended.

The East Asian miracle began during the cold war and in the context of U.S. hegemony.[89] Through the early 1970s, East Asia was divided into two camps: the free world and the communist bloc. The Korean War and the Vietnam War decided where the line was drawn. South Korea, Japan, Taiwan, the Philippines, Indonesia, Malaysia, Singapore, and Thailand belonged to the free world. North Korea, China, and Indochina belonged to the communist bloc.

Japan was dependent on the United States for security, oil, food, technologies, and market. The American Occupation authorities introduced economic measures to break up industrial concentration, which allowed greater competition. The Americans also introduced land reform, which improved agricultural production.

The American effort to democratize labor allowed higher wages for workers and thus greater domestic consumption. All these measures laid the foundation for Japan's rapid growth in later years.[90] The United States was also instrumental in shaping postwar Japanese political economy. The American Occupation authorities destroyed the military and weakened the prewar conglomerate *zaibatsu* but left the economic bureaucracy intact. In fact, now Japanese bureaucrats acquired greater ability to control the Japanese business community, something they had not been able to do before the war. With this autonomy, Japanese bureaucrats adopted the neomercantilist policies to restrict foreign imports and foreign investments while promoting exports to the rest of the world.[91]

The United States helped to conduct land reform in both Taiwan and South Korea, using aid as leverage. It was easier in Taiwan and South Korea to conduct land reform than in the Philippines or Latin America because of wars. The Chinese Nationalist government was an outsider government in Taiwan. The brief North Korean occupation in 1950 significantly weakened the power of landlords in the south. Through the early 1960s, both Taiwan and South Korea adopted import-substitution strategies and received significant economic and military aid from the United States. South Korea received $6 billion in 1946–1978 in economic aid. Taiwan and South Korea received $9.05 billion in military aid from the United States.[92] South Korea also received a significant amount of foreign exchange from the American forces and American procurements, which exceeded the country's merchandise exports in 1960–1961.[93]

The United States facilitated the flying geese formation discussed earlier by helping forge Japan's close economic ties with Taiwan, South Korea, and Southeast Asia. Once the U.S. government decided to rebuild Japan rather than punishing it, the American planners had two major concerns. One was the hegemonic concern to make sure that Japan would remain subordinate to the United States. The other was a hinterland concern, to find outlets for Japanese exports. China was Japan's largest trading partner before the war. Without access to Chinese materials and market, alternative sources had to be found in Southeast Asia. France and Britain did not like that idea because they wanted to maintain their colonial possessions in Southeast Asia, but the United States was not interested in supporting European colonial empires in Asia.[94] Japan's efforts to reconnect with Taiwan and South Korea were made easier by the fact that the United States was the protector for all three allies.

The U.S. wars in East Asia also benefited its allies economically. Japanese economic recovery received a major boost from U.S. procurement for the Korean War. Japan particularly benefited from the hard currencies earned, $590 million in 1951 and more than $800 million in 1952 and 1953, which accounted for 60 to 70 percent of Japanese exports at the time.[95] Other countries have also benefited from the Korean War. Malaysia, for instance, gained from a sharp rise in commodity prices for strategic materials such as rubber and tin.[96] Japan benefited proportionally less than other allies from the Vietnam War. Thailand's total earnings from U.S. military bases and from the "rest and recreation" expenditure of the U.S. military personnel increased from $27 million in 1963 to $318 million in 1968, equaling 45 percent of Thailand's exports and 5.8 percent of GDP that year.[97]

Starting in the early 1980s, the United States put pressure on its East Asian allies to liberalize their trade and finance. While negotiations appeared painfully drawn out at the time, American pressure did contribute to the liberalization of these economies, which in turn facilitated trade expansion and rising living standards.

In some way, the United States continues to be a dominant player in East Asian political economy. The United States was and still is the principal export market for East Asia. After the mid-1980s Japanese foreign direct investment in East Asia led to a greater share of manufactured products back to Japan, but it became clear in short order that Japan would not replace the United States as the destination market. There was a triangle of Japan, East Asia, and the United States, with the United States ending up with deficits. When the Asian financial crisis devastated major southeastern countries and South Korea, it was the United States rather than Japan that absorbed the distress goods from the region. While China has become a major market for East Asians, much of that is assembled for the final stop in the United States, a cycle that explains why China's surpluses with the United States ballooned while the surpluses of the rest of East Asia decreased proportionally.

Managing Rivals

Japan became the second largest economy in the free world in 1968 and was thus no longer a semiperiphery to the United States in economic terms. Japan also became a significant foreign aid donor in the 1970s, with virtually everything going to East Asia in the early stage. By the 1980s, Japan came to compete with the United States for economic dominance in East Asia. By the late 1980s, many in the United States and East Asia felt that Japan had replaced the United States as the economic leader in East Asia.

The United States responded with trade retaliation based on the notion of fair trade and put pressure on Japan, Taiwan, and South Korea to open their markets.[98] Negotiations were difficult, and it appeared at the time that little progress was made. In retrospect, however, things added up. The United States regained much ground. U.S. pressure also affected the shape of East Asian political economy. The Plaza Accord reached in 1985 to appreciate the yen against the dollar to reduce Japanese trade surpluses with the United States and the world resulted in a flood of Japanese investment to Southeast Asia. The U.S. pressure on South Korea and Taiwan in later years had the similar effect of channeling their investment to Southeast Asia and then China. In the 1990s, fortunes were reversed between Japan and the United States. The United States enjoyed a decade of economic boom while Japan was in an economic quagmire. Japan remains a formidable competitor, particularly its internationally competitive large firms. But U.S. attention is now turning to China.

Although China began growing rapidly after Deng Xiaoping launched the economic reform in 1979, people really began to pay close attention after the mid-1990s. China grew rapidly while the rest of East Asia slowed down. The country now has significant trade surpluses, and made-in-China products flood the world market. Foreign capital has flown to China, making the country one of the largest destinations of foreign capital.

We have discussed earlier in the chapter the hegemonic and hinterland considerations in U.S. thinking about Japan in the late 1940s. The two questions also apply to China. First, will China act as a hegemon, and what does that mean for East Asia and global political economy? Second, where will Chinese products go and where will China get natural resources? For both questions, it has become increasingly clear since the Asian financial crisis that China is an emerging great power in East Asia and is turning Southeast Asia and parts of the world into its hinterland for markets and resources.

Despite heated debates over China policy, the U.S. government has largely maintained an engagement policy toward China. The thrust of the policy is to integrate China into the global system. The United States controls some entry points. In particular, the United States could block China's accession to the WTO. By insisting on stringent conditions for China's membership, the U.S. policy helped to shape China's domestic political economy because it made it easier for foreign firms to participate in Chinese economy in a way far greater than in Japan and South Korea. Using its position as the largest source of Chinese trade surpluses and advanced technologies, the United States continues to exert pressure on China over a wide range of issues such as intellectual properties and exchange rates.

At the same time, the United States tries to influence the nature of China's interaction with the rest of the world.[99] The United States wants to maintain its primacy in East Asia and will work to deny China or any other countries a hegemonic position in East Asia, an economically and strategically important region in the world. The United States has adopted a hedging strategy of enhancing alliances with Japan and some key countries around China to deter a rising China. Put simply, by maintaining a strong military presence in East Asia and by controlling the shipping lanes for oil and goods, the United States is essentially creating a situation in which it is in China's own interest to focus on economic development rather than military adventures over Taiwan or territorial disputes with Japan, which would have a devastating effect on East Asian economy.

The United States and East Asian Regionalism

The United States was not that enthusiastic about regional integration, which partly explains the weak institutionalization of the region. U.S. dominance in the early years made it less necessary for its Asian allies to seek regional cooperation. Therefore, emerging regionalism since the end of the cold war partially resulted from a relative decline of U.S. hegemony in East Asia.[100] There was a view in East Asia that East Asian countries were justified to create their grouping given the efforts by the United States to form free trade agreements in North America, which might extend to South America.

China's rise factors heavily in American attitude toward East Asian regionalism at present. The U.S. position is becoming clearer with the regional efforts to create an East Asians–only grouping, which would mean a Chinese leadership. The U.S. displeasure, facilitated by Japan and other countries, has slowed down the process of regional integration, as will be discussed in Chapter 11. Looking into the near future, the nature and dynamic of U.S.-China relations and how regionalism will play out will be central to developments in East Asian political economy.

THE POLITICAL ECONOMY OF GROWTH

The economic growth in East Asia naturally makes one wonder how economic growth relates to politics. As should be made abundantly clear in my discussion above, the nature of East Asian politics has a profound impact on economic development. The capitalist system has won the competition against the socialist system in East Asia. While it is debatable whether the strong developmental state is a necessary condition for economic growth, the strong state and fast economic growth have largely correlated with each other in East Asia. Countries need to have a national consensus on economic development before they can do anything about it. Japan settled on an income-doubling strategy in 1961 after divisive politics over the alliance in the 1950s. Taiwan and South Korea turned to economic development in the early 1960s whereas they had previously focused more on survival and unification. China shifted attention from class struggle to economic development in the late 1970s. Moreover, a country's development strategy matters, as shown in East Asia's shift from import substitution to export promotion.

International politics affects economic growth. The American hegemony has contributed to the economic development of America's allies and friends. For Taiwan and South Korea, the cold war security reality was an important reason for the governments to mobilize resources to achieve economic growth as a matter of life and death. The security imperative also shaped the relationship between the state and the society, leading to the rise of the developmental state in Northeast Asia.[101] After a painful breakup with Malaysia and concern about serious unemployment threatening the country's political stability, Singapore saw rapid industrialization as central for its political survival.[102] With economic sanctions on China, Hong Kong had no choice but to turn to the global market in the 1950s. As a British colony, Hong Kong enjoyed an easy access to the British Commonwealth markets. Much of the capital and technologies flooded to the islands by refugees, particularly those from Shanghai, who fled from victorious communists in mainland China.

Economic development also affects politics. Starting with Martin Lipset in the 1950s, it has often been suggested that economic development leads to democratization.[103] But Samuel Huntington showed in the late 1960s that a transition period from developing to developed world often leads to political instability as people's expectations grow faster than the actual economic growth, which explains why one could observe the rise of military-techno authoritarian regimes in the world.[104] Huntington's thesis was borne out empirically in East Asia at the time. In South Korea, General Park Chung Hee justified his authoritarian regime on the inability of the old regime to end economic stagnation and achieve economic growth. To achieve economic growth, Park believed that the state should promote and control "millionaires" and used economic planning to achieve long-term goals of prosperity and income equality.[105] Ferdinand Marcos justified his martial law imposed on the Philippines in 1972 as necessary for achieving economic growth modeled after the Asian tigers. His message was taken seriously as some key technocrats joined the administration on that basis and the international aid and financial communities gave his administration initial strong support.[106]

When scholars came to talk about a global wave of democratization starting in the late 1980s, they were divided over whether economic development or political factors explained this global phenomenon. After all, democratization broke through in some economically underdeveloped countries.

Harold Crouch and James Morley proposed a reasonable analytical framework, what they called "the driven by growth model," to explain the dynamic between economic and political development. They argued that economic growth leads to social mobilization to political mobilization to regime change. Put simply, economic growth unleashes new social forces that become political overtime. These new social and political dynamics lead to regime change, although not necessarily democratization. While the authors avoided sounding deterministic about economic growth leading to full democracy, they pointed out such a general trend in East Asia.[107] There is no question that democracy has gained ground in East Asia in recent years and that economic growth, while not a sufficient condition, has clearly contributed to this transition.

CONCLUSION

East Asia has grown rapidly and has been transformed into a far more sophisticated economy. Most East Asian governments have been heavily interventionist but in a way that encourages exports after the early 1960s. The state-market interaction is at the core of the explanation for the East Asian economic miracle. The market was clearly important. Those East Asian nations that did not embrace the market did not fare well. At the same time, the state was also important in explaining the East Asian economic success in that it has gone beyond providing infrastructure, training labor force, and maintaining a good business environment. The East Asian miracle has been a regional phenomenon, with much mutual learning and positive externalities. The East Asian economic miracle has also taken place in the larger international environment, namely the cold war competition, U.S. hegemony, and a liberalizing global economic order. Last but not the least, whereas economic growth is not a sufficient condition for democratization, the East Asian experience does show a general tendency of rising income level leading to more responsible governance.

SUGGESTED READINGS

Asian Development Bank. *Emerging Asia: Changes and Challenges* (Manila: Asian Development Bank, 1997).

Balassa, Bela. *The Newly Industrializing Economies in the World Economy* (New York: Pergamon Press, 1981).

Berger, Peter L., and Michael Hsin-Huang Hsiao, eds. *In Search of an East Asian Development Model* (New Brunswick, N.J.: Transaction, 1988).

Bernard, Mitchell, and John Ravenhill. "Beyond Product Cycles and Flying Geese: Regionalization, Hierarchy, and the Industrialization of East Asia." *World Politics* 47, no. 2 (January 1995): 171–209.

Booth, Anne. "Initial Conditions and Miraculous Growth: Why Is South East Asia Different from Taiwan and South Korea?" *World Development* 27, no. 2 (February 1999): 301–321.

Chan, Anita, Benedict J. Tria Kerkvliet, and Jonathan Unger, eds. *Transforming Asian Socialism: China and Vietnam Compared* (Lanham, Md.: Rowman and Littlefield, 1999).

Chan, Steve, Cal Clark, and Danny Lam, eds. *Beyond the Developmental State: East Asia's Political Economies Reconsidered* (New York: St. Martin's Press, 1998).

Crone, Donald. "Does Hegemony Matter? The Reorganization of the Pacific Political Economy." *World Politics* 45, no. 4 (July 1993): 501–525.

Fei, John C.H., Gustav Ranis, Shirley W.Y. Kuo, with Yu-Yuan Bian and Julia Chang Collins. *Growth with Equity: The Taiwan Case* (New York: Oxford University Press, 1979).

Gray, H. Peter. "Culture and Economic Performance: Policy as an Intervening Variable." *Journal of Comparative Economics* 23, no. 3 (December 1996): 278–291.

Haggard, Stephan, and Euysung Kim. "The Sources of East Asia's Economic Growth." *Access Asia Review* 1, no. 1 (August 1997).

Haggard, Stephan. *Pathways from the Periphery: Politics of Growth in the Newly Industrializing Countries* (Ithaca: Cornell University Press, 1990).

Hsieh, Chang-Tai. "What Explains the Industrial Revolution in East Asia? Evidence from Factor Markets." *American Economic Review* 92, no. 3 (June 2002): 502–526.

Huff, W. G. *The Economic Growth of Singapore: Trade and Development in the Twentieth Century* (Cambridge: Cambridge University Press, 1994).

Hughes, Helen, ed. *Achieving Industrialization in East Asia* (Cambridge: Cambridge University Press, 1988).

Katzenstein, Peter J. *A World of Regions: Asia and Europe in the American Imperium* (Ithaca: Cornell University Press, 2005).

Krugman, Paul. "The Myth of Asia's Miracle." *Foreign Affairs* 73, no. 6 (November/December 1994): 62–78.

Lardy, Nicholas R. *Integrating China into the Global Economy* (Washington, D.C.: Brookings Institution Press, 2002).

Morley, James M., ed. *Driven by Growth: Political Change in the Asia-Pacific Region*, rev. ed. (Armonk, N.Y.: M. E. Sharpe, 1999).

Naya, Seiji F. *The Asian Development Experience: Overcoming Crises and Adjusting to Change* (Hong Kong: Asian Development Bank, 2002).

Noland, Marcus, and Howard Pack, *Industrial Policy in an Era of Globalization: Lessons from Asia* (Washington, D.C.: Institute for International Economics, 2003).

Ohno, Kenichi, and Izumi Ohno, eds. *Japanese Views on Economic Development: Diverse Paths to the Market* (London: Routledge, 1998).

Perkins, Dwight H. "There Are at Least Three Models of East Asian Development." *World Development* 22, no. 4 (April 1994): 655–661.

Petri, Peter A. *The Lessons of East Asia: Common Foundations of East Asian Success* (Washington, D.C.: World Bank, 1993).

Rawski, Thomas T. "What Is Happening to China's GDP Statistics?" *China Economic Review* 12, no. 4 (Annual 2001): 347–354.

Vogel, Ezra F. *The Four Little Dragons: The Spread of Industrialization in East Asia* (Cambridge: Harvard University Press, 1991).

Wade, Robert. *Governing the Market: Economic Theory and the Role of Government in East Asian Industrialization* (Princeton: Princeton University Press, 1990).

Wang, Shaoguang, and Angang Hu. *The Political Economy of Uneven Development: The Case of China* (Armonk, N.Y.: M.E. Sharpe, 1999).

Woo, Wing Thye. "The Art of Economic Development: Markets, Politics, and Externalities." *International Organization* 44, no. 3 (Summer 1990): 403–429.

World Bank. *The East Asian Miracle: Economic Growth and Public Policy* (New York: Oxford University Press, 1993).

Zoellick, Robert B. "Economics and Security in the Changing Asia-Pacific." *Survival* 39, no. 4 (Winter 1997–98): 29–51.

NOTES

1. World Bank, *The East Asian Miracle: Economic Growth and Public Policy* (New York: Oxford University Press, 1993), 2.
2. World Bank, *Global Economic Prospects: Economic Implications of Remittances and Migration* (Washington, D.C.: World Bank, 2006), 8.
3. World Bank, *East Asian Miracle*, 2–4.
4. John C. H. Fei, Gustav Ranis, Shirley W. Y. Kuo, with Yu-Yuan Bian and Julia Chang Collins, *Growth with Equity: The Taiwan Case* (New York: Oxford University Press, 1979); Edward S. Mason et al., *The Economic and Social Modernization of the Republic of Korea* (Cambridge: Harvard University Press, 1980).
5. Wang Shaoguang and Angang Hu, *The Political Economy of Uneven Development: The Case of China* (Armonk, N.Y.: M.E. Sharpe, 1999).
6. UNDP, *Human Development Report 2001* (New York: UNDP, 2001), 183.
7. UNDP, *Human Development Report 2006* (New York: UNDP, 2006), 336.
8. Calculated from Table 1.3 in World Bank, *Global Economic Prospects,* 9.
9. Nathan Rosenberg, and L. E. Birdzell Jr., *How the West Grew Rich: The Economic Transformation of the Industrial World* (New York: Basic Books, 1986), 6–9.
10. Maddison, *World Economy,* 260.
11. Gunnar Myrdal, *Asian Drama: An Inquiry into the Poverty of Nations* (New York: Twentieth Century Fund, 1968).
12. Simon S. Kuznets, "Economic Growth and Income Inequality," *American Economic Review* 45, no. 1 (March 1955): 1–28. See also Irma Adelman and Cynthia Talf Morris, *Economic Growth and Social Equity in Developing Countries* (Stanford: Stanford University Press, 1973), 187–189.

13. UNDP, *Human Development Report 1997* (New York: UNDP, 1997), 146. In 2004, the United Kingdom ($30,821) caught up with Hong Kong ($30,822) while surpassing Singapore ($28,077). UNDP, *Human Development Report 2006*, 283.

14. UNDP, *Human Development Report 2006*, 283–286.

15. Paul Krugman, "The Myth of Asia's Miracle," *Foreign Affairs* 73, no. 6 (November/December 1994): 62–78.

16. Alwyn Young, "Lessons from the East Asian NICs: A Contrarian View," *European Economic Review* 38, no. 3–4 (April 1994): 964–973 and "The Tyranny of Numbers: Confronting the Statistical Realities of the East Asian Growth Experience," *Quarterly Journal of Economics* 110, no. 3 (August 1995): 641–680.

17. Jong-il Kim and Lawrence J. Lau, "The Sources of Economic Growth of the East Asian Newly Industrializing Countries," *Journal of the Japanese and International Economies* 8, no. 3 (1994): 235–271.

18. Stephan Haggard and Euysung Kim, "The Sources of East Asia's Economic Growth," *Access Asia Review* 1, no. 1 (August 1997).

19. World Bank, *East Asian Miracle*, 46–69. The study recognized Young's finding on Singapore.

20. Seiji F. Naya, *The Asian Development Experience: Overcoming Crises and Adjusting to Change* (Hong Kong: Asian Development Bank, 2002), 37–44.

21. Chang-Tai Hsieh, "What Explains the Industrial Revolution in East Asia? Evidence from Factor Markets," *American Economic Review* 92, no. 3 (June 2002): 502–526.

22. Thomas T. Rawski, "What Is Happening to China's GDP Statistics?" *China Economic Review* 12, no. 4 (Annual 2001): 347–354.

23. Xinhua News Agency, December 20, 2005, http://finance.sina.com.cn/g/20051220/11152213055.shtml.

24. China News Agency, January 9, 2006, www.chinanews.com.cn/news/2006/2006-01-09/8/675577.shtml.

25. "A Survey of the World Economy," *The Economist*, October 2, 2004, 4.

26. Martin Fransman, ed., *Global Broadband Battle: Why the U.S. and Europe Lag While Asia Leads* (Stanford: Stanford University Press, 2006).

27. Ronald I. McKinnon, "Government Deficits and the Deindustrialization of America," *The Economists' Voice* 1, no. 3 (2004): 1, www.bepress.com/ev.

28. Dwight H. Perkins, "There Are at Least Three Models of East Asian Development," *World Development* 22, no. 4 (April 1994): 656.

29. World Economic Forum, www.weforum.org/site/homepublic.nsf/Content/Global+Competitiveness+Programme%5CGlobal+Competitiveness+Report.

30. John McMillan and Barry Naughton, eds., *Reforming Asian Socialism* (Ann Arbor: University of Michigan Press, 1996).

31. Harry Harding, *China's Second Revolution: Reform After Mao* (Washington, D.C.: Brookings Institution, 1987); Susan L. Shirk, *The Political Logic of Economic Reform in China* (Berkeley: University of California Press, 1993); Nicholas R. Lardy, *Integrating China into the Global Economy* (Washington, D.C.: Brookings Institution, 2002).

32. OECD, *Economic Survey of China 2005* (Paris: OECD, 2005), 81–86.

33. Melanie Beresford and Dang Phong, *Economic Transition in Vietnam: Trade and Aid in the Demise of a Centrally Planned Economy* (Northampton, Mass.: Edward Elgar, 2001); Anita Chan, Benedict J. Tria Kerkvliet, and Jonathan Unger, eds., *Transforming Asian Socialism: China and Vietnam Compared* (Lanham, Md.: Rowman and Littlefield, 1999); James W. Morley and Masashi Nishihara, eds., *Vietnam Joins the World* (Armonk, N.Y.: M. E. Sharpe, 1997).

34. Yves Bourdet, *The Economics of Transition in Laos: From Socialism to ASEAN Integration* (Northampton, Mass.: Edward Elgar, 2000); Toshiyasu Kato, Jeffrey A. Kaplan, Chan Sophal, and Real Sopheap, *Cambodia: Enhancing Governance for Sustainable Development* (Manila: Asian Development Bank, 2000); Ronald Bruce St. John, *Revolution, Reform, and Regionalism in Southeast Asia: Cambodia, Laos, and Vietnam* (New York: Routledge, 2005).

35. Doowon Lee, "North Korean Economic Reform: Past Efforts and Future Prospects," in *Reforming Asian Socialism,* ed. John McMillan and Barry Naughton (Ann Arbor: University of Michigan Press, 1996), 317–336; Chang-Ho Yoon and Lawrence J. Lau, eds., *North Korea in Transition: Prospects for Economic and Social Reform* (Northampton, Mass.: Edward Elgar, 2001); Young Whan Kihl and Hong Nack Kim, eds., *North Korea: The Politics of Regime Survival* (Armonk, N.Y.: M. E. Sharpe, 2006).

36. Perkins, "There Are at Least Three Models of East Asian Development." See also Anne Booth, "Initial Conditions and Miraculous Growth: Why Is South East Asia Different from Taiwan and South Korea?" *World Development* 27, no. 2 (February 1999): 301–321.

37. H. Peter Gray, "Culture and Economic Performance: Policy as an Intervening Variable," *Journal of Comparative Economics* 23, no. 3 (December 1996): 278–291; Ronald Dore, *Taking Japan Seriously: A Confucian Perspective on Leading Economic Issues* (Stanford: Stanford University Press, 1987); Tu Wei-Ming, ed., *Confucian Traditions in East Asian Modernity: Moral Education and Economic Culture in Japan and the Four Mini-Dragons* (Cambridge: Harvard University Press, 1996); Gilbert Rozman, *The East Asian Region: Confucian Heritage and Its Modern Adaptation* (Princeton: Princeton University Press, 1991); Francis Fukuyama, *Trust: The Social Virtues and the Creation of Prosperity* (New York: Free Press, 1995); Lawrence E. Harrison and Samuel P. Huntington, eds.,

Culture Matters: How Values Shape Human Progress (New York: Basic Books, 2000).

38. For a summary of the four schools of explanations, see Peter A. Petri, *The Lessons of East Asia: Common Foundations of East Asian Success* (Washington, D.C.: World Bank, 1993).

39. Bela Balassa, *The Newly Industrializing Economies in the World Economy* (New York: Pergamon Press, 1981); Anne O. Krueger, "The Experience and Lessons of Asia's Superior Exporters," in *Export-Oriented Development Strategies: The Success of Five Newly Industrializing Countries,* ed. Vittorio Corbo, Anne O. Kueger, and Fernando Ossa (Boulder: Westview Press, 1985), 187–248; Helen Hughes, ed., *Achieving Industrialization in East Asia* (Cambridge: Cambridge University Press, 1988).

40. World Bank, *East Asian Miracle,* 5.

41. Robert Gilpin, *Global Political Economy: Understanding the International Economic Order* (Princeton: Princeton University Press, 2001), 46–76.

42. Iyanatul Islam and Anis Chowdhury, *The Political Economy of East Asia: Post-Crisis Debates* (New York: Oxford University Press, 2000), 5–7.

43. For evolving theories of development, see Wing Thye Woo, "The Art of Economic Development: Markets, Politics, and Externalities," *International Organization* 44, no. 3 (Summer 1990): 403–429; Paul Krugman, "Cycles of Conventional Wisdom on Economic Development," *International Affairs* 71, no. 4 (October 1995): 717–732; Ian M. D. Little, *Economic Development: Theory, Policy, and International Relations* (New York: Basic Books, 1982).

44. Gunnar Myrdal, *Asian Drama: An Inquiry into the Poverty of Nations,* condensed by Seth S. King (New York: Pantheon Books, 1971); Raul Prebisch, *The Economic Development of Latin America and its Principal Problems* (New York: United Nations, 1950); Hans W. Singer, "The Distribution of Gains Between Investing and Borrowing Countries," *American Economic Review* 40, no. 2 (May 1950): 473–485.

45. Robert M. Solow, "A Contribution to the Theory of Economic Growth," *The Quarterly Journal of Economics* 70, no. 1 (February 1956): 65–94; Trevor Swan, "Economic Growth and Capital Accumulation," *The Economic Record* 32 (November 1956): 334–361.

46. Ian M. D. Little, Tibor Scitovksy, and Maurice Scott, *Industry and Trade in Some Developing Countries: A Comparative Perspective* (Oxford: Oxford University Press, 1970).

47. Anne O. Krueger, *Foreign Trade Regimes and Economic Development: Liberalization Attempts and Consequences* (New York: National Bureau of Economic Research, 1978).

48. Asian Development Bank, *Southeast Asia's Economy in the 1970s* (New York: Praeger, 1971).

49. Ronald I. McKinnon, *Money and Capital in Economic Development* (Washington, D.C.: Brookings Institution, 1973).

50. Gary S. Fields, "Employment, Income Distribution, and Growth in Seven Small Open Economies," *Economic Journal* 94, no. 373 (March 1984): 74–83.

51. John Williamson, "What Washington Means by Policy Reform," in *Latin American Adjustment: How Much Has Happened?*, ed. John Williamson (Washington, D.C.: Institute for International Economics, 1990), 7–38.

52. Paul M. Romer, "Increasing Returns and Long-Run Growth," *Journal of Political Economy* 94, no. 5 (October 1986): 1002–1037; Robert E. Lucas, "On the Mechanics of Economic Development," *Journal of Monetary Economics* 22, no. 1 (July 1988): 3–42.

53. Gene M. Grossman and Elhanan Helpman, *Innovation and Growth in the Global Economy* (Cambridge: MIT Press, 1991); Philippe Aghion and Peter Howitt, "A Model of Growth Through Creative Destruction," *Econometrica* 60, no. 2 (March 1992): 323–351.

54. Chung H. Lee and Seiji Naya, "Trade in East Asian Development with Comparative Reference to Southeast Asian Experience," *Economic Development and Cultural Change* 36, no. 3 (April 1988 Supp.): S123–S152.

55. Mancur Olson, *The Rise and Decline of Nations: Economic Growth, Stagflation, and Social Rigidities* (New Haven: Yale University Press, 1982).

56. Chalmers Johnson, *MITI and the Japanese Economic Miracle: The Growth of Industrial Policy, 1925–1975* (Stanford: Stanford University Press, 1982).

57. Chalmers Johnson, "Political Institutions and Economic Performance: The Government-Business Relations in Japan, South Korea, and Taiwan," in *Asian Economic Development: Present and Future*, ed. Robert A. Scalapino, Seizaburo Sato, and Jusuf Wanandi (Berkeley: University of California, 1985), 63–89.

58. Alice H. Amsden, *Asia's Next Giant: South Korea and Late Industrialization* (London: Oxford University Press, 1989); Wade, *Governing the Market*; Stephan Haggard, *Pathways from the Periphery: Politics of Growth in the Newly Industrializing Countries* (Ithaca, N.Y.: Cornell University Press, 1990). Also see Steve Chan, Cal Clark, and Danny Lam, eds., *Beyond the Developmental State: East Asia's Political Economies Reconsidered* (New York: St. Martin's Press, 1998).

59. W. G. Huff, *The Economic Growth of Singapore: Trade and Development in the Twentieth Century* (Cambridge: Cambridge University Press, 1994).

60. Anne Booth, *The Indonesian Economy in the Nineteenth and Twentieth Centuries: A History of Missed Opportunities* (London: Macmillan, 1998).

61. Iwan J. Azis, "Indonesia," in *The Political Economy of Policy Reform,* ed. John Williamson (Washington, D.C.: Institute for International Economics, 1993), 397–400.

62. Leroy Jones and Il SaKong, *Government Business and Entrepreneurship in Economic Development: The Korean Case* (Cambridge: Harvard University Press, 1980).

63. W. G. Huff, G. Dewit, and C. Oughton, "Building the Developmental State: Achieving Economic Growth Through Co-operative Solutions: A Comment on Bringing Politics Back In," *Journal of Development Studies* 38, no. 1 (October 2001): 147–151.

64. For a discussion of tests of government intervention, see Perkins, "There Are at Least Three Models of East Asian Development," 658–659.

65. Anne Emig, "Japan's Challenge to the World Bank: An Attempt at Intellectual Contribution," *The Japanese Economy* 27, no. 1 (January–February 1999): 46–96.

66. Toru Yanagihara, "Anything New in the Miracle Report? Yes and No," *World Development* 22, no. 4 (April 1994): 670.

67. Sanjaya Lall, "The East Asian Miracle: Does the Bell Toll for Industrial Strategy?" *World Development* 22, no. 4 (April 1994): 645–654.

68. For an overview of Japanese views, see Kenichi Ohno and Izumi Ohno, eds., *Japanese Views on Economic Development: Diverse Paths to the Market* (London: Routledge, 1998).

69. Asian Development Bank, *Emerging Asia: Changes and Challenges* (Manila: Asian Development Bank, 1997).

70. Marcus Noland and Howard Pack, *Industrial Policy in an Era of Globalization: Lessons from Asia* (Washington, D.C.: Institute for International Economics, 2003).

71. Naya, *Asian Development Experience,* 7–19.

72. Bruce Cumings, "The Origins and Development of the Northeast Asian Political Economy: Industrial Sectors, Product Cycles, and Political Consequences," *International Organization* 38, no. 1 (Winter 1984).

73. Petri, *Lessons of East Asia,* 7.

74. Naya, *Asian Development Experience,* 19.

75. Kiyoshi Kojima, *Japan and a New World Economic Order* (Boulder: Westview Press, 1977), 150–152; Pekka Korhonen, "The Theory of the Flying Geese Pattern of Development and Its Interpretations," *Journal of Peace Research* 31, no. 1 (February 1994): 93–108.

76. Raymond Vernon, "International Investment and International Trade in the Product Cycle," *Quarterly Journal of Economics* 80, no. 2 (May 1966): 190–207; Raymond Vernon, *Sovereignty at Bay: The Multinational Spread of U.S. Enterprises* (New York: Basic Books, 1971), 65–112.

77. Ippei Yamazawa, "Gearing the Japanese Economy to International Harmony," *Developing Economics* 28, no. 1 (March 1990): 3–15; Kojima Kiyoshi, "Japanese-Style Direct Foreign Investment," *Japanese Economic Studies* 14, no. 3 (Spring 1986): 52–82.

78. Cumings, "Origins and Development of the Northeast Asian Political Economy." See also Peter A. Petri, "The East Asian Trading Bloc: An Analytical History," in *Regionalism and Rivalry: Japan and the United States in Pacific Asia,* ed. Jeffrey A. Frankel and Miles Kahler (Chicago: University of Chicago Press, 1993), 21–48.

79. Mitchell Bernard and John Ravenhill, "Beyond Product Cycles and Flying Geese: Regionalization, Hierarchy, and the Industrialization of East Asia," *World Politics* 47, no. 2 (January 1995): 171–209.

80. Andrew MacIntyre and Barry Naughton. "The Decline of a Japan-Led Model of the East Asian Economy," in *Remapping East Asia: The Construction of a Region,* ed. T. J. Pempel (Ithaca, N.Y.: Cornell University Press, 2005), 77–100.

81. Bourdet, *Economics of Transition in Laos.*

82. Ungsuh Park, "Economic Development Model of Japan: Transferability to Korea and Taiwan," in *Asian Economic Development: Present and Future* (see note 57), 90–113.

83. Hadi Soesastro, "Japan 'Teacher'—ASEAN 'Pupils': Can It Work?" in *Asian Economic Development: Present and Future* (see note 57), 114–130.

84. K. S. Jomo and Chris Edwards, "Malaysian Industrialization in Historical Perspective," in *Industrializing Malaysia: Policy, Performance, Prospects,* ed. K. S. Jomo (London: Routledge, 1993), 28–29.

85. Maddison, *Chinese Economic Performance in the Long Run,* 159.

86. Jon-Wha Lee, "Policy Reforms and the Prospects of Economic Growth in North Korea," in *North Korea in Transition* (see note 35), 98.

87. Young Whan Kihl, "Staying Power of the Socialist 'Hermit Kingdom,'" in *North Korea: The Politics of Regime Survival* (see note 35), 4–5.

88. Peter J. Katzenstein, *A World of Regions: Asia and Europe in the American Imperium* (Ithaca, N.Y.: Cornell University Press, 2005).

89. Robert B. Zoellick, "Economics and Security in the Changing Asia-Pacific," *Survival* 39, no. 4 (Winter 1997–98): 30.

90. Takafusa Nakamura, *The Postwar Japanese Economy: Its Development and Structure,* trans. Jacqueline Kaminski (Tokyo: University of Tokyo Press, 1981), 23–30.

91. Johnson, *MITI and the Japanese Economic Miracle,* 41–82.

92. Cumings, "Origins and Development of the Northeast Asian Political Economy," 24. By contrast, Africa received $6.89 billion in economic aid and Africa and Latin America received $3.2 billion in military aid in the same period.

93. Charles R. Frank Jr., Kwang Suk Kim, and Larry E. Westphal, *South Korea* (New York: National Bureau of Economic Research, distributed by Columbia University Press, 1975), 231.

94. Cumings, "Origins and Development of the Northeast Asian Political Economy," 18–19. Also see Michael Schaller, *Altered States: The United States and Japan Since the Occupation* (New York: Oxford University Press, 1997).

95. Nakamura, *Postwar Japanese Economy*, 41. See also Yutaka Kōsai, *The Era of High-Speed Growth: Notes on the Postwar Japanese Economy*, trans. Jacqueline Kaminski (Tokyo: University of Tokyo Press, 1986), 65–67.

96. Alasdair Bowie and Danny Unger, *The Politics of Open Economies: Indonesia, Malaysia, the Philippines, and Thailand* (New York: Cambridge University Press, 1997), 72–73.

97. Asian Development Bank, *Southeast Asia's Economy in the 1970s*, 75–76.

98. For U.S.-Japan trade negotiations, see Leonard J. Schoppa, *Bargaining with Japan* (New York: Columbia University Press, 1997).

99. For samples of American strategic thinking, see Richard L. Armitage and Joseph S. Nye, *The U.S.-Japan Alliance: Getting Asia Right Through 2020* (Washington, D.C.: Center for Strategic and International Studies, February 16, 2007); Michael Armacost, "The Mismatch Between Northeast Asian Change and American Distractions," *NBR Analysis* 18, no. 1 (January 2007): 5–12.

100. Donald Crone, "Does Hegemony Matter? The Reorganization of the Pacific Political Economy," *World Politics* 45, no. 4 (July 1993): 501–525.

101. Meredith Woo-Cumings, "Back to Basics: Ideology, Nationalism, and Asian Values in East Asia," in *Economic Nationalism in a Globalizing World*, ed. Eric Helleiner and Andreas Pickel (Ithaca, N.Y.: Cornell University Press, 2005), 91–117.

102. Bee-Yan Aw, "Singapore," in *Liberalizing Foreign Trade*, Vol. II, ed. Demetris Papageorgiou, Michael Michaely, and Armeane M. Choksi (Cambridge: Blackwell, 1991), 350.

103. Seymour Martin Lipset, "Some Social Requisites of Democracy: Economic Development and Political Legitimacy," *American Political Science Review* 53, no. 1 (1959): 69–105.

104. Samuel P. Huntington, *Political Order in Changing Societies* (New Haven: Yale University Press, 1968).

105. Alice H. Amsden, *Asia's New Giant: South Korea and Late Industrialization* (Oxford: Oxford University Press, 1989), 48–52.

106. Shepherd and Alburo, "The Philippines," 226–228.

107. Harold Crouch and James W. Morley, "The Dynamics of Political Change," in *Driven by Growth: Political Change in the Asia-Pacific Region*, rev. ed., ed. James M. Morley (Armonk, N.Y.: M. E. Sharpe, 1999), 313–354.

CHAPTER 6

The Asian Financial Crisis

This chapter discusses the Asian financial crisis in 1997–1998, a momentous watershed in East Asian political economy. The crisis hit the region hard and wide. Standards of living, measured in U.S. dollars, dropped so dramatically for several crisis countries that decades of efforts appeared to have been for naught. The crisis also revealed some fundamental flaws in the East Asian political economy, appearing to ridicule the prior discussion of an impending Asian century in the new millennium. Thus, an analysis of the crisis helps us understand the nature of the contemporary East Asian political economy and the power of the contemporary global capital market.

The chapter answers two questions. First, how did the Asian financial crisis spread throughout the region? The crisis began in Thailand in July 1997 and spread like wildfire to the rest of East Asia and then outside the region. By tracing the sequence of events prior to and during the crisis, one will acquire not only a factual account of what happened but also an understanding of the reasons for the crisis. I will show the variation in the impact of the crisis on different countries and different policy choices made due to different institutional and political contexts.

Second, why did the crisis happen? The chapter introduces three main schools of thought. One school sees East Asia as a victim of the volatile global financial market. Another school attributes the crisis to misguided macroeconomic policies and weak financial and corporate sectors. The third school blames the crisis squarely on East Asian crony capitalism. Partly based on the process of tracing the crisis, the chapter argues that all three factors are necessary but none is sufficient in itself. The panic of the global financial market explains the timing of the crisis. At the same time, weak economic fundamentals and crony capitalism explain why some countries were affected more than others.

TRACING THE CRISIS

The Asian financial crisis was a global crisis, similar to the Latin American debt crisis in the 1980s. It was called the Asian financial crisis because it started in Asia and most of the affected countries were in East Asia. The Asian financial crisis was the third currency crisis of the 1990s, following the European Monetary System crisis of 1992–1993 and the Mexican peso crisis of 1994–1995. The crisis occurred in several waves, each aggravating the previous ones. For most crisis countries, the crisis followed a similar pattern: a foreign exchange crisis led to a sharp depreciation of the local currency, to a banking crisis, to a full economic crisis, to a social crisis, and to a political crisis.

In the first wave, the Asian financial crisis began as a foreign exchange crisis when Thailand's central bank was forced to float the Thai currency baht on July 2, 1997.[1] In retrospect, there were strong reasons that Thailand was the first to fall. Thailand had sought to create an international financial center in Bangkok in the early 1990s by liberalizing the financial sector without introducing effective oversight. Foreign capital inundated Thai financial institutions and companies, facilitated by the baht's peg to the U.S. dollar at a rate of 25 baht to one dollar since 1985, which minimized foreign exchange risk. Problems in the financial institutions began in 1994, but powerful politicians serving in a weak coalition government who were connected with the failing banks and finance companies prevented the government from implementing the declared financial restructuring measures, which weakened the confidence of investors.

The crisis began when speculators decided that Thailand would not be able to defend the peg and began selling the baht. The Thai central bank tried to defend the peg by purchasing the baht with U.S. dollars in its foreign reserve. Like any commodities, the value of a currency is determined by supply and demand. If the relative price of a currency against another currency is falling, the monetary authority may seek to prevent that by purchasing its own currency, which increases its demand, and selling the other currency, which increases its supply, provided that it has sufficient reserves to do so. In the end, the Thai central bank could not hold the line when its foreign reserve was exhausted. The baht lost 15 percent of its dollar value immediately and continued to fall, as shown in Figure 6.1. With a rapid flight of capital and currency depreciation, Thailand asked the International Monetary Fund (IMF) for help. The IMF offered a bailout package of $17.2 billion on August 11. As conditions for the loan, Thailand raised interest rates to prevent capital flight; additional measures were adopted in 1997 and 1998. A combination of sharp depreciation and high interest rates meant that the proportion of nonperforming loans increased as most Thai banks had unhedged dollar-denominated loans, much of which had been used for speculative property investments in a real estate bubble. A banking crisis now took place, which led to a crash in the stock market. A cheaper baht did not immediately facilitate exports. When the exchange rate is too unstable, economic transactions become problematic. With a banking crisis, exporters are also not able to get the credit they need for exports. In response to the crisis, the Thai government cut spending and citizens

FIGURE 6.1
Decline in East Asian Currencies (monthly average rates)

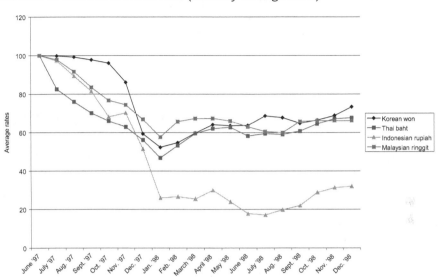

Source: Calculated based on data from Bank of Korea, http://ecos.bok.or.kr/EIndex_en.jsp.

lost much personal savings, leading to a demand-driven recession, a full-blown economic crisis. Social crisis was the next stage, when people lost their jobs and their savings in the stock market. In the third stage, Thailand experienced a power transfer. Prime Minister Chavalit Yongchaiyudh resigned on November 3, 1997.

The Thai currency crisis was infectious. Investors were now worried about the creditworthiness of other Southeast Asian countries that were perceived to be similar to Thailand. In a cascading effect, the Thai baht's collapse put competitive pressure on other currencies. Thus, in 1998 other Southeast Asian nations followed Thailand in floating their currencies, in the sequence of the Philippine peso on July 11, the Malaysian ringgit another three days later, and the Indonesian rupiah on August 14.

The Philippines was hit relatively less. As Figure 6.2 shows, the Philippines had a negative growth rate of 0.6 percent in 1998, much better than –10.5 percent for Thailand, –13.1 percent for Indonesia, –7.4 percent for Malaysia, and –6.9 percent for South Korea. The reform under President Fidel V. Ramos (1992–1998) contributed to the ability of the Philippines to weather the storm. Moreover, the Philippine business community had been more cautious than their Thai counterparts given their previous crises. But this was mainly a case in which the country

FIGURE 6.2
GDP Growth for East Asian Economies Affected by the Crisis, 1990–2004

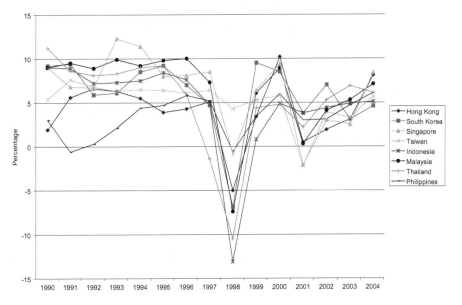

had not flown as high as Thailand, Malaysia, and Indonesia and therefore did not fall as hard either. Specifically, the Philippines was not as attractive a destination for foreign investments and accordingly did not suffer as much from capital flights.[2] As Figure 6.2 shows, the Philippines did not grow as fast as the tiger economies despite progress made under Ramos. Also, the IMF came to the Philippines' aid quickly, with a $1.1 billion aid package on July 14.

Malaysia took a different approach from Thailand, Indonesia, and South Korea.[3] Finance Minister Anwar Ibraham initially adopted a policy of fiscal and monetary austerity consistent with the IMF approach, but Prime Minister Mahathir reversed the course. Malaysia imposed selective capital controls in September 1998 to stem short-term portfolio flows and the ringgit offshore market in Singapore. Investors were required to have a one-year holding period for repatriation of portfolio capital flows. Mahathir essentially tried to insulate domestic economy from the global market. The day after introducing capital controls, Mahathir fired Anwar, which led to political instability. The capital controls allowed the Malaysian government to achieve some monetary expansion through lower interest rates. The government subsequently relaxed capital controls.

Indonesia suffered the most from the crisis.[4] Few observers had anticipated such an outcome. The perceived wisdom in the summer of 1997 was that Indonesia was in a stronger position than Thailand, with moderate inflation, relatively smaller current account deficit, absence of a bubble economy effect, and a more centralized decision-making structure.[5] The Indonesian government initially fended off attack on the rupiah by expanding the intervention band of the peg from 8 percent to 12 percent on July 11, but that effort made the country an easy target for speculators. After losing $1.5 billion of foreign exchange to defend the peg, half a billon on August 13 alone, the government floated the rupiah and increased the overnight interest rates from 19.5 percent to 36 percent to prevent capital flight on August 14. The depreciation and high interest rates led to a financial crisis because many banks and companies were heavily exposed to foreign exchange risks. The government adopted austerity measures following the IMF prescription in September. The government decided to seek IMF assistance on October 8 and secured a credit line of $23 billion (increasing to $38 billion later) in exchange for policy reforms on October 31. However, President Suharto began to send mixed signals about his resolve to implement promised reforms. The rupiah began declining again in November, partly in reaction to the Korean currency crisis. The political turmoil resulting from speculation that Suharto was seriously ill and might not seek reelection sent the currency downward again in December. The IMF and Suharto clashed in January 1998 when the IMF criticized his budget plan as breaching the targets agreed to with the Fund. Suharto was forced to sign a second IMF program on January 15. More clashing with the Fund ensued. The IMF withheld a $3 billion installment scheduled for disbursement on March 15 to force the Indonesian government to implement agreed reform measures. On May 4, Suharto raised the prices of fuel, gasoline, and electricity. On the same day, the IMF approved $1 billion as one-third of the $3 billion credit line. The IMF had wanted price increases. Protests and looting immediately broke out in the country. Indonesia now had a major social and political crisis. Suharto resigned on May 21. The IMF bailout package was augmented in July 1998.

In the second wave, Northeast Asian economies came under attack. Depreciation of Southeast Asian currencies meant competitive pressure on the rest of East Asia. Deciding not to intervene in support of the New Taiwan Dollar, Taiwan floated the currency on October 17, 1997. The Taiwan dollar fell by almost 20 percent in the next three months. The stock market lost more in percentage relative to the local currency in the same period. Nevertheless, in the end, Taiwan emerged largely unscathed by the crisis. Taiwan's economy grew by 4.8 percent in 1998, which was not as strong as in 1997 but surely much better than the crisis countries. Various reasons have been offered to explain Taiwan's performance, including sound economic fundamentals, limited reliance on foreign capital, conservative corporate financing, stronger stock market, a large holding of foreign exchange reserves, and effective institutions.[6]

Hong Kong became the next target.[7] Hong Kong created a currency board to peg the Hong Kong dollar to the U.S. dollar in 1983. Hong Kong held the peg, with Beijing's help; it was important for China to support Hong Kong right after Hong Kong's handover to China. Despite Hong Kong and China's few hundred billion dollars in foreign reserves, Hong Kong still took a beating in the stock market. The Hong Kong monetary authority drastically raised overnight interest rates to prevent capital flight, which led to a sharp fall in the stock market because Hong Kong was dominated by large development firms, whose profits are affected by changes in interest rates (high interest is detrimental for development firms). Hong Kong's Hang Seng index fell by 10.41 percent on October 23, the largest fall in the history of the Hong Kong market. The Hong Kong government intervened in the stock market by buying shares, breaking with its free-market tradition. The turmoil in Hong Kong affected global financial markets, particularly emerging markets. The Dow Jones industrial average lost 186.88 points or 2.33 percent that day.[8]

Facing a spreading crisis, investors became concerned about South Korea as well. South Korea was already in a weaker position starting in 1997 when several large corporations failed. S&P and Moody's, two leading international rating agencies, downgraded South Korea's credit rating in late October. Large South Korean conglomerates, or *chaebol,* had expanded globally based on foreign borrowing, resulting in weak balance sheets that investors could readily see. Foreign investors had already been selling stock shares from August. The Korean stock market price index lost 41 percent from June to November. Foreign bankers recalled their loans, which explained to a large extent South Korea's depleting foreign reserves, with merely $7.3 billion in November. The South Korean government gave up support for the Korean won on November 21. On December 3, South Korea agreed to reform measures in exchange for an IMF aid package of $58.4 billion. In the third quarter of 1998, the country saw a –6.8 percent economic growth rate and a 7.4 percent unemployment rate, which was a sharp reversal of fortunes considering its average growth rate of over 7 percent and an average unemployment rate of below 3 percent for the previous decade.[9] Of all the crisis-affected countries, South Korea took the strongest reform measures.

By the end of 1997, a full-blown crisis had developed in most East Asian nations. As shown in Figure 6.1, the Thai baht, Korean won, Indonesian rupiah, and Malaysian ringgit all lost significantly against the U.S. dollar. Only the Hong Kong dollar and the Chinese yuan maintained pegs to the U.S. dollar. The stock markets in the region also fell sharply. By the end of 1997, Thailand's stock market had lost 90 percent of its value, Indonesia 85 percent, Korea 80 percent, and Singapore 60 percent.[10]

The crisis did not spread evenly throughout the region; some countries were affected much more than others. Japan had already been in an economic recession and its economy did not fall in the crisis. Among the tigers Taiwan was affected less than South Korea. In Southeast Asia, Singapore was affected less than Malaysia partly because it had a managed-float exchange rate, which preempted the speculative attack. China largely escaped and emerged stronger after the crisis.[11] China had a large holding of foreign exchange reserves, and its capital control meant a limited short-term capital inflow in the first place. Moreover, China had attracted mostly direct investment in fixed assets rather than portfolio investment that can be pulled out in a hurry. Outside East Asia, India was in a similar situation with its capital controls system.

In the next wave the crisis moved beyond East Asia. Russia defaulted on its foreign debt in August 1998, and Brazil experienced serious difficulties in early 1999. The IMF orchestrated a $41 billion package for Brazil in November 1998. Even in the United States, the hedge fund Long-Term Capital Management collapsed in September 1998.

EXPLAINING THE CRISIS

There has been much heated debate between those who argue that the Asian financial crisis was caused by external speculative capital and those who argue that the crisis was due to East Asian crony capitalism.[12] The debate was particularly furious during the crisis because it was not just an intellectual debate. Rather, the outcome of the debate would affect politics and public policy. In a way, the political debate was about whom to blame for the crisis. Most Western observers and officials focused on crony capitalism, which was internal to East Asia. Many Asians, supported by some Western scholars, blamed the volatile global capital market and inappropriate IMF policy, although few went as far as Malaysia's Mahathir to blame Western investors such as George Soros.

With the benefit of hindsight, we may view the Asian financial crisis as a perfect storm. To understand why it happened, we need to consider both external and domestic factors and particularly how these factors interacted with each other to cause the outbreak of the crisis. Both exogenous and domestic factors are necessary and neither is sufficient. To simplify things, I divide these explanations into three interrelated broad categories: speculative capital, unsustainable economic policies in East Asia, and cozy government-business relations.

Speculative Capital

Speculative capital was obviously important for the Asian financial crisis. Without strong movements of speculative capital across national borders, it would be hard to see how there can be a regionwide financial crisis. Moreover, the countries that exercise greater capital control like China and Vietnam did not suffer as much as those with less capital control. Not only Asians blamed external factors; some prominent Western scholars also held such views. Jeffrey Sachs felt that the policy fundamentals in East Asia remained sound. The main problem was a financial panic.[13] Robert Wade maintained simply that with the surge in foreign capital movement, "even 'best practice' corporate governance and bank regulation in Asia would have been unlikely to stop the bubble and crash."[14]

The theoretical justification for free flow of capital is straightforward: It leads to a more efficient allocation of savings and investment because capital can be used where it generates the highest returns. Developing countries enjoy greater access to capital. An added benefit for them is that with deregulation and entry of foreign banks, the financial system may be better disciplined as foreign banks bring with them better accounting practices and create greater competition in the financial sector. Investors now can seek highest possible returns all around the world. They can also diversify the risk by spreading their investment portfolio.

The potential dangers of free flow of capital are also well understood. Free capital flow generates instability because of speculation. Speculators try to make money from the change in value of a currency by betting correctly on the direction and rate of change in the currency market. One cannot speculate unless one can trade in currencies easily. Because of lack of perfect information, people tend to influence each other, creating a herd effect. Thus, there is an overshoot in market adjustments, more than is justified by economic fundamentals. Speculators prey on easy targets, namely those governments that peg their currencies to a strong one without adequate foreign reserves. Speculators bet that the currency will depreciate and then attack the currency by dumping it on the market. To shore up the currency, the targeted government has to buy the currency with hard currency, which depletes official reserves.[15] What the Asian financial crisis shows is that although there were structural reasons such as crony capitalism, there was also a strong element of self-fulfilling panic leading to the crisis.

Panics are back.[16] A panic refers to a widespread fear about declining values of financial assets that leads to desperate sale of financial assets, which in turn causes an economic depression. Panics are caused by financial intermediaries, which borrow short (deposits) and lend long (investments). As a result, a run on banks takes place when everyone tries to take out their money before others, causing a self-fulfilling collapse of the bank. On the international level, investors may pull out of a country in a herd effect, causing the country's financial collapse. Then the financial crisis may spread to other countries, causing a global panic.

Financial panics used to be common but were largely absent from the 1930s to the 1980s. To prevent panic, the U.S. federal government, for instance, created three mechanisms: (a) deposit insurance to boost confidence of depositors, (b) regulations to prevent banks from risky investments (moral hazard), and (c) use of the central bank to act as lenders of last resort. These measures effectively prevented panics at the expense of an efficient allocation of savings to best investors.

In recent years, deregulation has made the financial market more efficient, but that also means that players take bigger risks to be competitive, which causes panics to recur. With a global capital market, when investors become nervous, they want the U.S. dollar. There is no best solution to financial crises. One has to make a tradeoff between efficiency and stability. The best we can hope for is to minimize the shock of a crisis through better monitoring and strengthening of domestic institutions. It is also important to remember that financial deregulation was partial and recent in Asia, which contributed to the crisis.

Thus, conditions for panic developed in East Asia. The most striking feature of East Asian political economy before the crisis was the massive flow of short-term speculative capital. The countries most affected by the crisis were largely those recently committed to the idea of free movement of capital. Table 6.1 shows the heavy inflow of capital into the five most seriously affected countries, namely Indonesia, Malaysia, the Philippines, South Korea, and Thailand, amounting to $92.8 billion of U.S. dollars in 1996. Only $7 billion of that amount was direct investment while the rest was debt.

At least five reasons explain why foreign investors had put their money in East Asia. First, there was much liquidity looking for investment in emerging markets in the 1990s. Second, investors could invest in East Asia since most East Asian governments deregulated capital controls. The Thai government, for example, created the Bangkok International Banking Facility to make Bangkok a regional financial center. While its original intent was to conduct transactions among nonresidents, Thai banks and firms ended up using the facility to borrow abroad.[17] Third, the prospect of high-growing East Asia was bright. Fourth, foreign investments

TABLE 6.1

External Financing of Indonesia, Malaysia, the Philippines, South Korea, and Thailand, 1994–1998 ($ billion)

	1994	1995	1996	1997	1998
Current account balance	−24.6	−41.3	−54.9	−26.0	17.6
Net external financing	47.4	80.9	92.8	15.2	15.2
Direct equity flows	4.7	4.9	7.0	7.2	9.8
Portfolio flows	7.6	10.6	12.1	−11.6	−1.9
Commercial bank lending	24.0	49.5	55.5	−21.3	−14.1
Nonbank private lending	4.2	12.4	18.4	13.7	−3.3
Net official flows	7.0	3.6	−0.2	27.2	24.6
Change in reserves	−5.4	−13.7	−18.3	22.7	−27.1

Source: United Nations Conference on Trade and Development, *Trade and Development Report, 1998,* 66.

appeared safe. Because the borrowers tended to be well connected politically, investors expected to be bailed out by the host governments or international financial institutions. There was also a perception of low foreign exchange risk since East Asian economies pegged their currencies to the U.S. dollar. Fifth, one does it because everybody else is doing it. But precisely because of such a herd effect, they would also retreat in a hurry. That is exactly what happened.

Investors pulled out quickly in 1997 because their assessment of East Asian fundamentals had shifted. As an early sign of weakening fundamentals, growth rates for East Asian merchandise exports fell dramatically in 1996, as shown in Figure 6.3, which indicated to investors that the Asian boom was ending.

Southeast Asia's position was further weakened by what was happening in Northeast Asia. Japan, which was sinking into economic stagnation in the early 1990s, failed to serve as a locomotive for regional economy. In fact, because of the need to improve balance sheets, Japanese companies pulled money from Southeast Asia, which was a contributing factor for the Asian financial crisis. Also, the yen depreciated against the U.S. dollar in the mid-1990s. Pegged to the U.S. dollar, the currencies of Southeast Asian nations suffered a real effective exchange rate over-

FIGURE 6.3
Growth Rates of East Asian Merchandise Exports, 1991–1996

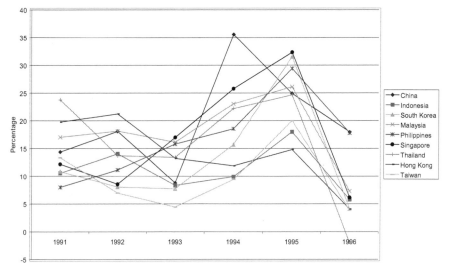

Source: World Development Indicators Database. Data for Taiwan are from Ministry of Finance of the Republic of China, www.mof.gov.tw/public/data/statistic/trade/2281.htm.

valuation measured against June 1987 to May 1997 averages, ranging from 4 to 12 percent for Indonesia, Thailand, Malaysia, and the Philippines. Although the overvaluation was not that large, it demonstrated the region's increasing weakness.[18]

The China factor also contributed to the crisis. The Chinese government depreciated the yuan against the dollar in 1994. More important, it became obvious by 1997 that China was more competitive than most Southeast Asian nations in the global market. In retrospect, it was not surprising that the crisis began in Thailand. Being pushed by China, Thailand needed to upgrade its economic structure but could not because of its poor public education system. It was difficult to establish factually that China was indeed taking away comparative advantage from Southeast Asia and the country's surging exports contributed to the meltdown in Southeast Asia, but there was such a perception by some analysts.[19] Perception matters for investors.

By discussing the Japan and China factors, I am not saying that Japan and China are responsible for the Asian financial crisis. What I am saying is that there was a regional dynamic to the extent that one cannot formulate policy in isolation from what is happening in other countries.

Unsustainable Economic Policies

Speculative capital preys on the weak. The Asian financial crisis took place also because of fundamental weaknesses found in many East Asian countries. An IMF study concluded that the Asian crisis resulted mainly from a combination of macroeconomic imbalances, external developments (appreciation of the U.S. dollar), and weakness in financial and corporate systems (unhedged foreign currency borrowing, excessive reliance on short-term external debt, risky investments in stocks and property, rapid expansion of domestic credit, pegged exchange rates, and weak supervision).[20]

To start with, the pegged exchange rate system became unstable for most East Asian countries. The early scholars of currency crises argue that exchange rate policy cannot conflict with other monetary and fiscal objectives and that a country's ability to export is important for a stable exchange rate regime.[21] If a country had a pegged exchange rate and an expansionist monetary policy at the same time, it would lead to reduction in foreign reserves. The reason is that those with excess domestic currency will exchange them for foreign securities or domestic interest-bearing bonds. The purchasing of foreign securities puts direct downward pressure on the domestic currency by increasing demands for foreign currencies and decreasing demands for the domestic currencies. The flow to domestic bonds will increase demands for the bonds and lead to decreasing yields, which will then result in a shift to better earning foreign assets, with the same depreciating effect on the domestic currency. The monetary authorities would have to float the domestic currencies as its foreign reserve is being depleted.[22] A key implication of the theory is thus that central bank borrowing to cover budget deficits, current account deficits, and increasing foreign debt may trigger a currency crisis when a fixed exchange rate regime is in place.

A second generation of currency models emphasizes the self-fulfilling interaction between investor expectations and policy choices. Put simply, if investors believe that a country may have to devalue its currencies, they would increase the cost of borrowing on their loans, which in a self-fulfilling prophecy increases the cost of defending the peg.[23] As Nouriel Roubini and Brad Setser argued, a third generation of models, learning from the Asian financial crisis, viewed the imbalance in the private sector as the cause of the crisis.[24] Factually, the East Asian crisis countries did not suffer from fiscal deficits or government debts prior to the crisis. Rather, they suffered from worsening current account deficits resulting from investment bubbles in the private sector.

Some analysts have zeroed in on the fixed-but-adjustable exchange rate regimes adopted in most East Asian countries before the crisis. W. Max Corden argued that this type of exchange rate regime, combined with high capital mobility and lack of political credibility, creates special problems and leads to recessions deeper than would occur under alternative exchange rate regimes. The key argument against the fixed exchange rate regime under the condition of capital mobility is that when speculators attack the peg, the affected country has to raise interest rates to fend off the attack, which hurts the country's financial sector.[25]

Before the 1997 crisis, most East Asian countries pegged their currencies to the U.S. dollar. It made sense. The U.S. economy is the strongest economy in the world. In addition, most of the economic transactions East Asian nations have with each other or with countries outside the region are denominated in the U.S. dollar. One pegs one's currency to a strong one for two simple reasons. The first and more important reason is to ensure financial stability. The second reason is to make it easier to trade and attract investments. But fixed exchange rates may also lead to problems, particularly in an era of globalization. It is now impossible for any governments to achieve the so-called "impossible trinity."

Robert Mundell came up with the notion of the impossible trinity in the 1960s, which basically says that it is impossible to have the following three simultaneously—namely a fixed exchange rate, financial openness, and autonomy in monetary policy—and that one can have only two of the three at any one point.[26] If we want to regulate markets and maintain sovereignty, integration with global financial markets will be compromised. If we want to maintain sovereignty but allow capital markets to integrate, we must accept an entirely free global financial market. If we want capital market integration and global regulation, we will sacrifice national sovereignty.

In the case of East Asia, fixed exchanged rates and deregulation of capital accounts created inflationary pressure because inflow of capital adds to money supply. Normally, a country should appreciate its currency to fend off inflationary pressure, but it cannot do so under a fixed exchange rate system (this would defeat the purpose of piggybacking on a stronger currency to control inflation in other cases). Some East Asian nations tried to adopt a monetary policy as an instrument while maintaining a pegged exchange rate and free capital movement. Take Thailand, for example. The Thai government tried to cool the economy by raising interest rates, but that led to a huge inflow of capital, which defeated the government's original purpose. In the first half of 1997, with a slowdown in economy, the Thai central bank provided financial support to domestic banks and other financial institutions, which effectively increased the base money by more than 66 percent. Investors began to see pressure on the peg and the Thai foreign reserves diminishing. Thus, their exit from baht-denominated assets began.

Another problem with a fixed exchange rate is that inflation, which means rising of the general price level, makes one's exports less competitive. This problem was compounded by two other factors. The first factor was that South Korea, Thailand, and Malaysia were already under wage pressure because of a shortage of skilled workers and greater freedom to form unions in a more democratic environment. The other factor was that the Japanese yen depreciated sharply against the U.S. dollar in the mid-1990s and China depreciated the yuan in 1994. Consequently, exports of Southeast Asian countries and South Korea began declining after the mid-1990s. Export performance is a fundamental for investors. A decline in export earnings means a decline in foreign reserves and thus decreasing ability to defend the peg. Once investors sense weakness (e.g., weakening exports and increasing public debt), they run and, worse, deliberately attack the currency to make money.

In the case of Thailand, the combination of pegged exchange rates and relaxed capital control meant that Thais could now raise capital overseas. In fact, as interest rates were lower on foreign loans, it was actually cheaper to borrow overseas. However, in the 1990s, there was not that much opportunity to invest in the exporting sector, so they invested in office building and executive apartments, which created a self-perpetuating bubble. Foreign investors lent because of "irrational exuberance." An added problem was that foreign investors believed that since Thai borrowers had strong political connections, loans were essentially guaranteed.

When several East Asian countries' current account balances deteriorated, it became clear to investors that they would not be able to defend the peg indefinitely. After all, the crisis countries had sizable current account deficits in 1996, measured as percentage of GDP. Thailand had a high 8.0 percent, the Philippines 5.9 percent, Malaysia 5.3 percent, South Korea 4.8 percent, and Indonesia 3.4 percent. In fact, these countries had high percentages for several years before 1996.[27]

The five crisis countries (Indonesia, Malaysia, the Philippines, South Korea, and Thailand) had a combined current account deficit of $24.6 billion in 1994, $41.3 billion in 1995, and $54.9 billion in 1996. As Figure 6.3 shows, East Asian exports declined sharply in growth rates in 1996.

East Asian corporations became vulnerable as a result of excessive borrowing. The debt-to-equity ratio for large Korean companies was exceedingly high, 577 percent for Hyundai Motor, 660 percent for Hyundai E&C, 438 percent for Samsung Corp., 341 percent for SK Telecom, 580 percent for LG Electronic, and 364 percent for Samsung Electronic. For Malaysia, the debt-to-equity ratio was 363 percent for Sime Derby and 148 percent for Petronas. By contrast, Taiwanese firms had low debt-to-equity ratios.[28]

Thus, the United Nations Conference on Trade and Development concluded in 1998 that the Asian financial crisis was not that different from the Latin American debt crisis in the 1980s, the European Monetary System crisis in 1992, and the Mexican peso crisis in 1994. There was much inflow of capital to take advantage of the differential interest rates, facilitated by the pegged exchange rates. The problem was a high percentage of short-term loans reaching maturity prior to the crisis.

Moreover, the heavy borrowing was related to a property bubble. Exposure to the property sector accounted for 15–20 percent of total bank loans in the Philippines, 15–25 percent in South Korea, 25–30 percent in Indonesia, 30–40 percent in Malaysia, Thailand, and Singapore, and 40–55 percent in Hong Kong. Worse, in Thailand and Indonesia, foreign borrowing was short term and denominated in foreign currency.[29] In a vicious cycle, depreciation of a currency led to an increase in nonperforming loans, which further pushed down the value of the currency.

Last but not the least, the financial sector in the crisis countries was poorly regulated and nontransparent. In fact, some analysts argue that the health of the financial sector and currency crisis are a mutually reinforcing pair.[30]

Crony Capitalism

For some analysts, the weaknesses described above are the logical outcomes of crony capitalism in East Asia. While recognizing the importance of panic in a global financial market, Paul Krugman argued that "crony capitalism in general, and moral hazard in banking in particular, created a 'bubble economy' that had to burst sooner or later."[31]

Crony capitalism refers to cozy government-business relations, a capitalist system based on political patronages. The term cronyism comes from the Western context in which a clear separation between the government and business is maintained and in which it is normally inappropriate for the relatives of government leaders to engage in business activities and receive government contracts.

TABLE 6.2
Maturity Distribution of Lending to East Asian Countries ($ million)

	All Loans			Under 1 Year			1 to 2 Years		
	June 1996	Dec. 1996	June 1997	June 1996	Dec. 1996	June 1997	June 1996	Dec. 1996	June 1997
Hong Kong	211,238	207,037	222,289	179,784	170,705	183,115	5,119	5,248	4,417
Indonesia	49,306	55,523	58,726	29,587	34,248	34,661	3,473	3,589	3,541
Malaysia	20,100	22,234	28,820	9,991	11,178	16,268	834	721	615
Philippines	10,795	13,289	14,115	5,948	7,737	8,293	531	565	326
South Korea	88,027	99,953	103,432	62,332	67,506	70,182	3,438	4,107	4,139
Singapore	189,195	189,235	211,192	176,080	175,228	196,600	2,707	1,799	1,719
Taiwan	22,470	22,363	25,163	19,405	18,869	21,966	585	483	236
Thailand	69,409	70,147	69,382	47,834	45,702	45,567	4,083	4,829	4,592

Source: United Nations Conference on Trade and Development, Trade and Development Report, 1998, 60.

Some analysts used to praise such a close government-business arrangement, a common feature in East Asian political economy, as evidence of a developmental state central to the East Asian miracle. For example, the East Asian governments typically pressured banks to lend to companies with good political connections or that were considered important for the country. While such a practice often channeled money into important sectors, it posed a moral hazard issue because investors or lenders felt that the state would bail out well-connected companies if they ran into difficulties. A weak financial system results from crony capitalism.

Another major issue is weak corporate governance in East Asia. In the countries most affected, large corporations tend to be controlled by families who prefer to borrow from banks rather than raising capital in the stock market. So these companies tend to be heavily in debt. On top of that, families who run these companies often have good political connections. The previous section has already discussed the unusually high debt-to-equity ratios for companies in some East Asian countries.

MANAGING THE CRISIS

As soon as the financial crisis broke out, the international community tried to fight it off. Some economies that had not been affected seriously, namely Taiwan and Singapore, relied on their own resources. Hong Kong had massive foreign reserves and could also count on Beijing's support. The focus of the international community was thus on the countries affected the most: Thailand, Indonesia, Malaysia, the Philippines, and South Korea. The IMF took the lead. The basic IMF approach is to provide standby loans for crisis countries. The Philippines was the first to receive the IMF help by extending an existing standby arrangement in July. Thailand arranged an agreement with the IMF in August, Indonesia in November, and South Korea in December. The packages the IMF orchestrated also included contributions from the World Bank, the Asian Development Bank (ADB), and bilateral donors. The three packages amounted to a total commitment of $125.3 billion (including augmentations), as shown in Table 6.3. However, not all committed funds were disbursed to the crisis countries, only $66.6 billion as of May 30, 2000. In return for loans, the IMF demanded restructuring programs, which typically involve deregulation, privatization, austerity measures, and tighter monetary policy (i.e., higher interest rates) to prevent currency depreciation and inflation spirals.

By contrast, Mahathir of Malaysia did not ask the IMF for help. Instead, on September 1, 1998, Malaysia fixed the exchange rate and imposed capital controls. With capital control, the Malaysian government could lower interest rates and introduce a stimulus package. To the surprise of many contemporary observers,

TABLE 6.3
IMF-Orchestrated Packages for Thailand, Indonesia, and South Korea ($ billion)

	Commitments				Disbursements as of May 30, 2000		
	IMF	WB&ADB	Bilateral	Total	IMF	Other	Total
Thailand	4.0	2.7	10.5	17.2	3.4	10.9	14.3
Indonesia	15.0	10.0	24.7	49.7	11.6	10.3	21.9
South Korea	21.1	14.2	23.1	58.4	19.8	10.6	30.4
Total	40.1	26.9	58.3	125.3	34.8	31.8	66.6

Source: Adapted from International Monetary Fund (IMF), "Recovery from the Asian Crisis and the Role of the IMF," June 2000, Table 1, www.imf.org/external/np/exr/ib/2000/062300.htm.

Note: WB&ADB refers to World Bank and Asian Development Bank. Commitment for Indonesia includes augmentations after July 1998.

Malaysia did not do badly. Malaysia's relative success and the fact that China, which had not completely deregulated its capital controls, had not been seriously affected by the Asian financial crisis allow some critics of the IMF to argue that free capital movement may not be the right approach under all conditions.[32]

Various criticisms of the IMF approach were offered even during the crisis, particularly in the case of Indonesia. Some suggested that the IMF had made mistakes by failing to recognize the large debts of the private sector and by forcing the Indonesian government to close sixteen insolvent banks in November 1997, which caused a banking panic and capital flight.[33] The IMF was accused of using the method developed to deal with the Latin American debt crisis to deal with the Asian financial crisis. However, the private sector accumulated large debt and there was little inflationary pressure. As a result, the high interest rates and austerity measures proposed by the IMF created deflationary consequences, resulting also in an outflow of capital.[34] Thus, Joseph Stiglitz, the World Bank's chief economist, argued that the IMF had made a key error when it imposed high interest rates on countries that were already headed for recession.[35]

The IMF did orchestrate large bailout packages, which compensated for the private capital outflow.[36] Without offsetting official inflow of capital, interest rates in East Asia would not have been able to come down, something crucial for stimulating production and consumption in the region. As Table 6.3 shows, the IMF itself put in about one-third of the total commitments but accounted for half of the disbursements of the funds as of May 30, 2000. The crisis countries did recover, and the IMF packages contributed to that recovery. At the same time, Malaysia, which did not follow the IMF prescription, also recovered. The debate thus continues.

East Asians mostly equated the IMF approach with the American approach. The Japanese resented what they saw as an American impulse to change Asian capitalism into the Anglo-Saxon form of capitalism. Rather than seeing the crisis as resulting from structural problems in Asia, they prefer to see the crisis as resulting from global capitalism.[37] Some non-Asian experts such as Robert Wade also argued that the U.S. factor contributed to the Asian financial crisis with its chronic current account deficits, which meant increased liquidity for East Asia. Moreover, the U.S. government pressured the East Asian governments to remove capital controls to allow free movement of capital.[38] At the same time, the United States played an important part in organizing bailout packages and contributed to the ones for Indonesia and South Korea. Equally important, the U.S. market was important for absorbing distress goods from the crisis countries while the Asian markets were weak.

Japan pumped billions of dollars into the region. Japan was the largest bilateral donor in the IMF packages and separately, totaling $42 billion, compared with $11 billion from the United States and $5.4 billion from Europe. Japan contributed to the crisis countries indirectly through its contributions to the IMF, the World Bank, and the ADB. Japan also created a separate facility, the New Miyazawa Initiative, of $30 billion for the distressed countries.[39] At the same time, Japan failed to serve as the market for distress goods and its public financing was offset by private Japanese capital leaving the region.

Unsatisfied with the IMF approach, Japan proposed an Asian Monetary Fund in August 1997 to deal with the crisis, with contributions from East Asia totaling $100 billion. The U.S. Treasury killed the idea for fear that the IMF's role would be diluted. China also failed to support the Japanese initiative.

China emerged from the Asian financial crisis a stronger power. Even though it contributed only $1.2 billion directly to the crisis countries, China's decision not to revaluate the yuan won praise from the countries in the region, which became a turning point in how it views East Asian regionalism.

THE CONSEQUENCES OF THE CRISIS

There are three reasons why East Asia's recovery was relatively fast.[40] First, the crisis reduced imports, which turned trade balances to surpluses, leading to increases in foreign reserves for the crisis countries. Second, the governments of the crisis countries, except the Philippines, stimulated economy in 1998. They also took over private debts and offered depositor insurance, which gradually restored investors' confidence. The exposure to short-term loans decreased. Official flows in the form of IMF packages compensated partially the loss of capital. Third, the booming U.S. economy helped to pull East Asia out of the crisis. Not surprisingly, when the U.S. economy began to slow down in mid-2001, the East Asian economy also suffered.

The Asian financial crisis had an impact on East Asian finance in that Asian governments were more interested in increasing their foreign reserves to prepare for another crisis. East Asian nations became capital exporters after the crisis because of decreased investment against higher ratios of savings. China is different from the crisis countries in that its investments as well as savings remain high and its increased foreign reserves have largely come from the government's purchase of dollars to maintain its exchange rates.[41] Yet even in China, saving/GDP ratios are higher than investment/GDP ratios, 50 percent versus 46 percent in 2005, reflecting in part the country's worsening production overcapacity.[42] Along with U.S. budget deficits, the crisis thus contributed to an enlarging global financial imbalance in the later years. Asian governments also became more interested in foreign direct investment (FDI), which is less risky than portfolio investment.

The Asian financial crisis has also led to greater interest in creating regional institutions in East Asia. Examples include the Asian Monetary Fund and free trade negotiations. There was much hope at the beginning of the crisis that the crisis might have presented an opportunity for further regional cooperation. Of the aid package for Thailand, more than half came from fellow Asian countries. The United States was noticeably absent from the list of bilateral donors.

In terms of strategic significance, the Asian financial crisis also created a regional impact. China's position improved. The crisis had a negative impact on Japanese companies in terms of market sales and profits.[43] There was a general sense that Japan had suffered from the crisis as its development model came to be discredited.[44]

There were many proposals to reform the IMF, but without much long-term impact on governance of international finance.[45] One school of thought focuses on an internationalized moral hazard created by the IMF bailout packages. Availability of such packages means that developing governments will have no incentives to conduct reforms and international speculators no incentives to avoid risky investments. There is also a perception that speculators largely escaped unhurt from the Asian crisis. Some prominent economists suggested allowing sovereign states to receive bankruptcy protection.[46]

Some senior IMF officials were also critical of the IMF approach. Stanley Fischer, the No. 2 man in the IMF, argued that the IMF could have lessened the crisis if it had not demanded fiscal tightening.[47] The Independent Evaluation Office of the IMF drew a similar conclusion in its evaluation of the IMF programs for Indonesia, Korea, and Brazil issued in July 2003. Considering the initial stock of debt, the report concluded that fiscal tightening in Indonesia and South Korea was not warranted. The report concluded that nonfinancial structural reform measures are beneficial in the long run but should not be part of immediate solutions to the crisis. The report also stated that it was inconclusive whether high interest rates are effective in stabilizing exchange rates.[48]

A consensus is emerging among analysts that private lenders should take a hit too because they have made risky decisions. So they should be involved in rescheduling, but not surprisingly they resist such an approach. Creditors took losses during the Latin American debt crisis but not in the Mexican peso crisis and the Asian financial crisis. It does not make sense for taxpayers to pay for lenders' mistakes. One concrete way to advance that objective is to allow debtor nations to declare bankruptcy and then follow the same procedure for debt adjustment as is done for firms in the United States. This way, it will give debtor nations time and also let creditors bear some of the losses.

THE POLITICAL ECONOMY OF THE CRISIS

Complementing the economic explanation of the crisis offered in the second section, I focus on the political economy explanation in a separate section consistent with the internal organization of the East Asian miracle chapter and all the upcoming issue chapters. The Asian financial crisis was as much a political event as an economic one. Political factors partly explained the onset of the crisis. As discussed earlier, crony capitalism has been cited by some as the main reason for the start of the crisis. Whether one uses that negative label or considers crony capitalism a sufficient condition for the crisis, the overly cozy government-business relations were clearly an important piece of the puzzle, a partial indictment of the developmental state. As Stephan Haggard has shown, the concentration of private economic power and close business-government relations in East Asia gave business great potential power to influence public policy. State intervention in the financial sector created a moral hazard problem in that financial institutions were less vigilant about monitoring their clients. Moreover, the concentration of private economic power means that the liberalization measures adopted by the governments were "captured" by private interests.[49]

Politics also mattered in the handling of the crisis. A government's policy choices may make things worse by creating greater uncertainties for investors. As a case in point, Indonesian President Suharto's mishandling of the implementation of the IMF package exacerbated the crisis. The case thus supports the arguments made by some economists that models of currency crises should include the interaction of policy and capital market, unlike the first generation of models that emphasize unsustainable economic policies and structural imbalances.[50] Andrew MacIntyre argued that policy rigidity (inability to adjust) and policy volatility (excessive policy shifts) at the extreme ends of a policy continuum create uncertainties for investors and are thus detrimental in a time of crisis. Of the four Southeast Asian crisis countries, Thailand suffered from policy rigidity because of a wide disperse of veto power in the political system, Malaysia and Indonesia experienced policy volatility because of a high concentration of veto power, and only the Philippines maintained a steady policy position because the country does not have a wide dispersal or a high concentration of veto authority.[51]

On first look, one may conclude that the type of political regime does not make that much difference when it comes to the Asian financial crisis since the crisis hit democratic South Korea and Thailand as well as semiauthoritarian Malaysia and Indonesia. Under further scrutiny, however, Haggard has shown that whereas democratic South Korea and Thailand indeed had a difficult time facing the crisis because of electoral pressure and coalition government, the democratic regimes had an advantage in forming new governments to launch reform based on public support. By contrast, while semiauthoritarian Malaysia and Indonesia could be more decisive in the absence of strong political constraints, they were also prone to offsetting policy blunders, particularly in the case of Indonesia. Furthermore, the succession problem, typical of authoritarian regimes, created great uncertainties in both Indonesia and Malaysia.[52] More broadly, as MacIntyre argued, most advanced industrial countries, with thick democracy, are able to avoid the two extremes of veto authority commonly found among developing nations.[53] Thus, a stronger democracy would have made a difference in whether a country could handle the Asian financial crisis more successfully.

All economic crises have political consequences. Crises strain a country's system of political economy and unleash social and political forces that generate political change. The Asian financial crisis was no exception. One striking feature of the political consequences of the Asian financial crisis was that the political forces unleashed largely pushed for greater accountability in the political system than for reversing to authoritarianism in the recently democratized countries like South Korea, the Philippines, and Thailand. For the democracies, the crisis led to newly elected governments under Kim Dae Jung in South Korea and Chavalit in Thailand, both of whom introduced reforms. Of the crisis countries, South Korea introduced the strongest reforms, which partly explained the country's subsequent return to strong economic growth. For both Malaysia and Indonesia, the crisis unleashed social forces for change. In Indonesia, the crisis led to violence and overthrow of the Suharto regime. By contrast, Mahathir managed to survive the crisis because of a strong political party and other political institutions to co-opt opposition.[54]

CONCLUSION

The Asian financial crisis resulted from the interplay of multiple factors. East Asian financial institutions and corporations accumulated large unhedged short-term loans denominated by foreign currencies because of the availability of international capital and perceived absence of foreign exchange risks from pegged exchange rates. Because of skewed incentives, weak corporate governance, and ineffective prudential regulations, much of the foreign currency borrowing went into nonproductive sectors such as real estate. With worsening current account balances, Thailand became vulnerable to speculation that its peg to the U.S. dollar would not hold. Thailand's inevitable foreign exchange realignment in the face of mounting attacks from speculative capital triggered a vicious cycle. Concerned about foreign exchange losses of their financial investments, investors fled from the region, which pushed down the values of the local currencies even further. Currency depreciation hit domestic companies hard because of their large foreign currency debt obligations. Failing financial institutions and companies created a banking crisis and a broad economic crisis.

When the Asian financial crisis occurred, some analysts were quick to suggest that the crisis revealed the fundamental flaws of the East Asian system of political economy. However, one crisis does not necessarily discredit a whole political economy system. As a case in point, the Great Depression did not discredit the whole capitalist system. Rather, reforms are called for in most crisis situations. The best way to evaluate the East Asian development model is that it served its historical purpose: The model was more or less successful, particularly compared with other developing nations. Massive input mobilization for rapid economic growth may eventually be limited, but it did generate a few decades of rapid growth. Cozy government-business relations also served their purpose. But now the model has exhausted itself to a large extent.

The cases of the crisis countries discussed in the chapter, limited though they might be, suggest that the democratic regimes are preferable to the authoritarian regimes in dealing with the crisis because they have strong institutions to represent public interests and their policies have stronger credibility because of the electoral and legislative support they enjoy. The crisis generated demands for economic and political reforms and strengthened East Asia's commitment to integration with the global market.

SUGGESTED READINGS

Cohen, Benjamin J. "The Triad and the Unholy Trinity: Problems of International Monetary Cooperation." In *Pacific Economic Relations in the 1990s: Cooperation or Conflict?* ed. Richard Higgott, Richard Leaver, and John Ravenhill (Boulder: Lynne Rienner, 1993), 133–158.

Corden, W. Max. "Exchange Rate Regimes for Emerging Market Economies: Lessons from Asia." *The Annals of the American Academy of Political and Social Science* 579 (January 2002): 26–37.

Dornbusch, Rudi. "A Primer on Emerging Market Crises." NBER Working Paper 8326 (Cambridge: National Bureau of Economic Research, June 2001).

Eichengreen, Barry. "Strengthening the International Financial Architecture: Where Do We Stand?" *ASEAN Economic Bulletin* 17, no. 2 (August 2000): 175–192.

Flynn, Norman. *Miracle to Meltdown in Asia: Business, Government, and Society* (Oxford: Oxford University Press, 1999).

Garnaut, Ross. "Exchange Rates in the East Asian Crisis." *ASEAN Economic Bulletin* 15, no. 3 (December 1998): 328–337.

Goldstein, Morris. *The Asian Financial Crisis: Causes, Cures, and Systemic Implications* (Washington, D.C.: Institute for International Economics, 1998).

Haggard, Stephan. *Political Economy of the Asian Financial Crisis* (Washington, D.C.: Institute for International Economics, 2000).

Hill, Hal. *The Indonesian Economy in Crisis: Causes, Consequences, and Lessons* (New York: St. Martin's Press, 1999).

Hughes, Christopher W. "Japanese Policy and the East Asian Currency Crisis: Abject Defeat or Quiet Victory." *Review of International Political Economy* 7, no. 2 (Summer 2000): 219–253.

International Monetary Fund. "Recovery from the Asian Crisis and the Role of the IMF." Issue Brief June 2000, *www.imf.org/external/np/exr/ib/2000/062300.htm*.

Islam, Iyanatul, and Anis Chowdhury. *The Political Economy of East Asia: Post-Crisis Debates* (New York: Oxford University Press, 2000).

Jackson, Karl D., ed. *Asian Contagion: The Causes and Consequences of a Financial Crisis* (Boulder: Westview Press, 1999).

Jomo, K.S., ed. *Malaysian Eclipse: Economic Crisis and Recovery* (London: Zed Books, 2001).

Kindleberger, Charles P. *Manias, Panics, and Crashes: A History of Financial Crises* (New York: Basic Books, 1978).

Krugman, Paul. "A Model of Balance-of-Payments Crises." *Journal of Money, Credit, and Banking* 11, no. 3 (August 1979): 311–325.

Lardy, Nicholas R. "China and the Asian Contagion." *Foreign Affairs* 77, no. 4 (July/August 1998): 78–88.

MacIntyre, Andrew. "Institutions and Investors: The Politics of the Economic Crisis in Southeast Asia." *International Organization* 55, no. 1 (Winter 2001): 81–122.

Noble, Gregory W., and John Ravenhill, eds. *The Asian Financial Crisis and the Architecture of Global Finance* (Cambridge: Cambridge University Press, 2000).

Obstefeld, Maurice. "Rational and Self-Fulfilling Balance of Payments Crises." *American Economic Review* 76, no. 1 (March 1986): 72–81.

Pempel, T. J., ed. *The Politics of the Asian Economic Crisis* (Ithaca, N.Y.: Cornell University Press, 1999).

Pesenti, Paolo, and Cédric Tille. "The Economics of Currency Crises and Contagion: An Introduction." *Economic Policy Review* 6, no. 3 (September 2000): 3–16.
Roubini, Nouriel, and Brad Setser. *Bailouts or Bail-Ins? Responding to Financial Crises in Emerging Economies* (Washington, D.C.: Institute for International Economics, 2004).
Sakakibara, Eisuke. "Crossing Swords with the Three Marketers." *Japan Echo* 26, no. 6 (December 1999): 18–22.
Stiglitz, Joseph E. *Globalization and Its Discontents* (New York: Norton, 2002).
Wade, Robert. "The U.S. Role in the Long Asian Crisis of 1990–2000." In *The Political Economy of the East Asian Crisis and Its Aftermath: Tigers in Distress,* ed. Arvid John Lukauskas and Francisco L. Rivera-Batiz (Northampton, Mass.: Edward Elgar, 2001), 195–226.
Warr, Peter, ed. *Thailand Beyond the Crisis* (New York: RoutledgeCurzon, 2005).
Woo, Wing Thye, Jeffrey D. Sachs, and Klaus Schwab, eds. *The Asian Financial Crisis: Lessons from a Resilient Asia* (Cambridge: MIT Press, 2000).
World Bank. *East Asia: Recovery and Beyond* (Washington, D.C.: World Bank, 2000).

NOTES

1. For studies of the baht crisis, see Andrew MacIntyre, "Political Institutions and the Economic Crisis in Thailand and Indonesia," in *The Politics of the Asian Economic Crisis,* ed. T. J. Pempel (Ithaca: Cornell University Press, 1999), 143–154; Ammar Siamwalla, "Anatomy of the Crisis," in *Thailand Beyond the Crisis,* ed. Peter Warr (New York: RoutledgeCurzon, 2005), 66–104.

2. Paul Hutchcroft, "Neither Dynamo nor Domino: Reforms and Crises in the Philippine Political Economy," in *The Politics of the Asian Economic Crisis* (see note 1), 162–183.

3. Mahani Zainal-Abidin, "Implications of the Malaysian Experience on Future International Financial Arrangements," *ASEAN Economic Bulletin* 17, no. 2 (August 2000): 135–47; K. S. Jomo, ed., *Malaysian Eclipse: Economic Crisis and Recovery* (London: Zed Books, 2001).

4. Anwar Nasution, "The Meltdown of the Indonesian Economy: Causes, Responses, and Lessons," *ASEAN Economic Bulletin* 17, no. 2 (August 2000): 148–62; Hal Hill, *The Indonesian Economy in Crisis: Causes, Consequences, and Lessons* (New York: St. Martin's Press, 1999).

5. MacIntyre, "Political Institutions and the Economic Crisis in Thailand and Indonesia," 154–161; Shinichi Watanabe, "Evolution of the Crisis in Indonesia: Part II," *Journal of Research Institute for International Investment and Development* 25, no. 3 (May/June 1999): 71–120.

6. Yun-han Chu, "Surviving the East Asian Financial Storm: The Political Foundation of Taiwan's Economic Resilience," in *The Politics of the Asian Economic Crisis* (see note 1), 184–202; Norman Flynn, *Miracle to Meltdown in Asia: Business, Government, and Society* (Oxford: Oxford University Press, 1999), 21.

7. Linda Y. C. Lim, "Free Market Fancies: Hong Kong, Singapore, and the Asian Financial Crisis," in *The Politics of the Asian Economic Crisis* (see note 1), 103–108.

8. The title of the headline story in *The Washington Post* on October 24, 1997, reads as follows: "Sell-Off in Hong Kong Shakes Global Markets: Dow Falls 187; Asia, Europe Hit Harder."

9. Jisoon Lee, "An Understanding of the 1997 Korean Economic Crisis," *EXIM Review* 19, no. 2 (July 1999): 41.

10. Flynn, *Miracle to Meltdown in Asia,* 7.

11. Nicholas R. Lardy, "China and the Asian Contagion," *Foreign Affairs* 77, no. 4 (July/August 1998): 78–88; Yu Yongding, "China's Deflation During the Asian Financial Crisis, and Reform of the International Financial System," *ASEAN Economic Bulletin* 17, no. 2 (August 2000): 163–174.

12. Stephan Haggard, *Political Economy of the Asian Financial Crisis* (Washington, D.C.: Institute for International Economics, 2000); Iyanatul Islam and Anis Chowdhury, *The Political Economy of East Asia: Post-Crisis Debates* (New York: Oxford University Press, 2000); Wing Thye Woo, Jeffrey D. Sachs, and Klaus Schwab, eds., *The Asian Financial Crisis: Lessons from a Resilient Asia* (Cambridge: MIT Press, 2000); Karl D. Jackson, ed., *Asian Contagion: The Causes and Consequences of a Financial Crisis* (Boulder: Westview Press, 1999); Gregory W. Noble and John Ravenhill, eds., *The Asian Financial Crisis and the Architecture of Global Finance* (Cambridge: Cambridge University Press, 2000).

13. Steven Radelet and Jeffrey D. Sachs, "The East Asian Financial Crisis: Diagnosis, Remedies, Prospects," *Brookings Papers on Economic Activity,* no. 1 (Spring 1998): 1–90.

14. Robert Wade, "The U.S. Role in the Long Asian Crisis of 1990–2000," in *The Political Economy of the East Asian Crisis and Its Aftermath: Tigers in Distress,* ed. Arvid John Lukauskas and Francisco L. Rivera-Batiz (Northampton, Mass.: Edward Elgar, 2001), 198.

15. Charles P. Kindleberger, *Manias, Panics, and Crashes: A History of Financial Crises* (New York: Basic Books, 1978); Robert Gilpin, *Global Political Economy: Understanding the International Economic Order* (Princeton: Princeton University Press, 2001), 264–267.

16. For a succinct comment on panics, see Paul Krugman, "Start Taking the Prozac," *Financial Times,* April 9, 1998, 26.

17. Morris Goldstein, *The Asian Financial Crisis: Causes, Cures, and Systemic Implications* (Washington, D.C.: Institute for International Economics, 1998), 13.

18. Goldstein, *Asian Financial Crisis,* 14–15.

19. Goldstein, *Asian Financial Crisis,* 16–17.

20. International Monetary Fund, "Recovery from the Asian Crisis and the Role of the IMF," Issue Brief, June 2000, *www.imf.org/external/np/exr/ib/2000/ 062300.htm.* See also Timothy Lane, "The Asian Financial Crisis: What Have We Learned?" *Finance and Development* 36, no. 3 (September 1999).

21. Paul Krugman, "A Model of Balance-of-Payments Crises," *Journal of Money, Credit, and Banking* 11, no. 3 (August 1979): 311–325; Robert P. Flood and Peter M. Garber, "Collapsing Exchange-Rate Regimes: Some Linear Examples," *Journal of International Economics* 17, nos. 1–2 (August 1984): 1–13.

22. Paolo Pesenti and Cédric Tille, "The Economics of Crises and Contagion: An Introduction," *Economic Policy Review* 6, no. 3 (September 2000): 4–5.

23. Pesenti and Tille, "The Economics of Crises and Contagion," 3–16. Also see Maurice Obstefeld, "Rational and Self-Fulfilling Balance of Payments Crises," *American Economic Review* 76, no. 1 (March 1986): 72–81 and "Models of Currency Crises with Self-Fulfilling Features," *European Economic Review* 40, nos. 3–5 (April 1996): 1037–1047; Allan Drazen and Paul Masson, "Credibility of Policies Versus Credibility of Policymakers," *Quarterly Journal of Economics* 109, no. 3 (1994): 735–754; Harold Cole and Patrick Keohoe, "A Self-Fulfilling Model of Mexico's 1994–95 Debt Crisis," *Journal of International Economics* 41, no. 3 (November 1996): 309–330.

24. Nouriel Roubini and Brad Setser, *Bailouts or Bail-Ins? Responding to Financial Crises in Emerging Economies* (Washington, D.C.: Institute for International Economics, 2004), 35–36. Also see Rudi Dornbusch, "A Primer on Emerging Market Crises," NBER Working Paper 8326 (Cambridge: National Bureau of Economic Research, June 2001).

25. W. Max Corden, "Exchange Rate Regimes for Emerging Market Economies: Lessons from Asia," *The Annals of the American Academy of Political and Social Science* 579 (January 2002): 26–37. See also Ross Garnaut, "Exchange Rates in the East Asian Crisis," *ASEAN Economic Bulletin* 15, no. 3 (December 1998): 328–337.

26. Robert A. Mundell, *International Economics* (New York: Macmillan, 1968); Benjamin J. Cohen, "The Triad and the Unholy Trinity: Problems of International Monetary Cooperation," in *Pacific Economic Relations in the 1990s: Cooperation or Conflict?,* ed. Richard Higgott, Richard Leaver, and John Ravenhill (Boulder: Lynne Rienner, 1993), 133–158.

27. United Nations Conference on Trade and Development, *Trade and Development Report,* 1998, 67.

28. Flynn, *Miracle to Meltdown in Asia,* 19–24.

29. Goldstein, *Asian Financial Crisis,* 8–9.

30. Graciela L. Kaminsky and Carmen M. Reinhart, "The Twin Crises: The Causes of Banking and Balance-of-Payments Problems," *American Economic Review* 89, no. 3 (June 1999): 473–500.
31. Krugman, "Start Taking the Prozac."
32. Joseph Stiglitz, *Globalization and Its Discontents* (New York: Norton, 2002), 122–125.
33. Paul Dibb, David D. Hale, and Peter Prince, "The Strategic Implications of Asia's Economic Crisis," *Survival* 40, no. 2 (Summer 1998): 11.
34. Robert Wade and Frank Veneroso, "The Resources Lie Within," *The Economist,* November 7, 1998, 19–20.
35. Stiglitz, *Globalization and Its Discontents,* 89–132.
36. For IMF's own defense, see International Monetary Fund, "Recovery from the Asian Crisis and the Role of the IMF."
37. Sakakibara Eisuke, "Crossing Swords with the Three Marketers," *Japan Echo* 26, no. 6 (December 1999): 18–22.
38. Wade, "U.S. Role in the Long Asian Crisis of 1990–2000," 195–226.
39. Ming Wan, *Japan Between Asia and the West: Economic Power and Strategic Balance* (Armonk: M. E. Sharpe, 2001), 88–94.
40. World Bank, *East Asia: Recovery and Beyond* (Washington, D.C.: World Bank, 2000), 5–6.
41. Taniuchi Mitsuru, "Ajia no shihon ryushutsunyu kozo no henka to kadai ajia kikigo no ajia keizai" [Changing Capital Flows in Asia—New Developments After the Asian Financial Crisis], *Journal of JBIC Institute* no. 28 (February 2006): 83–110.
42. The data come from the Chinese State Foreign Exchange Management Bureau, May 4, 2006, www.chinanews.com.cn/news/2006/2006-05-04/8/725785.shtml.
43. A large survey of the Japanese companies in May–June 1998 showed this effect. See Shigeki Tejima, "The Effects of Asian Crisis on Japan's Manufacturing FDI," *EXIM Review* 19, no. 3 (September 1999): 1–85.
44. For an opposing view, see Christopher W. Hughes, "Japanese Policy and the East Asian Currency Crisis: Abject Defeat or Quiet Victory," *Review of International Political Economy* 7, no. 2 (Summer 2000): 219–253.
45. Roubini and Setser, *Bailouts or Bail-Ins?* 4–5. See also Barry Eichengreen, "Strengthening the International Financial Architecture: Where Do We Stand?" *ASEAN Economic Bulletin* 17, no. 2 (August 2000): 175–192.
46. Anne Krueger, "International Financial Architecture for 2002: A New Approach to Sovereign Debt Restructuring," Speech at the National Economists' Club Annual Members' Dinner, American Enterprise Institute, Washington, D.C., November 26, 2001, www.imf.org/external/np/speeches/2001/

112601.htm; Stiglitz, *Globalization and Its Discontents*; Stanley Fischer, "On the Need for an International Lender of Last Resort," *Journal of Economic Perspectives* 13, no. 4 (Fall 1999): 85–104.

47. See his speech in Singapore on June 1, 2001, reported in *The Strait Times*, June 2, 2001, S17.
48. Independent Evaluation Office of the IMF, *The IMF and Recent Capital Account Crises: Indonesia, Korea, Brazil* (Washington, D.C.: IMF, 2003).
49. Haggard, *Political Economy of the Asian Financial Crisis*, 15–46.
50. Pesenti and Tille, "Economics of Crises and Contagion," 3–16.
51. Andrew MacIntyre, "Institutions and Investors: The Politics of the Economic Crisis in Southeast Asia," *International Organization* 55, no. 1 (Winter 2001): 81–122.
52. Haggard, *Political Economy of the Asian Financial Crisis*, 47–72.
53. MacIntyre, "Institutions and Investors," 118.
54. Haggard, *Political Economy of the Asian Financial Crisis*, 222–237.

CHAPTER 7

The Political Economy
of East Asian Production

This chapter examines the political economy of East Asian production. When one talks about East Asian political economy, one normally focuses on trade, foreign investment, and exchange rates. But production is at the core of East Asian political economy. To East Asians, modernization equates with industrialization, namely production of manufactured goods. To enjoy a higher living standard and to create a strong nation, one has to "produce" wealth. Reinforced practices and attitudes regarding production and vested interests created in the process of industrialization have helped to shape the contemporary East Asian political economy to the way it is today. For most East Asian governments, trade, foreign investment, and exchange rates follow the imperative of production. Such an obsession with production helps explain both the East Asian economic miracle and the subsequent economic crisis. Industrial policy to promote manufacturing production and exports is at the core of the debate over what explains the East Asian miracle. Production overcapacity was also an important reason for the Asian financial crisis.

This chapter addresses five questions. The first question is about the current state of East Asian production. The chapter shows that East Asia has become the factory of the world. Next, the chapter focuses on transnational production networks. Production leads off the issue chapters in the book to highlight the regional dimension of East Asian political economy. A principal form of East Asian regional integration is the production network across national borders. Industrial regional integration took place in East Asia prior to high-level political efforts for regional groupings. Third, the chapter examines how the East Asian governments pick winners to compete in the global market and their policies toward direct investment inflow and outflow. A discussion of the East Asian companies follows. Last, the chapter shows how production relates to politics in East Asia.

THE "FACTORY" OF THE WORLD

East Asian Industrialization

East Asia has enjoyed rapid industrialization, moving from labor-intensive to capital-intensive to high-tech products, but not at the same pace. Through the

1980s, a Japan-led flying geese formation moved up the industrial ladder in a tiered formation. Japan showed the way for other East Asian nations even if they did not exactly copy the Japanese model because of their own objectives and circumstances.

Japan was the first industrialized country in East Asia, a feat accomplished before the Second World War. Thus, unlike other East Asian nations but similar to Western Europe, Japan's postwar mission was more about reconstruction than development. Still, Japan lagged behind the West economically in the 1950s. Japan caught up with the West by the end of the 1960s and established itself as an economic superpower by the late 1980s. Japan was a world leader in labor-intensive products in the 1950s. It then moved up to capital-intensive manufacturing. By 1976, Japan had an impressive share of 90 percent of motorcycle exports by Organization of Economic Cooperation and Development countries, 70 percent in televisions and radios, 43 percent in ships, 29 percent in steel, 23 percent in watches, and 20 percent in motor cars.[1] Japan remains a world manufacturing leader in some areas and boasts some of the largest and most successful firms in the world. According to the *Consumer Reports* 2007 annual auto issue, the best models in ten categories in 2007 were all Japanese (Toyota 4, Honda 3, Infiniti 2, and Mazda 1).[2] Toyota surpassed General Motors as the world's largest automaker in the first quarter of 2007. Japan's Sony and Sharp took the number one position (14.6 percent) and number three position (13.6 percent), respectively, in world liquid crystal display (LCD) TV unit shares in 2004–2005. Holland's Philips was the second (14.2 percent) and South Korea's Samsung (11.6 percent) and LG (6.5 percent) were fourth and fifth.[3]

In the second wave, South Korea, Taiwan, Singapore, and Hong Kong industrialized. South Korea followed Japan's model the closest, building world-class companies with world-class brand names. Starting in the 1960s, South Korea took advantage of its competitiveness in labor-intensive sectors such as footwear and apparel. South Korea began to move up to capital-intensive heavy and chemical industries in the late 1960s, which remained the focus for the country through the 1970s. South Korea is now a major exporter of automobiles, machinery, and ships. In particular, South Korea has been the world's leader in shipbuilding. South Korea received orders for 14.5 million compensated gross tons (CGTs), a ship capacity measure, for 2005, or 38 percent of the world total. The European Union came second with 8.5 million CGTs, followed by China (7 million) and Japan (6.2 million).[4] South Korea began to export high-tech products such as semiconductors and electronics by the mid-1990s. South Korea is now the world's largest producer of dynamic random access memory chips (DRAMs).

Similar to Japan and South Korea, Taiwan's industrialization began with exports of textiles and apparel that expanded rapidly in the 1960s. Taiwan's petrochemical industry began in the 1950s and took off in the late 1960s. Similar to South Korea, Taiwan promoted heavy and chemical industries in the 1970s, but unlike South Korea the Taiwanese government relied heavily on public enterprises. The government decided to move away from energy-intensive industries after the second oil crisis. Instead, the government emphasized high-technology, high value-added, low energy-intensive "strategic industries" in the early 1980s. Taiwan's electronics industry became internationally competitive in the 1980s. Taiwan was one of the largest information technology (IT) hardware exporters in the world.[5] Its export has decreased in recent years only because it has shifted much production capacity to mainland China. Despite Taiwanese foreign direct investment (FDI) in IT manufacturing in the mainland, Taiwan remains a powerhouse for semiconductor production. Taiwan's industrialization differs from South Korea's in that Taiwanese companies are smaller than South Korean ones, Taiwan did not succeed in creating general trading companies like South Korea, and Taiwanese firms have not built as many international brands as South Korean firms. However, the more conservative nature of Taiwanese companies in contrast to debt-burdened South Korean ones was one reason that Taiwan did not suffer as much as South Korea in the Asian financial crisis.

Singapore has always depended on trade, as indicated by its annual trade volume exceeding its gross domestic product (GDP). But the Singaporean government began to shift from a port economy based on staples trade to an exporter of manufactured goods in 1960. Manufacturing became a leading sector in Singaporean economy by 1970. The share of nonpetroleum direct manufactured exports (not reexported) increased from 12.7 percent of GDP in 1966 to 47.1 percent in 1979 and 62.9 percent in 1990. The government depended on multinational corporations for industrialization. Wholly or majority-owned foreign firms accounted for 84.1 percent of direct manufactured exports in 1975 and 85.8 percent in 1990.[6] Unlike South Korea and Taiwan, Singapore could concentrate more on industrial development since it did not have an agricultural sector.

Similar to Singapore, Hong Kong is an urban economy. Adapting to the founding of the People's Republic of China in 1949 and a massive flow of refugees, Hong Kong made a successful transition from an entrepôt economy serving China to an export-based manufacturing economy in the 1950s and the 1960s.[7] Unlike the other three tigers, the British colonial government in Hong Kong did not actively engage in industrial policy. Rather, the government protected law and order, provided public goods, and kept tax low by relying on revenues from sale of public land for development. Hong Kong became a major producer of several manufactured products, particularly labor-intensive garments initially and electronics, watches, and toys later in the 1960s. Unlike other newly industrialized economies (NIEs) that engaged in industrial upgrading in the 1970s, Hong Kong maintained its labor-intensive industries even in the late 1970s because of "timely" immigrants from mainland China.[8] But as Hong Kong resumed its traditional entrepôt role after China reentered the world market in the late 1970s, its service sector became more prominent relative to manufacturing.[9]

In the third wave, Southeast Asia has been undergoing a fast pace of industrialization beginning in the early 1970s (the early 1980s for Indonesia). The region's manufacturing base has shifted from household to factories and has broadened from resource processing and simple consumer goods to capital goods, heavy processing, and more sophisticated consumer goods. Compared with Taiwan and South Korea, the Southeast Asian industrializing countries have depended heavily on FDI. The share of manufacture in Malaysia's GDP increased from 8.7 percent in 1960 to 20.5 percent in 1980. Owing to dependence on foreign capital, labor-intensive industries did not grow as fast as capital-intensive industries.[10] Malaysia's manufacturing sector grew further with a heavy industrialization drive that began in 1981. The manufacturing sector came to account for 30 percent of GDP by 2000.[11] Thailand also experienced industrialization, with shares of manufacturing in its GDP increasing from 16.0 percent to 21.7 percent in 1980, to 23.0 percent in 1988, and with shares of manufacturing in its exports increasing from 2.4 percent in 1961 to 68.6 percent in 1989.[12] Industry came to represent 46 percent of Thailand's GDP by 2006. The country has not been able to upgrade its industries that fast, however, and its manufacturing remains largely in raw material-based and labor-intensive industries.[13] Though not as successful as Malaysia and Thailand, Indonesia and the Philippines have also achieved some degree of industrialization.[14] Indonesia depended heavily on the petroleum industry but had to promote non-oil industries after a sharp drop of crude oil prices in the mid-1980s. The Filipino economy suffered from the corrupt Marcos authoritarian regime and the subsequent political instability in the 1980s and regained modest growth in the 1990s.

The East Asian socialist countries made a detour. Drastic contrasts can be seen particularly in the divided nations of China and Korea. East Asian communist countries also emphasized industrialization, but their industrialization based on socialist planning distorted the economic structure by emphasizing heavy industrialization at the expense of light industry and agriculture.[15] China initially put great emphasis on Soviet-style heavy industrialization. Mao Zedong then decided to mobilize masses to catch up with the West in steel production in 1958, which led to three years of the Great Famine. North Korea went further in heavy industrialization and collectivization of agriculture than China and Vietnam. North Korea achieved economic successes through the 1960s by mobilizing resources, often the case in the early stage of a planned economy, but began to suffer the consequences of distorted economic structure and exhaustion of resources by the 1970s.[16]

Similar to South Korea and Taiwan, the Chinese government initially shifted to labor-intensive industries to take advantage of the country's comparative advantage after Deng Xiaoping launched economic reform in the late 1970s. Despite being a late developer, China has been climbing up the ladder at a faster pace and in many fields at the same time. China is now a major producer of more and more manufactured products. As mentioned earlier in the context of South Korean shipbuilding success, China has become a world-class shipbuilder, trailing only South Korea and the European Union in 2005. China became the largest producer of crude steel in the world for the first time in 1996, with its share of world total crude steel production increasing from 13.5 percent in 1996 to 33.8 percent in 2006. Japan was the second largest producer in 2006, with production about one-quarter of China's.[17] Quality aside, China is now the fourth largest automobile producer in the world, trailing only the United States, Japan, and Germany, and may overtake Germany soon.[18] China became a net exporter of cars for the first time in 2005. While foreign firms produce cars in China for the domestic market, most Chinese exports are from Chinese firms like Chery Automobile Co.[19] As a measure of industrial upgrading, China conducted $415.96 billion of high-tech trade or 29.2 percent of its total trade in 2005.[20]

East Asian industrialization was at the core of the East Asian miracle. One way to measure the importance of industrialization is the structural change of East Asian economy. As shown in Table 5.3 in Chapter 5, the proportion of industry has increased dramatically in East Asia.

East Asia has become a center of manufacture in the world. China accounted for 7.40 percent of global manufacturing export in 2005, increasing from 1.79 percent in 1990. Japan's share was 5.73 percent in 2005 and 8.28 percent in 1990. China and Japan trailed only Germany and the United States in 2005.[21]

There are good economic reasons why East Asia has done well in manufacture. With a global industrial structural shift taking place, high-tech industries have become more important in advanced countries. It thus makes sense to move labor-intensive declining industries to developing nations. Compared with other developing regions, East Asia is well positioned to benefit from this global development. East Asia has a large, educated labor force and continues to have labor cost advantages in the high-tech sectors. For example, while it cost $300,000 to employ a computer chip design engineer in Silicon Valley in 2002 and $150,000 in Canada, it cost only $65,000 in South Korea, $60,000 in Taiwan, and $24,000–$28,000 in China.[22] High domestic savings and inflow of foreign investment provide the capital needed for industrial expansion. In a virtuous cycle, East Asian countries have learned by doing. Since the 1970s, East Asian industrialization has also come to be largely based on technologies. Technological innovations have been a driving force for Japan's economic success. The electronics industrialization in the NIEs in the 1970s and the 1980s was central to economic growth in East Asia. East Asia is a rising power in high-tech industries. In the IT industry, for instance, Asia consumed about 20 percent of the world total IT goods while producing about 40 percent of the total in 2003.[23] East Asia is better than other regions in terms of share of new products in their export mix.[24]

As in developed countries before them, East Asian manufacturers a concentrated in industrial clusters, often surrounding the countries' capitals. The share of manufacturing in the Bangkok area increased from 39.4 percent in 1970 to 54.6 percent in 1986.[25] Even though the Thai government began providing incentives to regions farther away from Bangkok in 1987, they have achieved only limited success. Given its massive size, China boasts three major manufacturing centers. The Pearl River delta (Guangdong) has become a major IT processing center and export base that exported $83.6 billion high-tech and new products in 2005. The Yangzi delta (Shanghai, Jiangsu, and Zhejiang) is now a center in telecommunications, software, and microelectronics that exported $94.8 billion for the year. The Bohai region (Beijing, Tianjin, Hebei, Liaoning, Shanxi, Shandong, and Inner Mongolia) specialized in mobile, aerospace, and integrated circuitry, exporting $29.5 billion. These three economic centers accounted for 95.3 percent of China's total exports in high-tech and new products in 2005.[26] Such industrial clusters are crucial for East Asian nations' success in attracting FDI or moving up the technological ladder.

East Asian production has been defined by intense domestic competition and regional competition, which often leads to excess production capacity. The impact of such overcapacity is a push toward foreign markets. We have seen such a pattern. Japanese firms, toughened at home, beat up foreign competitors. Now Chinese firms that have managed to reduce production costs as a result of brutal domestic competition meet few challenges overseas in sectors where they excel.

Foreign Direct Investment in East Asia

A large amount of FDI has flowed into East Asia, as shown in Table 7.1. China alone has attracted over $50 billion of FDI annually for the past few years. East Asian economies attracted 17.2 percent of world total FDI inflows in 2005.[27] FDI has been an important reason for East Asian industrialization, particularly for ASEAN and China. In fact, FDI was so important for Southeast Asia after the mid-1980s that some analysts used "FDI-led industrialization" to describe Southeast Asia's growth. As a case in point, the foreign share of Malaysia's manufacturing was basically above 45 percent in 1968–1991.[28] As shown in Table 7.2, FDI accounted for 97.0 percent of gross fixed capital formation in Hong Kong, 78.9 percent in Singapore, 15.2 percent in Malaysia, 11.3 percent in Vietnam, and 9.2

TABLE 7.1
Foreign Direct Investment (FDI) in East Asia ($ million)

FDI Flows	1985–1995 (Annual average)	2001	2002	2003	2004	2005
Japan						
Inward	642	6,241	9,239	6,324	7,816	2,775
Outward	24,214	38,333	32,281	28,800	30,951	45,781
China						
Inward	11,715	46,878	52,743	53,505	60,630	72,406
Outward	1,687	6,885	2,518	−152	1,805	11,306
South Korea						
Inward	697	3,692	3,043	3,892	7,727	7,198
Outward	1,278	2,420	2,617	3,426	4,658	4,312
Taiwan						
Inward	1,009	4,109	1,445	453	1,898	1,625
Outward	2,671	5,480	4,886	5,682	7,145	6,028
Hong Kong						
Inward	4,093	23,777	9,682	13,624	34,032	35,897
Outward	7,884	11,345	17,463	5,492	39,753	32,560
Singapore						
Inward	4,529	14,122	7,338	10,376	14,820	20,083
Outward	1,505	22,711	2,287	3,143	8,512	5,519
Malaysia						
Inward	2,924	554	3,203	2,473	4,624	3,967
Outward	676	267	1,905	1,370	2,061	2,971
Thailand						
Inward	1,428	3,886	947	1,952	1,414	3,687
Outward	213	346	106	486	125	246
Indonesia						
Inward	1,364	−2,978	145	−597	1,896	5,260
Outward	532	125	182	15	3,408	3,065
Philippines						
Inward	727	899	1,542	491	688	1,132
Outward	86	−160	65	303	579	162
Vietnam						
Inward	633	1,300	1,200	1,450	1,610	2,020
Outward	—	—	—	—	—	—
World						
Inward	182,438	825,925	617,732	557,869	710,755	916,277
Outward	203,256	743,465	539,540	561,104	813,068	778,725

Sources: Data for 1985–1995 and 2001 are from UNCTAD, *World Investment Report 2005,* country fact sheets. Data for 2002–2005 are from *World Investment Report 2006,* country fact sheets.

TABLE 7.2

*Foreign Direct Investment (FDI) as a Percentage
of Gross Fixed Capital Formation*

FDI Flows	1985–1995 (Annual average)	2001	2002	2003	2004	2005
Japan						
Inward	—	0.6	1.0	0.7	0.7	0.3
Outward	2.8	3.6	3.4	3.0	3.0	4.3
China						
Inward	6.0	10.5	10.4	8.6	8.0	9.2
Outward	0.9	1.5	—	—	0.2	1.4
South Korea						
Inward	1.0	2.6	1.9	2.1	3.8	3.1
Outward	1.6	1.7	1.6	1.9	2.3	1.9
Taiwan						
Inward	3.0	7.8	2.9	0.8	2.8	2.3
Outward	8.2	10.4	9.8	10.4	10.5	8.5
Hong Kong						
Inward	18.4	55.7	26.4	40.6	96.4	97.0
Outward	24.6	26.6	47.6	16.4	129.5	88.0
Singapore						
Inward	32.9	55.5	25.6	46.5	58.0	78.9
Outward	8.3	89.3	18.0	14.1	33.3	21.7
Malaysia						
Inward	13.8	2.5	14.5	10.8	19.1	15.2
Outward	3.0	1.2	8.6	6.0	8.5	11.4
Thailand						
Inward	4.2	14.6	3.3	5.7	3.4	7.2
Outward	1.1	1.3	—	1.4	0.3	0.5
Indonesia						
Inward	3.4	−9.4	—	−1.3	3.4	8.5
Outward	3.6	—	—	—	6.2	5.0
Philippines						
Inward	7.4	7.0	13.3	3.7	4.8	7.5
Outward	1.2	−1.3	—	2.3	4.1	1.1
Vietnam						
Inward	28.3	13.6	11.0	11.0	10.5	11.3
Outward	—	—	—	—	—	—
World						
Inward	3.8	12.0	10.6	7.3	7.7	9.4
Outward	4.3	10.8	9.7	7.4	9.3	8.3

Sources: Data for 1985–1995, 2001, and 2002 are from UNCTAD, *World Investment Report 2005,* country fact sheets. Data for 2003–2005 are from *World Investment Report 2006,* country fact sheets.

percent in China in 2005. In 2005 foreign firms exported from China $444.2 billion or 58.3 percent of China's total exports.[29] This is particularly the case in high-tech industries. Foreign firms accounted for 84.1 percent of China's high-tech trade in 2005.[30] By contrast, FDI has been less important for Japan and South Korea, accounting for only 0.3 percent and 3.1 percent of gross fixed capital formation, respectively, in 2005. The importance of foreign firms in local industrialization goes beyond their share of capital formation given their possession of technologies, management skills, and networks.

To highlight the importance of FDI for different countries, we can also measure inward FDI stocks as a percentage of GDP. As Table 7.3 shows, Hong Kong had a high 299.9 percent by 2005, Singapore 158.6 percent, Malaysia 36.5 percent, Thailand 33.5 percent, China 14.3 percent, and Taiwan 12.1 percent. By contrast, inward FDI stocks accounted for only 2.2 percent of GDP for Japan, and 8.0 percent for South Korea. This divergence reflects more deliberate policy choices as will be discussed in detail later in the chapter.

Since the end of the Second World War, there have been four waves of FDI into East Asia. The first wave took place in the 1960s and the early 1970s, with joint ventures in textiles and household electrical equipment to gain access to protected domestic markets. In the second wave in the 1970s, foreign investors moved in to establish import substitution operations and to export consumer electronics and semiconductors to the United States. The third wave took place in the mid-1980s in the wake of the sharp appreciation of the yen. Japan moved some manufacturing to East Asia. The second-tier economies South Korea and Taiwan also became major investors. In fact, Hong Kong, Taiwan, and Singapore accounted for 42 percent of total foreign investment in Thailand in 1990, more than Japan's share at 30 percent.[31] By the mid-1990s, Taiwan and Hong Kong had invested more in Vietnam than Japan, followed by Singapore and South Korea. In an even bigger wave than the third, FDI began to pour into China after the early 1990s.[32] China continues to be a major destination of FDI, attracting about one-third of all FDI into developing countries in 2002–2004.[33] In 2006, $69.5 billion of FDI flowed into China.[34]

The Investors of the World

East Asian firms have also invested heavily overseas. Outward FDI flows from East Asian economies amounted to 14.4 percent of the world total in 2005.[35] There are two main reasons for this. One is that East Asia has become a source of surplus capital based on strong exports and high domestic savings. The other reason is that East Asian firms need to have a global presence to be competitive with Western firms or with each other.

Japan leads East Asia in FDI outflows, which exploded after the 1985 Plaza Accord that sharply appreciated the yen against the dollar. *Endaka* (strong yen) led

TABLE 7.3
Foreign Direct Investment (FDI) Stocks as a Percentage of Gross Domestic Product ($ million and percentage)

FDI Stocks	1980		1990		2000		2003		2004		2005	
Japan												
Inward	3,270	—	9,850	—	50,322	1.1	89,729	2.1	96,984	2.1	100,899	2.2
Outward	19,610	1.8	201,441	6.6	278,442	5.8	335,500	7.8	370,544	7.9	386,581	8.5
China												
Inward	1,074	0.5	20,691	5.8	193,348	17.9	228,371	16.2	245,467	14.9	317,873	14.3
Outward	—	—	4,455	1.3	27,768	2.6	37,020	2.6	35,005	2.1	46,311	2.1
South Korea												
Inward	1,327	2.1	5,186	2.1	37,189	8.1	47,641	9.0	56,001	8.2	63,199	8.0
Outward	127	—	2,301	0.9	26,833	5.8	34,527	6.5	32,166	4.7	36,478	4.6
Taiwan												
Inward	2,405	5.8	9,735	6.1	17,581	5.7	37,131	13.0	40,304	13.2	41,929	12.1
Outward	13,009	31.4	30,356	19.0	66,655	21.5	84,092	29.4	91,265	29.8	97,293	28.1
Hong Kong												
Inward	21,175	74.3	45,073	60.3	455,469	275.4	381,342	239.2	453,031	275.2	532,956	299.9
Outward	146	0.5	11,920	15.9	388,380	234.9	339,649	213.0	403,094	244.9	470,458	264.7
Singapore												
Inward	6,203	52.9	30,468	83.1	112,571	123.1	144,363	160.2	166,844	156.2	186,926	158.6
Outward	3,718	31.7	7,808	21.3	56,766	62.1	90,242	100.1	105,413	98.7	110,932	94.1
Malaysia												
Inward	5,169	20.7	10,318	23.4	52,747	58.6	41,667	40.4	43,804	37.2	47,771	36.5
Outward	197	0.8	2,671	6.1	21,276	23.6	11,735	11.4	41,508	35.2	44,480	34.0
Thailand												
Inward	981	3.0	8,242	9.7	29,915	24.4	47,534	33.3	52,855	32.9	56,542	33.5
Outward	13	—	418	—	2,203	1.8	3,031	2.1	3,701	2.3	3,947	2.3
Indonesia												
Inward	4,680	6.0	8,855	7.7	24,780	16.5	10,329	5.0	15,858	7.0	21,118	7.7
Outward	6	—	86	0.1	6,940	4.6	—	—	10,670	4.7	13,735	5.0
Philippines												
Inward	1,281	3.9	3,268	7.4	12,810	16.9	12,216	15.2	12,896	14.9	14,028	14.4
Outward	171	0.5	155	—	1,597	2.1	1,194	1.5	1,877	2.2	2,039	2.1
Vietnam												
Inward	1,398	32.9	1,650	25.5	20,596	65.7	27,505	71.8	29,115	63.5	31,135	61.2
Outward	—	—	—	—	—	—	—	—	—	—	—	—
World												
Inward	530,244	5.0	1,768,589	8.4	5,780,846	18.3	7,980,317	22.0	9,544,887	23.3	10,129,739	22.7
Outward	570,125	5.8	1,785,264	8.7	6,148,284	19.7	8,731,240	24.3	10,325,240	25.2	10,671,889	23.9

Sources: Data for 1980, 1990, 2000, and 2003 are from UNCTAD, *World Investment Report 2005*, country fact sheets. Data for 2004–2005 are from *World Investment Report 2006*, country fact sheets.

to a drastic increase in Japanese FDI in advanced economies. Japanese FDI in the United States amounted to $113 billion in 1987–1991, or three times the total in 1951–1986. Japan was America's largest foreign investor in 1992. Japanese FDI to Europe in 1987–1993 more than doubled its total prior to 1986.[36] Japan's FDI overseas increased again in the early 1990s due to the second endaka. But Japanese FDI outflows this time around were more concentrated in East Asia. Some large Japanese companies have invested heavily overseas, partly to get around protectionist pressure on Japanese exports. Japanese automobile companies, for example, have become largely "domestic" in the U.S. market. Nissan produced 950,000 of 985,000 vehicles sold in the United States in 2004 in its factories in Tennessee and Mississippi.[37] Japan continues to invest heavily overseas, more than $30 billion a year for the past few years, as Table 7.1 shows.

In the second wave, the four tigers also engaged in outward investments beginning in the 1980s.[38] They poured much investment into Southeast Asia, actually surpassing Japanese investments in some Southeast Asian countries, as discussed previously. As calculated from Table 7.1, the four economies invested an annual average of $39.1 billion overseas in 2001–2005, surpassing Japan's $35.2 billion.

Hong Kong has been the largest source of FDI into China. Taiwanese firms have moved much of Taiwan's manufacturing to the mainland. Since much of Taiwanese investment was disguised as from Hong Kong or the Virgin Islands, Taiwan is probably the largest investor in China right now. Taiwanese companies are estimated to employ 10 million people in the mainland. Taiwanese investment has turned China into a major power in production of IT equipment. In 2002 China became the world's second largest IT hardware producer, trailing only the United States. At the same time, the mainland has imported a large quantity of IT components from Taiwan.[39] South Korea has become a major investor in China as well.

China is also investing overseas, with a sharp increase from less than half a billion U.S. dollars in 2000 to $16 billion in 2006. China's total FDI abroad reached $73 billion at the end of 2006.[40] China's leading firms are venturing overseas, making headline-catching moves. For example, International Business Machines Corp. (IBM) agreed to sell its personal computer business, the ThinkPad line of notebook computers, for $1.75 billion to China's largest computer maker Lenovo Group Ltd. on December 7, 2004. The most controversial case of Chinese acquisition of foreign assets was the failed attempt by China's National Offshore Oil Corporation (CNOOC) to purchase Unocal Corp. The Chinese firm made an $18.5 billion bid for the American oil firm on June 22, 2005. If successful, this purchase would become the largest purchase of a foreign firm by a Chinese firm. Chevron, which had already bid for Unocal, sweetened its bid to more than $17 billion. The Chinese bid invited strong congressional and media criticism. On August 2, 2005, CNOOC withdrew its bid.[41]

Chinese firms are moving overseas because they want to outflank considerable trade barriers on Chinese products, following the examples of Japan and South Korea. In addition, the China market has become so competitive that Chinese firms have to move overseas just to remain competitive at home. Unlike Japanese and South Korean firms, however, Chinese firms are seeking to take a shortcut in upgrading their products from low-cost to brand premium by acquiring foreign brands.

REGIONALIZATION OF PRODUCTION

What is striking about contemporary East Asian political economy is the regionalization of production. In the third section of Chapter 5, I have discussed at length the flying geese formation theory and the product cycle theory to explain the regional dimension of the East Asian economic miracle. Those two theories are used to explain intraregional movement of direct investment and how FDI has contributed to East Asia's rapid economic growth. My discussion in the previous section has also shown how important foreign capital has been for the capital formation and exports of East Asian economies, particularly ASEAN and China. Put simply, firms increasingly organize production on a regional or global rather than national basis, which means that much of the business they conduct is actually on an intrafirm basis.

Regionalization of production is more than FDI, however. In recent years, some scholars have used the term *cross-border production networks* (CPNs) or *international production networks* (IPNs) to analyze a new form of market organization in the contemporary global economy. By cross-border production networks, Michael Borrus, Dieter Ernst, and Stephan Haggard meant "the inter- and intra-firm relationships through which the firm organizes the entire range of its business activities: from research and development (R&D), product definition and design, to supply of inputs, manufacturing (or production of a service), distribution, and support services."[42] Thus, CPNs include not only firms and their affiliates and subsidiaries but also suppliers, subcontractors, service providers, and other participants in cooperative arrangements, particularly in R&D.

Traditionally, a firm vertically organizes all its R&D, production, distribution, and services using affiliates based in the country of origin. In the 1970s, brand name companies in the garment, footwear, furniture, and toy industries began outsourcing their manufactures to IPN partners. The electronics industry began outsourcing in the mid-1980s. Cisco represents the other extreme. Cisco does not do R&D. It focuses on definition of product and some software development. It relies on alliances (no equities) for production, design, and development. Its products are done by contract manufacturers in Asia and the United States.

Regionalization of production results from globalization of production. In a globalized economy, companies increasingly have to form transnational interfirm alliances to remain competitive. That is the case for East Asian companies. When we talk about production networks, we need to discuss both the production networks created by Asian firms and those by non-Asian firms. The fact that many production networks have been created by non-Asian firms shows that East Asian production networks should be seen as part of the global networks. IPNs thus characterize the changing division of labor in East Asia. More and more, firms enter the region not just to take advantage of cheaper resources and labor and to expand markets but also to take advantage of heterogeneous local technological capabilities in the region. The variation in these local technologies resulted from both transfer of technologies by multinational companies and local governments' policies.[43]

Studies of specific sectors show an increasing regionalization of production in East Asia, particularly in the electronics sector. However, it is harder to measure regionalization of production than regional trade interdependence. One useful measure is to look at components and parts trade statistics. East Asian trade in components has grown faster than Europe and North America's. By the end of the 1990s, components accounted for about 20 percent of East Asian manufacturing exports. Intraregional components trade has grown faster than global trade expansion. The Asian financial crisis did not stop this development.[44] While parts and components exports as shares of total exports increased worldwide from 1980 to 2002, East Asia saw the greatest increase.[45] The degree of production sharing is particularly high in the electronics industry.[46]

Using sophisticated tools of block multiplier decomposition and path decomposition to analyze detailed trade data, David Roland-Holst showed that global supply chains that have grown rapidly in recent years due to Western and East Asian FDI connect autonomous East Asian firms as intermediate suppliers situated at different nodes of these chains. He found that the majority of value creation and trade often comes from these linkages.[47]

It is largely private companies that have established intraregional linkages to seek competitive advantages in the global market. The dominant players that have created production networks in East Asia are Japanese, American, European, South Korean, and ethnic Chinese firms. Constraint of space does not allow a nuanced comparison of the various systems here. Rather, I will offer a stylized contrast of the Japanese, American, and Chinese systems, viewing them as prototypes, the South Korean system as similar to the Japanese system, and the European system as close to the American model.

Japanese firms tend to be centralized. Compared with Western firms, Japanese firms are less willing to share technologies and more hesitant to employ local managers. Japanese subsidiaries source most components from parent firms in

Japan. When they increase local sourcing, it often comes from Japanese suppliers that had invested in the country as well. Japanese firms replicate their domestic production networks overseas to internationalize their ownership-specific advantages while keeping R&D at home.[48] Moreover, the reverse exports of the Japanese subsidiaries to Japan tend to displace exports from domestically owned firms in Taiwan and South Korea. In key sectors such as electronics, the Japanese companies have followed a similar approach in Southeast Asia and then in China.[49]

By contrast, American subsidiaries in East Asia are more willing to transfer technologies and often assign the task of R&D for local as well as global markets.[50] U.S. firms that are less centralized in decision making follow open and flexible strategies. These national differences have historical and social roots. They also reflect national policy.

For example, Japanese and Western electronics firms follow different strategies in Malaysia. While Japanese and Western firms started out to exploit cheap labor, Western firms turned to localization to exploit new Malaysian potentials and Japanese firms largely remained unchanged in their focus. As a result, Japanese firms have largely taken a production-cost focused, status-quo position on investment in Malaysia while Western firms have been more aggressive in committing investment in the country.[51]

The Japanese and Chinese networks in East Asia are different. Unlike the Japanese, the Chinese have had a much longer and deeper social root in Southeast Asia. The Chinese networks are familial/clannish, horizontal, loose, and open. A survival mentality and the Confucian tradition have shaped the first generation of Chinese entrepreneurs. They emphasize thrift, trust family members irrespective of their competency, and prefer an imperial organization in which professional managers have limited authority. The Chinese network is flexible and open, connecting with the outside world as well.[52] It is also important to recognize that Chinese capitalism is dynamic and has been subject to globalizing forces.[53]

The organization of IPNs should have important implications for the competitiveness of different countries. As a case in point, the U.S. electronics firms benefited from their alliances in East Asia in competition with the Japanese firms. American firms were dominant in the global electronic market in the 1950s. Japanese firms such as Matsushita and Hitachi that emulated American firms and excelled in lean production techniques prevailed over American consumer electronics producers by the late 1970s and came to challenge the U.S. lead in other areas by the early 1980s. But technologies shifted by the mid-1980s. Firms using microelectronics technologies now wanted their systems to interoperate. As a result, technical standards became intellectual properties available for others in the value chain to produce components, systems, or software. This meant a shift of market power from assemblers to those who control product standards, such as

Intel for microprocessors and Microsoft for operating systems. Now U.S. firms linked with Asian suppliers to form alternative production networks to reduce dependence on Japanese supplies. They began to invest in electronics in non-Japan East Asia in the 1960s largely for exports back to the United States and Europe, a purpose that necessitated sustained effort to help their Asian partners upgrade their technological capability. By contrast, Japanese firms invested in East Asia to enter the local market, which meant transfer of technologies just enough for a less demanding market. By the 1990s, American firms became competitive against Japanese firms by focusing on new product definition and design while relying on contract producers in Taiwan and Singapore for production.[54] In a way, a combination of American and ethnic Chinese firms in East Asia helped erode Japanese dominance in electronics in Asia and to lead to a resurgence of U.S. dominance in the industry.

But how effective a system is ultimately depends on circumstances, such as the type of sector which partly explains why we do not see a convergence of a single organizing form of regional production networks. The close and exclusionary networks Japanese firms have built yield good results in the automobile sector because of the host countries' protectionist, industrial policy to promote the sector and because of the incremental innovation nature of the sector. By contrast, the Japanese firms have not been that successful in the computer accessories sector, which the Asian governments have not sought to protect and because of sudden and dramatic innovations of the sector.[55]

Japanese firms are facing tougher competition even in their strongholds. Japan's auto parts investment in Thailand is a case in point. While Japanese auto parts makers invested heavily in Thailand to create a strong network, they faced a changed business environment in the late 1990s when American and European auto parts manufacturers became rivals in the Thai market. The Japanese companies also began to adopt a new, Western-style procurement policy (away from a Japanese-style business association or *keiretsu*). A key development is that Japanese automobile makers such as Isuzu, Mazda, and Mitsubishi are now partnered with Western firms so they adopt a Western-style procurement policy. It is estimated that now 70 percent of Thai auto production is using the Western-style procurement policy.[56]

THE EAST ASIAN STATE AND PRODUCTION

The East Asian state has been heavily involved in production politics. The East Asian developmental state model essentially views the manufacturing sector as central to rapid economic growth and transformation. This section examines how different East Asian nations have dealt with the challenge of creating and maintaining manufacturing industries.

Picking the Winners

East Asian nations virtually all strive to create and maintain national champions and boost industrial production through industrial policy. The essence of industrial policy is selective state intervention. Marcus Noland and Howard Pack defined industrial policy as "an effort by a government to alter the sectoral structure of production toward sectors it believes offer greater prospects for accelerated growth than would be generated by a typical process of industrial evolution according to static comparative advantage."[57] Thus, we may call industrial policy simply picking the winners.

Japan was the first East Asian nation to adopt industrial policy and set a successful example for others.[58] Japan recognized the need to build a competitive manufacturing sector by restructuring industry from labor-intensive to capital-intensive to knowledge-intensive industries and by adopting aggressive domestic and international business strategies.[59] Japan created a powerful industrial bureaucracy to execute a production-oriented export policy, channel scarce capital to targeted industries, and protect the domestic turf from foreign competition. While internationalization has weakened Japan's industrial policy, Japanese bureaucrats continue to adopt industrial policy in high-tech sectors.[60]

South Korea took industrial policy to another level. South Korean strategies have been somewhat different from the Japanese model, adapting to local conditions. The South Korean government began to adopt industrial policy in the early 1960s, when the government channeled money into infrastructure, labor-intensive export industries, and import substitution of chemical, petroleum, and steel production. In the 1970s, the government expanded labor-intensive exports and chemical industry and initiated industries of consumer electronics, automobiles, and shipbuilding. The government allocated financial resources to sectors or firms it deemed central for the country's economic growth.[61] While South Korea turned more to market forces in the 1980s and the 1990s, it retained some key features of industrial policy.[62] The flip side of the state support for large companies was that large companies threatened by bankruptcy could hide behind court-administered rehabilitation procedures based on social values (i.e., employment) and prospect for improvement. Such a system began to cause problems of misallocation of resources beginning in the early 1990s.[63]

The 1997 Asian financial crisis was a turning point for South Korea. Losing cost competitiveness to China and some other countries, the South Korean government has chosen to move beyond skilled, low-labor, cost-based manufacturing to a knowledge-based information and communications technology (ICT) sector. The South Korean government has invested heavily in ICT infrastructure, such as high-speed computer links between cities and free access to broadband Internet service and education and training in ICT for millions of citizens.[64] The government also reformed its bankruptcy system to lower exit barriers for large companies by emphasizing the criteria of efficiency.[65]

Taiwan also engaged in state intervention although it does not have an economic bureaucracy as centralized and as powerful as the South Korean industrial planning bureaucracy.[66] The Taiwanese government encouraged industrial upgrading to heavy industries in the mid-1970s through fiscal incentives, control over trade regime, and public funding for select industries. As Taiwan only achieved success in some heavy industries because of rising oil prices, the government began to shift to technology-intensive industries in the late 1970s. The government created the Hsinchu Science-Based Industrial Park in 1980, which has helped to make some domestic firms world leaders. The Hsinchu Park is similar to Silicon Valley in California in many ways. Numerous Taiwanese entrepreneurs used to work in Silicon Valley. But unlike Silicon Valley, Hsinchu has been the product of deliberate government policy.[67] By the mid-1980s, the Taiwanese government resorted more to market forces, which proved successful as electronic and information industries came to drive Taiwan's exports in the late 1980s and the early 1990s.[68] Similar to South Korea in the face of mainland China's challenge, Taiwan now needs to move from manufacturing to knowledge-based industries. Taiwan has identified the semiconductor, the thin-film transistor LCD flat-screen industries, digital content, and biotechnology as the next phase of economic development.[69]

The Singaporean government has also used public enterprises to boost industrialization. In July 1967, the British government announced its plan to withdraw all military forces from Singapore by the mid-1970s. The British military bases had employed about 16 percent of Singapore's labor force and contributed 13–20 percent of its GDP. In response, the Singaporean government decided the next year on a dramatic expansion of government investment in manufacturing. By the end of 1970, the government held about one-quarter of all shareholders' funds in the economy. One-third of the loans went to the electrical machinery and petroleum products industries, resulting in a large increase in the labor force employed in manufacturing and values added in the two selected industries. With that initial success, the Singaporean government continued to promote industry and economy, using government corporations and statutory boards. By the 1980s, the Jurong Town Corporation had built dozens of industrial parks and export processing zones. The government had a complete ownership or a majority control in manufacturing firms in chemicals and petrochemicals, iron and steal, shipbuilding and repair, food, textiles, and printing. The government financed investment in manufacturing with loans and could afford to finance public investment projects by keeping current expenditure lower than revenues by borrowing from the country's Central Provident Fund. The Central Provident

Fund was established as a social security agency in 1955 to mandate savings for retirement. In addition to domestic investment, the government began to encourage foreign investment in 1968 with tax incentives and strict restrictions on labor's right to negotiate with management.[70] Singapore emphasized financial and business services after 1978, continuing its success in selective government intervention. While the Singaporean government still welcomes foreign capital, it now also seeks to develop domestic capital, particularly in biotechnology. The government has committed billions of U.S. dollars to the endeavor, attracting top researchers from around the world with top-of-the-line research facilities and strong government support without meddling.

Unlike other East Asian governments, the Hong Kong government has had limited intervention in the economy while adopting measures to keep production cost low. The government basically had low taxes and limited regulations to provide a suitable business environment for all firms, local or foreign. The government does not get involved in the manufacturing sector. Simply put, Hong Kong has been a showcase of free market economy.

The Malaysian government also emphasized manufacturing, introducing import substitution industrialization from the late 1950s to the end of the 1960s, shifting to an export-led industrialization in the early 1970s, and resorting to a protectionist heavy industrialization in the early 1980s.[71] Datuk Seri Mahathir bin Mohamad, who became prime minister in 1980, launched a heavy industrialization drive in 1981, largely modeled after South Korea. In 1986 the government launched the Industrial Master Plan, an industrial policy with plans for targeted industries.[72] Since Mahathir was also talking about "learning from Japan" for Malaysia's modernization drive, his plan was to seek Japan's capital and technology for heavy industrialization, particularly in automobile and steel sectors.[73] In this context, Malaysia formed a national automobile company, Perusahaan Otomobil Nasional (Proton), in collaboration with Japan's Mitsubishi to produce Malaysia's national car, the Proton Saga, which is really a remodeled Mitsubishi Lancer. Mahathir saw the Proton Saga as a symbol of Malaysia's status as an industrializing country in the world. The term was favorable to Mitsubishi, which controlled technologies and faced little competition from other foreign carmakers, including loans guaranteed by the Malaysian government and import duties on foreign cars. The Japanese firm also came to occupy top management positions in Proton.[74]

The Thai government has not engaged in industrial policy as actively as Northeast Asian countries, but it set up the Board of Investment in 1959 to promote private investment. The Ministries of Industry, Commerce, and Finance and the Bank of Thailand have adopted policies to facilitate industrial development.[75] Thailand has also adopted an open attitude toward FDI, which increased dramatically in

Thailand after the mid-1990s, led by Japanese, Taiwanese, Korean, and Hong Kong firms in labor-intensive industries largely because of low labor costs in Thailand.[76]

Indonesia followed a socialist economic approach from 1950 to 1965, a period referred to as the Old Order, when the government sought to control the "commanding heights" of industries by turning the nationalized Dutch enterprises into state-owned enterprises (about 20 percent of the country's GDP), which denied sales of these firms to economically powerful ethnic Chinese businessmen and allowed patronage of political supporters. That policy was not successful. In the early 1970s, Indonesia grew economically thanks to its drastically increased oil revenues. The oil windfall had a negative effect on non-oil tradable goods, namely reducing their competitiveness against foreign firms, due to the real appreciation of the currency. The Indonesian government responded by increasing protection of domestic industries. Using oil revenues, the government launched an import substitution industrialization plan and resorted to export promotion only after the mid-1980s.[77]

The Chinese government promoted heavy industrialization in the 1950s, first following the Soviet planned economy model and then the Chinese mass mobilization model. When reform began in the late 1970s, initial emphasis was placed on the agricultural and light-industry sectors to adjust the distorted economic structure. With a growing economy and the need to reform state enterprises, the Chinese government decided to create its own national champions, initially modeled after the South Korean *chaebol*. Similar to Japan and South Korea, the Chinese government channels cheap credit to the championed enterprises, provides tax breaks, and helps them secure business deals at home and abroad. But unlike Japan and South Korea, China has far more control over state enterprises. The Chinese government created the State-Owned Asset Supervision and Administration Commission under the State Council in March 2003 to be in charge of large state enterprises, now around 170. Unlike Japan and South Korea, China has invited foreign companies to operate in China, which has explained partly the explosive growth of Chinese manufacturing. In recent years, the Chinese government has allowed some foreign acquisition of Chinese companies while maintaining severe restrictions. At the same time, some Chinese are increasingly concerned about technology dependency on Western and Japanese firms. As a sign of greater industrial ambition, in March 2007, the Chinese State Council announced that the Chinese government would push for R&D of large civilian planes. With a greater technological base and capital, China is essentially taking on Airbus and Boeing in a strategic sector.

There have been debates over the effectiveness of industrial policy. Critics point out that the states have often picked wrong winners. From a different angle, based on an examination of Japan, South Korea, and Taiwan, Noland and Pack concluded that these countries' industrial policy had only a modest positive impact on economic growth while creating unintended negative effects. Industrial policy tends to breed corruption. It is in any case difficult now for developing nations to adopt that model in the changed international economic system we have today: The United States and other developed nations are more driven by economic interests after the cold war ended, and selective subsidies are harder to implement also because of a stronger enforcement mechanism of the World Trade Organization.[78] The flip side of picking winners is creating "losers." From an economic perspective, state intervention distorts allocations of resources, resulting in inefficiency. Overemphasis on one sector leads to relative underdevelopment of other sectors. Also, the practice of channeling soft credit to manufacturing firms from government-controlled or government-guided banks has resulted in shallow financial markets in East Asia as well as nonperforming loans in most East Asian countries. A focus on the manufacturing sector often means a weak services sector. As a case in point, China's financial support for state-owned champions has resulted in insufficient financing for private firms that are generally more efficient than state-owned enterprises. More broadly, a bias toward manufactured exports at the expense of domestic consumption has contributed to a global financial imbalance.

Foreign Direct Investment Policies

Inward investments. There has been a sharp difference between East Asian nations in terms of inward investments. Japan and South Korea largely discouraged FDI in their countries. The government and the companies preferred to acquire technologies through licensing rather than FDI.[79] The South Korean government allowed FDI in the light-industry export sector but discouraged foreign ownership in the import substitution and heavy industry sectors. The government encouraged FDI in the high-tech sectors in the 1970s but the share of FDI in these sectors remained low.[80] After the Asian financial crisis, South Korea changed course and now encourages FDI into the country.[81] As Table 7.1 shows, inward FDI for South Korea increased from an annual average of $697 million in 1985–1995 to $7,198 million in 2005. However, as shown by recent South Korean backlash against American investors' attempt to take over South Korea's KT&G, formerly the Korean Tobacco & Ginseng, South Korea has yet to be truly welcoming to foreign investors.[82] Former Japanese Prime Minister Koizumi hoped to double FDI by 2008, but legislators in his own ruling party frustrated his effort to reduce barriers to FDI. Resistance to FDI remains strong in Japan.[83] As Table 7.2 shows, FDI accounted for only 0.3 percent of Japan's gross capital formation in 2005.

Other East Asian economies welcome foreign investment, although mainly in the manufacturing sector. Hong Kong follows a laissez-faire approach to FDI. In fact, the British colonial government did not distinguish between foreign and domestic firms.[84] Taiwan welcomed FDI with selective prohibitions. Singapore provided incentives to foreign firms. Southeast Asia actively sought an FDI-led industrialization starting in the late 1980s. Thailand was cautious at first but became more welcoming. In fact, a 2005 World Bank study found Thailand having a better investment climate than China, India, and most East Asian countries. For example, firm managers in Thailand spend the fewest working hours dealing with bureaucrats and regulators.[85] The Philippines also were somewhat cautious. Indonesia saw the most dramatic shifts, from nationalization (1950–1965) to openness (1967–1973) to restrictive policies (1974–1984) and then back to openness in the early 1990s.[86] Malaysia has welcomed FDI. For political reasons, the Malaysian government encouraged foreign investors at the expense of economically powerful local Chinese enterprises.[87] Similar to the Thai case, a World Bank study in 2005 found Malaysia's investment climate better than even the advanced regions in China judging by criteria such as customs clearance time.[88]

China enacted a joint venture law in 1979 and has also provided major incentives for foreign investors since the 1980s. In fact, the Chinese laws and regulations have treated foreign firms better than private Chinese companies although not as well as state-owned enterprises.[89] The Chinese government has also used its market potential as leverage to achieve technology transfers, but this has not been that effective. Even the effort of purchasing foreign brands will be only a temporary relief for state enterprises. There has been growing concern in China in the past few years that FDI has not helped China upgrade technologies as foreign firms continue to control core technologies. The Chinese government is hoping to turn the country into a manufacturing powerhouse, not just a production base. Since 2005 there has been a nationalist backlash against perceived foreign firms purchasing core Chinese industrial enterprises to monopolize the Chinese market. The Chinese government announced in August 2006 that starting on September 9, 2006, foreign acquisition of key Chinese enterprises has to be reported to the Ministry of Commerce, a signal that Beijing may tighten regulations in the name of national economic security.

The Vietnamese government now also actively seeks FDI, following the Chinese and ASEAN models. North Korea issued a similar law in 1984 and enacted a few new business laws in the early 1990s to encourage foreign investors and established the Rajin-Sonbong Economic and Trade Zone.[90]

Outward investments. Japan led in outward investments. Japanese firms expanded overseas initially to obtain primary products and to promote exports. The Japanese government encouraged FDI overseas in mineral and energy sectors through tax breaks and financing from the Japan Export-Import Bank. As Kojima noted in the late 1970s, Japanese FDI was "trade-oriented," meant to complement Japan's comparative advantage position. Specifically, Japanese firms that established production operation in Southeast Asia, where labor cost was cheaper than in Japan, could substitute export of final products with exports of machinery, equipment, and technological know-how.[91] But with concerns over protectionist pressure in North America and Western Europe, Japanese firms invested in these markets. Japanese firms also turned to East Asia to avoid restrictions and to reexport to the United States and Europe. The Japanese model was followed by South Korea, Taiwan, and Singapore.

The Chinese government now also encourages outward FDI. It follows the pattern established by Japan and the NIEs. Pushed by insufficient demand at home, this new twist began around 2000 and is meant to acquire natural resources, promote exports, and contract projects. When purchasing foreign firms, Chinese firms tend to pledge to keep the managers and labor force, unlike Western multinational corporations that would immediately consolidate the new purchases. The reason is that Chinese firms need technology and management skills, which is part of the reason that they are moving overseas in the first place. The Chinese government has supported the efforts of the large state enterprises with funding; after all, these companies mostly have narrow profit margins and are not that competitive globally but for state support.[92]

EAST ASIAN COMPANIES

East Asian companies are the engines of East Asian economic growth and economic transformation, and they have become more prominent globally. Japan led the way. Brand names by globally competitive Japanese firms abound, including Sony, Toshiba, Toyota, Honda, Nissan, Mitsubishi, and Nintendo. As Table 7.4 shows, Japan accounts for more global brands than any other East Asian country. While Japan has experienced a decade of economic slowdowns and recessions, leading Japanese firms remain competitive internationally. Through incremental reforms, Japanese companies have reduced debt by saving more and by adopting more flexible labor policies, such as hiring part-timers and contract workers who cost far less than regular workers.

Six large Japanese industrial groups or keiretsu (it literally means sequence) dominate Japanese industries: Mitsubishi, Mitsui, Sumitomo, Fuyo, Daiichi-Kangyo, and Sanwa. Mitsubishi, Mitsui, and Sumitomo are based on the prewar family-controlled business conglomerates or *zaibatsu,* which the American Occupation authorities disbanded. A keiretsu has member companies operating in various industries, which are organized around a main bank and a trading company. The member companies are connected through cross-shareholdings.[93] The Japan-

TABLE 7.4
Asia and Global Brands

Brand	Rank in 2006	Rank in 2005	Rank in 2004	Rank in 2003	Country of Ownership	Brand Values ($ million) 2006
Coca-Cola	1	1	1	1	U.S.	67,000
Microsoft	2	2	2	2	U.S.	56,926
IBM	3	3	3	3	U.S.	56,201
GE	4	4	4	4	U.S.	48,907
Intel	5	5	5	5	U.S.	32,319
Nokia	6	6	8	6	Finland	30,131
Toyota	7	9	9	11	Japan	27,941
Disney	8	7	6	7	U.S.	27,848
McDonald's	9	8	7	8	U.S.	27,501
Mercedes-Benz	10	11	11	10	Germany	21,795
Honda	19	19	18	18	Japan	17,049
Samsung	20	20	21	25	South Korea	16,169
Sony	26	28	20	20	Japan	11,695
Canon	35	35	35	39	Japan	9,968
Nintendo	51	50	46	32	Japan	6,559
Hyundai	75	84	New		South Korea	4,078
Panasonic	77	78	77	79	Japan	3,977
Nissan	90	85	90	89	Japan	3,108
Lexus	92	New			Japan	3,070
LG	94	97	New		South Korea	3,010

Source: Interbrand, in Business Week, August 7, 2006, 60–66; August 1, 2005, 90–94; and August 9–16, 2004.

Note: Among the top 100 brands in 2006, 52 belong to American firms (including Accenture, which relocated to Bermuda), 37 to European companies, and 11 to East Asian firms.

ese keiretsu system has made it difficult for foreign or domestic firms to enter their turf. However, things have begun to change in recent years. In a celebrated case, Renault SA of France merged with Japan's Nissan Motor Co. in 1999, and Carlos Ghosn, who came to lead both companies, became a symbol of change. Then in July 2006, as a first, a major blue-chip company, Oji Paper Co., mounted a $1.2 billion hostile bid for another blue-chip company, Hokuetsu Paper Mills Ltd. That bid failed shortly when Mitsubishi Corp. increased its stake to almost 25 percent with Hokuetsu's sale of shares to Mitsubishi below market price and when Nippon Paper Group Inc., number 2 paper maker in Japan, also increased its share.

South Koreans have followed Japan's example with a similar set of manufacturing firms, such as Hyundai, Samsung, Daewoo, LG (formerly Lucky Goldstar), and SK (formerly Sun Kyung), the so-called *chaebol* (financial clique), which refer to business groups consisting of large companies in different sectors controlled by family members.[94] These large chaebol have powered South Korean economic growth. Proportionally, South Korean chaebol are more dominant in domestic economy than Japanese keiretsu. Unlike prewar Japanese zaibatsu, a chaebol does not have a main bank at its core although it does have a general trading company similar to the Japanese system.

Some South Korean brands have received much international media exposure, an indicator of their rising name recognition. As Table 7.4 shows, South Korea's Samsung, Hyundai, and LG rank among the top 100 global brands in 2006. Samsung ranks number 20, trailing only Toyota and Honda among Asian firms. Samsung Electronics has also built a brand name of cutting-edge technologies and design in recent years. Since the Asian financial crisis, the company has restructured itself and spent billions of U.S. dollars on research and marketing to build a brand name that is now close to that of Sony.[95] Detroit automakers now consider Hyundai a serious rival similar to Japan's major carmakers in the 1980s. Hyundai was introduced in the United States in the 1980s. Its products were initially considered shoddy, but Hyundai has become more competitive. It became the world's seventh largest carmaker in 2004, overtaking Honda and Nissan. In 2004 Hyundai tied for second place with Honda in the United States in overall quality in a J.D. Power and Associates survey, trailing only Toyota but ahead of Mercedes-Benz.[96]

Taiwanese companies are largely small and family-owned, partly because the government continued their practice from mainland days to be highly restrictive of large firms. As a result, businesses chose to establish new small firms rather than expanding existing ones. Taiwanese companies now realize the importance of having their own brands. Unlike South Korean firms, Taiwanese firms such as BenQ Corporation that makes consumer electronics and mobile phones have chosen to make IT products for other firms that own the brands, a practice known as original design manufacturing or original equipment manufacturing. As a result, Taiwan has no entry on the list of the top 100 global brands reported by the consultancy Interbrand. Taiwan now faces competition from China, more intense competition for consolidated brand-name IT firms, and the burst of the IT bubble. Since around 2001, some large Taiwanese firms have been trying to create their own brands. Acer, for instance, has been selling more products under its own brand.[97]

Unlike South Korea, public or state-owned enterprises have played an important role in Taiwan's economic life, particularly strong in utilities, heavy industry, and infrastructure projects such as transportation. Taiwan's share of state-owned enterprises in nonagricultural GDP was around 21 percent in the 1950s–1960s and 14–17 percent in the 1980s–1990s, a level close to India and Indonesia. Public and state-owned enterprises basically focused on the domestic market, whereas most exporting firms were private.[98]

As China is emerging as an economic superpower, its companies have also become more active globally and attracted much international attention. The Chinese government has been trying to privatize its state-owned enterprises.[99] At the same time, the government has been trying to create 30–50 state-owned national champions that are globally competitive by 2010. To advance this objective, the government provides land, labor, and cheap credits from state banks. The government also facilitates the companies in their overseas activities. Now they have succeeded in creating some large companies that rank among Fortune Magazine's Global 500 measured by revenues. Nineteen Chinese companies (not including one from Hong Kong) were listed among Fortune 500 in 2005, an increase of three over the previous year. SINOPEC, China's largest company for the year, ranked 23rd in the world. By comparison, the U.S. had 170 companies and Japan had 70. Of the top 10 companies in Asia, Japan had 6, China 3, and South Korea 1.[100]

But are these Chinese firms truly competitive internationally? Most of these firms are large because they enjoy monopoly or near monopoly in China and because they are commodity producers for a fast growing market. The 19 Chinese firms listed among Fortune 500 are all state companies in oil, power, banking, telecommunications, steel, and chemistry. If one looks at the brand names or technological capacity, the Chinese firms have not been that successful. They cannot truly compete with Western, Japanese, or South Korean consumer brand names. Some of the foreign purchases were designed to buy brand names. However, this does not solve the basic problem of lack of technological innovation inherent in the Chinese firms. As China's own statistics show, although China's exports of high-tech products have increased drastically, less than 10 percent came from China's own brands in 2004.[101] Only 0.03 percent of the Chinese firms control their core technologies. Ninety-nine percent of the firms have not applied for patent, and 60 percent of the firms do not have their own brands.[102] According to UNCTAD, China's PetroChina was the largest spender on R&D among China firms, but it ranked only 219 in the world in 2003. By contrast, 4 Japanese firms (Toyota Motor, Matsushita Electric, Sony, and Honda Motor) ranked among the top 20 in the world. South Korea's Samsung Electronics ranked the 33rd. China had only 2 firms among the world's 700 largest R&D spending firms in 2003. The United States had 296 firms, Japan 154, South Korea 10, and Taiwan 8.[103]

Similar to Taiwanese and Hong Kong companies, ethnic Chinese companies in Southeast Asia are family firms that tend to be flexible and diversified in various businesses. Prominent firms include the Pico Group in Singapore, Wee Cho Yaw's United Overseas Bank in Singapore, Robert Kuok's Shangri-La Hotel in Malaysia, Liem Sioe Liong's Salim Group in Indonesia, and Charoen Pokphand Group in Thailand.[104] The 500 largest local public companies controlled by ethnic Chinese had total assets over $500 billion in the 1990s, and Chinese firms accounted for

73 percent of market capitalization in Indonesia, 81 percent in Singapore, 90 percent in Thailand, 60 percent in Malaysia, and 50 percent in the Philippines in the same period.[105] To be sure, market capitalization does not equate to a nation's wealth. One should not forget about a large public sector, the presence of foreign capital, the land, and other assets controlled by the *bumiputras* or sons of the soil.[106] But few would dispute that the ethnic Chinese firms are major economic forces in Southeast Asia.

Successful non-Chinese companies also abound in Southeast Asia.[107] But they face challenges. For example, a survey of the Malaysian firms finds them suffering from a serious shortage of skills and lacking innovation.[108] Similar to China, Southeast Asia often sees large state enterprises in manufacturing, mining, and energy. State companies such as Malaysia's Proton, Perwaja Steel, and Petronas (petroleum) and Indonesia's Pertamina (petroleum) are international players.

The behavior of companies has important implications for the politics and economy of East Asian countries as elsewhere. From an economic perspective, Japan's recession in the past decade can be explained in part by the efforts of Japanese companies to balance their sheets by reducing debt in a time of economic slowdown.[109]

East Asian businesses traditionally recognize the legitimacy of state interference or accept it as an unpleasant reality. At the same time, these companies are gradually becoming more independent and powerful in domestic politics. This is particularly the case for those internationally competitive companies. The government depends on them to deliver economic growth and jobs. Unlike in the United States that has a strong antitrust tradition, the chance of breaking a national champion company in East Asia is not good.

As East Asian countries have become more integrated into the global market, globalization has affected how these firms operate in terms of governance and organization.[110] International norms and practices of business are diffusing into East Asia through networks of production and also international education. Asian companies often hire non-Asian managers, and Asians work in non-Asian companies. Many Asian businesspersons, particularly the second generation, have been educated in the West.

DOMESTIC POLITICAL ECONOMY OF PRODUCTION

How does East Asian production relate to East Asian political economy? The first question that needs to be addressed is why production has been so important for East Asia. In some ways, all countries want production because they want a strong economic base for national power and the employment that manufacturing provides. Thus, Paul Kennedy warned that the United States was losing manufacturing, which indicated that the country was declining like all previous great powers.[111]

It is obvious why a developing nation might want to emphasize manufacturing production. When developing nations began economic development, they easily concluded that the gap with advanced countries was the degree of industrialization. Early intellectual leaders also told them that they could not depend on agricultural commodities because of deteriorating terms of trade caused by decreasing input ratio in the industrialized countries; the share of agriculture became smaller and smaller and technological advance meant that industrialized countries would not need as much input, both of which make agricultural exports less profitable.[112] The state then needs to give industrialization a big push, nurturing and protecting national industries. Thus, late industrializers or late-late industrializers tend to adopt centralized, state interventionist political economy regimes.[113] What made East Asia different was not ideologies but that they made far more progress than other developing regions.

Politics matters in policy toward production. Who doesn't want the rent from state protection and state support, which are by definition scarce commodities? State favors have led to crony capitalism to different degrees in various East Asian economies.

Corruption aside, the East Asian governments seek various objectives in their industrialization plan. Taiwan's heavier dependence on public and state-owned enterprises than South Korea's was partly due to the political logic that Taiwan's Nationalist government had political interest not to turn mainlander-dominated public enterprises to the private sector dominated by native Taiwanese businessmen.[114]

As another striking example, the Malaysian government has sought to enhance the economic position of the indigenous Malay population in its foreign-capital-based industrialization. The Malaysian government adopted an import substitution industrialization strategy beginning in the late 1950s, but the Malay population did not benefit that much. A widening income gap contributed to mounting racial tensions that erupted in anti-Chinese riots in May 1969.[115] Mahathir's main purpose for industrialization was to elevate his country to the rank of the four Asian tigers and to help achieve the goal of the New Economic Policy adopted in 1970 to enhance the economic status of the indigenous Malays vis-à-vis more affluent ethnic Chinese and Indian communities in Malaysia.[116] Thus, Malaysia's picking of winners were not "the true winners" in the domestic context since Chinese firms were not favored and the Japanese firms have enjoyed a privileged position in this relationship.

For political economy of production, political concerns factor into decisions regarding FDI. One of the reasons for Singapore's early encouragement of FDI into the country was that the government wanted foreign powers to have a stake in Singapore to enhance the country's survival. The Malaysian government encouraged FDI to dilute the Chinese control of the economy in the country.[117]

The flip side of picking the winners is to create losers. Unlike the Western states that have developed social welfare systems, East Asian governments have largely relied on a growth-with-equity philosophy, informal social support mechanisms, and control or repression of opposition. As discussed in Chapter 5, East Asia's rapid growth has benefited many. At the same time, as revealed by the Asian financial crisis, there are limitations in this model. A new social contract is needed and demanded.[118]

Japan has performed the best in East Asia in maintaining social stability. In the Japanese system, the state has followed the logic of a rising tide lifting all boats. To soften potential opposition, the government has provided side payments for losing sectors.[119] The government has also tried to shield weak sectors from international competition. While bureaucrats may be credited with picking winners for growing sectors, they have not been able to resist political pressure from troubled industries.[120] However, foreign pressure makes it increasingly difficult to support losing sectors. Other East Asian countries face far greater challenges than Japan in this regard.

The irony is that the government helps create stronger companies and industrial associations, which over time have acquired greater bargaining capacity vis-à-vis the state. This is particularly the case in a time of globalization when companies now respond more to the market than to bureaucratic directives. The large Japanese firms that have moved overseas now may raise funds abroad and become less beholden to bureaucrats. Take Taiwan's textile industrialists for another example. The government actually became more involved in helping the textile industry to upgrade as a result of greater external protectionist pressure and competition. At the same time, with greater funds available and greater technological expertise, the textile manufacturers became stronger players, challenging the state policies, especially in the 1980s.[121]

The bigger picture is that economic success combined with changes in external environment leads to a changed situation. For example, when a country has become more successful economically, it loses comparative advantages in labor-intensive industries. The more skilled labor force also provides conditions for structural shift. From a political economy perspective, a simple story would be one between "the old forces" and "the new forces." An important intervening variable is ideas. Again, take Taiwan for an example. The government gradually shifted to liberalization and high-tech industries in the early 1980s because of new economic and social interests, the policy suggestions of U.S.-based Taiwanese neoclassical economists, and the experience of Taiwanese returnees, particularly those who worked in Silicon Valley. One should also recognize the crucial leadership role played by President Chiang Ching-kuo in economic and political liberalization in Taiwan.[122] Such transitions are easier said than done. It is inherently difficult to reconcile conflicting, evolving interests and ideas.

CONCLUSION

East Asia has industrialized rapidly and has become a major center of manufacturing in the world. The state has played a prominent role in shaping production in East Asia. On one extreme, the South Korean state has been the most detail-oriented interventionist, learning from Japan and moving to another level. On the other extreme, the Hong Kong government has basically adopted a free-market approach. Most East Asian governments clearly have a strong tendency toward state intervention. Nowhere is state intervention more visible than in the issue of industrial policy. There has been much debate over the benefits of industrial policy. But the fact remains that East Asia has become industrialized and the state has played a central role in shaping the nature of East Asian industrialization, for better or for worse.

At the same time, there are market forces at work in East Asian production. East Asia has excelled because of advantages in production cost, proximity, and skills. Market forces are also reflected in that foreign firms have found it important and to their advantage to invest in the region. With greater integration into the global market, it is no longer easy for the state to control firms.

A production bias has skewed the East Asian political system, which has had unintended negative economic and political consequences. From an economic perspective, picking winners creates losers and an imbalance of the economic structure. From a political perspective, industrial firms have acquired too much economic and political power without being checked by financial institutions, which have been kept weak. More broadly, dominance of big business contributes to authoritarian regimes.

SUGGESTED READINGS

Amsden, Alice. *Asia's Next Giant: South Korea and Late Industrialization* (London: Oxford University Press, 1989).

Borrego, John, Alejandro Alvarez Bejar, and K. S. Jomo, eds. *Capital, the State, and Late Industrialization: Comparative Perspectives on the Pacific Rim* (Boulder: Westview Press, 1996).

Borrus, Michael, Dieter Ernst, and Stephan Haggard, eds. *International Production Networks in Asia* (London: Routledge, 2000).

Chen, Edward K. Y., and Peter Drysdale, eds. *Corporate Links and Foreign Direct Investment in Asia and the Pacific* (Pymble, Australia: HarperEducation, 1995).

Clark, Rodney. *The Japanese Company* (New Haven: Yale University Press, 1979).

Encarnation, Dennis J., ed. *Japanese Multinationals in Asia: Regional Cooperation in Comparative Perspective* (New York: Oxford University Press, 1999).

Graham, Edward M. *Reforming Korea's Industrial Conglomerates* (Washington, D.C.: Institute for International Economics, 2003).

Haggard, Stephan, Wonhyuk Lim, and Euysung Kim, eds. *Economic Crisis and Corporate Restructuring in Korea: Reforming the Chaebol* (New York: Cambridge University Press, 2003).

Ho, Yin-Ping. *Trade, Industrial Restructuring, and Development in Hong Kong* (Honolulu: University of Hawaii Press, 1992).

Hsueh, Li-min, Chen-kuo Hsu, and Dwight H. Perkins. *Industrialization and the State: The Changing Role of the Taiwan Government in the Economy, 1945–1998* (Cambridge, Mass.: Harvard Institute for International Development, 2001).

Huang, Yasheng. *Selling China: Foreign Direct Investment During the Reform Era* (New York: Cambridge University Press, 2003).

Huff, W. G. *The Economic Growth of Singapore: Trade and Development in the Twentieth Century* (Cambridge: Cambridge University Press, 1994).

Jesudason, James V. *Ethnicity and the Economy: The State, Chinese Business, and Multinationals in Malaysia* (Singapore: Oxford University Press, 1989).

Jomo, K. S., ed. *Industrializing Malaysia: Policy, Performance, Prospects* (London: Routledge, 1993).

Noland, Marcus, and Howard Pack. *Industrial Policy in an Era of Globalization: Lessons from Asia* (Washington, D.C.: Institute for International Economics, 2003).

Pekkanen, Saadia M. *Picking Winners? From Technology Catch-Up to the Space Race in Japan* (Stanford: Stanford University Press, 2003).

Rowen, Henry S., Marguerite Gong Hancok, and William F. Miller, eds. *Making IT: Asia's Rise in High Tech* (Stanford: Stanford University Press, 2007).

Tsai, Terence, and Bo-Shiuan Cheng, eds. *The Silicon Dragon: High-Tech Industry in Taiwan* (Northampton, Mass.: Edward Elgar, 2006).

van Hoesel, Roger. *New Multinational Enterprises from Korea and Taiwan: Beyond Export-Led Growth* (London: Routledge, 1999).

Warr, Peter G., ed. *The Thai Economy in Transition* (Cambridge: Cambridge University Press, 1993).

Williamson, Peter J. *Winning in Asia: Strategies for Competing in the New Millennium* (Cambridge: Harvard Business School Press, 2004).

Yeung, Henry Wai-chung. *Chinese Capitalism in a Global Era: Towards Hybrid Capitalism* (London: Routledge, 2004).

Yoshihara, Kunio. *Philippine Industrialization: Foreign and Domestic Capital* (Singapore: Oxford University Press, 1985).

Yusuf, Shahid, Kaoru Nabeshima, and Dwight H. Perkins. *Under New Ownership: Privatizing China's Enterprises* (Stanford: Stanford University Press, 2006).

NOTES

1. Ira C. Magaziner and Thomas M. Hout, *Japanese Industrial Policy* (Berkeley: University of California, Institute of International Studies, 1980), 11.
2. Consumer Reports.org, April 2007, www.consumerreports.org/cro/cars/new-cars/top-picks-for-2007-4-07/overview/0704_top-picks-2007.htm.
3. The data come from DisplaySearch, a world leader in display market research, February 23, 2006, www.displaysearch.com/press/?id=584.
4. Clarkson Plc., a ship broker and research firm based in London, cited in Agence France Press (AFP), "South Korea Sweeps Global Shipbuilding Orders in 2005," February 2, 2006.
5. Terence Tsai and Bo-Shiuan Cheng, eds., *The Silicon Dragon: High-Tech Industry in Taiwan* (Northampton, Mass.: Edward Elgar, 2006).
6. Huff, *Economic Growth of Singapore*, 299–322.
7. Yin-Ping Ho, *Trade, Industrial Restructuring, and Development in Hong Kong* (Honolulu: University of Hawaii Press, 1992).
8. Tai-lok Lui and Stephen W. K. Chiu, "Merchants, Small Employers, and a Non-Interventionist State: Hong Kong as a Case of Unorganized Late Industrialization," in *Capital, the State, and Late Industrialization: Comparative Perspectives on the Pacific Rim,* ed. John Borrego, Alejandro Alvarez Bejar, and K. S. Jomo (Boulder: Westview Press, 1996), 221–246.
9. Ho, *Trade, Industrial Restructuring, and Development in Hong Kong,* 34–40.
10. Anuwar Ali, *Malaysia's Industrialization: The Quest for Technology* (Singapore: Oxford University Press, 1992), 14–20.
11. World Bank, *Malaysia: Firm Competitiveness, Business Climate, and Growth,* Report No. 26841-MA, June 30, 2005, 9–10.
12. Somsak Tambunlertchai, "Manufacturing," in *The Thai Economy in Transition,* ed. Peter G. Warr (Cambridge: Cambridge University Press, 1993), 119.
13. Kaspar Richter, "Thailand's Growth Path: From Recovery to Prosperity," World Bank Policy Research Working Paper No. 3912 (May 2006), 17.
14. Kunio Yoshihara, *Philippine Industrialization: Foreign and Domestic Capital* (Singapore: Oxford University Press, 1985); Geoffrey Shepherd and Florian Alburo, "The Philippines," in *Liberalizing Foreign Trade,* vol. II, ed. Demetris

Papageorgiou, Michael Michaely, and Armeane M. Choksi (Cambridge, Mass.: Basil Blackwell, 1991), 133–308; Booth, *Indonesian Economy in the Nineteenth and Twentieth Centuries.*

15. Barry M. Richman, *Industrial Society in Communist China* (New York: Random House, 1969); Melanie Beresford and Dang Phong, *Economic Transition in Vietnam: Trade and Aid in the Demise of a Centrally Planned Economy* (Northampton, Mass.: Edward Elgar, 2001); Chang-Ho Yoon and Lawrence J. Lau, eds., *North Korea in Transition: Prospects for Economic and Social Reform* (Northampton, Mass.: Edward Elgar, 2001); St. John, *Revolution, Reform and Regionalism in Southeast Asia.*

16. Marcus Noland, *Avoiding Apocalypse: The Future of the Two Koreas* (Washington, D.C.: Institute for International Economics, 2000).

17. International Iron and Steel Institute, "World Produces 1,239.5 mmt of Crude Steel in 2006," January 22, 2007, www.worldsteel.org/?action=news detail&id=182.

18. *Guangzhouribal* [Guangzhou Daily], November 6, 2006, http://auto.chinanews.com.cn/auto/zcsc/news/2006/11-06/816229.shtml.

19. Gordon Fairclough, "Chinese Auto Exports Raise Fresh Concerns for Detroit," *The Washington Post,* February 16, 2006, D6.

20. Department of Scientific and Technological Development and Trade in Technology of Chinese Ministry of Commerce, January 27, 2006, http://kjs.mofcom.gov.cn/aarticle/bn/bs/200601/20060101437606.html.

21. World Bank, World Development Indicators database.

22. United Nations Conference on Trade and Development (UNCTAD), *World Investment Report 2005,* 174.

23. Henry S. Rowen, "An Overview," in *Making IT: Asia's Rise in High Tech,* ed. Henry S. Rowen, Marguerite Gong Hancok, and William F. Miller (Stanford: Stanford University Press, 2007), 1.

24. World Bank, *Global Development Prospects: Trade, Regionalism, and Development* (2005), 47–48.

25. Somsak Tambunlertchai, "Manufacturing," in *The Thai Economy in Transition* (see note 12), 123.

26. Department of Scientific and Technological Development and Trade in Technology of Chinese Ministry of Commerce, January 27, 2006, http://kjs.mofcom.gov.cn/aarticle/bn/bs/200601/20060101437606.html.

27. UNCTAD, *World Investment Report 2006,* country fact sheets. East Asia here includes Southeast Asia, Japan, China, South Korea, Taiwan, Hong Kong, and Macao.

28. Rajah Rasiah, "State Intervention, Rents, and Malaysian Industrialization," in *Capital, the State, and Late Industrialization* (see note 8), 152–153.

29. China Ministry of Commerce, February 10, 2006, http://gcs.mofcom.gov .cn/aarticle/Nocategory/200602/20060201484567.html.

30. Department of Scientific and Technological Development and Trade in Technology of Chinese Ministry of Commerce, January 27, 2006, http://kjs .mofcom.gov.cn/aarticle/bn/bs/200601/20060101437606.html.

31. Peter G. Warr, "The Thai Economy," in *The Thai Economy in Transition* (see note 12), 68.

32. Peter A. Petri, "The Interdependence of Trade and Investment in the Pacific," in *Corporate Links and Foreign Direct Investment in Asia and the Pacific,* ed. Edward K. Y. Chen and Peter Drysdale (Pymble, Australia: HarperEducation, 1995), 34–40.

33. World Bank, *Global Development Finance* 2005, 16.

34. China Ministry of Commerce, January 16, 2007, www.mofcom.gov.cn/ aarticle/tongjiziliao/v/200701/20070104307380.html.

35. UNCTAD, *World Investment Report 2006,* country fact sheets. East Asia here includes Southeast Asia, Japan, China, South Korea, Taiwan, Hong Kong, and Macao.

36. Mark Mason, *Europe and the Japanese Challenge: The Regulation of Multinationals in Comparative Perspective* (New York: Oxford University Press, 1997), 1.

37. "Raw Nerves in Motown," *The Economist,* January 15, 2005, 58.

38. Roger van Hoesel, *New Multinational Enterprises from Korea and Taiwan: Beyond Export-Led Growth* (New York: Routledge, 1999).

39. "On Shoring: Taiwan Is Shifting Much of Its Manufacturing to the Mainland," *The Economist: A Survey of Taiwan,* January 15, 2005, 7–9.

40. China News Agency, January 17, 2006, www.chinanews.com.cn/news/2006/ 2006-01-17/8/679552.shtml; China Ministry of Commerce, January 24, 2007, www.mofcom.gov.cn/aarticle/ae/ai/200701/20070104310215.html.

41. For a discussion of the national security dimension of China's direct investment in the United States, see Edward M. Graham and David M. Marchick, *U.S. National Security and Foreign Direct Investment* (Washington, D.C.: Institute for International Economics, 2006), 95–121.

42. Michael Borrus, Dieter Ernst, and Stephan Haggard, "Introduction," in *International Production Networks in Asia: Rivalry or Riches?* ed. Michael Borrus, Dieter Ernst, and Stephan Haggard (London: Routledge, 2000), 1.

43. Borrus, Ernst, and Haggard, eds., *International Production Networks in Asia.*

44. Francis Ng and Alexander Yeats, "Production Sharing in East Asia: Who Does What for Whom and Why?" World Bank Policy Research Working Paper No. 2197, October 1999.

45. World Bank, *Global Economic Prospects* 2005, 46–47.

46. Naya, *Asian Development Experience,* 189.

47. David Roland-Holst, "Global Supply Networks and Multilateral Trade Linkages: A Structural Analysis of East Asia," in *New East Asian Regionalism: Causes, Progress, and Country Perspectives,* ed. Charles Harvie, Fukunari Kimura, and Hyun-Hoon Lee (Northampton, Mass.: Edward Elgar, 2005), 39–70.

48. Lynne E. Guyton, "Japanese Manufacturing Investments and Technology Transfer to Malaysia," in *Capital, the State, and Late Industrialization* (see note 8), 171–201; K. S. Jomo, ed., *Japan and Malaysian Development: In the Shadow of the Rising Sun* (London: Routledge, 1994); Dieter Ernst, "Mobilizing the Region's Capabilities? The East Asian Production Networks of Japanese Electronics Firms," in *Japanese Investment in Asia: International Production Strategies in a Rapidly Changing World,* ed. Eileen M. Doherty (San Francisco: Asia Foundation and Berkeley: Berkeley Roundtable on the International Economy, 1995), 29–55.

49. Eric Harwit, "Japanese Investment in China," *Asian Survey* 36, no. 10 (October 1996): 978–994.

50. Michael Borrus, "Left for Dead: Asian Production Networks and the Revival of U.S. Electronics," in *Japanese Investment in Asia* (see note 48), 125–146.

51. Takeshi Kasuga et al., "Report on a Survey of Investment Climate Assessments by Japanese and Western Electrical Equipment and Electronics Companies in Malaysia," *JBICI Review,* no. 11 (June 2005): 37–66.

52. John Kao, "The Worldwide Web of Chinese Business," *Harvard Business Review,* March–April 1993, 2–11. See also Dajin Peng, "Ethnic Chinese Business Networks and the Asia-Pacific Economic Integration," *Journal of Asian and African Studies* 35, no. 2 (May 2000): 229–250.

53. Henry Wai-chung Yeung, *Chinese Capitalism in a Global Era: Towards Hybrid Capitalism* (London: Routledge, 2004).

54. Michael Borrus, "The Resurgence of U.S. Electronics: Asian Production Networks and the Rise of Wintelism," in *International Production Networks in Asia* (see note 42), 57–79.

55. Walter Hatch, "When Strong Ties Fail: U.S.-Japanese Manufacturing Rivalry in Asia," in *Beyond Bilateralism: U.S.-Japan Relations in the New Asia Pacific,* ed. Ellis S. Krauss and T. J. Pempel (Stanford: Stanford University Press, 2004), 154–175.

56. Takeshi Kasuga et al., "The Expansion of Western Auto Parts Manufacturers into Thailand, and Responses by Japanese Auto Parts Manufacturers," *JBICI Review,* no. 11 (June 2005): 1–35.

57. Marcus Noland and Howard Pack, *Industrial Policy in an Era of Globalization: Lessons from Asia* (Washington, D.C.: Institute for International Economics, 2003), 10.

58. Kozo Yamamura, "Caveat Emptor: The Industrial Policy of Japan," in *Strategic Trade Policy and the New International Economics,* ed. Paul R. Krugman (Cambridge: MIT Press, 1986), 169–209.

59. Magaziner and Hout, *Japanese Industrial Policy,* 5.

60. Saadia M. Pekkanen, *Picking Winners? From Technology Catch-Up to the Space Race in Japan* (Stanford: Stanford University Press, 2003).

61. Russell Mardon, "The State and Industrial Transformation in the Republic of Korea," *Journal of Social, Political, and Economic Studies* 15, no. 4 (Winter 1990): 457–482.

62. Edward M. Graham, *Reforming Korea's Industrial Conglomerates* (Washington, D.C.: Institute for International Economics, 2003).

63. Lim Youngjae, "Bankruptcy Policy Reforms and Corporate Restructuring in Postcrisis Korea," *Korea's Economy 2006* 22 (2006): 37–41.

64. Sang M. Lee, "South Korea: From the Land of Morning Calm to ICT Hotbed," *Academy of Management Executive* 17, no. 2 (2003): 7–18.

65. Lim, "Bankruptcy Policy Reforms and Corporate Restructuring in Postcrisis Korea."

66. Yun-han Chu, "State Structure and Economic Adjustment of the East Asian Newly Industrializing Countries," *International Organization* 43, no. 4 (Autumn 1989): 647–672.

67. John A. Matthews, "A Silicon Valley of the East: Creating Taiwan's Semiconductor Industry," *California Management Review* 39, no. 4 (Summer 1997): 26–54.

68. Li-min Hsueh, Chen-kuo Hsu, and Dwight H. Perkins, *Industrialization and the State: The Changing Role of the Taiwan Government in the Economy, 1945–1998* (Cambridge, Mass.: Harvard Institute for International Development, 2001), 3–4.

69. "Moving On: Manufacturing Is Out, Knowledge-Based Industries Are In," *The Economist: A Survey of Taiwan,* January 15, 2005, 9–11.

70. Alwyn Young, "A Tale of Two Cities: Factor Accumulation and Technical Change in Hong Kong and Singapore," in *NBER Macroeconomics Annual 1992* (Cambridge: MIT Press, 1992), 13–54.

71. Jomo and Edwards, "Malaysian Industrialization in Historical Perspective," 14–39.

72. Ali, *Malaysia's Industrialization.*

73. Kit G. Machado, "Malaysian Cultural Relations with Japan and South Korea in the 1980s: Looking East," *Asian Survey* 27, no. 6 (June 1987): 638–660; Kit G. Machado, "Japanese Transnational Corporations in Malaysia's State Sponsored Heavy Industrialization Drive: The HICOM Automobile and Steel Projects," *Pacific Affairs* 62, no. 4 (Winter 1989–1990): 504–531.

74. Kit G. Machado, "ASEAN State Industrial Policies and Japanese Regional Production Strategies: The Case of Malaysia's Motor Vehicle Industry," in *The Evolving Pacific Basin in the Global Political Economy: Domestic and International Linkages*, ed. Cal Clark and Steve Chan (Boulder: Lynne Rienner, 1992), 169–202.

75. Warr, "Thai Economy," 38–39.

76. T. Shale, "Southeast Asia: A New Crop of Tigers," *Euromoney*, September 1989, 91–92.

77. Booth, *Indonesian Economy in the Nineteenth and Twentieth Centuries*, 172–202.

78. Noland and Pack, *Industrial Policy in an Era of Globalization.*

79. Dennis J. Encarnation, *Rivals Beyond Trade: American Versus Japan in Global Competition* (Ithaca, N.Y.: Cornell University Press, 1992); Mark Mason, *American Multinationals and Japan: The Political Economy of Japanese Capital Controls, 1899–1980* (Cambridge: Harvard University Press, 1992); Mardon, "State and the Effective Control of Foreign Capital," 111–138.

80. Amsden, *Asia's Next Giant: South Korea and Late Industrialization*, 72–76.

81. Florence Lowe-Lee, "Economic Trends," *Korean Insight* 7, no. 1 (2005): 2.

82. "Repel Boarders," *The Economist*, March 4, 2006, 59. For a broader discussion of South Korean society's suspicion of foreign ownership, see Judith Cherry, "Killing Five Birds with One Stone: Inward Foreign Direct Investment in Post-Crisis Korea," *Pacific Affairs* 79, no. 1 (Spring 2006): 9–27.

83. David Pilling, "Koizumi's Campaign to Attract FDI Dealt Blow," *Financial Times*, March 11, 2005, http://news.ft.com/cms/s/7fcdf90e-9210-11d9-bca5-00000e2511c8.html.

84. Ho, *Trade, Industrial Restructuring, and Development in Hong Kong*, 133–139.

85. Cited in Richter, "Thailand's Growth Path," 28.

86. Booth, *Indonesian Economy in the Nineteenth and Twentieth Centuries*, 311–326.

87. James V. Jesudason, *Ethnicity and the Economy: The State, Chinese Business, and Multinationals in Malaysia* (Singapore: Oxford University Press, 1989); K. S. Jomo, "Introduction," in *Industrializing Malaysia: Policy, Performance, Prospects*, ed. K. S. Jomo (London: Routledge, 1993), 11.

88. World Bank, *Malaysia*, 16–22.

89. Yasheng Huang, *Selling China: Foreign Direct Investment During the Reform Era* (New York: Cambridge University Press, 2003).

90. Lee, "Policy Reforms and the Prospects of Economic Growth in North Korea"; Icksoo Kim, "The Rajin-Sonbong Economic and Trade Zone (RSETZ): The Sources of Difficulties and Lessons for the Future," in *North Korea in Transition: Prospects for Economic and Social Reform*, ed. Chang-Ho Yoon and Lawrence J. Lau (Northampton, Mass.: Edward Elgar, 2001), 301–333.

91. Kojima, *Japan and a New World Economic Order*, 75–91.

92. Friedrich Wu, "The Globalization of Corporate China," *NBR Analysis* 16, no. 3 (December 2005): 16–17.
93. Rodney Clark, *The Japanese Company* (New Haven: Yale University Press, 1979), 73–87.
94. Stephan Haggard, Wonhyuk Lim, and Euysung Kim, eds., *Economic Crisis and Corporate Restructuring in Korea: Reforming the Chaebol* (New York: Cambridge University Press, 2003).
95. "As Good as It Gets," *The Economist,* January 15, 2005, 64–66.
96. Greg Schneider, "Hyundai Now a Contender," *The Washington Post,* January 18, 2005, E1.
97. "Moving On: Manufacturing Is Out, Knowledge-Based Industries Are In," *The Economist: A Survey of Taiwan,* January 15, 2005, 9–11.
98. Hsueh, Hsu, and Perkins, *Industrialization and the State,* 102–111.
99. Shahid Yusuf, Kaoru Nabeshima, and Dwight H. Perkins, *Under New Ownership: Privatizing China's Enterprises* (Stanford: Stanford University Press, 2006).
100. *Fortune,* July 2006, http://money.cnn.com/magazines/fortune/global500/2006.
101. China News Agency, January 13, 2005, www.chinanews.com.cn/news/2005/2005-01-13/26/528022.shtml.
102. China News Agency, January 2, 2006, www.chinanews.com.cn/news/2005/2006-01-02/8/673049.shtml.
103. UNCTAD, *World Investment Report 2005,* 120–121.
104. Kao, "Worldwide Web of Chinese Business."
105. Yeung, *Chinese Capitalism in a Global Era,* 12–14.
106. Wang Gungwu, *China and Southeast Asia: Myths, Threats, and Culture* (Singapore: World Scientific Publishing and Singapore University Press, 1999), 7–10.
107. Michael Alan Hamlin, *Asia's Best: The Myth and Reality of Asia's Most Successful Companies* (Singapore: Prentice Hall, 1998).
108. World Bank, *Malaysia,* 22–23.
109. Richard C. Koo, *Balance Sheet Recession: Japan's Struggle with Uncharted Economics and its Global Implications* (Singapore: Wiley, 2003).
110. Frank-Jürgen Richter, *Redesigning Asian Business: In the Aftermath of Crisis* (Westport, Conn.: Quorum Books, 2002); Michael Alan Hamlin, *The New Asian Corporation: Managing for the Future in Post-Crisis Asia* (San Francisco: Jossey-Bass, 2000); Peter J. Williamson, *Winning in Asia: Strategies for Competing in the New Millennium* (Cambridge: Harvard Business School Press, 2004); Henry Wai-chung Yeung, "The Dynamics of Asian Business Systems in a Globalizing Era," *Review of International Political Economy* 7, no. 3 (September 2000): 399–433.
111. Paul Kennedy, *The Rise and Fall of the Great Powers* (New York: Random House, 1987).

112. Raul Prebisch, *The Economic Development of Latin America and Its Principal Problems* (New York: United Nations, 1950); H. W. Singer, "The Distribution of Gains Between Investing and Borrowing Countries," *American Economic Review* 40, no. 2 (May 1950): 473–485.

113. One may argue that the stage of industrial development in the product cycle may have important political consequences. The first textile industry was correlated with a liberal England. The second wave of textile industrialization in Prussia and Austria was not strong enough to overcome the agrarian upper class. The steel industry tended to lead to authoritarian political regimes since the industry required a high degree of capital mobilization. The automobile industry had a mixed impact on politics. James R. Kurth, "The Political Consequences of the Product Cycle: Industrial History and Political Outcomes" *International Organization* 33, no. 1 (Winter 1979): 1–34. It has been argued in recent years that IT industry has a democratic effect.

114. Hsueh, Hsu, and Perkins, *Industrialization and the State,* 106–107.

115. Jomo and Edwards, "Malaysian Industrialization in Historical Perspective," 24–25.

116. R. S. Milne, "Malaysia: Beyond the New Economic Policy," *Asian Survey* 26, no. 12 (December 1986): 1364–1382.

117. K. S. Jomo, "Introduction: Southeast Asia's Ersatz Miracle," in *Southeast Asian Paper Tigers? From Miracle to Debacle and Beyond,* ed. K. S. Jomo (London: Routledge, 2003), 8.

118. Haggard, *Political Economy of the Asian Financial Crisis,* 183–237.

119. Kent E. Calder, *Crisis and Compensation: Public Policy and Political Stability in Japan, 1949–1986* (Princeton: Princeton University Press, 1988).

120. Robert M. Uriu, *Troubled Industries: Confronting Economic Change in Japan* (Ithaca, N.Y.: Cornell University Press, 1996).

121. Ying-yi Tu, "The Textile and Apparel Industries," in *Industrialization and the State: The Changing Role of the Taiwan Government in the Economy, 1945–1998,* ed. Li-min Hsueh, Chen-kuo Hsu, and Dwight H. Perkins (Cambridge, Mass.: Harvard Institute for International Development, 2001), 219–223.

122. Hsueh, Hsu, and Perkins, *Industrialization and the State,* 50–80.

CHAPTER 8

The Political Economy of East Asian Trade

This chapter examines the political economy of East Asian trade. Trade is the most politically sensitive economic issue, and trade calculations have been important for East Asian governments. As discussed previously, the East Asian economic miracle has been partly based on strong export performance, and a sharp slowdown in exports among some Southeast Asian countries contributed to the Asian financial crisis.

The chapter answers two questions. First, what are the basic characteristics of East Asian trade and why did they develop? East Asia has experienced the world's fastest growth in trade due to both market forces and government policies. A global trade expansion brought about by trade liberalization and new technologies has provided a favorable external environment for East Asians, who have responded better than other developing regions because East Asian governments promote trade or are at least less restrictive than others.

Second, what trade policies have East Asian nations adopted and why? Is there anything unusual about East Asian trade politics? East Asian nations have created almost a cult of export. Starting with Japan, they have relied heavily on exports, which were highly beneficial at first but came to have a negative effect later on. But in a path dependent logic, it has been difficult to shift course. A country's trade policy includes its handling of disputes with trading partners and its participation in the multilateral institutions, which will also be discussed in the chapter.

TRADE PATTERNS IN EAST ASIA

Rapid Expansion in Trade

East Asian trade has expanded rapidly, which is a powerful engine for the region's economic success. Based on the World Bank statistics, China, Hong Kong, Indonesia, South Korea, Malaysia, the Philippines, Singapore, Taiwan, and Thailand achieved an 11.5 percent average annual growth rate in trade in 1970–1995, twice as fast as the world average of 5 percent. Their share in world trade increased from 4 percent to 16 percent in the same period.[1] Merchandise exports have been particularly important for East Asian economic growth. World merchandise exports expanded 82.1 times from 1960 to 2005.[2] But as shown in Figure 8.1, Japan's merchandise exports expanded 146.9 times, the four tigers 492.9 times (including Hong Kong and Singapore's reexports), ASEAN 4 (Indonesia, Malaysia, the Philippines, and Thailand) 123.6 times, and a latecomer China 296.4 times.

East Asian economies have become major trading powers, which can be measured by exports as shares of world import markets. As shown in Table 8.1, Japan's share tripled from 3.0 percent in 1960 to 8.1 percent in 1990 but decreased to 5.6 percent in 2005. The combined share of the four tigers, ASEAN 4, and China increased from less than 6 percent in 1960 to 20 percent in the same period. China surpassed Japan as the world's third largest trading nation in 2004, trailing the United States and Germany. As shown in Table 8.2, China, Japan, Hong Kong, South Korea, Taiwan, Singapore, and Malaysia ranked among the top 25 exporters and importers in the world in 2005. Four other East Asian countries ranked among the top 50 that year.

As another indicator of East Asia's growing importance in the global trade, if we look at maritime transport, 27.4 million twenty-foot equivalent units (TEU)

FIGURE 8.1
East Asian Expansion in Merchandise Exports, 1960–2005

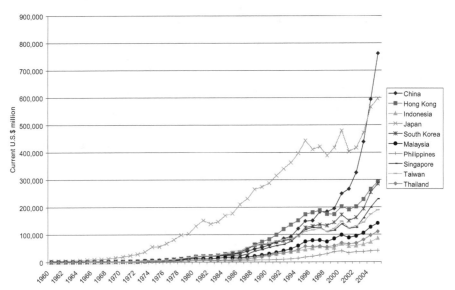

Source: World Bank, World Development Indicators Database. Data for Taiwan's export growth rates in 1969–1990 are from Council for Economic Planning and Development of the ROC, Taiwan Statistical Data Book 1996, 1-1b, and data for 1991–2005 come from Ministry of Finance of the ROC, www.mof .gov.tw/public/data/statistic/trade/2281.htm.

TABLE 8.1
East Asian Export Shares of World Imports

Economies	1960	1970	1980	1990	1995	2000	2005
Japan	3.05	6.02	6.41	8.10	8.49	7.21	5.59
Four Tigers	1.52	1.99	3.79	7.53	10.13	9.94	9.35
South Korea	0.02	0.26	0.86	1.83	2.40	2.59	2.67
Taiwan	0.12	0.46	0.97	1.89	2.14	2.23	1.78
Singapore	0.85	0.48	0.95	1.49	2.27	2.07	2.16
Hong Kong	0.52	0.78	1.00	2.32	3.33	3.05	2.74
ASEAN 4	2.30	1.42	2.32	2.43	3.70	4.10	3.55
Malaysia	0.89	0.53	0.64	0.83	1.42	1.48	1.32
Indonesia	0.63	0.35	1.08	0.72	0.87	0.98	0.81
Thailand	0.31	0.22	0.32	0.65	1.08	1.04	1.03
Philippines	0.47	0.32	0.28	0.23	0.34	0.60	0.39
China	1.93	0.72	0.89	1.75	2.85	3.75	7.15

Source: World Development Indicators Database. Data for Taiwan's export growth rates in 1969–1990 are from Council for Economic Planning and Development of the ROC, Taiwan Statistical Data Book 1996, 1–1b, and data for 1991–2005 come from Taiwan's Ministry of Finance, www.mof.gov.tw/public/data/statistic/trade/2281.htm.

left East Asian ports in 2002, accounting for 45.0 percent of the global container transport (60.9 million TEU), and 19.7 million TEU arrived in East Asian ports or 32.3 percent of the world total. Intraregional container flow amounted to 8.9 million TEU. In terms of containers handled, East Asia had the top six ports in the world in 2004, namely Hong Kong (21.9 million TEU), Singapore (20.9 million), Shanghai of China (14.6 million), Shenzhen of China (13.7 million), Busan of South Korea (11.3 million), and Kaoshiung of Taiwan (9.7 million), ahead of Rotterdam (8.3 million), Los Angeles (7.3 million), Hamburg (7.0 million), and Long Beach (5.8 million). Shanghai and Shenzhen grew faster than the others in 2001–2004 by 131.7 percent and 174.0 percent, respectively.[3] East Asia also had four of the ten top air freight airports in the world in 2003, namely Hong Kong (2), Tokyo (3), Seoul (5), and Singapore (10), among Memphis (1), Anchorage (4), Los Angeles (6), Frankfurt (8), and Miami (9).[4]

Merchandise trade has been important for East Asia, which can be measured by increasing merchandise trade as shares of gross domestic product (GDP), as shown in Figure 8.2. Although Japan is a major trading nation, its exposure to international trade actually did not change much, hovering around 20 percent in 1960–2005. Not surprisingly, Hong Kong has a high exposure to international trade. A city state, Singapore, not shown in the figure, is as dependent on trade as Hong Kong. China's merchandise trade as shares of GDP increased dramatically from 5.0 percent in 1970 to 63.6 percent in 2005. Of the five countries most affected by the Asian financial crisis, Indonesia's ratio increased from 21.8 percent

TABLE 8.2
Leading Exporters and Importers in World Merchandise Trade, 2005 ($ billion and percentages)

Rank	Exporters	Value	Share	Annual % Change	Rank	Importers	Value	Share	Annual % Change
1	Germany	969.9	9.3	7	1	U.S.	1,732.4	16.1	14
2	U.S.	904.4	8.7	10	2	Germany	773.8	7.2	8
3	China	762.0	7.3	28	3	China	660.0	6.1	18
4	Japan	594.9	5.7	5	4	Japan	514.9	4.8	13
5	France	460.2	4.4	2	5	UK	510.2	4.7	8
6	Netherlands	402.4	3.9	13	6	France	497.9	4.6	6
7	UK	382.8	3.7	10	7	Italy	379.8	3.5	7
8	Italy	367.2	3.5	4	8	Netherlands	359.1	3.3	12
9	Canada	359.4	3.4	14	9	Canada	319.7	3.0	15
10	Belgium	334.3	3.2	9	10	Canada	318.7	3.0	12
11	Hong Kong	292.1	2.8	10	11	Hong Kong	300.2	2.8	10
	Domestic	20.1	0.2	0		Retained	28.1	0.3	3
12	South Korea	284.4	2.7	12	13	South Korea	261.2	2.4	16
14	Singapore	229.6	2.2	16	15	Singapore	200.0	1.9	15
	Domestic	124.5	1.2	17		Retained	94.9	0.9	16
16	Taiwan	197.8	1.9	8	16	Taiwan	182.6	1.7	8
19	Malaysia	140.9	1.4	11	22	Thailand	118.2	1.1	25
25	Thailand	110.1	1.1	14	24	Malaysia	114.6	1.1	9
31	Indonesia	86.2	0.8	22	31	Indonesia	69.5	0.6	27
44	Philippines	41.3	0.4	4	40	Philippines	47.4	0.4	8
50	Vietnam	31.6	0.3	23	43	Vietnam	36.5	0.3	17
	World total	10,431.0	100.0	13		World total	10,783.0	100.0	13

Source: World Trade Organization, International Trade Statistics 2006, 17.

FIGURE 8.2
East Asian Merchandise Trade as Shares of GDP, 1960–2005

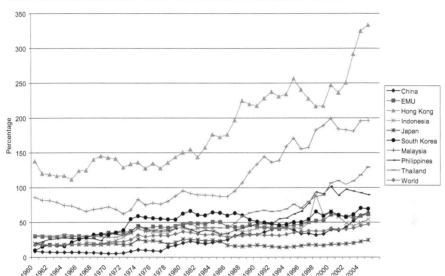

Source: World Development Indicators Database.

Note: EMU refers to the European Monetary Union.

in 1970 to 54.2 percent in 2005, South Korea from 31.7 percent to 69.3 percent, the Philippines from 34.1 percent to 89.5 percent, Thailand from 28.3 percent to 129.3 percent, and Malaysia from 72.2 percent to 196.1 percent. As a contrast, the world exposure to merchandise trade increased only from 20.4 percent to 47.3 percent.

East Asian trade expansion has resulted from an expanding and liberalizing global market to which East Asia has also contributed. One should thus not attribute the success of East Asian trade solely to East Asian trade policies, which are discussed in the next section.

At the same time, increasing dependence on trade creates vulnerability to the changing global market. As Figure 8.3 shows, East Asian exports suffered with the first oil crisis in the early 1970s and the second oil crisis in the early 1980s. In particular, Southeast Asian nations experienced severe economic difficulties during most of the 1980s. As discussed in Chapter 6, a significant slowdown in exports in 1996 was an important contributing factor to the Asian financial crisis. East Asian exports bounced back after the crisis. The Asian financial crisis had revealed the danger of relying too much on exports, thus Southeast Asian governments adopted measures to boost domestic consumption as an engine of growth, but they came

FIGURE 8.3

Growth Rates of East Asian Merchandise Exports, 1961–2005

Source: World Development Indicators Database. Data for Taiwan's export come from Ministry of Finance of the ROC, www.mof.gov.tw/public/data/statistic/trade/2281.htm.

short. Exports have grown much faster than domestic consumption. The flip side is that global economic ups and downs would affect the region more. The economic difficulties experienced in the developed countries after the terrorist attacks in the United States on September 11, 2001, had a large negative impact on Hong Kong, Singapore, and Taiwan, which had largely escaped from the Asian financial crisis.

The merchandise export performance of East Asian economies varies over time. As shown in Table 8.1, while Chinese export was about two-thirds of Japan's in 1960, that ratio decreased to about one-seventh by 1980. In the same period, the share for the four tigers increased dramatically, from smaller than China's in 1960 to over four times in 1980. ASEAN 4 maintained their shares, widening the gap with China from 20 percent to 2.6 times. China's declining export performance was due to disastrous domestic politics and increasing isolation from the global market. China's fortune began to change with Deng Xiaoping's reform and opening policy adopted in 1978. By 2005, China had a significantly larger share than Japan and ASEAN. While China's share in 2005 was smaller than that of the four tigers, much of trade by Hong Kong and increasingly by Taiwan was transshipment trade with China. The four tigers saw the most dramatic rise in exports. In particular, South Korea's shares increased from 0.02 percent in 1960 to 2.67 percent in 2005.

As shown in Table 8.1, the share of East Asia excluding Japan of world trade increased dramatically after the mid-1980s, which has had much to do with a drastic increase in Japanese foreign direct investment (FDI) after the Plaza Accord as well as FDI from Western nations and other East Asian economies. In particular, China's exports are increasingly conducted by foreign firms operating in China, more than half by Beijing's own estimates. Production networks discussed in the previous chapter mean that increasingly we need to take a regional perspective of East Asian exports because of exports transferring from one country to another through direct investments.

Structural Change in Trade

Structural change in trade refers to change in the composition of trade. East Asia shifted from export of primary commodities and resource-intensive manufactures to labor-intensive manufactures, and some advanced economies in the region are now moving toward capital-intensive and technology-intensive manufactures. As Figure 8.4 shows, the shares of manufactures in merchandise exports increased dramatically for East Asian economies from 1962 to 2005. Industrialized Japan and Hong Kong always had a high percentage. South Korea's shares increased from 18.2 percent in 1962 to 90.8 percent in 2005. Singapore jumped from 26.2 percent to 81.1 percent. Malaysia, the Philippines, and Thailand increased their shares from below 5 percent to 74–90 percent in the same period. China nearly doubled its shares from 47.7 percent in 1984 to 91.9 percent in 2005. Another transitional country, Vietnam started much later than China and saw modest gains. Vietnam's new World Trade Organization (WTO) membership achieved in November 2006 is expected to facilitate Vietnamese manufacturing exports, particularly in the textile sector.

The nonsocialist East Asian nations diversified exports in the 1970s to reduce dependence on products such as clothing and raw materials such as iron ore and wood.[5] This structural change has accelerated since the 1980s when foreign investment came into the region to take advantage of low-cost labor and to enter domestic markets.

To illustrate a sharp structural shift in trade in individual economies, we can use the example of Taiwan, not listed in Figure 8.4. Taiwan exported sugar and rice to Japan during the Japanese colonial period. Primary and processed agricultural products accounted for 91.9 percent of Taiwan's exports in 1952. Once Taiwan shifted to export promotion and currency devaluation in the late 1950s, the structure of Taiwanese exports changed rapidly. The share of industrial products in exports

FIGURE 8.4

Manufacture Exports as Shares of Merchandise Exports, 1962–2005

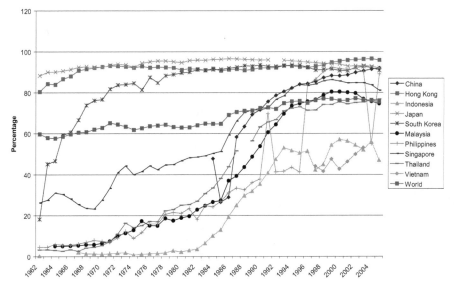

Source: World Development Indicators Database.

increased to 78.6 percent in 1970 and 90.8 percent in 1980. Based on its comparative advantages, Taiwan's early industrial exports concentrated in labor-intensive
light industrial products such as textiles, clothing, shoes, umbrellas, and toys. Even
its agricultural exports were labor-intensive.[6] Now Taiwan has become a major
exporter of high-value-added goods, particularly in information technologies.

As another example, Thailand had a large service sector in the 1950s, at around
45 percent of GDP. But manufacturing expanded at the expense of agriculture,
which decreased from about 40 percent in the 1950s to below 10 percent in 1996.
Manufacturing accounted for 30 percent of exports in the early 1980s, 80 percent
in 1993, and 87 percent in 2004.[7]

One striking feature of East Asian trade after the mid-1980s was a sharp
increase in exports of high-value-added products such as electronics and machinery. For China, high-tech and new products accounted for 29 percent of China's
total exports in 2006.[8] Figure 8.5 shows an increase of high-technology exports as
shares of manufactured exports for East Asia in 1988–2005 (information before
1987 not available). The high-technology exports statistics are reported by nation-
states. With that caveat, the technology component of East Asian exports has
clearly increased, reflecting industrial upgrading of regional economies.

FIGURE 8.5

High-Technology Exports as Shares of Manufactured Exports for East Asia, 1988–2005

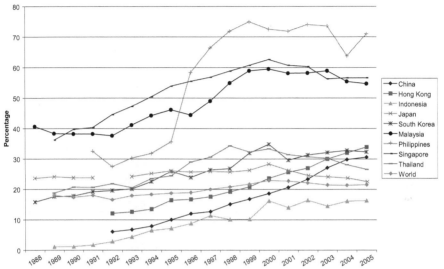

Source: World Development Indicators Database.

Surplus with the World

East Asia's rapid trade expansion has contributed to the global economy by offering greater opportunities for trade and investment. At the same time, East Asia's continuous large trade surpluses put political pressure on the governments in other regions. As Figure 8.6 shows, most East Asian economies now have large surpluses in merchandise trade with the world. Japan had huge trade surpluses since the late 1970s except during the second oil crisis in 1979–1980. The rest of East Asia increased their surpluses significantly after the early 1990s. In particular, China caught up with Japan by 2005 and posted a startling $117.5 billion surplus in 2006. Conversely, Figure 8.7 shows sharp, continuous increases of American trade deficits since the late 1970s.

From an economic perspective, East Asia's trade surpluses have largely resulted from the region's high savings and the low savings of countries like the United States. But from a political perspective, the non-Asian governments find it easier to blame the trade imbalances on the "unfair" trading practices of East Asian economies.

Japan sets the trend. There was much complaint about Japanese trading practices, particularly Japan's low levels of intraindustry trade unlike some major

FIGURE 8.6
Merchandise Trade Balances for East Asia, 1960–2006

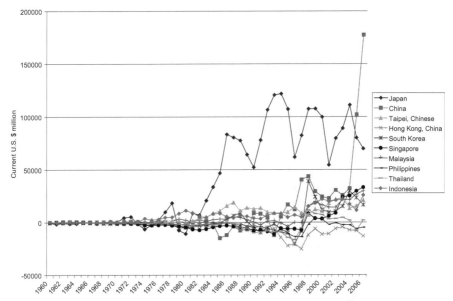

Source: Calculated from World Trade Organization, Statistics Database.

FIGURE 8.7
Merchandise Trade Balances for the United States, 1960–2006

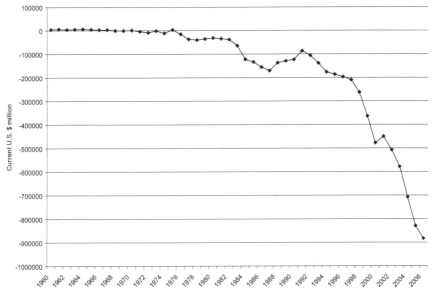

Source: Calculated from World Trade Organization, Statistics Database.

Western trading nations.[9] Japan's bilateral trade tensions with the United States cooled in the late 1990s. But as Figure 8.8 shows, Japan's surpluses as shares of U.S. trade deficits remain high. Statistics on bilateral trade flows can be misleading because countries are involved in multilateral trade; thus a country may have a large trade surplus with another country while maintaining a balanced trade with other parts of the world. The challenge of many East Asian economies lies in the large trade surpluses with the world in contrast to America's even larger deficit with the world. Japan had a much larger share than China's until 2005, peaking at slightly over 100 percent in 1992. Given the regionalization of production discussed in the previous chapter, much of the surplus has been transferred to China. Following in Japan's footstep, South Korea and Taiwan also began to accumulate trade surpluses with the United States, leading to U.S. pressure on them as well. In recent years China has increased its pressure on the rest of the world in labor-intensive, low-tech products, reaching 12.3 percent of U.S. deficits in 2005 and 20.1 percent in 2006. As will be discussed later in the chapter, China's surging trade surpluses against the United States and the world reflect to a large extent the transfer of exports from other East Asian economies to China. Unlike Japan, China is embracing foreign capital into the country, which accounts for more than half of its exports.

FIGURE 8.8
East Asian Merchandise Trade Balances as Shares of U.S. Trade Deficit, 1976–2006

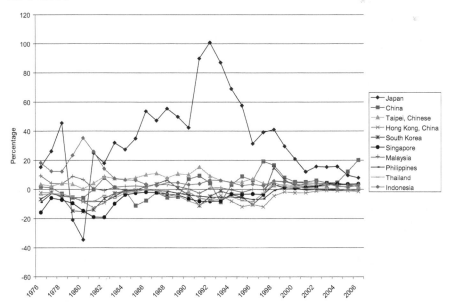

Source: Calculated from World Trade Organization, Statistics Database.

Trade surpluses with the world are linked to regionalization, to be discussed in the following paragraphs. Protectionist pressure partly explains FDI from Japan and then the four tigers to the rest of East Asia as well as to the rest of the world. Investors have essentially transferred their exports from their home economies to host economies.

Greater Regional Trade Interdependence

East Asian economies have turned increasingly to each other for trade. The share of world exports of East Asia excluding Japan almost tripled from 1975 (4.4 percent) to 2001 (12.1 percent) while the share of exports to each other increased more than sixfold (from 1.0 percent to 6.5 percent), at a faster pace than the North American Free Trade Agreement (NAFTA) region and the European Union.[10] Based on intraregional trade as a share of total trade, East Asia has become more interdependent in trade to the extent that East Asia now begins to look like the European Union. East Asian economies sent 31 percent of their total exports to the other economies in the region and imported 32 percent from them in 1981. The export and import ratios increased to 41 percent and 50 percent, respectively, in 2001.[11]

Increased intraregional trade does not mean that East Asian economies discriminate against nonregional countries. East Asia's share of the global trade has increased so they should trade with each other more proportionally. To control for the expanding size of East Asian trade, we can use a trade intensity index, which measures whether East Asian economies have traded more or less than predicted by their shares of world trade.[12] East Asia has intense intraregional trade even adjusted for distance and that intensity increased from 1985 to 1995 to 2001. East Asian economies also became more complementary in trade over this period.[13] But another study shows that trade intensity for East Asia (Japan, South Korea, Taiwan, Hong Kong, China, and ASEAN-10) declined slightly from 2.5 in 1980 to 2.2 in 2003, making it smaller than the NAFTA region (2.5) but larger than the European Union (1.7) in 2003. ASEAN-10 had a high intensity index of 4.1 in 2003 although smaller than its index of 4.8 in 1980.[14]

China has become a major destination for East Asian exports. At the same time, much of that import into China ends up in Chinese exports to the outside world, particularly to the United States, a phenomenon called *export-transferring*. Production networks are important channels for trade flows as well. Foreign firms operating in China exported $444.2 billion in 2005, accounting for 58.3 percent of China's total exports.[15] More important politically, foreign firms accounted for 83 percent of China's $101.9 billion trade surplus in 2005.[16]

Regionalization has resulted for several reasons. It makes economic sense because of increasing shares of East Asian trade in the global market, geographical proximity, and FDI-based production networks. Also, most East Asian governments have become more open in their economic orientation, which facilitates trade. In particular, they encourage FDI, which creates a positive nexus with trade, pulling each other up. A higher degree of intraregional trade is also the flip side of greater economic integration of the European Union, which has a discriminatory effect on East Asian exports.[17] The formation of the NAFTA and other regional free trade agreements (FTAs) are having a similar effect on East Asian regionalization.

EAST ASIAN TRADE STRATEGIES

The trade strategies of East Asian economies have gone through roughly three stages: import substitution, export-led growth, and liberalization. But this has not been a neat sequence. While export promotion replaced import substitution, some economies have at times gone backward. Malaysia adopted a more laissez-faire economic policy in the 1960s and reversed to a more protectionist policy in the 1970s. Malaysia then adopted an import substitution heavy industrialization plan in 1981. The Indonesian government practiced trade liberalization in 1966–1971 but resorted to protectionism after the 1973 tariff reform.[18] The Taiwanese government shifted from export-led growth to another round of import substitution in the textile industry in the 1970s.[19] While Taiwan began export promotion in the late 1950s, the government promoted heavy and chemical industries in the Sixth Four-Year Economic Plan (1974–1979) to substitute imports of intermediate materials and capital goods and introduced the second period of import substitution after the first oil crisis.[20] Hong Kong followed a free trade policy from the beginning, and some East Asian economies began partial liberalization even before the early 1980s. Resource-rich countries of Indonesia, Malaysia, Thailand, and the Philippines depended on exports of primary products through the 1970s, and their trade policy was thus heavily focused on the terms of trade. Socialist countries like China followed a totally different path of following import and export plans that covered virtually all their foreign trade. Most East Asian economies still pursue plans to create national champion industries to replace foreign imports.

Import Substitution

Like most other developing nations, East Asian noncommunist economies largely adopted an import substitution strategy (henceforth referred to as IS strategy) in the early stage of economic development after the Second World War. The dominant intellectual thinking at the time was that developing nations needed to protect their infant industries. The state-led development thinkers also wanted to have overvalued currencies based on the argument that cheap currencies would worsen the terms of trade and make inflation worse. As a major exception, Hong Kong followed a free trade policy.

While Japan had low GDP per capita in the early 1950s, it had been an economic powerhouse before the war and still possessed a highly educated labor force and strong managerial skills. Japan essentially adopted an IS strategy in the 1950s, selecting what the government considered to be potential industrial winners, such as steel, electric power, chemicals, and newer industries. Some of these industries began to export in the 1960s.[21] Japan would continue to protect its domestic market while nurturing internationally competitive industries.

Of the four tigers, Taiwan and South Korea adopted an IS strategy early. The Chinese Nationalist government moved to Taiwan after losing the mainland in 1949 and spent the first three years controlling high inflation and settling refugees. The government adopted an IS strategy in its first four-year plan (1953–1956), focusing on cement, glass, fertilizer, and textiles based on state targeting of industries, recruitment of private businesses for the preferred projects, and state-directed credit. The government particularly emphasized labor-intensive textile industry, providing materials and purchasing finished products in 1951–1953. The government temporarily stopped imports of cotton fabrics and cotton yarn, raised tariffs on imports, controlled domestic production and sales and restricted new production capacity, and used a multiple exchange rate system to allow favorable rates for imports of materials and machinery for the protected textile industry.[22] The government did not promote merchandise exports, although it did encourage exports of traditional products such as sugar, tea, canned pineapple, and rice.[23]

South Korea adopted an IS strategy after the Korean War ended in 1953. The Korean government used high tariffs to protect substituting sectors, mainly consumer products. The government did try to promote exports as well, but these exports were mainly agricultural and primary products. With such a strategy, South Korea initially achieved some growth, but the strategy was not successful owing to a weak domestic market and a strong need to import materials. South Korea had a trade deficit. The government's emphasis turned to export promotion after 1963. While import substitution contributed to 24.2 percent growth of manufactured output in 1955–1960, such contribution decreased to 0.9 percent in 1960–1963, 14.4 percent in 1963–1966, and –0.1 percent in 1966–1968. By contrast, export expansion contributed to 5.1 percent growth in 1955–1960, 6.2 percent in 1960–1963, 29.4 percent in 1963–1966, and 13.0 percent in 1966–1968.[24]

Traditionally an entrepôt trade port, Singapore became autonomous only in 1959 and followed an IS strategy after 1961. The government introduced protective tariffs and quotas in the early 1960s, and the protected items increased from 8 before Singapore's 1963 merger with Malaysia to 183 by the end of 1965. Import substitution appeared to make sense since Singapore would benefit from a larger protected market within the Federation of Malaysia. Singapore turned outward after its involuntary separation from Malaysia and after it was denied the access to the larger Malaysian market.[25]

In the rest of Southeast Asia, the Philippines underwent the easy stage of import substitution in the 1950s and suffered slow industrial growth and balance of payments difficulties in the 1960s. With comprehensive and high tariffs and nontariff barriers, the Philippines had higher effective protection rates, 86 percent in 1965 and 77 percent in 1974, than most other Southeast Asian countries (20 percent in 1965 and 17 percent in 1970 for Malaysia, and 45 percent in 1974 for Thailand). Only Indonesia was more protected, with effective protection rates of 137 percent in 1975 and 58 percent in 1980.[26] Thailand went through the easy phase of import substitution in the 1960s. Similar to Thailand, Malaysia lagged behind Northeast Asia in economic development by a decade. Malaysia launched import substitution industrialization based on tax incentives and high effective protection in the late 1950s, which was exhausted toward the end of the 1960s. Unlike Japan and South Korea, the majority of Malaysian import substitution industries were controlled by foreign firms. After a decade of export-led industrialization in the 1970s, Malaysia went back to protective import substitution heavy industrialization that relied heavily on foreign capital.[27] Indonesia adopted an IS strategy until the early 1980s, employing policies like import tariffs, higher import sales taxes, and nontariff restrictions. Exports of certain products were restricted to meet domestic needs.[28]

As became clear, IS strategy is biased against manufactured exports as well as agriculture because of greater incentives to focus on protected domestic markets and because of overvalued currencies. Moreover, the East Asian economies exhausted import substitution quickly as a result of their limited domestic markets. To move from a simpler stage of import substitution of nondurable consumer goods to durable consumer goods, intermediate goods, and capital goods would be more difficult for East Asia because of limited economies of scale and dependence on foreign technologies. Thus, most East Asian economies, starting with Taiwan and South Korea, moved to export promotion.

China followed an extreme case of import substitution industrialization in its trade policy before its launch of reform in 1978. China imported capital goods or materials to support its industrialization plans and organized exports to pay for imports. As a socialist country, the state monopolized imports and exports and used overvalued currency to make it cheaper to import what was needed for its industrialization plans. As typical of a planned economy, the Chinese government set prices for materials, intermediate goods, and final products, resulting in a separation of domestic and international prices, which offered little incentive for Chinese firms to export.[29]

Export Promotion

Export-led strategy (henceforth referred to as EL strategy) proved better than IS strategy. Exporting firms may take advantage of economies of scale given a far larger external market. Tougher competition also forces exporting firms to perform better than nonexporting firms, with much higher productivity and better wages although exporters were often good firms before they turned to export and exporting is not a panacea for firm performance.[30] A 2005 World Bank study showed that Malaysia's exporting firms enjoy a 4 percent Total Factor Productivity advantage over nonexporting firms. While the lead in Malaysia is not as significant as in some other countries, this may have resulted from the fact that a large number of exporting firms that have operated for a long time have allowed diffusion of knowledge and productivity to nonexporting firms.[31] As discussed in Chapter 5, East Asia's successful shift to an EL strategy from an IS strategy, compared to difficulties in doing so in other developing regions, particularly Latin America, has been explained as resulting from the presence of a strong developmental state.

Japan had emphasized exports all along because of the country's almost total dependence on imports of energy and materials. In a way, the whole Japanese political economy system was geared toward merchandise exports. Japan understood that to be successful in catching up with developed nations and to expand trade, a company must ensure that its domestic costs are lower than international prices and that the quality of the product must be good.[32] The Japanese state was involved heavily in promoting exports. Take exports of the consumer electronics industry for an example. The Japanese government protected the domestic market with nontariff barriers and allowed the major firms to engage in collusion and price fixing to charge higher prices for the same products at home than in overseas markets.[33] Japan developed general trading companies (GTCs) with extensive operations overseas to identify Japan's niches, organize exports, and promote FDI aimed at increasing exports. GTCs had certain advantages over individual firms marketing their products overseas because of their extensive knowledge of the foreign market, financing of export production, reduction of risks and transaction costs for exporting firms, and organization at times of new products for export. And they have adapted to the new business environment with more open markets.[34]

The Taiwanese government made a shift from import substitution to export promotion in 1959. To encourage exports, the government provided rebates for import duties, supplied low-interest export credit, made it less costly to import components or capital goods needed for export, and devalued the currency. In the first stage of export promotion, Taiwan focused on exports of processed imported materials and processed agricultural products such as canned pineapples and canned mushrooms to take advantage of Taiwan's comparative advantage in labor and skills.[35] Taiwan's protected textile industry became saturated in cotton fabrics by the mid-1950s. The government began providing incentives for exports, removed the restrictions on founding new textile factories, and allowed freer textile trade.[36] Taiwan was an early innovator in custom export processing zones, setting the first one in East Asia in Kaohsiung in December 1966. Investing firms in the zone enjoyed simplified regulations, relaxed foreign exchange and foreign trade control, and preferential tax treatment. The government created two more zones in 1972. Taiwan's highly successful experience with export zones helped the spread of various versions of export zones to other economies in East Asia and elsewhere in later years.[37]

The South Korean government adopted an EL strategy after the 1961 military coup, with subsidized long-term loans and export subsidies in the form of a large difference between official exchange rates and export-effective exchange rates (exporters received far more won than they would from the official exchange rates). President Park Chung Hee strongly urged exports in his State of the Nation message on January 16, 1965. The Korean government combined subsidies and heavy-handed pressure on enterprises (such as setting export targets). At the same time, the government used a variety of methods to restrict imports into the Korean market.[38] The government initially put emphasis on light industries to take advantage of educated but cheap labor in the country and then moved up to heavy industries in the 1970s. One strategy adopted was to set up highly specialized industrial zones to produce competitive products for export. The government also supported some trading companies modeled after the Japanese GTCs, starting in 1975. Unlike Taiwan, the South Korean government did not set up public enterprises but actively promoted national champion industries to lead the export drive.

Hong Kong was the first East Asian economy to adopt an export-oriented trade policy. Hong Kong shifted from entrepôt trade for China to processing of imported materials out of sheer necessity. The victory of the Chinese Communist Party in the mainland and the UN embargoes on China after outbreak of the Korean War virtually cut off Hong Kong's trade with the mainland. Hong Kong could not export primary products or follow an IS strategy given its small domestic market. Hong Kong built a manufacturing sector, and its exports increased rapidly based on the entrepreneurial and managerial talent and capital in the economy (from many who fled from Shanghai), a cheap labor force from over a million refugees from the mainland, and a favorable external environment since Hong Kong was part of the British Commonwealth. Unlike the rest of East Asia, however, the Hong Kong government did not adopt any industrial policy. Rather, it maintained law and order and kept taxes low for a stable business environment. Hong Kong was arguably the freest economy in the world, with no tariffs on imports and virtually no restriction on foreign investment.[39]

In Southeast Asia, Singapore was the first to adopt an EL development strategy in 1968 although the government began to promote exports as early as 1965. With the Economic Expansion Incentives Act adopted in 1967, the government collected only 4 percent of the profits from government-approved manufactures and products for export of "pioneer" firms instead of 40 percent for a typical firm. Singapore also welcomed foreign capital. The government set criteria for tax benefits and took away the pioneer status when necessary—labor-intensive industries, for instance, lost the status in the early 1970s. It also made preferential loans available for targeted industries.[40]

Malaysia followed suit in the early 1970s. The government introduced free trade zones in 1972, attracting mainly foreign capital rather than domestic capital, unlike free trade zones in Taiwan and South Korea. The country's emphasis on heavy industries led to less attention to exports in the early 1980s. But Malaysia intensified export promotion again after 1986, following losses in the heavy industrialization plan and a recession.[41] The Philippines adopted the Export Incentives Act in 1970 and promoted nontraditional exports in the 1970s. The government essentially provided export subsidies in the form of tax deductions and other incentives for exporters. The government also introduced export taxes on leading exports, which combined with export incentives to favor nontraditional manufactured exports over traditional agricultural and mining exports.[42] Thailand continued import substitution industrialization in the 1970s. But the government also began to promote exports actively from 1972 with the adoption of the Investment Promotion and Export Promotion Acts. It offered exporting firms tax exemption on imported inputs, tax rebates, and short-term loans.[43] Indonesia enjoyed high oil prices in the 1970s, with oil counting as two-thirds of its exports and government revenues by the early 1980s, and only began to promote non-oil products actively in the early 1980s when oil prices dropped.[44]

Trade Liberalization

Trade liberalization refers to a process by which a government reduces its intervention in trade by lowering tariffs or simplifying trade regulations and takes more of a neutral stance, favoring neither exports nor imports. Within a global free trade regime, the East Asian economies have gradually opened up their markets either by choice or under external pressure. Through the 1950s, most East Asian nations adopted protectionist IS strategies. Their shift to EL strategies starting in the early 1960s did not mean that these governments liberalized imports as well. However, they knew that protection of some industries might hurt exports. This happens because protected sectors draw primary factors of production away from the export sector and raise the prices of nontradable goods, some of which are important inputs for export. East Asian governments sought to correct the distortion by providing export subsidies or exemptions of duties on imports used for export. They also set up export-free zones. However, export subsidies and duty exemptions can also create biases, and export zones have long-term limitations when surplus capital is used up. The most efficient way is to liberalize imports as well as exports.[45]

There were early liberalizers in East Asia. Hong Kong has been a free trader all along. As Table 8.3 shows, Hong Kong's mean tariffs rates have been 0.0 percent. Singapore started out the same as Hong Kong. Singapore's autonomy from Great Britain and then merger with the Federation of Malaysia led to a period of import substitution. An EL strategy followed Singapore's breakup with Malaysia in 1967. But Singapore's export promotion went hand in hand with import liberalization. The government replaced quantitative import quotas with tariffs between 1968 and 1969 and then reduced tariffs and eventually abolished all quotas in 1970–1973.[46] As Table 8.3 shows, Singapore had a mean tariff rate of 0.3 percent in 1980. Indonesia experimented with liberalization in 1966–1971 after seven years of "guided economy," an Indonesia-style socialist policy that led to an economic crisis by the mid-1960s, but trade protection measures reappeared and accelerated after 1971.[47]

TABLE 8.3
Lowering Tariffs in East Asia

	Taxes as % of Exports and Imports				Mean Tariff Rates			
	1980	1990	2000	2004	1980	1990	2000	2004
East Asia								
Japan	0.9	0.9	1.5	1.5	9.5	6.9	4.5	2.9
S. Korea	4.1	3.4	1.3	1.3	20.4	13.3	8.7	9.3
Taiwan	3.6	2.1	1.5	0.8	—	9.7	8.8	6.9
Hong Kong	0.5	0.4	0.3	0.0	0.0	0.0	0.0	0.0
Singapore	0.4	0.1	0.1	0.0	0.3	0.4	0.4	0.0
Philippines	6.8	6.6	2.7	2.5	38.0	24.3	7.6	4.4
Indonesia	2.9	2.4	0.5	1.0	29.0	20.3	8.4	6.4
Malaysia	7.7	3.2	1.6	0.6	10.6	13.0	9.2	7.4
Thailand	6.9	5.4	1.4	1.3	32.3	40.8	17.0	13.3
China	5.7	3.7	1.5	1.8	49.5	40.3	16.3	9.8
Comparison								
India	15.5	21.1	8.4	5.7	74.3	79.2	32.5	28.1
Pakistan	15.3	15.2	5.6	3.9	77.6	58.8	46.6	16.1
Brazil	10.0	3.7	4.2	4.2	—	30.0	14.4	13.1
Argentina	9.5	9.9	3.1	7.4	27.8	20.5	12.6	11.4
United States	1.1	1.5	0.8	0.9	7.3	6.2	4.0	3.2

Sources: James Gwartney and Robert Lawson, *Economic Freedom of the World: 2006 Annual Report* (Vancouver: The Fraser Institute, 2006) and the 2005 report. Data retrieved from www.freetheworld.com.

The rest of East Asia has gradually reduced import tariffs since the early 1980s. Taiwan began liberalization around 1986, partly due to American pressure. The Taiwanese government removed many of the previous restrictions on imports and FDI. Formal tariffs were drastically reduced, informal barriers such as local content requirements were removed, and import procedures were simplified. Similar to Taiwan, South Korea began import liberalization as early as 1965 by relaxing import quotas, but the country's liberalization stalled in the 1970s because of balance of payments difficulties.[48] As shown in Table 8.3, South Korea's mean tariff rates dropped by half from 1980 to 2004.

Trade liberalization took place throughout Southeast Asia. The Philippines introduced a major policy program of tariff reduction and liberalization of residual import controls (import controls were removed in the early 1960s) in 1981. The reform stalled after the economic crisis in the early 1980s and was resumed in 1986.[49] Indonesia's trade liberalization was part of a package of reforms to deal with the crisis triggered by the worldwide economic recession of 1982–1983 and the sharp fall of oil prices in 1983–1986. The government simplified its trade protection regime and lowered tariffs on manufacturing imports while keeping the system of monopoly importing rights in place. Indonesia also devalued its currency by 28 percent in March 1983 and 31 percent in September 1986. The reform yielded results as the country's non-oil exports increased from $5 billion in 1983 to $14.4 billion in 1990.[50] Thailand also began liberalization in the early 1980s, facing much domestic resistance.[51] Malaysia introduced a significant reduction in tariffs and relaxation of requirements for ownership in manufacturing and financial sectors from the mid-1980s. In the 1990s the government also began to reduce tariffs on import substitution industries. However, as Malaysia was also promoting exports with subsidies, the proportion of imports did not increase drastically.[52]

The East Asian socialist countries belatedly joined other East Asian economies in export promotion and trade liberalization. After China adopted a policy of economic reform and openness in 1978, the Chinese government began to shift away from trade plans, which constituted a process of liberalization. China promoted exports with export credits and other measures in the 1980s, although not well publicized given China's decision to apply for a General Agreement on Tariffs and Trade (GATT) membership in 1986. China's adjustment of exchange rates to a more realistic level also facilitated Chinese exports. At the same time, the Chinese government maintained a relatively high tariff and used licenses and quotas to restrict imports through the 1980s.[53] China began trade liberalization in 1992 by cutting tariffs, which fell to about 15 percent prior to China's entrance into the WTO in January 2002. China also sharply decreased use of import licenses and quotas from about half of all imports at the end of the 1980s to 18 percent by 1992 and 8 percent by 2001. In addition, the government extended the right to engage in foreign trade, and the number of firms authorized to engage in foreign trade increased from 12 in 1978 to 5,000 in 1988 and 35,000 in 2001. Much of China's import goes into export processing. Thus, China's effective tariffs are actually lower than the statutory rates suggest.[54] China has embraced globalization more than Japan and Korea because of low tariffs, high imports as a share of GDP, and an open FDI regime. Similarly, Vietnam joined the WTO on November 7, 2006, after twelve years of negotiations.

Trade liberalization is often used as a measure for globalization, along with foreign trade as a share of GDP. China, Thailand, South Korea, and a number of East Asian countries are globalizers, with positive results to show for it. By contrast, Myanmar is a nonglobalizer. David Dollar of the World Bank argued that globalizers that adopted liberalization policies in the 1980s and the 1990s grew faster than nonglobalizers.[55] By contrast, Dani Rodrik argued that the integration of globalizers like China and South Korea came from their social and economic development, and only gradually, rather than following the policy prescriptions of the World Bank and the International Monetary Fund. Countries should first put emphasis on institutions and good policy. Global integration at present demands a long list of administrative requirements for developing nations and thus distorts their policy priorities.[56] Nevertheless, while global integration may not be a sufficient condition for strong economic performance, it has been an important contributing factor.

East Asian trade liberalization results from a combination of factors. First, a global trend of trade liberalization in the framework of the GATT/WTO, regional, and bilateral preferential trade arrangements has had an impact on East Asia, which in turn feeds into it. As Table 8.3 shows, other emerging countries have also been reducing their formal trade barriers. Intellectually, East Asia has been influenced by the ideas coming out of respected international organizations such as the World Bank. For example, Southeast Asian governments were convinced by exhaustive studies done by the World Bank and domestic think tanks that showed the negative effect of protectionism.[57] Moreover, international organizations such as the GATT/WTO had a long list of binding requirements. China agreed to comply with a long list of liberalization measures in phases to join the WTO. Vietnam had to adopt similar measures. Moreover, regional and bilateral trade agreements have all included targeted trade liberalization.

Second, using the access to the largest market in the world as a bargaining chip, the U.S. government has won concessions from East Asian economies, first Japan, then the four tigers, and now China. The next section will discuss this issue in greater detail.

Third, trade liberalization serves East Asia's own interests. Much of East Asia's trade liberalization has taken place unilaterally because the governments have decided that liberalization would help improve the productivity of their industries by testing their enterprises in the international market. In fact, as a World Bank study on regionalism calculated, unilateral cuts accounted for 66 percent of the 21 percentage point reduction in average weighted tariffs for all developing nations between 1983 and 2003. The commitment associated with the Uruguay Round accounted for 25 percent of the reduction while regional trade agreements (RTAs) explained the remainder 10 percent.[58] China and Vietnam both sought WTO membership, with all its liberalization commitments, as a logical outcome of years of economic reforms, which was viewed correctly as essential to their prosperity.

As East Asian economies have matured, their interest also began to shift. Some of their industries have become highly competitive in the global market, no longer justifying state protection. Rising living standards and labor costs have led to shifting comparative advantages. More important, as East Asia depends so much on exports, global trade liberalization would be most beneficial for the region. In accordance with the reciprocity principle embedded in the global trade regime, East Asia has to liberalize trade in exchange for liberalization elsewhere.

Trade liberalization so far has not put East Asia's fundamental interests at risk. The Chinese government, for example, concluded three years after joining the WTO that Chinese industries had not suffered more serious a shock than anticipated. According to a senior official at the Chinese Commerce Ministry, although China was still in a transitional period, its economy had grown rapidly and sustained no serious setbacks in the three years.[59] In fact, Long Yongtu, the Chinese chief negotiator for the WTO, gave a high mark to the results of joining the WTO in the past three years. China's internal and external business environments had improved.[60] Factually, China's trade volume increased sharply to over $1 trillion in the period. Such an assessment reinforced the resolve of the government to continue trade liberalization.

FACING THE WORLD

As discussed previously, East Asia has sizable trade surpluses with the world, particularly with the United States, and these trade imbalances have triggered trade disputes. There have also been disputes among East Asian economies, but they are less serious than those with countries outside East Asia. East Asia's trade relations with the world are not just disputes, of course. This section will also discuss the role of East Asia in the global trade regime.

Managing Trade Disputes

As East Asian economies became trading powers, their increased exports led to trade disputes with other countries. The United States initiated most disputes with East Asia. Since 1974 the U.S. government employed Section 301 of the 1974 Trade Act (amended a few times later) to pressure trade partners. The law gave the administration the legal power to investigate, negotiate, and retaliate against what the U.S. government considers to be unfair trading practices. East Asian economies were major targets. Besides actually bringing countries to disputes, the Office of the United States Trade Representative (USTR) also puts some countries on its Section 301 priority watch list as a way to exert pressure. Often, the threat of Section 301 is sufficient to make trading partners promise change.[61]

Japan was the first East Asian country to encounter a backlash, and its labor-intensive textile industry was the first serious battleground. The United States initiated the first trade dispute with Japan over textiles in the late 1960s.[62] Japan-U.S. trade disputes intensified and broadened after that until the issue subsided in the late 1990s when Japan had been in an economic slowdown for several years. Japan's strategy for negotiating with the United States combined stalling, brinkmanship, last-minute concessions, and large market-opening packages for their public relations effect.[63] The Japanese negotiators also used the American pressure to serve their bureaucratic interests at home and to exploit domestic divisions in the United States.[64] At the height of U.S.-Japan trade tensions, negotiations seemed drawn out, and agreements seemed to have yielded little result. Frustrated American officials and scholars began to view Japan as different from the United States and therefore constituting a threat to the United States.[65]

Since Japan had trade surpluses with virtually every country except oil exporters, Japan also had trade disputes with Western Europe and other trading partners. Japan responded with some market-opening measures, side payments in terms of official development assistance (ODA), and investment capital. Japan's shifting strategy from exporter to investor affected East Asian political economy of production. Japan also agreed to appreciate the yen sharply in accordance with the 1985 Plaza Accord. A stronger yen furthered Japanese investment flows to East Asia and elsewhere. As will be discussed in the next chapter, however, the Japanese monetary authority's loose-money policy to encourage outflow of capital to reduce pressure on the yen to appreciate further, along with a tightening budget, contributed to a stock market and real-estate bubble in the late 1980s. The burst of the bubble in the early 1990s led to a decade-long economic stagnation.

Despite being a free trade port, Hong Kong came under American pressure for voluntary export restraint (VER) on cotton products. With Japan agreeing to a VER earlier, Hong Kong's exports to the United States increased rapidly. Unlike Japan, Hong Kong refused to yield in negotiations with the United States in 1959–1960. America's failure allowed Hong Kong to benefit from export growth in the short run, but Hong Kong suffered a long-term loss when the U.S. government used a newly created bargaining power, the Short-Term Arrangement of

October 1961, to severely restrict Hong Kong's cotton manufacture exports. Hong Kong had to agree to restrict exports by 30 percent below the 1960 level.[66]

Compared with Hong Kong, Taiwan and South Korea were subject to U.S. trade pressure in far more cases.[67] Taiwan and South Korea were the principal targets of Section 301, second only to Japan. Similar to Japan, the South Koreans and Taiwanese engaged in tough negotiations with the Americans. In the end, the United States achieved results close to their specific objectives. South Korea and Taiwan essentially traded short-term concessions for long-term access to the all-important U.S. market. But they also limited the damage by using negotiation strategies such as problem redefinition, looking for legal loopholes, and transnational coalition-building.[68] The South Koreans and Taiwanese undoubtedly studied Japan's handling of trade disputes with the United States. Taiwan sent delegations to the United States to purchase large-ticket items. In the scheme of things, the South Koreans and Taiwanese yielded to American pressure because their overall exports continued to expand, particularly to the U.S. market. Similar to Japan, South Korea and Taiwan appreciated their currencies after the mid-1980s, which also led to outflow of capital to lower-cost countries. In later years, even though China has attracted more attention, Japan, South Korea, and Taiwan continue to be watched by the United States and be subject to Section 301. The U.S. antidumping charge against the steel exports of Japan, South Korea, and a number of other countries in the late 1990s is a case in point.[69]

New in the trade dispute game, Beijing reacted angrily to Washington's decision to restrict Chinese textile exports to the United States in 1982–1983 and retaliated with restrictions on American agricultural products to China. But like Japan and the tigers before it, China has learned to handle trade disputes pragmatically. For China, trade pressure also comes from other developed nations as well as fellow developing nations that compete with China in labor-intensive products.[70] Many of the antidumping cases brought against Chinese exports are from emerging countries like India, Argentina, Mexico, Brazil, and Peru. China has learned from other East Asian economies about negotiating trade disputes. China also sends delegations to the United States to purchase politically sensitive large items such as Boeing airplanes. China has been under pressure to appreciate the yuan. Partly reflecting on Japan's experience with the 1985 Plaza Accord, the Chinese government has sought to manage a gradual appreciation. Trade disputes have emerged as an important issue between the United States and China.[71]

Global Rules, Asian Plays

East Asian trade has expanded dramatically since the end of the Second World War in the context of an increasingly free global trade regime. East Asians are eager participants in the GATT/WTO that has managed global trade. That is not surprising. If one focuses on exports, one wants to have a stable trading arrangement. Virtually all East Asian economies are now WTO members. China's decade-long effort to join the GATT/WTO reveals the attractiveness of such a membership, which China saw as important for its modernization program and for its standing and influence in the international community. From a domestic political economy perspective, China's reformers wanted to lock in reform policy by joining a rule-based global trade regime.[72]

At the same time, the fact that it took China such a long time to join the GATT/WTO shows that the global trade regime demands serious commitments from member states. The GATT/WTO requires several norms, namely nondiscrimination, liberalization, reciprocity, safeguards, and development. The difficult negotiations over China's entrance centered on China wanting to join as a developing nation while the United States and some other developed nations wanted China to join as a developed nation that would require greater liberalization, and large developing nations wanted safeguards against a potential surge in Chinese exports. Interests aside, the United States wanted China to meet the global standard, namely rules-based, tight legal procedures acceptable to the international community.[73] In China's GATT/WTO negotiations, the most difficult ones were conducted with the United States and the European Union, powers outside East Asia. By contrast, the talks with Japan were far easier.[74] Expected to adopt global trade rules, Vietnam also had to meet the demands mainly by non-East Asian nations. Both China and Vietnam had to adapt to WTO norms and rules, not the other way around.

Earlier East Asian members of the GATT/WTO did not have that much impact on the creation of global trade rules either. As the only developed nation in the region, Japan was a principal player along with the United States, Western Europe, and Canada. But even Japan had little impact on the rules of the game and was often criticized as deviant from the international norms. South Korea was a far less prominent player than Japan. Taiwan was not even a formal member of the GATT. Even though the Nationalist government was one of the 23 founding members of the GATT, it was forced to withdraw in 1950, after losing the civil war in mainland China. Taiwan was an observer in the GATT until 1971, reapplied to join in 1990, and joined the WTO immediately after China. ASEAN nations were on the sideline of the rounds of multilateral trade negotiations before the Uruguay Round.[75]

East Asian economies have recently achieved some success in the WTO. After heavy lobbying and tough negotiation, Supachai Panitchpakdi of Thailand split terms as the WTO director general with Mike Moore of New Zealand. Moore served first in 1999–2002 and Panitchpakdi followed in 2002–2005. At the same time, East Asian economies have not been that active in the current Doha Round of negotiations. While the United States and the European Union remain dominant players and large developing nations such as India and Brazil have asserted themselves to counter Western domination, the East Asian voice is barely visible. At the WTO meeting held in Hong Kong in December 2005, for instance, as a semihost, although the Chinese delegation played a more visible role than before, China recognized that it was not nearly as active as India and Brazil. The reasons cited for China's low-key style were China's status as an inexperienced latecomer, a shortage of competent negotiators, and Beijing's unwillingness to take the lead for the developing nations to challenge the West because China's own commercial interests have diverged from those of the developing world.[76] At a meeting that suspended the Doha Round in Geneva in July 2006, the only East Asian nation present was Japan.

East Asia's less than prominent place in the global trade organization is not the principal reason for East Asian economies to seek regional trade integration. After all, many analysts view regionalism as building blocks for a global free trade regime. In that sense, East Asia largely wants both global free trade and regional integration. In fact, one important reason for accelerated efforts in East Asia to create free trade arrangements is the stalled global trade negotiations.

Some other analysts have pointed out that East Asian regionalism may be detrimental to global free trade, citing the greater illiberal tendencies in East Asia. The United States violates its own liberal trade principles from time to time but the principles are held. By contrast, the natural instinct in East Asia is protectionism. Take Japan, for example. Japan has more nontariff barriers to keep foreign imports away and has the least FDI in the country, which facilitates foreign imports. If that is the case for the largest economy in the region, how can East Asian regionalism be a liberal project?[77] Another criticism is that East Asians are less willing to enforce global rules and prefer to free ride on the global system.

But as will be discussed later, earnest government policies aside, East Asian regionalism remains largely open, partly as a hedge against growing regionalism in other regions. East Asia would have the most to lose from an eroded global trade regime and would have little to rely on to deal with intraregional trade tensions. As a result, key East Asian countries are likely to prefer global trade regime to regional trade arrangements for a long time.

Moreover, East Asians can use global rules to defend their trade interests. With its dispute settlement mechanism, the WTO commands respect as a useful multilateral institution.[78] Greater familiarity with and trust in the WTO mean that Japan finds the WTO expanding its options to manage trade disputes. Japan has won some important battles against the United States, particularly the 1994–1995 Japan-U.S. auto and auto parts negotiations.[79] Japan has also filed two cases against Indonesia. Similarly, South Korea shifted from its traditional aversion of legal settlements at the GATT to a more legalistic approach at the WTO because of greater trust in a strengthened dispute settlement mechanism at the WTO and because of its emerging deficits with major trading partners.[80] China has also come to view the WTO as an important instrument for defending its economic interests.[81] As a latecomer, China committed much energy to negotiations for entrance into the GATT/WTO because it viewed the organization as beneficial. China is the respondent of four cases, two from the United States and one each from the European Union and Canada. China is the complainant of one case against the United States.[82] The WTO is an equal-opportunity arena for dispute settlements for major East Asian trading powers.

EAST ASIAN TRADE REGIONALISM

East Asian regionalism has evolved in the past decades. Since the Asian financial crisis, East Asian regionalism has moved away from an open, institutionally weak regionalism to a more exclusive, institutionally stronger regionalism. Also, rather than a single project, East Asian regionalism has attempted regionalism projects at broader and narrower levels, with all their promises and weaknesses.

East Asian regionalism has been discussed in different circles for decades. The decisive moment came when the Asia-Pacific Economic Cooperation (APEC) forum was launched in 1989. The first APEC leaders' meeting was held in Seattle in 1993 at President Clinton's suggestion. APEC includes ten-member ASEAN, Australia, Canada, Chile, China, Hong Kong, Japan, South Korea, Mexico, New Zealand, Papua New Guinea, Peru, Russia, Chinese Taipei (Taiwan), and the United States. At the 1994 Bogor summit in Indonesia, the APEC members agreed to reduce tariffs to 0–5 percent by 2010 for the developed members and by 2020 for the developing members. But APEC has stalled in trade liberalization. Japan's opposition to the Early Voluntary Sectoral Liberalization (EVSL) was a major reason. Japan's powerful agricultural sector was opposed to inclusion of fishery and forestry in a whole package to be implemented. Some other major players in the APEC also contributed to the eventual failure of EVSL due to divergent interests and expectations.[83]

APEC differs from the WTO. As a global trade organization, the WTO has explicit obligations and procedures to prevent cheating. By contrast, APEC has a voluntary compliance structure, which will not have any legally binding commitments from member states.[84]

ASEAN was the most successful regional organization in East Asia, but it started out more as a political rather than economic organization. ASEAN became engaged in industrial cooperation and trade liberalization in the 1980s. The ASEAN early six (Brunei, Indonesia, Malaysia, the Philippines, Singapore, and Thailand) initiated the ASEAN Free Trade Area (AFTA) in January 1992, aiming at reducing tariffs in phases by 2008. The four new members, Vietnam (1995), Laos and Myanmar (1997), and Cambodia (1999), agreed to join AFTA although with a longer period to fulfill the required obligations. AFTA was later accelerated to be completed by 2003. After the Asian financial crisis, the ASEAN early six decided to push forward the completion date to 2002. AFTA was designed to make Southeast Asia more attractive for foreign investors rather than to create an exclusive regional bloc. The main mechanism for AFTA, the Common Effective Preferential Tariff (CEPT), requires reduction of tariffs on ASEAN products with at least 40 percent ASEAN content to 0.5 percent by 2002/2003 (2006 for Vietnam, 2008 for Laos and Myanmar, and 2010 for Cambodia). CEPT is supposed to cover 98 percent of the tariff lines. But AFTA allows a large number of exceptions: temporary exclusions, sensitive agricultural products till 2010, and general exceptions for reasons a member considers important such as national security, public morality, and health. For example, Malaysia employed temporary exclusion in 2000 to delay tariff reductions on automobiles. The problem is that exporting firms have to apply for tariff cuts and need to comply with complex country-of-origin rules.

APEC and AFTA do not correspond to East Asia as defined in this book, with APEC much broader and AFTA much narrower. Malaysian Prime Minister Mahathir tried to create an East Asian trading group, the East Asia Economic Caucus, but did not succeed. However, that project has revived under the guise of the "ASEAN Plus Three." In yet another turn, ASEAN has signed FTAs with China, Japan, and South Korea separately as well as with countries outside East Asia before an ASEAN Plus Three FTA.

What explains the growth of East Asian regionalism? Chapter 11 will offer a more detailed analysis of East Asian regionalism in general. This section provides specific explanations for East Asian trade regionalism. East Asian trade regionalism has grown both because of a perceived need for greater regional cooperation and in reaction to the global trends. First, a greater trade regionalization, as discussed earlier, makes it logical to form mechanisms to better coordinate trade policies. The Asian financial crisis, which was partly attributed to forces outside East Asia, has also convinced many in the region of the necessity of achieving greater regional cooperation.

Second, there has been a dramatic increase in regional trade agreements (RTAs) since the early 1990s. The RTAs in force quadrupled from 50 in 1990 to almost 230 by the end of 2004. Another 60 are under negotiation.[85] East Asia has fallen behind other regions. Developing East Asia and the Pacific region have only two RTAs per country, trailing all the other regions in the world. The world average is five.[86] Western European nations took the lead. The United States shifted its position on RTAs from avoidance to participation in the early 1990s. The U.S. government has become more active in RTAs since 2002 when it received trade promotion authority. Also, the global free trade negotiations have experienced difficulties, which help to channel energy to easier RTAs.

A detailed 2005 World Bank study on regionalism explains the pros and cons for RTAs. RTAs may have a positive effect on regional economies. First, with fewer members, RTAs are easier to make than multilateral ones. Second, RTAs may lower institutional and policy barriers to trade, which would help expand trade. Third, RTAs may address issues not done by global negotiations, such as standards. Fourth, these arrangements contribute to regional stability and domestic reform, both of which offer a better environment for economic development. On the other hand, RTAs may incur economic costs by discriminating against more efficient products from outside the region. Moreover, as a country participates in overlapping RTAs with different rules regarding origins of country and other procedures, this may lead to longer processing times. Delay means reduction of trade for the whole economy. The report concludes that the RTAs most conducive to wealth creation follow open regionalism, namely low external tariffs, few exceptions, nonrestrictive rules of origins, measures to promote across-border competition, large regional markets, and appropriate rules on investment and intellectual property.[87]

AFTA has much lower external tariffs than its counterparts in Latin America, Africa, and South Asia. AFTA's external tariffs are only somewhat higher than those of NAFTA.[88] At the same time, some of the deals have so many exceptions that they become less meaningful. For example, South Korea excluded rice from its FTA deal with ASEAN in May 2006, which Thailand has refused to sign.

The diversity of East Asian regionalism projects can be explained by the fact that regional countries have different interests and concerns. On the trade front, even though most countries recognize that it is in their mutual interests to lower trade barriers, they all want other countries to make more concessions while protecting their own pet industries, such as automaking for Malaysia and agriculture and fisheries for Japan and South Korea.

Moreover, East Asian regionalism is more than trade interests. It has been tied to geopolitical interests of the major players in the region. This is particularly the case when China's rise has led to alarm in countries like the United States and Japan. The great power rivalries, particularly one between China and Japan, are hindering the growth of East Asian regionalism. Chapter 11 will discuss this issue.

DOMESTIC POLITICAL ECONOMY OF TRADE

Trade has always been highly political. People often equate trade surpluses with job creation and deficits with job losses. Many also blame wage stagnation in developed nations on cheap imports from developing nations.[89] Trade policy and domestic politics have a mutual impact on each other. On the one hand, trade policy results from domestic politics. On the other hand, trade affects domestic politics.

In terms of how politics affects trade, one question we may ask is as follows: If free trade is so logically beneficial and protectionism has logically and empirically proven to be disastrous for the states involved and the international community, why is it so difficult for states to practice free trade? One explanation is that the state may follow a particular economic philosophy. Import substitution strategy is a case in point. Another explanation based on strategic interaction among states is that states have the incentives to free ride on the international free trade system, namely letting others reduce their trade barriers more than their own. These two reasons are often used to explain East Asian trade policies that tend to be less liberal than those of the West.

A domestic political economy explanation is that even if the state endorses free trade in principle, it seeks exceptions to the rules. This is particularly the case in domestic political economy where losers will fight politically to fend for their interests. A minority group with a direct stake in the issue tends to be better organized and fights harder than the majority, which has diffuse interests in the issue. Thus, the minority group often wins. As issue minorities are numerous, the free trade regime may be picked to a skeleton. Even if a state is interested in free trade, it sometimes has to balance between the larger interest and special interest by giving in somewhat to protectionist pressure to prevent larger damage to the free trade regime.[90] In addition, political leaders often decide that short-term noneconomic reasons are more important than the general liberalization principle. Put simply, economic policy distortions are often politically efficient. Political efficiency means increased chance for a political party to be elected.[91] For example, politicians may need the votes of the agricultural sector and have to protect the groups politically important for their electoral success. Sometimes, the state may also have legitimate political reasons to adopt inefficient economic policies. After all, the business of the state is not just business. Inclusion, fairness, and other goals are important, particularly for democracies. In fact, political arrangements in the domestic arena (welfare state) and in the international arena (international organizations) are necessary for a successful global free trade regime.[92]

The explanation above has been used to contrast East Asia and other developing nations in terms of policy adjustment. As discussed in Chapter 5, it has been suggested that most successful East Asian economies have a strong state insulated from special interests. Thus, unlike Latin America where entrenched special interests limited state options, the East Asian economies like Taiwan and South Korea could make a decisive shift from import substitution strategy to export-led strategy and to liberalize their trade regime more than other developing nations to the benefit of the nations. However, one should not push the strong state argument too far. Sectoral interests played an important role in shaping trade policy in South Korea and Taiwan. For example, the quota system imposed by the Multi-Fiber Agreement introduced in the early 1970s led to serious disputes between the state and the industries in Taiwan in the early 1980s. The government argued that it was within its right to distribute quotas, whereas the industrialists argued that the quotas were private properties because they had invested in the equipment. Although the government won, it also made adjustments in its quota system.[93] In addition, a strong state does not necessarily engage in free trade, as revealed in East Asia's own experience.

Moreover, the East Asian experience does not suggest a strong correlation between how insulated a government is and how open its trade is. After all, democratic countries that are "weak" as measured by the degree of societal influence on the state have more open trade policies than the developmental states in East Asia. Using the United States as an example, some scholars have shown that institutional arrangements created to structure trade conflict help promote free trade policy.[94]

Democratic or not, the East Asian state has to play a two-level political game to balance its trade policy. An example is Japan's policy toward FTAs with East Asian nations. It is well known that the Japanese government was hesitant to strike deals because of opposition from its politically powerful agricultural sector. However, China's activism in this area means that the Japanese government views FTAs—or, as Japan prefers to call them, economic partnership agreements (EPAs)—as something strategically important. Not surprisingly, the Japanese government tries to have its cake and eat it too, namely to have deals without hurting its agricultural sector. The Japanese government has also begun to offer some benefits from EPAs for farmers to reduce political resistance to free trade. In July 2004, the Japanese negotiators requested that Malaysia remove tariffs on some Japanese agricultural exports such as apples, pears, mandarin oranges, and other items. This was the first time the Japanese government had made such a request. This shift reflected the government's desire to move from protecting farming to promoting exports.[95]

In another important area where sectors lobby governments for actions, East Asian economies have increasingly taken on a fair trade approach, using the WTO to level the field in protected markets. Again using Japan as an example, the automobile and steel sectors have managed to file most of the Japanese complaints at the WTO. This is because the two sectors are particularly motivated politically and advantaged institutionally in the Japanese system.[96]

Trade affects domestic politics as well. First, the degree of exposure to global trade and the size of the countries affect the nature of the political system. It is sometimes argued that small but highly trade-dependent states like Singapore need to have a highly disciplined government to allow them to make timely adjustments.

Larger states like Japan may adopt a strategic stance to anticipate future shifts in the global markets.[97]

Second, trade is linked to economic performance and thus political legitimacy in a developmental state commonly found in East Asia. Trade policies matter in that they help determine a country's economic performance. The student demonstrations in South Korea in March 1960 had something to do with the weak economic performance under President Lee, which was in part caused by an unsuccessful import substitution strategy. General Park, who seized power after the May 1961 coup, realized the importance of economic development and shifted South Korea's development strategy. In Indonesia, a collapse of the economy under President Sukarno's guided democracy in 1958–1965 facilitated Suharto's success in acquiring political power after the 1965 coup attempt and the following bloody crackdown and contributed to the New Order's sudden shift to a more liberalized economy after 1966.[98] In China, the share of exports in goods and services to GDP increased from 6.6 percent in 1978 to 34.0 percent in 2004.[99] The Chinese government believed that exports contributed 2 percent to its annual GDP growth.[100] This puts foreign firms and the political economic interests they represent squarely within the Chinese domestic context. Trade exposure thus affects public policy as it becomes difficult to restrain foreign firms. This dynamic has become even more important as East Asia has become more exposed to trade.

Third, trade policy can also lead to shifting political power. As a case in point, the Sukarno government adopted an Indonesianization program in the 1950s that discriminated against ethnic Chinese businesses in terms of allocation of import rights. This policy helped to create a new class of indigenous traders that depended on and supported Sukarno's Partai Nasional Indonesia (PNI).[101] More broadly, an import substitution or export-led strategy favors import-substituting and exporting firms, respectively, and enhances their political influence relative to others.

CONCLUSION

This chapter shows that East Asian trade has expanded dramatically since the end of the Second World War, which has obviously contributed to the East Asian miracle. East Asian success in exports has resulted both from market forces and government strategies. East Asian economies have capitalized on their comparative advantages and an expanding global trade. However, government policies also matter. After all, East Asia's own experience shows that those that hinder market forces have failed, as shown by the import substitution strategy and the socialist countries. The basic feature of East Asian state policies toward trade is a retreating illiberal strategy in a global free trade regime.

East Asian export prowess has led to trade disputes with the rest of the world, particularly the United States. At times, trade disputes dominated some bilateral relationships, for example, the U.S.-Japan relationship in the early 1990s. Although it is a major force in the marketplace of global trade, East Asia continues to punch below its weight in the global trade regime, reflecting both institutional weaknesses as latecomers and a tendency to avoid conflict and to free ride on others. Despite skepticism by many outside the region, East Asian governments have shown amazing enthusiasm for regional cooperation. While a latecomer in this game, East Asia is moving forward and is well positioned to become a more coherent third center of global economic power.

Domestic and trade policy influence each other. The resistance of "losing" sectors or industries in a country explains the tendency of a government to endorse free trade in principle but to demand exceptions in practice. The relative insulation of the state from society in some East Asian economies explains East Asia's shift from an import substitution strategy to an export-led strategy although the strong state may and has often adopted unwise economic policies. Trade with the outside world has also affected East Asian politics. High exposure to the global market partly explains why the political regime in small states like Singapore is disciplined and tough in order to allow flexible adjustments. Trade performance also affects the political legitimacy of a developmental state.

SUGGESTED READINGS

Ahn, Dukgeun. "WTO Dispute Settlements in East Asia." NBER Working Paper Series No. 10178, December 2003.

Amirahmadi, Hooshang, and Weiping Wu. "Export Processing Zones in Asia." *Asian Survey* 35, no. 9 (September 1995): 828–849.

Ariff, Mohamed, and Tan Loong Hoe, eds. *The Uruguay Round: ASEAN Trade Policy Options* (Singapore: Institute of Southeast Asian Studies, 1988).

Bernard, Andrew B., and J. Bradford Jensen. "Exceptional Export Performance: Cause, Effect, or Both?" *Journal of International Economics* 47, no. 1 (February 1999): 1–25.

Corbo, Vittorio, Anne O. Kueger, and Fernando Ossa, eds. *Export-Oriented Development Strategies: The Success of Five Newly Industrializing Countries* (Boulder: Westview Press, 1985).

Destler, I. M., Haruhiro Fukui, and Hideo Sato. *The Textile Wrangle: Conflict in Japanese-American Relations, 1969–1971* (Ithaca, N.Y.: Cornell University Press, 1979).

Drysdale, Peter, and Ross Garnaut. "The Pacific: An Application of a General Theory of Economic Integration." In *Pacific Dynamism and the International Economic*

System, ed. C. Fred Bergsten and Marcus Noland (Washington, D.C.: Institute for International Economics, 1993), 183–223.

Hufbauer, Gary Clyde, Yee Wong, and Ketki Sheth. *U.S.-China Trade Disputes: Rising Tide, Rising Stakes* (Washington, D.C.: Institute for International Economics, 2006).

Lardy, Nicholas R. *Foreign Trade and Economic Reform in China, 1978–1990* (New York: Cambridge University Press, 1992).

Lincoln, Edward J. *East Asian Economic Regionalism* (Washington, D.C.: Brookings Institution Press, 2004).

Lincoln, Edward J. *Japan's Unequal Trade* (Washington, D.C.: Brookings Institution, 1990).

Ng, Francis, and Alexander Yeats. "Production Sharing in East Asia: Who Does What for Whom and Why?" World Bank Policy Research Working Paper No. 2197, October 1999.

Okamoto, Jiro, ed. *Trade Liberalization and APEC* (New York: Routledge, 2004).

Pekkanen, Saadia M. "International Law, Industry, and the State: Explaining Japan's Complainant Activities at the WTO." *The Pacific Review* 16, no. 3 (September 2003): 285–306.

Prestowiz, Clyde V. *Trading Places: How We Allowed Japan to Take the Lead* (New York: Basic Books, 1988).

Ravenhill, John. "APEC and the WTO: Which Way Forward for Trade Liberalization?" *Contemporary Southeast Asia* 21, no. 2 (August 1999): 220–237.

Ryan, Michael P. *Playing by the Rules: American Trade Power and Diplomacy in the Pacific* (Washington, D.C.: Georgetown University Press, 1995).

Schoppa, Leonard J. *Bargaining with Japan: What American Pressure Can and Cannot Do* (New York: Columbia University Press, 1997).

Scollay, Robert, and John P. Gilbert. *New Regional Trading Arrangements in the Asia Pacific?* (Washington, D.C.: Institute for International Economics, 2001).

Wan, Ming. "The U.S., Japan, and the EU: Comparing Political Economic Approaches to China." *The Pacific Review* 20, no. 3 (September 2007), 397–421.

Warr, Peter G. "Export Processing Zones and Trade Policy." *Finance and Development* 26, no. 2 (June 1989): 34–36.

Woo, Wing Thye. "Recent Claims of China's Economic Exceptionalism: Reflections Inspired by WTO Accession." *China Economic Review* 12, no. 2 (Summer 2001): 107–136.

World Bank. *Global Economic Prospects: Trade, Regionalism, and Development* (Washington, D.C.: World Bank, 2005).

Yoffie, David B. *Power and Protectionism: Strategies of the Newly Industrializing Countries* (New York: Columbia University Press, 1983).

NOTES

1. World Bank, *East Asia: Recovery and Beyond* (Washington, D.C.: World Bank, 2000), 45.
2. Calculated from World Development Indicators Database.
3. Judith Rehak, "Every Port in a Storm," *International Herald Tribune*, March 25–26, 2006, 16. Information for containers comes from the Containerization International Web site.
4. "Shifting Trade Patterns: How Will They Impact Infrastructure Needs in East Asia and Pacific Region?" *Kaihatsu kinyu kenkyushoho* [Journal of JBIC Institute] 25 (July 2005): 29–31. The airfreight information comes from Airport Council International Web site.
5. Chung H. Lee and Seiji Naya, "Trade in East Asian Development with Comparative Reference to Southeast Asian Experience," *Economic Development and Cultural Change* 36, no. 3 (April 1988 Supp.), S123–S152.
6. S. C. Tsiang, "Foreign Trade and Investment as Boosters for Take-Off: The Experience of Taiwan," in *Export-Oriented Development Strategies: The Success of Five Newly Industrializing Countries,* ed. Vittorio Corbo, Anne O. Kueger, and Fernando Ossa (Boulder: Westview Press, 1985), 39–40.
7. Kaspar Richter, "Thailand's Growth Path: From Recovery to Prosperity," World Bank Policy Research Working Paper No. 3912, May 2006, 15–17.
8. China Ministry of Commerce, February 5, 2007, www.mofcom.gov.cn/ aarticle/ae/ai/200702/20070204354875.html.
9. Edward J. Lincoln, *Japan's Unequal Trade* (Washington, D.C.: Brookings Institution, 1990).
10. Francis Ng and Alexander Yeats, "Major Trade Trends in East Asia: What Are Their Implications for Regional Cooperation and Growth?" World Bank Policy Research Working Paper No. 3084, June 2003, 4.
11. Edward J. Lincoln, *East Asian Economic Regionalism* (Washington, D.C.: Brookings Institution Press, 2004), 45.
12. Peter A. Petri, "The Interdependence of Trade and Investment in the Pacific," in *Corporate Links and Foreign Direct Investment in Asia and the Pacific,* ed. Edward K. Y. Chen and Peter Drysdale (Pymble, Australia: HarperEducation, 1995), 32.
13. Ng and Yeats, "Major Trade Trends in East Asia," 21–28. East Asia is defined as including Cambodia, China, Hong Kong, Indonesia, Korea, Malaysia, the Philippines, Singapore, Taiwan, Thailand, and Vietnam.
14. Masahiro Kawai and Taizo Motonishi, "Is East Asia an Optimum Currency Area?" in *Financial Interdependence and Exchange Rate Regimes in East Asia,* ed.

Masahiro Kawai, conference proceedings, Korea Institute for International Economic Policy and Policy Research Institute of Japan Ministry of Finance, December 2–3, 2004, Tokyo, 167, www.mof.go.jp/english/soken/kiep2005/kiep2005_04.pdf.

15. China Ministry of Commerce, February 10, 2006, http://gcs.mofcom.gov.cn/aarticle/Nocategory/200602/20060201484567.html.

16. China News Agency, February 15, 2006, www.chinanews.com.cn/news/2006/2006-02-15/8/690649.shtml.

17. Peter Drysdale and Ross Garnaut, "The Pacific: An Application of a General Theory of Economic Integration," in *Pacific Dynamism and the International Economic System,* ed. C. Fred Bergsten and Marcus Noland (Washington, D.C.: Institute for International Economics, 1993), 202.

18. Booth, *Indonesian Economy in the Nineteenth and Twentieth Centuries,* 222–227.

19. Ying-yi Tu, "The Textile and Apparel Industries," in *Industrialization and the State: The Changing Role of the Taiwan Government in the Economy, 1945–1998,* ed. Li-min Hsueh, Chen-kuo Hsu, and Dwight H. Perkins (Cambridge, Mass.: Harvard Institute for International Development, 2001), 203.

20. Ying-yi Tu, "The Petrochemical Industry," in *Industrialization and the State* (see note 19), 239–240.

21. Hugh Patrick and Henry Rosovsky, "Japan's Economic Performance: An Overview," in *Asia's New Giant: How the Japanese Economy Works,* ed. Hugh Patrick and Henry Rosovsky (Washington, D.C.: Brookings Institution, 1976), 12–13.

22. Tu, "Textile and Apparel Industries," 188–190.

23. Hsueh, Hsu, and Perkins, *Industrialization and the State,* 14–17.

24. Charles R. Frank Jr., Kwang Suk Kim, and Larry E. Westphal, *South Korea* (New York: National Bureau of Economic Research, distributed by Columbia University Press, 1975), 92.

25. Aw, "Singapore," 335–341; Huff, *Economic Growth of Singapore,* 307–309.

26. Romeo Bautista, *Development Policy in East Asia* (Singapore: Institute of Southeast Asian Studies, 1992), 30.

27. Jomo and Edwards, "Malaysian Industrialization in Historical Perspective," 18–34.

28. Richard R. Barrichello and Frank R. Flatters, "Trade Policy Reform in Indonesia," in *Reforming Economic Systems in Developing Countries,* ed. Dwight H. Perkins and Michael Roemer (Boston: Harvard Studies in International Development, 1991), 275–279.

29. Nicholas R. Lardy, *Foreign Trade and Economic Reform in China, 1978–1990* (New York: Cambridge University Press, 1992), 16–36.

30. Empirical research generally supports this claim. See Andrew B. Bernard and J. Bradford Jensen, "Exceptional Export Performance: Cause, Effect, or Both?" *Journal of International Economics* 47, no. 1 (February 1999): 1–25.

31. World Bank, *Malaysia: Firm Competitiveness, Business Climate, and Growth,* Report No. 26841-MA, June 30, 2005, 30–31.

32. Kojima, *Japan and a New World Economic Order,* 152–153.

33. Yamamura, "Caveat Emptor," 178–185.

34. Lawrence B. Krause and Sueo Sekiguchi, "Japan and the World Economy," in *Asia's New Giant* (see note 21), 389–398; Alan T. Shao and Paul Herbig, "The Future of Sogo Shosha in a Global Economy," *International Marketing Review* 10, no. 5 (December 1993): 37–55; Tom Roehl, "Markets Nurture Relationships: Changing Relationship Patterns of Japanese GTCs in the Post-Bubble Era," *Asian Business & Management* 3, no. 4 (December 2004): 417–434.

35. Little, *Industry and Trade in Some Developing Countries,* 254–258.

36. Tu, "Textile and Apparel Industries," 195–196.

37. Hooshang Amirahmadi and Weiping Wu, "Export Processing Zones in Asia," *Asian Survey* 35, no. 9 (September 1995): 828–849. Ireland was actually the first to create an export-processing zone in 1959, followed by India in 1965.

38. Amsden, *Asia's New Giant,* 64–70.

39. Ho, *Trade, Industrial Restructuring, and Development in Hong Kong,* 4–9.

40. Aw, "Singapore," 349–354.

41. Rajah Rasiah, "Free Trade Zones and Industrial Development in Malaysia," in *Industrializing Malaysia: Policy, Performance, Prospects,* ed. K. S. Jomo (London: Routledge, 1993), 118–146, and "Pre-Crisis Economic Weaknesses and Vulnerabilities," in *The Malaysian Eclipse: Economic Crisis and Recovery,* ed. K. S. Jomo (London: Zed Books, 2001), 48–51.

42. Shepherd and Alburo, "The Philippines," 214–217.

43. Narongchai Akrasanee and Juanjai Ajanant, "Manufacturing Industry Protection in Thailand: Issues and Empirical Studies," in *The Political Economy of Manufacturing Protection: Experiences of ASEAN and Australia,* ed. Christopher Findlay and Ross Garnaut (Sydney: Allen and Unwin, 1986), 79–80.

44. Barrichello and Flatters, "Trade Policy Reform in Indonesia."

45. Peter G. Warr, "Export Processing Zones and Trade Policy," *Finance and Development* 26, no. 2 (June 1989): 34–36.

46. Aw, "Singapore," 409.

47. Mark M. Pitt, "Indonesia," in *Liberalizing Foreign Trade,* vol. 5, ed. Demetris Papageorgiou, Michael Michaely, and Armeane M. Choksi (Cambridge, Mass.: Basil Blackwell, 1991), 1–196.

48. Kwang Suk Kim, "Korea," in *Liberalizing Foreign Trade,* vol. 2 (see note 47), 1–131.

49. Shepherd and Alburo, "The Philippines," 240–263.
50. Iwan J. Azis, "Indonesia," in *The Political Economy of Policy Reform*, ed. John Williamson (Washington, D.C.: Institute for International Economics, 1993), 387–415; Barrichello and Flatters, "Trade Policy Reform in Indonesia," 279–291.
51. Akrasanee and Ajanant, "Manufacturing Industry Protection in Thailand," 91–92.
52. Rasiah, "Pre-Crisis Economic Weaknesses and Vulnerabilities," 50.
53. Lardy, *Foreign Trade and Economic Reform in China, 1978–1990*, 37–82.
54. Lee Branstetter and Nicholas Lardy, "China's Embrace of Globalization," Woodrow Wilson International Center for Scholars, *Asia Program Special Report* 129 (July 2005): 6–12.
55. David Dollar and Aart Kraay, "Spreading the Wealth," *Foreign Affairs* 81, no. 1 (January/February 2002): 120–133.
56. Dani Rodrik, "Trading Illusions," *Foreign Policy* no. 123 (March 2001): 54–62.
57. Christopher Findlay and Ross Garnaut, *The Political Economy of Manufacturing Protection Policy in ASEAN and Australia* (Sydney: Allen and Unwin, 1986); Mohamed Ariff and Tan Loong Hoe, eds., *The Uruguay Round: ASEAN Trade Policy Options* (Singapore: Institute of Southeast Asian Studies, 1988).
58. World Bank, *Global Economic Prospects: Trade, Regionalism, and Development* (Washington, D.C.: World Bank, 2005), 42.
59. China News Agency, December 10, 2004, www.chinanews.com.cn/news/2004/2004-12-10/26/515406.shtml.
60. *Renmin ribao*, December 7, 2004, http://news.sina.com.cn/c/2004-12-07/05485143054.shtml.
61. Michael P. Ryan, "USTR's Implementation of 301 Policy in the Pacific," *International Studies Quarterly* 39, no. 3 (September 1995): 333–350.
62. I. M. Destler, Haruhiro Fukui, and Hideo Sato, *The Textile Wrangle: Conflict in Japanese-American Relations, 1969–1971* (Ithaca, N.Y.: Cornell University Press, 1979).
63. Ming Wan, *Japan Between Asia and the West: Economic Power and Strategic Balance* (Armonk, N.Y.: M. E. Sharpe, 2001), 60–61.
64. Leonard J. Schoppa, *Bargaining with Japan: What American Pressure Can and Cannot Do* (New York: Columbia University Press, 1997).
65. Clyde V. Prestowiz, *Trading Places: How We Allowed Japan to Take the Lead* (New York: Basic Books, 1988).
66. David B. Yoffie, *Power and Protectionism: Strategies of the Newly Industrializing Countries* (New York: Columbia University Press, 1983), 64–79.
67. Michael P. Ryan, *Playing by the Rules: American Trade Power and Diplomacy in the Pacific* (Washington, D.C.: Georgetown University Press, 1995).

68. John S. Odell, "The Outcomes of International Trade Conflicts: The U.S. and South Korea, 1960–1981," *International Studies Quarterly* 29, no. 3 (September 1985): 263–286; Steve Chan, "The Mouse that Roared: Taiwan Management of Trade Relations with the United States," *Comparative Political Studies* 20, no. 3 (October 1987): 251–292.

69. Hidetaka Yoshimatsu, "U.S.-East Asian Trade Friction: Exit and Voice in the Steel Trade Regime," *Asian Affairs: An American Review* 30, no. 3 (Fall 2003): 200–217.

70. Ming Wan, "The U.S., Japan, and the EU: Comparing Political Economic Approaches to China," *The Pacific Review* 20, no. 3 (September 2007), 397–421; Franco Algieri, "EU Economic Relations with China: An Institutionalist Perspective," *China Quarterly* 169 (March 2002): 64–77.

71. Gary Clyde Hufbauer, Yee Wong, and Ketki Sheth, *U.S.-China Trade Disputes: Rising Tide, Rising Stakes* (Washington, D.C.: Institute for International Economics, 2006).

72. Wing Thye Woo, "Recent Claims of China's Economic Exceptionalism: Reflections Inspired by WTO Accession," *China Economic Review* 12, no. 2 (Summer 2001): 107–136.

73. Mark A. Groombridge and Claude E. Barfield, *Tiger by the Tail: China and the World Trade Organization* (Washington, D.C.: American Enterprise Institute, 1999).

74. Wan, "U.S., Japan, and the EU: Comparing Political Economic Approaches to China."

75. Mohamed Arif, "Multilateral Trade Negotiations: ASEAN Perspectives," in *The Uruguay Round: ASEAN Trade Policy Options,* ed. Mohamed Ariff and Tan Loong Hoe (Singapore: Institute of Southeast Asian Studies, 1988), 1–37.

76. *Jingji Guanchabao* [Economic observation], December 17, 2005, http://news .sina.com.cn/c/2005–12-17/17088609164.shtml.

77. Lincoln, *East Asian Economic Regionalism,* 33.

78. Dukgeun Ahn, "WTO Dispute Settlements in East Asia," NBER Working Paper Series No. 10178, December 2003.

79. Saadia M. Pekkanen, "Aggressive Legalism: The Rules of the WTO and Japan's Emerging Trade Strategy," *The World Economy* 24, no. 5 (May 2001): 707–737, and "International Law, Industry, and the State: Explaining Japan's Complainant Activities at the WTO," *The Pacific Review* 16, no. 3 (September 2003): 285–306.

80. Dukgeun Ahn, "Korea in the GATT/WTO Dispute System: Legal Battle for Economic Development," *Journal of International Economic Law* 6, no. 3 (September 2003): 597–633.

81. Youngjin Jung, "China's Aggressive Legalism: China's First Safeguard Measure," *Journal of World Trade* 36, no. 6 (December 2002): 1037–1060.
82. WTO, www.wto.org/english/thewto_e/countries_e/china_e.htm (accessed July 10, 2006).
83. Jiro Okamoto, ed., *Trade Liberalization and APEC* (New York: Routledge, 2004).
84. John Ravenhill, "APEC and the WTO: Which Way Forward for Trade Liberalization?" *Contemporary Southeast Asia* 21, no. 2 (August 1999): 220–237.
85. World Bank, *Global Economic Prospects: Trade, Regionalism, and Development,* 28.
86. World Bank, *Global Economic Prospects: Trade, Regionalism, and Development,* 30.
87. World Bank, *Global Economic Prospects: Trade, Regionalism, and Development,* xi-xiii. See also Seiji F. Naya, *The Asian Development Experience: Overcoming Crises and Adjusting to Change* (Hong Kong: Asian Development Bank, 2002).
88. World Bank, *Global Economic Prospects: Trade, Regionalism, and Development,* xii.
89. For criticism of those views, see Paul Krugman, *Pop Internationalism* (Cambridge: MIT Press, 1996), 35–48.
90. Robert O. Keohane, "Reciprocity in International Relations," *International Organization* 40, no. 1 (Winter 1986): 1–28.
91. Stephen P. Magee, William A. Brock, and Leslie Young, *Black Hole Tariffs and Endogenous Policy Theory: Political Economy in General Equilibrium* (Cambridge: Cambridge University Press, 1989).
92. John Gerard Ruggie, "International Regimes, Transactions, and Change: Embedded Liberalism in the Postwar Economic Order," *International Organization* 36, no. 2 (Spring 1982): 379–416.
93. Tu, "Textile and Apparel Industries," 212–214.
94. Michael A. Bailey, Judith Goldstein, and Barry R. Weingast, "The Institutional Roots of American Trade Policy: Politics, Coalitions, and International Trade," *World Politics* 49, no. 3 (April 1997): 309–338.
95. "Japan Wants Tariffs Removed from Farm Exports to Malaysia," *The Japan Times,* July 22, 2004, www.japantimes.com/cgi-bin/getarticle.pl5?nb 20040722a2.htm.
96. Pekkanen, "International Law, Industry, and the State."
97. For the logic and evidence, see Peter J. Katzenstein, *Small States in World Markets: Industrial Policy in Europe* (Ithaca, N.Y.: Cornell University Press, 1985); Ronald Rogowski, "Trade and the Variety of Democratic Institutions," *International Organization* 41, no. 2 (Spring 1987): 203–223.
98. Mark M. Pitt, "Indonesia," in *Liberalizing Foreign Trade* (see note 47), 1–196.
99. World Bank, World Development Indicators Database.
100. China Ministry of Commerce, January 4, 2005, www.chinanews.com.cn/ news/2004/2005-01-04/26/523941.shtml.
101. Pitt, "Indonesia," 13–14.

CHAPTER 9

The Political Economy of East Asian Finance

Finance connects people who have savings with those who need capital. Financial systems include direct finance through financial markets and indirect finance through financial intermediaries such as banks and financial companies. The financial sector is central to the whole economy. According to Joseph Stiglitz et al., "Financial markets essentially involve the allocation of resources. They can be thought of as the 'brain' of the entire economic system, the central locus of decision-making: if they fail, not only will the sector's profit be lower than would otherwise have been, but the performance of the entire economic system may be impaired."[1] My previous discussion in the book bears this out. The East Asian miracle had much to do with the allocation of resources to speed up economic growth, and the Asian financial crisis devastated most East Asian economies.

This chapter studies how East Asian economies have mobilized domestic financial resources. They created financial systems that were largely effective in pooling domestic resources for industrialization, but those systems now need serious reforms. The chapter also discusses international finance, which means the movement of capital across national borders. East Asian nations started out capital-poor and needed foreign capital. International capital flows include foreign aid, short-term (one year or less) trade credit, medium-term suppliers' credit, direct foreign investment, portfolio investment (investment by purchase of securities, which are claims on companies' future incomes such as bonds), and medium- to long-term bank loans. Financial globalization means that national markets are being integrated.

This chapter discusses the following questions. First, what are the basic features of East Asian finance? Second, how have East Asian governments handled their financial affairs? Third, how is East Asia situated in the global financial system? Fourth, is there a regional financial system in East Asia? I discuss East Asian finance in the global context before discussing regional context for a good reason. Globalization of finance has affected the region far more than regionalization of finance.

EAST ASIAN FINANCE

The basic features of East Asian finance since World War II are high capital accumulations intended for high economic growth and dependence on banks rather than financial markets, except for Hong Kong and Singapore. Most East Asian economies have experienced serious nonperforming loan problems. East Asian financial markets have grown over time but remain troubled with serious problems.

East Asian Capital Accumulation

To achieve development, a country needs to accumulate capacity for growth. Accumulation includes three components: human capital, savings, and investments. I will focus on the last two components in this chapter.

Chapter 7 has discussed East Asia as a destination of foreign direct investment (FDI). At the same time, East Asia has become an important source of global finance thanks to high domestic savings that feed into high capital formation. As Table 9.1 shows, East Asia's saving rates have been consistently higher than the world average since the mid-1970s. Japan was the trendsetter in East Asia. As shown in Figure 9.1, which traces select East Asian countries yearly, Japan's savings/GDP ratio increased from 34.1 percent in 1965 to 41.1 percent in 1970 and

FIGURE 9.1
Gross Domestic Savings as Shares of GDP, 1965–2005

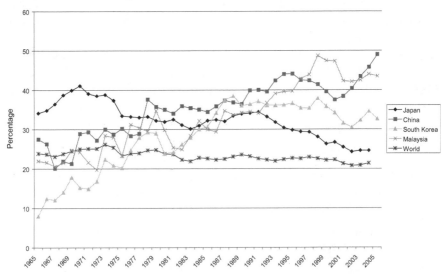

Source: World Bank, World Development Indicators Database.

TABLE 9.1
East Asian Gross Domestic Savings (percentage of GDP)

	1965	1970	1975	1980	1985	1990	1995	2000	2003	2004	2005
Japan	34.1	41.1	33.4	31.9	32.2	34.1	29.8	26.7	24.6	24.6	—
China	27.5	28.9	30.2	35.0	34.4	39.9	44.1	37.5	43.4	45.8	49.0
South Korea	8.0	15.2	20.2	23.9	30.6	36.4	36.6	34.2	32.3	34.6	32.6
Taiwan	20.7	25.6	26.7	32.3	32.9	27.6	25.7	24.3	24.0	23.7	23.0
Singapore	9.9	18.4	29.4	38.1	40.7	44.0	50.1	46.9	43.7	47.0	48.6
Hong Kong	31.5	28.2	28.6	34.4	31.7	35.7	29.6	32.0	31.2	30.7	33.0
Indonesia	7.9	14.3	26.6	38.0	29.7	32.3	30.6	32.8	32.7	27.9	26.6
Malaysia	22.0	24.3	23.3	29.8	29.9	34.5	39.7	47.3	42.5	44.0	43.5
Philippines	20.8	21.9	24.8	24.2	16.5	18.4	14.6	23.1	10.9	12.9	10.5
Thailand	18.6	21.2	22.1	22.9	25.5	33.8	35.4	31.5	31.7	31.8	30.1
Vietnam	—	—	—	—	—	3.3	18.0	27.1	27.4	28.3	30.2
World	23.9	25.0	23.3	23.8	22.6	23.2	22.7	22.3	20.9	21.4	—

Source: World Bank, World Development Indicators Database. The data for Taiwan in 1965–1980 that measure gross national savings as percentage of GNP are from the Council for Economic Planning and Development (Taiwan), Taiwan Statistical Databook (1996), 1. The data for Taiwan from 1985 are from the Asian Development Bank Statistical Database System: Key Indicators, various years.

began a slow decline after the 1973–1974 oil crisis but maintained rates over 30 percent until 1995. Japan's savings rate decreased to 24.6 percent in 2004, but it was still higher than the world average of 21.4 percent. Japan remains a net saver as its investment has decreased even more.

For the four tigers, as shown in Table 9.1, while Hong Kong always had high savings rates comparable with those of Japan, South Korea and Singapore started below 10 percent and Taiwan just over 20 percent in 1965. The three economies caught up with Japan in the 1980s. Malaysia followed a similar trajectory as South Korea. For the rest of the six original ASEAN members, Indonesia and Thailand came to have high savings rates in the 1990s, a decade behind the tigers. As an outlier, the Philippines began with savings rates comparable with its neighbors but saw them declining to below 20 percent mostly starting in the mid-1990s. China had high savings rates all along but came to have over 40 percent in the past few years, among the highest in the world. Vietnam's savings rate was a low 3.3 percent in 1990 but reached 30.1 percent in 2005.

The World Bank's 1993 *East Asian Miracle* report concluded that East Asian high savings largely resulted from rather than caused the high economic growth. Also, falling birth rates meant higher savings rates because of lower needs to support children and the elderly. The report also credited the governments' policies of keeping down inflation to encourage savings and of maintaining high public savings through restrained public expenditure. The East Asian governments also adopted measures to remove hindrances to savings, such as lack of insurance and high transaction costs. Some governments used mandatory pension plans to force savings although the report could not find sufficient evidence that these measures actually work.[2] At the same time, as discussed in Chapter 5, developmental state theorists go much further to explain the role of the state in facilitating high savings for investment.

East Asian high savings have gone into investment. Table 9.2 shows high domestic capital formation for East Asian economies. The World Bank miracle report argues that there has been a virtuous cycle of high growth, high savings, and high investment in East Asia.[3] As shown in Figure 9.2, Japan's shares began to decrease significantly since the early 1990s, reflecting its economic slowdown. Capital investment in Malaysia and South Korea has decreased significantly since the Asian financial crisis. On the other hand, China continues its trend of high savings and high investment, reflecting its continuous economic boom.

East Asia's savings and capital formation have not matched neatly over time and across economies. As Table 9.3 shows, Taiwan had a significant mismatch in the 1980s owing to large trade surpluses and domestic savings against decreasing investment opportunities. But the mismatch did not last into the 1990s. South Korea and Singapore had sizable deficits between domestic savings and domestic

TABLE 9.2
East Asian Gross Fixed Capital Formation (percentage of GDP)

	1965	1970	1975	1980	1985	1990	1995	2000	2003	2004	2005
Japan	30.4	36.2	33.1	32.2	28.1	32.5	28.0	25.2	22.9	22.9	—
China	20.4	24.2	29.4	29.3	29.8	26.0	34.4	34.1	39.4	40.7	42.3
South Korea	15.4	25.6	26.9	32.2	28.8	37.1	37.3	31.1	29.9	29.5	29.3
Taiwan					18.8	22.4	24.8	23.5	18.2	21.2	20.4
Singapore	21.1	32.5	36.0	40.7	42.4	32.9	33.8	30.6	24.1	23.8	21.8
Hong Kong	34.3	19.7	21.5	32.2	21.0	26.1	30.0	26.4	21.2	21.3	20.9
Indonesia	—	—	—	21.6	22.7	28.3	28.4	19.9	19.3	21.7	22.0
Malaysia	16.4	18.2	25.6	29.9	28.7	33.0	43.6	25.6	22.0	20.4	20.0
Philippines	17.6	18.1	24.6	27.2	16.5	23.1	22.2	21.2	16.8	16.1	14.9
Thailand	18.8	23.7	22.9	27.8	27.2	40.4	41.1	22.0	24.0	25.9	29.0
Vietnam	—	—	—	—	—	—	25.4	27.6	33.4	33.4	33.1
World	22.0	23.0	23.5	24.1	21.9	22.6	21.4	21.7	20.3	20.8	—

Source: World Bank, World Development Indicators Database. The data for Taiwan are calculated from the Asian Development Bank Statistical Database: Key Indicators, various years.

FIGURE 9.2
Gross Fixed Capital Formation as Shares of GDP, 1965–2005

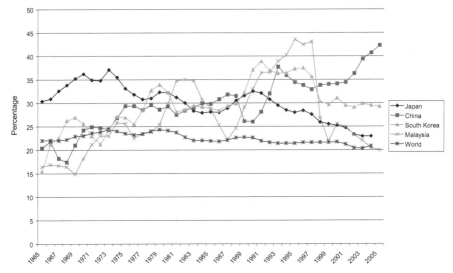

Source: World Bank, World Development Indicators Database.

capital formation through the early 1980s. China is investing heavily, but it is saving even more. Chinese households save because of rising income, weak pension
plans, and financial needs for health and education. The government saves by
investing in infrastructure and transferring capital to state firms. Chinese firms
also save although they spend much as well.

What is striking about the saving-investment ratios for East Asia in recent years
is a savings glut, as shown in Table 9.3. China had a net savings ratio minus investment ratio at 6.7 percent of GDP in 2005, although the country had always had
large ratios. Singapore and Malaysia had incredibly high ratios of 26.8 percent and
23.5 percent, respectively, in 2005. The Asian financial crisis started this trend
when the crisis countries simultaneously sought to increase reserves to prepare for
another financial crisis and saw investment decreasing. I will address this issue of
savings glut in the larger global context later in the chapter.

East Asian Banking

Savings need to be put into use. Financial intermediation handles the process of
linking the ultimate savers and the ultimate investors. East Asian financial assets
have grown rapidly, particularly compared with other developing regions. Their
growing financial depth can be measured by increasing ratio of M2 (currency,

TABLE 9.3
East Asian Savings-Investment Gap (percentage of GDP)

	1965	1970	1975	1980	1985	1990	1995	2000	2003	2004	2005
Japan	3.7	4.9	0.3	-0.3	4.1	1.6	1.8	1.5	1.7	1.7	—
China	7.1	4.7	0.8	5.7	4.6	13.9	9.7	3.4	4.0	5.1	6.7
South Korea	-7.4	-10.4	-6.7	-8.3	1.8	-0.7	-0.7	3.1	2.4	5.1	3.3
Taiwan	—	—	—	—	14.1	5.2	0.9	0.8	5.8	2.5	2.6
Singapore	-11.2	-14.1	-6.6	-2.6	-1.7	11.1	16.3	16.3	19.6	23.2	26.8
Hong Kong	-2.8	8.5	7.1	2.2	10.7	9.6	-0.4	5.6	10.0	9.4	12.1
Indonesia	—	—	—	16.4	7.0	4.0	2.2	12.9	13.4	6.2	4.6
Malaysia	5.6	6.1	-2.3	-0.1	1.2	1.5	-3.9	21.7	20.5	23.6	23.5
Philippines	3.2	3.8	0.2	-3.0	0.0	-4.7	-7.6	1.9	-5.9	-3.2	-4.4
Thailand	-0.2	-2.5	-0.8	-4.9	-1.7	-6.6	-5.7	9.5	7.7	5.9	1.1
Vietnam	—	—	—	—	—	—	-7.4	-0.5	-6.0	-5.1	-2.9
World	1.9	2.0	-0.2	-0.3	0.7	0.6	1.3	0.6	0.6	0.6	—

Source: Calculated from Tables 9.1 and 9.2.

demand deposit, time deposit, and savings deposit)/GDP. But observers came to recognize that East Asian finance was weak and needed reforms, an assessment confirmed by the 1997–1998 financial crisis. East Asian finance has been too dependent on banking rather than equity and debt securities. Hong Kong and Singapore are exceptions. Moreover, East Asian banking and financial markets have serious problems, particularly weak financial institutions such as corporate governance, disclosure, prudential regulations, and auditing practice. East Asia has made significant progress in financial reforms since the crisis, but much remains to be done.[4]

The Japanese government created a financial system that separated long-term banking from short-term banking and banks from security firms, with specialized banks and administrative guidance from the Ministry of Finance. Unlike in the United States where banks keep an arm's length from firms, the Japanese created a keiretsu, or an industrial group system, in which groups of companies were built around a main bank at the core. The banks and firms had an interlocking long-term relationship with cross-shareholdings. Japanese nonfinancial sectors received most external funding through bank loans (45–63 percent in 1954–1984) and trade credits (20–36 percent) rather than stocks (4–15 percent) or bonds (2–5 percent). The shares of stocks actually decreased from 15 percent in 1954–1958 to 6.1 percent in 1979–1983.[5] While this Japanese financial system offered Japanese competitive advantages and ensured access to financing and financial services from banks through the 1980s, it came to hurt the Japanese economy given the institutional tendency of the main banks to continue to lend to troubled affiliated firms, aggravating a nonperforming loan problem. In fact, the Japanese financial system has been blamed as a principal reason for Japan's great stagnation since 1990.[6]

The South Korean government turned private commercial banks to public enterprises in the early 1960s. The government introduced a principal transactions bank system in 1974, essentially assigning a principal commercial bank for a business group. Unlike the main bank system in Japan, the transactions bank did not hold cross-sharing arrangements with the companies; its business relationship with the firm was solely through government regulations. Through the 1970s, the government used banks as a policy instrument for channeling funds to preferred industries and companies. Along with foreign loans guaranteed by the government, bank loans accounted for two-thirds of external funding for South Korean firms until the mid-1980s. The state privatized several commercial banks and allowed establishment of nonbank financial institutions in the 1980s. Although securities became a more important source of external funding than bank loans after the mid-1980s, credits actually remained the dominant form of funding since bonds and commercial papers were largely guaranteed by financial institutions.[7]

State-owned banks dominated in Taiwan's banking sector, and the government controlled the banking sector tightly, setting interest rates and restricting entry of new banks. The government then channeled bank credit to favored state enterprises and exporting firms. The government adopted a new policy to move away from financial repression in 1989, and new banks were created starting in 1992.[8] For the formal financial sector, bank loans accounted for 70 percent of the total financing from money market, capital market, and domestic banks in 1977 and 60.7 percent as late as 1984.[9]

Banks also dominated in financial sectors in Southeast Asia. In Malaysia, banks dominated till the 1990s. Of the funds raised by the private sector, 67 percent in 1980–1985 and 51 percent in 1991–1996 came from bank loans. The stock market has gained in importance since the end of the 1980s, with the shares of funds raised from the equity market increased from 9 percent in 1980–1985 to 19 percent in 1990–1996.[10] Commercial banks dominate in Thailand as well. In terms of total assets, total savings mobilized, and total credit, commercial banks continued to be dominant, taking up close to or above 70 percent through the 1980s. The Thai banking sector was also highly concentrated, with the top four banks accounting for three-fifths of the banking industry.[11]

As Southeast Asia has over 200 million Muslims, there also exists an early stage of Islamic banking. Islamic banking is characterized by rejection of predetermined interest-bearing transactions and by an emphasis on sharing of profit and loss between the lender and user. But Muslims can trade stocks that are real assets. While informal financial arrangements consistent with the Shariah principles have always existed in the Muslim communities in Southeast Asia, formal Islamic banking in the region is not yet as advanced as in the Middle East. Islamic banking was introduced in Malaysia in 1983 and allowed in Indonesia in 1992. Islamic banking assets accounted for 9.4 percent of the banking sector in Malaysia and only 0.12 percent in Indonesia in 2003. The Malaysian government now wants to turn Kuala Lumpur into a regional hub of Islamic banking, particularly based in the Labuan International Offshore Financial Centre. Singapore is also hoping to tap into the Islamic financial market.[12]

China depends on bank loans even more than any other East Asian economy. Bank loans accounted for 85.1 percent of the funds raised in the domestic financial market in 2003 and 78.1 percent in 2005. By contrast, treasury bonds accounted for 9.5 percent in 2005, corporate bonds 6.4 percent, and stocks merely 6.0 percent.[13] China's banking system is deep, as measured by total credit divided by GDP. However, most bank credits go to state and listed sectors. Chinese companies are turning more to share and debt markets. There is also some indication that Chinese firms lend to each other informally even though Chinese law does not allow it.[14]

East Asian banks have nonperforming loan (NPL) problems. NPLs are bad loans that will not be repaid to lenders. NPLs are costly for a country's economy because the affected banks need to be recapitalized, often with public money. NPLs have to be dealt with to ensure the stability and functioning of the banking system.[15] Asian banks are having NPL problems because governments make banks lend to companies that may not be profitable and because banks themselves lend irresponsibly for risky projects.[16]

It is difficult to get accurate data since most countries tend to undercount their NPL problem, but it is generally agreed that virtually all East Asian economies have had a serious NPL problem at one time or continuously. According to World Bank statistics, as shown in Table 9.4, China, Indonesia, Malaysia, the Philippines, and Thailand have remained troubled by NPLs since 2000. As a contrast, the United States does not have any problem with NPLs, which is below 1 percent of total loans, and the world average has decreased from 9.5 percent in 2000 to 4.4 percent in 2005. The World Bank data are based on official reports and cover only the period from the year 2000. Some independent estimates put East Asia's NPLs at a much higher level.

Shallow Financial Markets

East Asian financial markets have grown, but they still need better financial intermediation to allocate their growing financial assets more efficiently. East Asia also needs to manage risks and enhance risk sharing (derivative markets). My discussion here focuses on the equity and bond markets.

TABLE 9.4
East Asian Nonperforming Loans (share of total loans)

	2000	2001	2002	2003	2004	2005	2006
China	22.4	29.8	25.6	20.1	15.6	10.5	9.8
Hong Kong	7.3	6.5	5.0	3.9	2.3	1.5	1.3
Indonesia	34.4	31.9	24.0	19.4	14.2	15.6	—
Japan	5.3	8.4	7.2	5.2	2.9	1.8	—
South Korea	8.9	3.4	2.4	2.6	1.9	1.2	1.2
Malaysia	15.4	17.8	15.8	13.9	11.8	9.9	9.5
Philippines	24.0	27.7	26.5	26.1	24.7	20.0	—
Singapore	3.4	8.0	7.7	6.7	5.0	3.8	3.8
Thailand	17.7	11.5	16.5	13.5	11.8	11.1	8.9
United States	1.1	1.3	1.4	1.1	0.8	0.7	0.7
World	9.5	8.5	7.9	6.7	5.5	4.4	—

Source: World Bank, World Development Indicators Database.

Not all East Asian economies are problematic. Hong Kong has been a highly efficient financial center for the region and is one of the most important in the world.[17] Hong Kong's success lies in open financial institutions, a stable currency, a location right between the European and American capital markets, large flow of capital into Hong Kong, low taxes, and a good legal structure. Hong Kong has one of the three largest gold exchanges in the world. It has well-functioning financial markets of foreign exchange, gold, stocks, and futures. It is also developing a bond market. Hong Kong firms have handled many consortium loans in the Asian Pacific region. Along with London, Hong Kong surpassed the New York Stock Exchange in initial public offerings in 2006. New York's relative decline was due to litigations, more stringent regulations that increase costs of doing business in the city, and tighter immigration rules after September 11, 2001.[18]

Trying to outdo Hong Kong, Singapore has also been successful in creating a strong financial sector since the early 1960s. Singapore is now a major financial center in East Asia, along with Tokyo and Hong Kong.[19] Based on stable politics, highly favorable regulatory environment, low taxes, skilled labor force, and no barriers to the entry and repatriation of capital, Singapore has attracted a large number of leading foreign financial institutions that offer a wide array of financial instruments. Singapore is now the fourth largest foreign exchange trading center in the world, trailing only London, New York, and Tokyo. The city state has created the first derivatives market in Asia and is part of the global futures markets. It is also building a formidable asset and wealth management industry that may rival Switzerland in the future.

East Asian equity markets. The East Asian stock markets have grown in East Asia as measured by capitalization of listed companies. East Asia, including here China, Hong Kong, Indonesia, South Korea, Malaysia, the Philippines, Singapore, and Thailand but excluding Japan, increased its capitalization of listed companies from $334 billion (2.9 percent of the world total) in 1989 to $3,139 billion (7.2 percent) in 2005, as shown in Table 9.5. In particular, China began with $2 billion capitalization in 1991 and came to have a market capitalization of $781 billion in 2005. East Asia, not including Japan, has had a major increase in equity market capitalization since the Asian financial crisis, the 2005 amount being more than two times that in 1996. Japan saw a dramatic fall in relative shares of market capitalization, from a high $4.4 trillion (125.1 percent of the U.S. and 37.5 percent of the world total) in 1989 to $4.7 trillion (27.9 percent of the U.S. and 10.9 percent of the world total) in 2005. Japan's equity market capitalization went down as low as $2.1 trillion in 2002. While China, Japan, and Indonesia still have a bank-based financial system, South Korea, Malaysia, the Philippines, and Thailand had adopted a market-based financial system by the mid-1990s.[20]

TABLE 9.5
Market Capitalization of Listed Companies (current U.S. $ billion)

	1989	1990	1991	1992	1993	1994	1995	1996	1997	1998	1999	2000	2001	2002	2003	2004	2005	2006
China	—	—	2	18	41	43	42	114	206	231	331	581	524	463	681	640	781	2,426
Hong Kong	77	83	122	172	385	270	304	449	413	343	609	623	506	463	715	861	1,006	—
Indonesia	2	8	7	12	33	47	67	91	29	22	64	27	23	30	55	73	81	139
Japan	4,390	2,920	3,130	2,400	3,000	3,720	3,667	3,089	2,217	2,496	4,547	3,157	2,252	2,126	3,041	3,678	4,737	—
South Korea	141	111	96	107	139	192	182	139	46	121	396	172	220	250	330	429	718	835
Malaysia	40	49	59	94	220	199	223	307	94	99	145	117	120	124	168	190	181	235
Philippines	12	6	11	15	40	57	59	81	31	35	42	26	21	19	24	29	40	68
Singapore	36	34	48	49	133	135	148	150	106	94	198	153	117	102	146	172	208	—
Thailand	26	24	36	58	131	131	142	100	24	35	58	29	36	46	119	115	124	140
United States	3,510	3,060	4,090	4,490	5,136	5,067	6,858	8,484	11,309	13,451	16,635	15,104	13,855	11,098	14,266	16,324	16,998	—
World	11,714	9,404	11,347	10,938	14,017	15,116	17,788	20,253	23,117	26,924	36,109	32,188	27,888	23,489	32,602	39,120	43,642	—

Source: World Bank, World Development Indicators Database.

The Japanese stock market was initially meant to protect companies. The Tokyo stock market was designed not for companies to raise funds but to allow them to form long-term relationships with cross-share holdings in the keiretsu system. Unlike the American system, the Japanese equity market was also designed to protect the weak from unfriendly takeovers.[21]

As a British colony, Malaysia had share trading as early as the 1870s. Public share trading began with the Malayan Stock Exchange established in May 1960. The Kuala Lumpur Stock Exchange and the Stock Exchange of Singapore operated as a unified exchange with separate locations in Kuala Lumpur and Singapore. The Kuala Lumpur Stock Exchange was used by the government as a policy tool of the New Economy Policy introduced in 1970. After 1976, all listed firms had to sell 30 percent of the shares below market prices to native bumiputra. The two markets split in 1990. The Kuala Lumpur Stock Exchange grew rapidly after that. The equity market came to be as important a source of corporate finance as bank loans in the early 1990s. But much of the funds raised went into privatization of public sector assets rather than into expansion of production capacities. With financial liberalization, foreign investors came to acquire about one-quarter of the stock in the market by early 1997.[22]

China created the Shanghai Stock Exchange and the Shenzhen Stock Exchange in 1990. The main purpose of the Chinese stock markets in the 1990s was to help channel capital to state enterprises. Controlled by the provincial governments, the markets were poorly regulated and plagued by manipulation by professional investors. Moreover, prices and behavior of investors do not reflect the fundamental values of listed companies. The Chinese stock market is inefficient despite its rapid expansion and stronger regulations from the central government in recent years. The cost for nonstate enterprises to list is high. The Chinese state companies issue both tradable and nontradable shares. The nontradable shares are owned by the state institutions or other public institutions. A large proportion of the shares owned by the government create uncertainties for investors. If prices go up, government agencies may purchase the share and stop the rise. The boards that include government officials are selected secretly. The government is both the regulator and the holder of large numbers of shares. Outside investors have little influence on the management of the firms, and the state or family-owned companies tend to underpay the dividends to shareholders.[23]

East Asian bond markets. Since the Asian financial crisis, much attention in East Asia has been given to development of local currency bond markets. Local currency bond markets prevent a currency mismatch where a firm has assets in local currencies but liabilities in a foreign currency. Such a mismatch makes a country vulnerable to fluctuations in exchange rates.[24] A currency mismatch explained the

TABLE 9.6
Asian Local Currency Bond Markets ($ billion outstanding, percentage of GDP)

	Dec. 1995		Dec. 2000		Dec. 2005		Dec. 2006	
	$ billion	% GDP	$ billion	% GDP	$ billion	% GDP	$ billion	% GDP
China	66.7	9.5	265.6	24.6	606.8	27.3	1,350.6	52.9
South Korea	227.3	43.8	269.1	52.6	656.4	83.4	959.0	109.3
Malaysia	62.6	70.5	74.7	82.8	124.0	94.8	121.3	82.5
Thailand	15.3	9.1	32.4	26.4	81.0	45.9	112.0	37.4
Singapore	21.0	24.9	44.7	48.2	81.9	70.2	99.2	74.3
Hong Kong	26.4	18.6	60.5	35.9	85.6	48.0	96.2	51.0
Indonesia	3.2	1.4	53.7	32.4	50.5	18.0	53.4	15.2
Philippines	25.8	34.7	21.0	27.7	40.6	41.2	43.5	37.2
Vietnam	–	–	–	–	4.3	8.1	4.9	8.9
Total	448.3	96.8	821.7	133.6	1,731.1	436.9	2,840.1	468.7
Japan	5,092.1		6,209.1		8,855.2	194.0	7,096.1	159.0

Source: Asian Development Bank, Asian Bonds Online: Asia Bond Indicators, http://asianbondsonline.adb.org/asiabondindicators/default.php.

spiraling 1997–1998 financial crisis because the local currency's depreciation worsened the balance sheets for the government and the private sector. Analysts often add another mismatch of maturity between long-term investment goals and short-term capital flows. A logical solution is then to develop a long-term local financing source denominated in local currencies.[25]

East Asian bond markets have grown since the Asian financial crisis. As Table 9.6 shows, East Asia excluding Japan increased its local currency bond outstanding from $448.3 billion by the end of 1995 to $2,840.1 billion by the end of 2006. While growing slowly, Japan had 2.5 times bonds outstanding than the rest of East Asia by end of 2006.

More broadly, East Asian economies have turned to domestic debt more than elsewhere since the Asian financial crisis. Asia as a whole has switched from external debt to domestic debt. The ratio of domestic to external debt increased from about parity in 1997 to three times in 2002. As a dramatic example, Indonesia's domestic debt increased from extremely low before the crisis to about 42 percent of GDP at present while its public sector external debt decreased from 70 percent to 40 percent.[26]

Despite their growth, East Asian bond markets are still underdeveloped. The size of the markets is still relatively small as measured by bonds outstanding as a percentage of GDP. East Asian bond markets are also dominated by the government issues rather than corporate issues. East Asian firms do not depend on bond markets to raise capital.

At the end of 2005, East Asia excluding Japan had less than $2 trillion in bonds in local currencies (plus $135 billion in dollar-denominated bonds) compared with $7 trillion of Japanese bonds and $22 trillion American bonds. In the big picture, what all this means is that most of East Asian foreign reserves end up being invested in U.S. financial markets, particularly the Treasuries, which then cycle back to East Asia in the form of portfolio investments and FDI. The East Asian governments increasingly question the wisdom of such a situation and urge development of national and regional bond markets. Dependence on foreign financial markets makes the region vulnerable to international investors, and it makes sense to shift some savings from bank accounts to investments. At the same time, American bonds are safe and liquid, and moving away from them necessarily leads to a greater concentration of risks.[27]

EAST ASIAN FINANCIAL POLICIES

Mobilizing Domestic Capital

A rapid expansion in East Asian capital accumulation comes from the success of the East Asian governments to mobilize domestic capital. East Asian governments were able to avoid long-term fiscal deficit and to restrain inflation, creating a positive environment for savings. Moreover, East Asian governments monitored banks to achieve the same results as deposit insurance. They simultaneously restricted deposit and lending rates. Most East Asian economies, following Japan's lead, also created postal savings systems to lower the transaction costs for smaller and distant savers. The governments could also force savings by creating pension plans such as Singapore's Central Provident Fund.

East Asian governments then used development banks and other specialized financial institutions to channel high savings as long-term financing to targeted areas. East Asia has been far more successful than other regions in using development banks. East Asian development banks have tried to use commercial banking principles and create institutions to minimize political intervention. The governments provided tax incentives for investment, tax holidays, credits, accelerated depreciation, and special exemptions. Also, they held down the relative price of capital goods. They created risk-sharing mechanisms for private investors, but firms were monitored for performance. Lastly, they restricted outflows of capital to more attractive foreign financial instruments.[28]

An active role by the state to direct cheap credits to favored industrial projects was at the core of the East Asian miracle discussed in Chapter 5. Without effective mobilization of resources, the developmental state theorists argue, East Asia would not have been able to grow as rapidly as it did. By contrast, other developing regions fell behind because their governments were far less effective in this regard. At the same time, as discussed in Chapter 6, East Asia's approach toward savings and investments came to be viewed as a principal problem for the Asian financial crisis and Japan's economic stagnation before then. While the East Asian system might have contributed to strong economic growth in the catch-up stage, the system that distorts economic structure has become more detrimental to the whole economy when East Asian economies have come to possess surplus capital. Japan is a primary example in this regard.

The Japanese government has been highly effective in channeling high savings to projects deemed important for the country. The best-known Japanese financial institution to serve this purpose is the Japan postal savings system invented in 1875. Japan Post not only handles mail but also serves as a bank and insurance provider for Japanese households. It has ¥386 trillion ($3.6 trillion) in savings and insurance assets, which makes Japan Post the largest financial institution in the world.[29] The Japanese government has created a secondary budget based on the deposits to fund important projects. Besides Japan Post, Japan has other state-owned financial institutions, which possessed a total of ¥143.7 trillion in loans outstanding as of December 2004.[30]

More than specific measures to boost savings, the Japanese system was structured to promote investment to catch up with the West, which meant rationing cheap credits to target industries to spur faster economic growth. The flip side was relatively low personal consumption. While a relatively lower consumption as share of GDP was understandable during high-growth years that necessarily relied on investment, Japan became an outlier among developed nations after the 1973–1974 oil crisis when its personal consumption declined further.[31] As Yukio Noguchi put it succinctly, the bubble of the late 1980s was created in the following sequence. Japanese economic growth and productivity gains led to a stronger yen, which should allow consumers to benefit from cheaper imports. However, the producers and distributors captured the yen appreciation benefits and they then channeled the profits into financial speculation (so-called zai-tech). They could raise money easily because of their rising stocks and then speculated in land deals, which pushed up further land and stock prices.[32]

South Korea took the directed credit approach to another level. The South Korean government simply took over private commercial banks to channel domestic savings at cost to preferred industries or companies. Given that South Korean companies typically had a high debt-asset ratio and that their principal source of financing was bank credit, they had strong incentives to follow state directives. Unlike the other three tigers, South Korea had a serious foreign debt burden by the early 1980s because the country needed foreign borrowings to pay for current account deficits in the 1970s. But the state was still in control since it guaranteed all the foreign loans, which made it necessary to monitor corporate activities. Unlike Taiwan, the South Korean government favored large corporations as champions of its big push for rapid industrialization.[33] The flip side of a state-controlled financial system was a thriving informal private money market, with high risks and high returns for small businesses.[34] South Korea did achieve rapid industrialization partly thanks to its development strategies. At the same time, South Korea paid a heavy price for this development model in the Asian financial crisis.

In Taiwan's case, the government realized early on the importance of boosting saving rates for long-term economic development. In the 1950s the orthodoxy among development economists was that the government should keep interest low to encourage investment and to prevent cost-push effect on inflation. However, the Taiwanese government decided to raise the real interest rate as early as 1950. Since the inflation rate was over 100 percent, the Bank of Taiwan adopted a special system of savings deposits with a nominal interest of 125 percent a year. As a result, savings grew rapidly and the inflation level came down. The government then gradually lowered the interest rates. The government also adopted other measures such as tax incentives. Taiwan's domestic savings exceeded the need of capital investment in 1963. Taiwan became a capital exporter by the mid-1970s.[35] Similar to South Korea, the government's direction of relatively cheap credit to large companies meant that small and medium-sized companies had no choice but to turn to the informal financial market for funding. The informal financial sector provided 32.9 percent of domestic borrowing by private firms but only 3.2 percent of public enterprises in 1964–1994.[36]

In the 1980s, Taiwan saw a mismatch of high domestic savings and large trade surplus vis-à-vis relatively low domestic investment. Similar to Japan, investors looked for alternative ways to invest their money, leading to a real estate and stock market boom as well as to investment overseas. But unlike Japan, the mismatch did not last long in Taiwan as savings and trade surpluses began to decline by the 1990s and the economy continued to grow despite the burst of the bubble.[37] Taiwan's healthier financial sector was an important reason that it was not affected by the Asian financial crisis as much as South Korea and some other regional economies.

Singapore managed to run budget surpluses as public sector savings, which were used as loans to finance the government investment projects for industrialization and economic growth. Singapore's public sector savings increased from 22.8 percent of gross national savings in 1974 to 66.8 percent in 1985. Also, Singapore established the Central Provident Fund in 1955 as a scheme to force private savings. The government collected and invested savings from employees to be used as retirement payments. The government borrowed from the fund with low interest rates to finance construction of infrastructures, which in turn attract foreign companies to invest in the city state.

In Malaysia, Bank Negara, the central bank established in 1959, focused on the mobilization of domestic savings by creating confidence in the national banking system through stronger bank regulations and spread of government bank branches into smaller towns. The government also created the state-owned National Savings Bank, which originated from the Post Office Savings Banks, and the compulsory savings fund the Employees Provident Fund. The government was less interventionist in allocation of bank credits than Japan and South Korea, although Bank Negara did urge credits to various categories of borrowers such as bumiputra, small businesses, and low-cost housing. Also unlike Northeast Asian countries, the Malaysian government did not seek to repress interest rates partly because, as part of the Sterling Area until 1973, Malaysia, Singapore, and Brunei allowed free movement of capital.[38] Malaysia's capital accumulation maintained a high level in the 1990s, but much of the expansion took place in nontradable property markets. Malaysia's investment outpaced savings in the 1990s prior to the Asian financial crisis, with the gap filled by inflows of foreign capital. But increasingly short-term foreign capital inflows covered Malaysia's current account deficits, which in turn were caused mainly by growing imports of input and equipment for nontradable infrastructure and property.[39] This situation contributed to Malaysia's sharp fall during the Asian financial crisis.

The Philippines under the Marcos regime sought to follow a state-led development strategy in the second half of the 1970s, more for political than economic reasons, by directing credits to the favored and protected business groups. Without sufficient domestic savings, the government relied on foreign borrowings to finance public infrastructure and energy development projects, which worsened the trade and current account balances and led to a debt crisis in the early 1980s.[40]

The socialist countries used more direct measures to force savings for industrialization. China, for example, saw rapid industrialization as a priority. Besides receiving aid from the Soviet Union in the early years, the Chinese government extracted resources from forced savings and indoctrination of frugality among citizens to keep consumption low and free up resources for industrial investment, keeping a high investment to national income ratio.[41] This was a typical socialist approach.

Since the reform, the Chinese government on all levels has been boosting production based on high savings and high investments following the East Asian model. Similar to Japan before the bubble, much of the profits have been captured by the Chinese companies, particularly monopoly state enterprises, rather than consumers. China's investments as share of GDP were above 40 percent in 2005. Much of this investment boom comes from retained earnings of Chinese state-owned companies. While state-owned enterprises often lost money in the early 1990s, they are largely profitable now because of their monopoly of strategic sectors. Since they do not pay dividends to the state, their savings have grown dramatically. Investment generates more investment. But this investment-driven growth model is not sustainable since it depends on exports to the rest of the world, which invites trade protectionism and strains the world markets in energy and materials. In the end, despite two decades of reform, the Chinese investment system still exhibits some of the features of a planned economy, leading to seasonal fluctuations, low returns, excess capacity, and distorted factor prices.[42]

Financial Liberalization

In the 1980s there was a global movement for financial liberalization. East Asia was no exception. Financial liberalization refers to liberalization of the financial market aimed at allowing domestic and foreign capital to flow to the most profitable investment opportunities according to market forces. Financial liberalization includes measures such as liberalization of interest rates, capital account transactions, and the financial services sector to foreign firms. The intellectual arguments for free flow of capital are that a more efficient allocation of savings and investment results when capital goes where it generates the highest returns. Developing countries enjoy greater access to capital. Investors now can seek the highest possible returns all around the world. Also, investors can diversify the risk by spreading their investment portfolio more widely. However, economists have been less united in opposing capital control than trade protectionism.[43] In fact, while promoting trade liberalization through the 1960s, advanced countries mostly imposed capital controls. In the Bretton Woods system that ensured stable exchange rates, capital control was seen as necessary for a stable exchange rate system since capital flows would create balance of payments problems.

The theory of financial liberalization rejects financial repression, a practice of keeping a ceiling on interest rates through regulations of the financial market. Financial repression is based on the notion that since developing nations are capital scarce, the market will have overly high interest rates. The practice was dealt a serious blow by the intellectual contributions of Ronald I. McKinnon and Edward S. Shaw in the early 1970s.[44] They pointed out that financial repression explains low savings rates and underdevelopment of the financial sector in many developing nations because there is less interest in financial assets, and this creates a moral hazard for investors, who become less careful. Governments should liberalize domestic financial markets to let the market determine interest rates. McKinnon argued that monetary reform is more important for development than trade liberalization, tax reform, or incentives to attract foreign capital.

The intellectual influence of the Shaw and McKinnon theory aside, one important reason for financial liberalization for developing nations was the debt crisis in the early 1980s when flows of external loans changed from positive to negative. This major shift helped to convince the developing countries that they needed to shift from an interventionist financial policy to one based more on market forces. Some East Asian economies had become more modern and complex, which made it necessary to reform the financial sector that was now increasingly inefficient. The international organizations and the Western governments also encouraged financial liberalization as a natural follow-up to trade liberalization.

Most Asian governments have introduced financial reform. Limited financial reform began in the 1970s. The reforms that began after 1985 were more serious. For most East Asian economies, financial liberalization had made significant progress by the mid-1990s. According to some estimates, Hong Kong, Indonesia, South Korea, Malaysia, the Philippines, Taiwan, and Thailand had the same level of domestic financial liberalization as most Western European countries. Japan and South Korea announced "Big Bang" reforms in the mid-1990s, modeled after the British Big Bang. The 1997 Asian financial crisis paved the way for further reforms.[45]

Japan began financial reform as a result of both external and internal pressure. There was increasing external pressure on Japan to change its economic structure to reduce trade surpluses. Moreover, by the 1980s, large Japanese corporations had shifted much of their financing from Japanese banks to corporate bonds in the international market. With a shrinking operational base, major Japanese banks were forced to enter new business areas such as real estate financing. Japan also introduced the internationalization of its domestic bond market after the mid-1980s. The Financial Reform Act of 1993 allowed banks to establish securities subsidiaries and securities companies and trust banks to create banking and securities subsidiaries. To indicate a break from the past gradualist approach, Japanese Prime Minister Hashimoto Ryutaro announced in November 1996 the Big Bang reform to make the Japanese markets free (liberalization of entry, products, and pricing), fair (transparency and investor protection), and global (a global market with monitoring and accounting systems), aimed at a comprehensive deregulation of Japan's financial services by 2001.[46] The aim of the Big Bang was to make Tokyo as prominent an international financial center as New York and London. One wants a financial center because it is more costly to raise money overseas and because a financial center attracts financial firms to locate nearby. However, although almost all the measures have been implemented, the position of the Tokyo financial market has declined in recent years.[47]

While Japan was not one of the crisis countries in the Asian financial crisis, it came close to a meltdown. In fact, Japan's financial problems that emerged in 1994 and intensified in the spring of 1997 were a prelude to the crisis. The government had to bail out some failing financial institutions. Then the Long Term Credit Bank (LTCB) failed in the fall of 1998. LTCB was one of the largest banks in the world, and its collapse revealed the depth of Japan's banking crisis. In response, the government injected public money and created an independent regulator, the Financial Services Agency. Japan made much progress in putting bad loans under control after Koizumi Junichiro became prime minister in 2001. By September 2005, his banking reforms had managed to reduce by half the $480 billion bad loans reported in 2002.[48] As an indicator of progress, net bank lending increased again in 2005. Koizumi also managed to pass a bill for reforming Japan Post, which would partly privatize the system by 2017.

One major development in the Japanese banking sector is consolidation of major banks into three megabanks. Of the fourteen big commercial banks that existed before the Asian financial crisis, some collapsed and the rest merged into MUFG (a merger of Bank of Tokyo-Mitsubishi and UFJ), Mizuho (a merger of Industrial Bank of Japan, Dai-Ichi Kangyo Bank, and Fuji Bank), and SMBC (a merger of Sumitomo Bank and Mitsui Bank).

The South Korean government introduced financial reforms in the early 1980s. One reason for liberalization measures was that the state-directed credit to promote heavy and chemical industries in the mid-1970s led to excess production capacities and to large current account deficits. The government privatized some commercial banks and allowed establishment of new commercial banks and nonbank financial institutions. The equity market also grew.[49] The government liberalized FDI in the 1980s and financial capital flows in the 1990s. But there were limits to the financial liberalization of the 1980s, and the weaknesses of the financial system were revealed later in the Asian financial crisis.

In return for an IMF standby arrangement in December 1997, the South Korean government committed to drastic reform measures of closing nonviable financial institutions, restructuring and recapitalizing viable ones, disposing of NPLs, creating a limited deposit insurance plan, and improving banks to international standards. South Korea created new financial supervisory institutions and followed through on the promised reform measures, including closure of 30 percent of the banks and 21 percent of nonbanking financial institutions.[50]

Taiwan liberalized FDI and financial capital flows at a similar pace as South Korea's. The government adopted several measures in the 1980s to liberalize the banking sector and the financial market. Following interest rate liberalization, the government relaxed restrictions on foreign banks after the mid-1980s. The Banking Law of 1989 privatized the banking sector. Foreign investors were allowed to participate in the Taiwanese stock market after March 1996. The money market and the capital market became more important sources of funds for companies.[51]

In Malaysia, financial reforms largely began in the 1980s and continued in the 1990s. Reform measures included deregulation and development of the financial sector. The stock market expanded in the early 1980s. The market turnover increased rapidly in the late 1980s and the early 1990s to the extent that companies now could turn to the market more for financing. The government control over the direction of bank credits weakened and the state's role in direct lending and transfer to the private sector decreased after the mid-1980s.[52] In 1990, the Malaysian government also created an offshore banking facility, the Labuan International Offshore Financial Centre, which has attracted some leading international financial institutions such as Standard Chartered Bank, Hongkong and Shanghai Bank, Bank of Tokyo-Mitsubishi, Dresdner Bank AG and Deutsche Bank AG, and Citibank Malaysia. Like South Korea and Thailand, Malaysia liberalized financial capital flows in the 1990s. As discussed in Chapter 6, Malaysia chose capital control during the Asian financial crisis, thus diverging from most other East Asian economies.

The Philippines began financial sector reform in 1980, aiming to increase competition, encourage savings, and expand financial markets. Financial deepening took place but mainly because of transfer of savings from the informal financial sector to the formal sector. Not accompanied by prudent banking regulations, the reform was not very successful. After the fall of the Marcos regime in 1986, the Philippines continued financial sector reforms, focusing on introduction of new financial products in the 1990s. The Filipino financial sector made progress but failed to develop a corresponding institutional infrastructure.[53]

The Indonesian government adopted some financial reform measures in the 1980s, particularly the lifting of interest rate ceilings in 1982 and the permission for new banks to enter the financial sector and the simplification of procedures for opening new bank branches in 1988.[54] Indonesia suffered the most from the Asian financial crisis. None of the seven original state banks and the ten largest commercial banks were solvent. The net cost of cleaning up the banking sector was estimated to be at least 40 percent of GDP. The government established the Indonesian Bank Restructuring Agency (IBRA) under the Finance Ministry in January 1998. It offered guarantees for bank depositors. IBRA nationalized and recapitalized some of the failed banks to rid them of NPLs (reaching 38 banks by 1999) and removed top management from the failed national banks. The public funding came from government bonds larger than the total liabilities of the banking system. Nationalized banks sold to domestic and foreign investors were allowed to operate again in 2003.[55] But in the scheme of things, the Indonesian financial reform has been slow.

Thailand began financial liberalization with current account transactions in May 1990. The government then liberalized capital account transactions in April 1991 and relaxed controls on outward FDI and travel expenses.[56] In the 1990s Thailand also sought to create the Bangkok International Bank Facility (BIBF), an offshore banking system that allowed Thai companies to have access to foreign-denominated loans, and BIBF loans, mostly short term, increased drastically and accounted for two-thirds of the new external debt in 1992–1996. Due to weak oversight, much of BIBF lending went to nontraded sectors.[57] The conditions for the Asian financial crisis were thus laid. In the aftermath of the crisis, the Thai government closed or forced mergers of dozens of financial companies and commercial banks and needed further capital injection to recapitalize the financial institutions.

China has introduced more market mechanisms into its economy. Creation of a stock market has been part of that overall strategy. But the Chinese government sought to use the stock market to advance its policy objectives of finding new sources of funding for state-owned enterprises in the areas that it deemed essential for the state industrialization. In fact, the provincial governments captured the Chinese stock markets based in Shenzhen and Shanghai to serve their local political and economic agenda. Private Chinese enterprises found it difficult to list in the Chinese stock market.[58]

Starting in 2000, the Chinese government sought to recentralize the Chinese stock market and to better enforce regulations. Some progress has been made. The Chinese government has also used the stock market as a way to privatize a large number of Chinese state enterprises in a stealth fashion.[59] At the same time, the

Chinese stock markets are still troubled by the chronic problems of lack of disclosure by listed companies, the stripping of list company assets, disregard for minority shareholders, and political interference. The government has become more determined since August 2005 to improve the stock market, and the volume is increasing. The current government's strategy is to allow listed state enterprises to gradually convert previously nontradable shares, about two-thirds of the total shares, to ordinary shares and then sell them to investors. As an indicator of a more active stock market, mergers and acquisition deals involving Chinese companies have increased drastically, reaching $62 billion in the first seven months of 2006, twice as much as in the same period in 2005, with $28 billion involving only Chinese firms.[60]

China has also been trying to reform banks since 1997, paying particular attention to NPLs.[61] In August 1998, Premier Zhu Rongji injected 270 billion yuan ($32.6 billion) as special government bonds into the four state-owned commercial banks. In 1999, China created four state asset management companies (AMCs) for the four state commercial banks (the China Construction Bank, the Bank of China, the Agricultural Bank of China, and the Industrial and Commercial Bank of China). The AMCs purchased 1.4 trillion yuan ($169 billion) of NPLs from the four banks at full book value, using government bonds. The government thus simply transferred bad loans from one government agency to another. The Chinese government has been hesitant to force bankruptcy of thousands of state enterprises, which would create unemployment and social unrest. The AMCs were not as effective as initially envisioned given a lack of government guarantee for their bonds. It was thus not surprising that the Chinese government has had to revisit the NPL problem. Using a newly created investment wing, the People's Bank of China has injected $60 billion of foreign reserves for equity into the four state commercial banks since late 2003. After 2004, the People's Bank of China purchased 780 billion yuan from three state banks and then auctioned them off at 26–40 percent of the book values to the AMCs. The Chinese taxpayers have essentially paid for the huge costs of NPLs.

Since 2002 the Chinese government has adopted a new strategy of attracting foreign capital to help improve Chinese banks and diversify their ownership. Foreign financial institutions have been encouraged to purchase equity stakes in the Chinese state banks, which will then list in stock markets. Declared FDI amounted to $16.5 billion, or 15 percent of the core capital of the Chinese banking system, by the end of 2005.[62] More has taken place since then.

The Asian financial crisis has taught East Asians a lesson. The crisis shows that the transitional countries like Malaysia, Thailand, and South Korea were vulnerable. The availability of international capital allowed East Asian financial institutions and companies to borrow large amounts of short-term, unhedged foreign currency credit. The flight of foreign capital created pressure on the pegged exchange rates and triggered the crisis. Although financial liberalization is a desirable policy, governments need to monitor it closely and to create legal and institutional infrastructure and stronger domestic financial markets.[63]

Intellectually, some scholars have pointed out the danger of capital market liberalization accompanied by certain types of exchange rate regimes. Capital market liberalization, which essentially means elimination of restrictions on short-term capital flows across national borders, can hurt unprepared developing nations. The basic argument is that high growing countries like China and India did not liberalize the financial sector. Growth is based on increasing investment rather than speculative capital moving in and out of a country quickly. Speculative capital causes volatility that makes investment less attractive. With capital market liberalization, a fixed exchange rate regime becomes vulnerable to speculative attacks.[64] Some maintain that financial liberalization creates too much risk while delivering small benefits. As a result, it makes sense to adopt a cautious approach toward capital account liberalization, which is what China has been doing.[65] In fact, as some analysts have argued based on the experience of East Asian economies, even a gradualist approach does not allow a liberalizing country to avoid volatility once it passes a certain threshold of openness.[66] In response, some noted that financial liberalization is still beneficial in the long run. Besides, repressed East Asian economies also experienced banking problems.[67]

EAST ASIA IN GLOBAL FINANCE

East Asian political economy of finance cannot be understood outside the context of global politics and finance. East Asian economies have developed their distinct mobilization systems partly out of a perceived weak position in the global system, and the variation in institutional setup and performance reflects more variation in capacity than in desire. But the persistence of East Asian patterns, particularly high domestic savings, has been made possible by low savings in other parts of the world, particularly the United States. Put simply, the high savings in East Asia and high spending in the United States reinforce each other.

Cross-Border Capital Flows

Flow of foreign capital includes foreign aid, export credit, bank loans, FDI, and portfolio investment. East Asian economies typically first received foreign aid from developed countries or multilateral aid organizations, followed by export credit, direct investment, portfolio investment, and short- to medium-term bank loans. What type of capital one attracts is largely consistent with one's stage of development. Much of foreign capital is private, and private investors calculate risk. The higher the stage of development, the more confidence foreign investors will have in investing in the country. In the first stage, a developing country is in a weak position to attract private capital and has to depend on aid money. Once a developing nation has grown and become more capable of attracting private foreign capital, that nation will normally graduate from foreign aid. The more advanced East Asian economies have shifted from net capital importers to capital exporters.

Government aid was important for most East Asian nations in the 1950s. The United States offered massive aid to Japan, South Korea, Taiwan, the Philippines, and others. As a case in point, U.S. aid was equivalent to 6.6–9.5 percent of Taiwan's GDP and about half of its imports in the 1950s.[68] Great Britain also offered aid to Malaya and subsidized the Hong Kong administration until the 1960s. For the socialist camp, China, North Korea, and North Vietnam received significant aid from the Soviet Union. The Soviet Union helped China build some strategic turnkey enterprises. The newly independent Indonesian government under President Sukarno also received aid from the Soviet bloc as he followed a socialist policy and allied with the Indonesian Communist Party. Beijing also provided considerable aid in cash and goods to East Asian communist countries and to a lesser extent to developing countries through the 1970s. According to recently declassified Chinese diplomatic archives, China offered 4.028 billion yuan from 1950 to mid-1960, of which 3.539 billion yuan went to fellow socialist countries, mostly to Vietnam, Mongolia, and North Korea. The total Chinese aid amounted to one-tenth of the national capital construction investment in the first Five-Year Plan (1953–1957).[69]

In the 1960s, the U.S. aid to Northeast Asia decreased significantly. These economies now received much financial assistance from the World Bank. Japan was the second largest recipient of World Bank loans, next only to India. Starting in the 1960s, Japan transferred capital to East Asia in the form of reparations. The Europeans also became significant donors, although they paid more attention to regions elsewhere. The Soviet Union stopped aid to China after its quarrels with China escalated, but Soviet aid continued to flow to North Korea and North Vietnam. China began the self-reliance phase and also began giving aid to other Asian socialist countries.

In the 1960s, East Asia also began borrowing from foreign banks as it became worthy of private loans. Industrial countries used packages of FDI, suppliers' credit, and bank loans to facilitate projects in East Asia.

In the early 1970s, Hong Kong, Singapore, and Taiwan graduated from foreign aid and began attracting foreign capital. Foreign capital accounted for a large percentage of capital formation. East Asia benefited from capital inflows. This is particularly the case for exporting sectors of primary sources, traditional sectors such as textiles, and other manufacturing sectors. FDI also contributes in transfer of technologies and skills.

South Korea was particularly dependent on foreign capital for fixed capital formation. In the early 1960s, the government selected major five-year plan projects that needed foreign capital and sent missions to advanced countries to solicit foreign financing. The government approved and guaranteed foreign loans and provided favorable treatments such tax concessions as incentives. Foreign capital was crucial for South Korea's rapid industrialization, accounting for 78.3 percent of total investment and 8.5 percent of GNP in 1960 and 26.7 percent of investment and 5.6 percent of GNP in 1972.[70] But foreign capital came in the form of loans rather than direct investment. Japan and South Korea have been different from the rest of East Asia in that they have not really encouraged FDI because of nationalist sentiment against foreign ownership. Korea's heavy dependence on foreign capital explains why South Korea had a more serious foreign debt burden than most other East Asian nations.

In the early 1980s, East Asia continued to attract foreign capital, unlike Latin America that was experiencing a serious debt crisis. The main source of capital flows was commercial bank credit, followed by official development assistance. After the mid-1980s, FDI into East Asia became more significant than before while commercial bank loans continued to grow.[71] Except for Japan and South Korea, all East Asian governments tried to attract FDI. China entered the reform stage, adopting a new policy of accepting bilateral and multilateral aid, attracting foreign investments, and raising funds in international capital markets.

Increasingly, capital inflows into East Asian economies came from other East Asian economies. Japan led the way, recycling its large foreign capital. Japan emerged as a significant source of capital for global economy after the 1985 Plaza Accord. Following Japan's footsteps, several newly industrialized economies in East Asia became significant capital exporters in the late 1980s. Taiwan became a net exporter in FDI and portfolio investment. South Korea emerged as a net FDI exporter but also a major recipient of portfolio investments after the early 1990s. In a reversal, Singapore became a major portfolio investor overseas while a major destination of FDI.[72]

With financial liberalization and pegged exchange rates, hot money flowing into East Asia increased dramatically, which was an important reason for the Asian financial crisis. Right before the crisis, the five crisis countries increased their foreign reserves mainly through private commercial borrowings of short-term debt rolled over year after year. Net interbank lending to the five crisis countries increased from $14 billion per year in 1990–1994 to $43 billion in 1995–1996. Two-thirds of the short-term loans in 1995–1996 had maturities of less than a year. By contrast, FDI was $11 billion and $17 billion over the same periods.[73] One major difference between East Asia in the mid-1990s and Latin America in the 1980s is that the foreign borrowing was done mainly by the private sector for investment in the East Asian case.

With the Asian financial crisis, $88.4 billion of commercial bank capital fled from Indonesia, South Korea, Malaysia, and Thailand in the second half of 1997 and 1998. For the whole of East Asia, $93.4 billion left in the same period.[74] Foreign capital has returned to East Asia since 1998. In 2004, the Asian Pacific region was a principal destination of international private capital flows, attracting $146 billion in net capital flows compared with $97 billion to the emerging markets in Europe, $26 billion to Latin America, and $9.2 billion to Africa and the Middle East, according to a report by the Institute of International Finance Inc. released on January 19, 2005.[75]

One notable feature of East Asian finance is that the central banks of Japan and developing East Asia have moved their hard-earned currencies to the United States, mainly in the form of low-interest U.S. Treasury bills. In fact, most developing nations have been building up their reserves for the past few years to be better prepared for a repeat of the Asian financial crisis. They purchase U.S. treasuries with the dollars earned from exports to the United States and other countries. Former U.S. Treasury Secretary Lawrence Summers has argued that the problem for the developing nations is that their foreign reserve increase has been excessive, as defined by reserves above the amount of foreign debts due for the year. Summers estimated that developing nations now have $2 trillion in excess reserves, increasing from less than $500 billion in 1997, which could have generated much higher yields if invested more productively.[76] As will be shown below, such a pattern of capital flows creates problems.

Global Saving Glut

One important debate at present is whether East Asian countries and some others have saved too much and thus caused a global imbalance. The conventional argument is that overspending in the United States has caused a global imbalance in trade and current accounts. However, Ben Bernanke, who became the chairman of the Federal Reserve in January 2006, raised the issue of "a global saving glut" at a meeting in Virginia on March 10, 2005. Excessive savings mean that a strong economy does not have to lead to higher interest rates to prevent inflation and that the United States has been able to finance its high annual current account deficits.[77] Essentially, the growing U.S. current account deficits have been financed partly through foreign reserve accumulations of countries like Japan and China.

Current account balances measure trade in goods and services, income, and unilateral net current transfers. As Table 9.7 shows, the United States suffered a deficit of $805.0 billion in 2005, an increase from $668.1 billion in 2004. By con-

TABLE 9.7
East Asian Current Account Balances (current U.S. $ million)

	1970	1975	1980	1985	1990	1995	2000	2004	2005
Japan	—	—	-10,750	51,129	44,078	111,044	119,660	172,059	165,783
China	—	—	—	-11,417	11,997	1,618	20,518	68,659	160,818
South Korea	—	—	-5,312	-795	-2,014	-8,665	12,251	27,613	16,559
Taiwan	—	—	—	9,203	10,923	5,474	8,851	18,493	16,366
Singapore	—	-584	-1,563	-4	3,122	14,708	11,936	27,897	33,265
Hong Kong	—	—	—	—	—	—	6,993	15,728	19,706
Indonesia	—	—	—	-1,923	-2,988	-6,431	7,992	3,108	929
Malaysia	—	-491	-266	-600	-870	-8,644	8,488	14,871	19,877
Thailand	—	-606	-2,076	-1,537	-7,281	-13,582	9,313	6,857	-3,719
Philippines	—	—	-1,904	-36	-2,695	-1,980	6,258	2,080	2,354
Bahrain	—	-203	184	39	70	237	830	415	—
Iran	—	—	-2,438	-476	327	3,358	12,481	—	—
Oman	—	57	942	-10	1,106	-801	3,129	443	—
Saudi Arabia	—	14,385	41,503	-12,932	-4,147	-5,318	14,317	51,926	87,131
EMU	932	123	-52,488	16,984	4,079	45,004	-38,838	76,142	-17,886
UK	1,970	-3,465	6,862	3,314	-38,811	-14,291	-36,684	-42,973	-57,616
U.S.	2,620	17,880	2,150	-124,470	-78,960	-113,664	-415,996	-668,074	-804,961

Source: World Bank, World Development Indicators Database. The data for Taiwan are from the Asian Development Bank (ADB) Statistical Database: Key Indicators, various years. The data for China, South Korea, Singapore, Indonesia, Malaysia, and the Philippines in 2005 are also from ADB Key Indicators.

Note: EMU is the European Monetary Union that evolved into the euro area, which currently includes Belgium, Germany, Greece, Spain, France, Ireland, Italy, Luxembourg, the Netherlands, Austria, Portugal, and Finland.

trast, East Asian economies have enjoyed large current account surpluses. Japan, China, South Korea, Taiwan, Singapore, Hong Kong, and Malaysia had a combined current account surplus of $432.4 billion in 2005, or more than half of the U.S. current account deficit that year.

To measure the magnitude of current accounts, we can look at their shares of GDP. As Figure 9.3 shows, East Asia has collectively moved to highly positive since the Asian financial crisis, except the Philippines in 1999–2002 and Thailand in 2005. In 2005, Singapore had 28.4 percent and Malaysia 15.3 percent; in contrast, the United States had a negative 6.4 percent. Not included in the figure, the United Kingdom suffered from deficits of –2.6 percent and Saudi Arabia had a high surplus of 28.1 percent in 2005.

With sharply increasing budget deficits during the Bush administration, the United States has become increasingly dependent on foreign financing. According to the latest U.S. Treasury report, including short-term debt securities, the United States had a total of $7,779 billion worth of U.S. securities held by foreigners as of June 30, 2006, of which Japan (ranked first) had $1,106 billion, China (2) $699 billion, Singapore (15) $163 billion, Taiwan (16) $135 billion, South Korea (17) $124 billion, and Hong Kong (19) $110 billion. Five emerging East Asian economies ($1,231 billion) surpassed Japan's holdings of U.S. securities. The six East Asian economies accounted for 30 percent of the total foreign holdings of U.S. securities. While Middle East oil exporting nations (Bahrain, Iran, Iraq, Kuwait, Oman, Qatar, Saudi Arabia, and United Arab Emirates) had a large current account surplus on par with East Asia, they actually financed only $243 billion of U.S. debt securities.[78] Through purchase of U.S. debt securities, the East Asian governments have sought to prevent an appreciation of their currencies, which will be discussed in detail in the next chapter.

Much of East Asian financing of U.S. debt securities is reflected in a sharp increase in foreign reserves. One way to see how much East Asia has accumulated these assets is to tally the combined foreign reserves, which amounted to $2.57 trillion in 2005, as calculated from Table 10.2 in the next chapter.

The danger of such an international financial imbalance is that it will sooner or later become unsustainable. A sharp adjustment would most likely cause serious global economic difficulties. A likely scenario is that foreign investors would reduce purchase of U.S. securities when they become concerned about the growing U.S. debt burden due to continuing current account deficits. Put differently, capital inflow into the United States would stop or even reverse. If this shift takes place too suddenly, the value of the U.S. dollar will drop sharply. With sharp dollar depreciation, the interest rates would go up and the stock market would fall. A recession would follow and would affect the global market.[79] Another problem is

FIGURE 9.3
Current Account Balances (percentage of GDP), 1970–2005

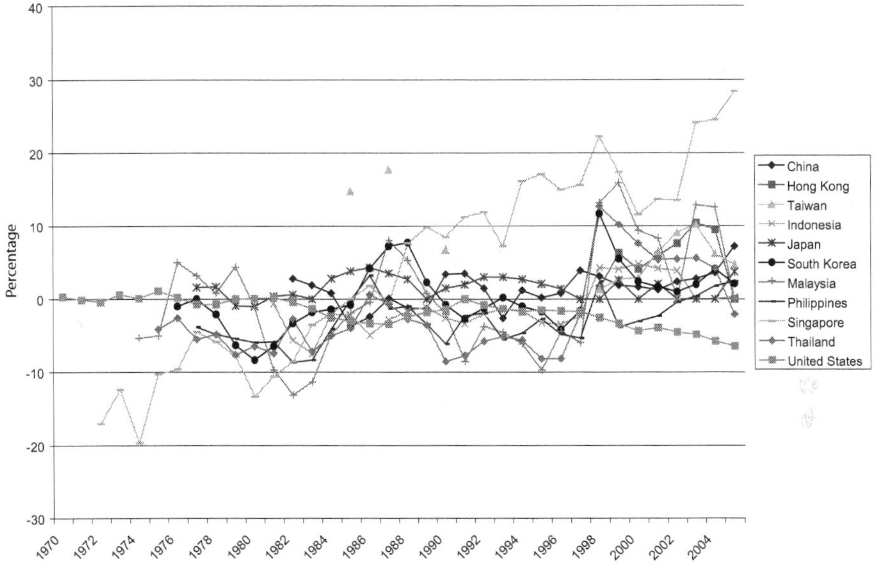

Source: World Bank, World Development Indicators Database. The data for Taiwan are from Asian Development Bank Statistical Database: Key Indicators, various years.

that the developing nations should put more resources into their own infrastructure and social development rather than exporting capital to the rich countries in the form of safe but low-yielding U.S. treasuries.

EAST ASIAN FINANCIAL REGIONALISM

East Asia is trying to integrate financially. The Asian financial crisis was a main catalyst for regional financial cooperation.[80] The East Asian economies participated actively in supporting each other, particularly in the first bailout package for Thailand, while the United States failed to lend money. The crisis revealed common challenges facing East Asian nations, which require cooperation to prevent future currency crises. Moreover, East Asia's relative weight in the international financial system has increased. Trade links are another factor. For all these reasons, financial integration makes sense for East Asia.

East Asia appears to have a different approach toward international finance. In fact, some analysts see East Asia trying to create an alternative financial structure to the West-dominated IMF system.[81] On the other hand, some other scholars suggest that East Asian financial regionalism, as it is evolving now, is compatible with the global financial institution.[82] In fact, most East Asian economies have continued to anchor their currencies to the U.S. dollar since the crisis.[83]

Any discussion of East Asian financial integration has to begin with a failed attempt, namely the Asian Monetary Fund (AMF), which Japan proposed at the Asia-Europe Meeting (ASEM) in Thailand in September 1997. Japan wanted to create a $100 billion fund on the argument that regional countries needed to pool resources together to deal with the Asian financial crisis. The Japanese Ministry of Finance lobbied actively for the proposal. However, the United States and the IMF opposed the idea for fear of undermining the influence of the IMF. The Chinese government was also hesitant, because the bureaucracy needed time to form a consensus and the country was not yet ready for ambitious regional integration projects. The Japanese proposal basically died in a meeting in Manila in November 1997. However, the desire for a regional framework did not die with the AMF. The Japanese government announced the New Miyazawa Initiative in October 1998 to facilitate recovery from the crisis among the five crisis-affected countries with a commitment of $30 billion.[84]

Of various measures taken, the Chiang Mai Initiative has drawn much attention because the initiative is often viewed as a revival of the AMF in disguise.[85] The initiative was launched at the ASEAN Plus Three meeting in Chiang Mai, Thailand, in May 2000. The initiative extended the existing ASEAN swap arrangements to cover the ASEAN Plus Three region, supported by Japan as the main supplier of swap funds. Since May 2000, the ASEAN Plus Three member countries have concluded a large number of bilateral swap agreements, ranging from $1 billion to $7 billion, with the Japan-Korea agreement the largest. Japan was the dominant player since the power specific for this arrangement is based on foreign reserves. Japan had more foreign reserves than any of the other regional economies at the time. Half of the money is from Japan. Japan is now supporting local currency bond markets because the Japanese institutions want to play a major role in the region. China was viewed as a lender rather than a borrower. As of now, the program is small and has a high threshold for tapping into the swap funds. With growing foreign reserves, East Asian economies do not expect much from the program. Without IMF approval, it is hard to tap into the money. There is a need to clarify the activation process and improve surveillance. Nevertheless, the key word about the Chiang Mai Initiative is its potential.

East Asia now has two main initiatives to promote regional bond markets, namely the Asian Bond Markets Initiative (ABMI) and the Asian Bond Fund (ABF). The ASEAN Plus Three financial officials created the ABMI in Chiang Mai in December 2002 to deal with the mismatch between supply and demand of funds by increasing regional supplies of bonds. ABMI has created a number of working groups to study how to improve domestic and regional bond markets. The Asian Development Bank provides technical assistance to the groups.

ABF was created by the Executives Meeting of East Asia and Pacific Central Banks and Monetary Authorities (EMEAP) in June 2003. EMEAP comprises Australia, China, Hong Kong, Indonesia, Japan, South Korea, Malaysia, New Zealand, the Philippines, Singapore, and Thailand. ABF pooled $1 billion of reserves from members to purchase U.S. dollar-denominated bonds from eight members. EMEAP created a second fund called ABF2, which pooled $2 billion of reserves to invest in local currency sovereign or quasi-sovereign bonds issued by the governments in the same eight economies. Unlike ABF, ABF2 is open to retail investors.[86] EMEAP asked the Bank for International Settlements (BIS) to manage the fund.

Both ABMI and ABF are still small, and there is still limited regional interest in purchasing regional assets. Some analysts have called on the East Asian governments to take an active role in promoting the development of local currency bond markets with ideas such as Asian basket currency bonds (against a collection of individual East Asian local currencies). Others argue that purchasing of other Asian bonds does not help East Asian economies to diversify their debt portfolios since they share similar business cycles. Moreover, owing to the lack of transparency and poor accounting and auditing of East Asian corporations, empirically East Asians do not exhibit a regional bias in favor of the bonds issued by other economies in the region. Therefore, a market-based strategy is preferable to a state-led strategy.[87]

All this shows that it is harder to achieve regional financial integration because of the gravity of financial globalization. Ever since the crisis, East Asian stock markets have largely correlated more closely with the American stock market than previously, but there is also some sign of regional integration.[88] Many agree that East Asian finance is connected closely to New York and London rather than regionally. East Asian financial liberalization has made East Asian economies develop stronger financial ties with advanced countries than with each other.[89] At the same time, one has to ask why the East Asian governments have been so interested in regionalization since the Asian financial crisis. There are clearly political reasons and drivers behind all this.[90] Some have argued that East Asian financial integration is greater than one might think judging by the share of bonds underwritten and loans syndicated going to East Asians.[91]

EAST ASIAN POLITICAL ECONOMY OF FINANCE

Politics has always been important for financial policy. Finance is about allocation of capital within the economy, which is at the heart of state power. After all, politics can be understood as allocation of scare resources. The importance of politics was particularly prominent through the 1960s when capital was scarce in most East Asian economies. With financial globalization, East Asian firms and individuals have acquired greater abilities to evade state control, but the state remains important albeit in a changed way.

With the exception of Hong Kong, all East Asian governments made sure that they controlled the flow of capital. Thus, where the money went reflected the governments' political agenda and political calculations. The East Asian governments' preference for a bank-based financial system rather than a securities-based system reflects their desire for rapid industrialization.[92] As a late developer, the Japanese government channeled capital to selected companies to enable them to compete in the international market. As a late-late developer, the South Korean government went all out for the biggest company groups. Being homogeneous, the Japanese and South Korean governments did not have to worry about ethnic divisions. The mainlander Taiwanese government had no incentives to strengthen the economic power of the Taiwanese businesses and channeled money to state enterprises that controlled the key infrastructure, utilities, and industries. The Malaysian government wanted to help improve the economic power of the indigenous population relative to ethnic Chinese starting in the early 1970s.

China adopted a socialist planned economy that was the opposite of the market economy. With reform launched in 1978, the Chinese government tried to reform its financial sector, letting banks run more like commercial banks and nurturing the financial market. However, the government did not have the natural instinct for a market economy. Rather, they fundamentally see the financial sector as one of the instruments to advance their policy. The finance and economy are one of several *xitongs* in the Chinese political. Politics explains why state-owned enterprises receive most of the state economic resources even though they are the least efficient firms. By contrast, more efficient Chinese private firms receive the least support.[93] Despite reforms, Chinese state banks continue to offer loans to losing state-owned enterprises, which leads to accumulation of bad loans. Private firms have found it difficult to borrow loans from state banks and have to resort to higher risk and legally murky informal financial institutions.[94] The government has also used the financial market unabashedly as an instrument to support state-owned enterprises with additional resources in the 1990s and for privatization of many state-owned enterprises since 2000. The bureaucrats determine which firms can list in the Chinese stock markets. Given the priority and vested interests, it is thus not surprising that private firms find it difficult to list in the Chinese stock markets.

State-directed credit can work, as demonstrated by the East Asian development experience. Mobilization of domestic resources could help promote faster growth. But politics may go wrong. The governments needed to benefit as broad a population base as possible. The overemphasis on political cronies in the Philippines shows that a strong state could do evil as well as good. Another lesson is that a politics-in-command approach without any regard for underlying economic dynamic is bound to fail. The ultimate failure of socialist countries is a case in point.

Equally important, the state intervention in the financial sector also creates long-term problems by distorting incentives, as shown by the experiences of Japan and others in the region. The fact that the state in East Asia mobilized finance to advance state objectives necessarily meant that the practice created institutions to favor certain political actors at the expense of others. Vested political interests make the necessary financial reform difficult if not impossible. In the case of Japan, entangled political and institutional interests have slowed down the pace of financial reforms.[95] For example, Japan Post gave the state the option to seek state objectives without going to the taxpayers. But the system favored the ruling Liberal Democratic Party (LDP) by funding projects that helped LDP win votes. Prime Minister Koizumi had to threaten to destroy the LDP itself and waged a huge fight against the rebels of his postal reform within his own party to win a watered-down reform package in 2005.

Financial reforms cannot escape politics either. Malaysia's financial reform in the 1980s and the 1990s was partly based on political favoritism, particularly bumiputra businesses connected with the ruling party. Cronies pocketed large profits from preferential allocation of stock shares.[96] For example, the reform and expansion of the Kuala Lumpur Stock Exchange in the early 1990s led to a casino atmosphere. Much of the funds raised in the market went into privatization of public sector assets.[97]

While politics affects financial policy, domestic and global financial markets affect politics in return. Financial capital is a highly liquid asset, which provides both opportunities and challenges for the state. Integration into the global capital market creates both winners and losers in the domestic context.

On the domestic front, once created, a country's financial sector constrains its policy. For example, the Chinese government has been trying unsuccessfully to restrict high investments in recent years to prevent an overheated economy. The country's investment as share of GDP approached an impossibly high 50 percent in 2005 and may well exceed 50 percent in 2006.[98] Preventing an overheated economy and a resulting economic collapse is a fundamental political interest for the party, but its ability has been constrained.

Financial difficulties also serve as catalyst for political and institutional change. Japan's burst of the economic bubble and the long stagnation were reasons that led to institutional change, including a significant weakening of the power of the Ministry of Finance, which lost its Japanese name Okurasho (Great Treasury Ministry) at the end of 2000. The bureaucrats were blamed for their mishandling of money.

The global financial market makes it difficult for national governments. As Robert Mundell reasoned in the 1960s, it is impossible to achieve a fixed exchange rate, free capital movement, and national sovereignty at the same time. A government can hope to achieve two objectives at a given time. For example, if a government wants to maintain national autonomy in financial policy but also wants to fully integrate with the global financial market, it will have no choice but to adopt a free-float exchange rate system.

Financial globalization means that foreign financial institutions are becoming increasingly powerful players in a country's domestic financial market. For example, with its entry in the WTO, foreign banks were allowed to operate in China in December 2006.

One direct impact on the state institutions is that the challenge to manage the global capital market means that the central banks often need to be shielded from interest-group-based politics. There are historical and institutional backgrounds to the national central banks that have generated much research.[99] However, a more independent central bank does not necessarily mean that all problems have been solved. In fact, one may argue that the resistance of the Bank of Japan to increase money supply to fight off deflation contributed to a painfully slow economic recovery in Japan.[100]

Also, the nature of financial issues has affected decision making. As a case in point, advanced nations sought to liberalize capital controls while showing less enthusiasm for trade liberalization in the 1970s and the 1980s. Two reasons cited for this difference are low political visibility of financial issues compared with more politically charged trade issues and the inherent difficulty in controlling capital movement given capital's mobility and fungibility.[101]

Last but not least, a bank-based financial system affects domestic politics in that it favors exporters and investment and consequently also a stable, and preferably undervalued, exchange rate regime. By contrast, a securities-based financial system does not really favor domestic producers.[102]

CONCLUSION

East Asia has experienced a virtuous cycle of high savings, high investment, and high growth. Deliberate government policies have played a prominent role in forcing savings and channeling savings to targeted investments. The state has served a role of financial intermediation, relying heavily on the banking sector. This strategy of capital accumulation and directed credit largely worked in that it enabled East Asian economies during their catch-up stage. However, the example of the Philippines shows that the state-directed credit strategy could also be used for supporting political cronies, with disastrous consequences. Even if directed credits reached the "right" sectors, this strategy still created a number of long-term negative results, namely bad-loan problems and weak financial markets. A combination of dependence on bank loans and pegged exchange rates meant that domestic firms sought short-term foreign bank loans, leading to greater exposure to foreign debt and consequently an important reason for the Asian financial crisis. A more developed and diversified financial sector that offered greater investment opportunities would have alleviated the threat of a financial crisis triggered by sharp shifts in short-term capital flows.

East Asia has transformed from a capital-poor to a capital-rich region. High savings and relatively low investment for a large number of East Asian economies since the Asian financial crisis have contributed to a major global financial imbalance in which East Asia with a large current account surplus lends to the United States troubled with large current deficits. This unsustainable situation threatens the long-term prosperity of the global economy. Whereas the United States should gradually reduce its budget deficits, East Asian economies also need to put greater emphasis on domestic demands. East Asia has also made some progress in financial regional integration since the Asian financial crisis, but East Asian financial regionalism remains limited because East Asia is really part of financial globalization.

Finance is at the core of a country's political economy system because it is about distribution of scarce resources. Political agenda and political calculations of the East Asian governments have shaped their developmental state approach to mobilize financial capital to achieve rapid industrialization in the early years and how they have approached financial liberalization in the later years. As a highly liquid asset, finance has also affected the nature of East Asian political economy and East Asian policymaking.

SUGGESTED READINGS

Amyx, Jennifer A. *Japan's Financial Crisis: Institutional Rigidity and Reluctant Change* (Princeton: Princeton University Press, 2004).

Ariff, Mohamed, ed. *Islamic Banking in Southeast Asia: Islam and the Economic Development of Southeast Asia* (Singapore: Institute of Southeast Asian Studies, 1988).

Bryant, Ralph C. *International Financial Intermediation* (Washington, D.C.: Brookings Institution, 1987).

de Brouwer, Gordon, with Wisarn Pupphavesa, eds. *Asia Pacific Financial Deregulation* (New York: Routledge, 1999).

Ghosh, Swati R. *East Asian Finance: The Road to Robust Markets* (Washington, D.C.: World Bank, 2006).

Goldstein, Morris, and Philip Turner. *Controlling Currency Mismatches in Emerging Markets* (Washington, D.C.: Institute for International Economics, 2004).

Green, Stephen. *The Development of China's Stock Market, 1984–2002* (London: Routledge, 2004).

Hamilton-Hart, Natasha. *Asian States, Asian Bankers: Central Banking in Southeast Asia* (Ithaca, N.Y.: Cornell University Press, 2002).

Helleiner, Eric. "Free Money: Why Have States Been More Willing to Liberalize Capital Controls Than Trade Barriers?" *Policy Sciences* 27, no. 4 (December 1994): 299–318.

Henning, C. Randall. *East Asian Financial Cooperation* (Washington, D.C.: Institute for International Economics, 2002).

Hiwatari, Nobuhiro. "Embedded Policy Preferences and the Formation of International Arrangements After the Asian Financial Crisis." *The Pacific Review* 16, no. 3 (September 2003): 331–359.

Hutchison, Michael M., and Frank Westermann, eds. *Japan's Great Stagnation: Financial and Monetary Policy Lessons for Advanced Economies* (Cambridge: MIT Press, 2006).

Ito, Takatoshi, and Anne O. Krueger, eds. *Financial Deregulation and Integration in East Asia* (Chicago: University of Chicago Press, 1996).

Jomo, K. S., ed. *The Malaysian Eclipse: Economic Crisis and Recovery* (London: Zed Books, 2001).

Lardy, Nicholas R. *China's Unfinished Economic Revolution* (Washington, D.C.: Brookings Institution Press, 1998).

McKinnon, Ronald I. *Money and Capital in Economic Development* (Washington, D.C.: Brookings Institution, 1973).

Noguchi, Yukio. "The 'Bubble' and Economic Policies in the 1980s." *Journal of Japanese Studies* 20, no. 2 (Summer 1994): 291–329.

Park, Yung Chul, Takatoshi Ito, and Yunjong Wang, eds. *A New Financial Market Structure for East Asia* (Northampton, Mass.: Edward Elgar, 2005).

Rawski, Thomas T. "Will Investment Behavior Constrain China's Growth?" *China Economic Review* 13, no. 4 (December 2002): 361–372.

Shaw, Edward S. *Financial Deepening in Economic Development* (New York: Oxford University Press, 1973).

Tett, Gillian. *Saving the Sun: A Wall Street Gamble to Rescue Japan from Its Trillion-Dollar Meltdown* (New York: HarperBusiness, 2003).

Tsai, Kellee S. *Back Alley Banking: Private Entrepreneurs in China* (Ithaca, N.Y.: Cornell University Press, 2002).

Tsurumi, Masayoshi, ed. *Financial Big Bang in Asia* (Aldeshot, England: Ashgate, 2001).

Venardos, Angelo M. *Islamic Banking and Finance in Southeast Asia* (Singapore: World Scientific, 2005).

NOTES

1. Joseph E. Stiglitz, Jaime Jaramillo-Vallejo, and Yung Chal Park, "The Role of the State in Financial Markets," *Proceedings of the World Bank Annual Conference on Development Economics 1993: Supplement to World Bank Research Observer* (1993), 23.
2. World Bank, *East Asian Miracle,* 203–221.
3. World Bank, *East Asian Miracle,* 221–242.
4. Swati R. Ghosh, *East Asian Finance: The Road to Robust Markets* (Washington, D.C.: World Bank, 2006).
5. Koichi Hamada and Akiyoshi Horiuchi, "The Political Economy of the Financial Market," in *The Political Economy of Japan,* vol. 1, *The Domestic Transformation,* ed. Kozo Yamamura and Yasukichi Yasuba (Stanford: Stanford University Press, 1987), 224–228.
6. Michael M. Hutchison, Takatoshi Ito, and Frank Westermann, "The Great Japanese Stagnation: Lessons for Industrial Countries," in *Japan's Great Stagnation: Financial and Monetary Policy Lessons for Advanced Economies,* ed. Michael M. Hutchison and Frank Westermann (Cambridge: MIT Press, 2006), 1–32.
7. Bon-Ho Koo, "Industrial Policy and Financial Reforms in Korea," in *Financial Sector Reforms in Asia and Latin American Countries: Lessons of Comparative Experience,* ed. Shakil Faruqi (Washington, D.C.: World Bank, 1993), 167–178; Sang-Woo Nam, "The Principal Transactions Bank System in Korea and a Search for a New Bank-Business Relationship," in *Financial Deregulation and Integration in East Asia,* ed. Takatoshi Ito and Anne O. Krueger (Chicago: University of Chicago Press, 1996), 277–306; Sang Yong Park, "Financial Reform and Its Impact on Corporate Organization in Korea," in *Asia Pacific Financial Deregulation,* ed. Gordon de Brouwer with Wisarn Pupphavesa (New York: Routledge, 1999), 207–231.
8. Hsueh, Hsu, and Perkins, *Industrialization and the State,* 78–79.
9. Ya-Hwei Yang and Jia-Dong Shea, "Evolution of Taiwan's Financial System," in *East Asia's Financial Systems,* ed. Seiichi Masuyama, Donna Vandenbrink, and Chia Siow Yue (Singapore: Institute of Southeast Asian Studies, 1999), 272.
10. Chin Kok Fay and K. S. Jomo, "Financial Liberalization and System Vulnerability," in *The Malaysian Eclipse: Economic Crisis and Recovery,* ed. K. S. Jomo (London: Zed Books, 2001), 91–108.

11. Naris Chaiyasoot, "Commercial Banking," in *The Thai Economy in Transition*, ed. Peter G. Warr (Cambridge: Cambridge University Press, 1993), 226-264.

12. Angelo M. Venardos, *Islamic Banking and Finance in Southeast Asia* (Singapore: World Scientific, 2005); Mohamed Ariff, ed., *Islamic Banking in Southeast Asia: Islam and the Economic Development of Southeast Asia* (Singapore: Institute of Southeast Asian Studies, 1988).

13. People's Bank of China, China Monetary Policy Report, 2004 Quarter 4, www.pbc.gov.cn/english//detail.asp?col=6612&ID=27, 30; 2005 Quarter 4, 21.

14. "Chinese Capital Markets: Out of the Shadows," *The Economist*, December 16, 2006, 78-79.

15. Andrew Sheng, ed., *Bank Restructuring: Lessons from the 1980s* (Washington, D.C.: World Bank, 1999).

16. As a case in point, Chinese state banks made policy loans to money-losing state enterprises, which is the root problem for China's NPL problem. See Nicholas R. Lardy, *China's Unfinished Economic Revolution* (Washington, D.C.: Brookings Institution Press, 1998).

17. Yiping Huang, "Can Hong Kong Survive as an International Financial Center?" in *A New Financial Market Structure for East Asia*, ed. Yung Chul Park, Takatoshi Ito, and Yunjong Wang (Northampton, Mass.: Edward Elgar, 2005), 194-209.

18. "Down on the Street," *The Economist*, November 25, 2006, 69-71.

19. Manuel F. Montes, "Tokyo, Hong Kong, and Singapore as Competing Financial Centers," in *Asia Pacific Financial Deregulation* (see note 7), 151-170; Ngiam Kee Jin, "Recycling Asian Savings Within the Region: The Role of Singapore," in *A New Financial Market Structure for East Asia* (see note 17), 210-228; Eiji Ogawa, "Tokyo Financial Market as a Financial Center in East Asia," in *A New Financial Market Structure for East Asia* (see note 17), 167-193.

20. Yung Chul Park, Wonho Song, and Yunjong Wang, "Finance and Economic Development in East Asia," in *A New Financial Market Structure for East Asia* (see note 17), 20-27.

21. Gillian Tett, *Saving the Sun: A Wall Street Gamble to Rescue Japan from Its Trillion-Dollar Meltdown* (New York: HarperBusiness, 2003), 8-10.

22. Fay and Jomo, "Financial Liberalization and System Vulnerability," 100-108.

23. For studies of the Chinese stock markets, see Carl E. Walter and Fraser J. T. Howie, *Privatizing China: The Stock Markets and Their Role in Corporate Reform* (Singapore: Wiley, 2003); Stephen Green, *The Development of China's Stock Market, 1984-2002* (London: Routledge, 2004).

24. Morris Goldstein and Philip Turner, *Controlling Currency Mismatches in Emerging Markets* (Washington, D.C.: Institute for International Economics, 2004).
25. Takatoshi Ito and Yung Chul Park, "Overview: Challenges and Strategies," in *Developing Asian Bond Markets,* ed. Takatoshi Ito and Yung Chui Park (Canberra: Asia Pacific Press, 2004), 1–15.
26. World Bank, *Global Development Finance: Mobilizing Finance and Managing Vulnerability* (Washington, D.C.: World Bank, 2005), 78–79.
27. "Asian Bond Markets: Think Global, Act Local," *The Economist,* June 3, 2006, 73–74.
28. World Bank, *East Asian Miracle,* 203–241.
29. *The Economist,* June 11, 2005, 41.
30. "Japanese Finance: The State as Sugar Daddy," *The Economist,* July 30, 2005, 68–69.
31. Richard Katz, *Japan: The System That Soured* (Armonk, N.Y.: M. E. Sharpe, 1998), 199–210.
32. Yukio Noguchi, "The 'Bubble' and Economic Policies in the 1980s," *Journal of Japanese Studies* 20, no. 2 (Summer 1994): 299.
33. Russell Mardon, "The State and the Effective Control of Foreign Capital: The Case of South Korea," *World Politics* 43, no. 1 (October 1990): 111–138; Jung-en Woo (Meredith Woo-Cummings), *Race to the Swift: State and Finance in Korean Industrialization* (New York: Columbia University Press, 1991); Koo, "Industrial Policy and Financial Reforms in Korea," 167–178.
34. Edward S. Shaw, *Financial Deepening in Economic Development* (New York: Oxford University Press, 1973), 135–137.
35. S. C. Tsiang, "Foreign Trade and Investment as Boosters for Take-Off: The Experience of Taiwan," in *Export-Oriented Development Strategies: The Success of Five Newly Industrializing Countries,* ed. Vittorio Corbo, Anne O. Krueger, and Fernando Ossa (Boulder: Westview Press, 1985), 42–48.
36. Yang and Shea, "Evolution of Taiwan's Financial System," 264–269.
37. Hsueh, Hsu, and Perkins, *Industrialization and the State,* 52–53.
38. K. S. Jomo and Natasha Hamilton-Hart, "Financial Regulation, Crisis, and Policy Response," in *The Malaysian Eclipse* (see note 10), 68–75.
39. K.S. Jomo, "From Currency Crisis to Recession," in *The Malaysian Eclipse* (see note 10), 3–4.
40. Fritz-Krockow, "Savings and Financial Intermediation in the Philippines," 90–94.
41. Barry M. Richman, *Industrial Society in Communist China* (New York: Random House, 1969), 311–312, 495–502.

42. Thomas T. Rawski, "Will Investment Behavior Constrain China's Growth," *China Economic Review* 13, no. 4 (December 2002): 361–372.

43. Eric Helleiner, "Free Money: Why Have States Been More Willing to Liberalize Capital Controls Than Trade Barriers?" *Policy Sciences* 27, no. 4 (December 1994): 299.

44. McKinnon, *Money and Capital in Economic Development;* Shaw, *Financial Deepening in Economic Development.*

45. Barry Eichengreen and Yung Chul Park, "Financial Liberalization and Capital Market Integration in East Asia," in *A New Financial Market Structure for East Asia* (see note 17), 46–81; Masayoshi Tsurumi, ed., *Financial Big Bang in Asia* (Aldeshot, England: Ashgate, 2001).

46. Akiyoshi Horiuchi, "Financial Fragility in Japan," in *Asia Pacific Financial Deregulation* (see note 7), 235–252; Takao Saga, "Financial Reform in Japan," in *Financial Big Bang in Asia* (see note 45), 37–62.

47. Eiji Ogawa, "Tokyo Financial Market as a Financial Center in East Asia," in *A New Financial Market Structure for East Asia* (see note 17), 167–193.

48. Anthony Faiola, "Koizumi Supported in Difficult Mission," *The Washington Post,* September 13, 2005, A20.

49. Koo, "Industrial Policy and Financial Reforms in Korea," 170–176; Won-Am Park, "Financial Liberalization: The Korean Experience," in *Financial Deregulation and Integration in East Asia* (see note 7), 247–273.

50. Dong Won Kim and Inn Won Park, "Financial Reform in the Republic of Korea: Past and Present," in *Financial Big Bang in Asia* (see note 45), 63–88.

51. Yang and Shea, "Evolution of Taiwan's Financial System," 271–272; Tsun-Siou Lee, "Economic Development and Financial System Reform in Taiwan," in *Financial Big Bang in Asia* (see note 45), 89–107.

52. Jomo and Hamilton-Hart, "Financial Regulation, Crisis, and Policy Response," 75–79.

53. Fritz-Krockrow, "Savings and Financial Intermediation in the Philippines," 101–107; Hidenobu Okuda, "The Roles of Domestic Banks in the FDI-Led Industrialization: A Case Study of Philippine Commercial Banks," *EXIM Review* 18, no. 1 (1998): 1–26.

54. Anwar Nasution, "Financial Policy and Financial Sector Development in Indonesia Since the 1980s," in *Financial Big Bang in Asia* (see note 45), 191–223.

55. George Fane and Ross H. McLeod, "Banking Collapse and Restructuring in Indonesia, 1997–2000," *The Cato Journal* 22, no. 2 (Fall 2002): 277–295; Hidenobu Okuda and Yasushi Take, "Economic Reforms and Financing Structure of Indonesian Listed Companies After the Asian Crisis: Corporate Finance Issues and the Solutions," *JBICI Review* 12 (August 2005): 1–31.

56. Pakorn Vichyanond, "Dealing with Debt: NPLs and Debt Restructuring," in *Thailand Beyond the Crisis*, ed. Peter Warr (New York: RoutledgeCurzon, 2005), 211.

57. Donald Hanna, "Restructuring Asia's Financial System," in *The Asian Financial Crisis: Lessons for a Resilient Asia*, ed. Wing Thye Woo, Jeffrey D. Sachs, and Klaus Schwab (Cambridge: MIT Press, 2000), 56–57.

58. Green, *Development of China's Stock Market*; Walter and Howie, *Privatizing China*.

59. Green, *Development of China's Stock Market*; Walter and Howie, *Privatizing China*.

60. "Chinese M&A: Playing at Home," *The Economist*, August 5, 2006, 65.

61. Guonan Ma, "Sharing China's Bank Restructuring Bill," *China and World Economy* 14, no. 3 (2006): 19–37.

62. Ma, "Sharing China's Bank Restructuring Bill," 26–27.

63. Jia-Dong Shea and David C. Y. Sun, "Financial Crisis and the Prudential Regulation of Financial Institution," in *Asia Pacific Financial Deregulation* (see note 7), 67–85.

64. Joseph E. Stiglitz, "Capital Market Liberalization and Exchange Rate Regimes: Risk Without Reward," *Annals of the American Academy of Political and Social Science* 579 (January 2002): 219–248.

65. Guonan Ma and Robert McCauley, "Introduction: China's Capital Account Liberalization: International Perspective," *BIS Papers* 15 (April 2003): 1–6.

66. Shinji Takagi, "Capital Account Liberalization: Lessons from Two Giants and Four Tigers," in Masahiro Kawai, ed., *Financial Interdependence and Exchange Rate Regimes in East Asia*, conference proceedings, Korea Institute for International Economic Policy and Policy Research Institute of Japan Ministry of Finance, December 2–3, 2004, Tokyo, 103–129, www.mof.go.jp/english/soken/kiep2005/kiep2005_03.pdf.

67. Gordon de Brouwer, *Financial Integration in East Asia* (Cambridge: Cambridge University Press, 1999), 29–41.

68. Hsueh, Hsu, and Perkins, *Industrialization and the State*, 20–21.

69. Xinmin wanbao [New people nightly], July 29, 2006, http://news.sina.com.cn/c/2006-07-29/145210571641.shtml.

70. Frank, Kim, and Westphal, *South Korea*, 101–107.

71. Akira Kohsaka, "Interdependence Through Capital Flows in Pacific Asia and the Role of Japan," in *Financial Deregulation and Integration in East Asia* (see note 7), 107–142.

72. Kohsaka, "Interdependence Through Capital Flows in Pacific Asia and the Role of Japan," 117–118.

73. Pierre Poret, "Liberalising Capital Flows: Lessons from Asia," *OECD Observer* 214 (October–November 1998): 1–3.

74. World Bank, *East Asia: Recovery and Beyond,* 26.

75. Institute of International Finance Inc., press release, "Major Gains Seen in Capital Flows to Emerging Markets," January 19, 2005, www.iif.com/press/pressrelease.quagga?id=99 (accessed January 20, 2005).

76. Quoted in Paul Blustein, "Advice to Invest Less in U.S. Bonds," *The Washington Post,* June 22, 2006, D1. Summers gave a speech at the Center for Global Development on June 13, 2006, www.cgdev.org/content/article/detail/8373/.

77. Remarks by Governor Ben S. Bernanke at the Sandridge Lecture, Virginia Association of Economics, Richmond, Virginia, March 10, 2005, www.federalreserve.gov/boarddocs/speeches/2005/200503102/default.htm.

78. U.S. Department of the Treasury, March 30, 2007, "Preliminary Report on Foreign Holdings of U.S. Securities at End-June 2006."

79. Mitsuru Taniuchi, "Global Imbalances and Asian Economies," *JBICI Review* 14 (March 2006): 10.

80. Ghosh, *East Asian Finance,* 29–43.

81. Lincoln, *East Asian Economic Regionalism*; Takeshi Terada, "Constructing an 'East Asian' Concept and Growing Regional Identity: From EAEC to ASEAN+3," *The Pacific Review* 16, no. 2 (June 2003): 251–277.

82. Jennifer Amyx, "What Motivates Regional Financial Cooperation in East Asia Today?" *Asia Pacific Issues,* no. 76 (Honolulu: East-West Center, February 2005). For advocacy of linking Asian financial regionalism to the IMF framework, see Yunjong Wang, "The Asian Financial Crisis and Its Aftermath: Do We Need a Regional Financial Arrangement?" *ASEAN Economic Bulletin* 17, no. 2 (August 2000): 205–217.

83. Nobuhiro Hiwatari, "Embedded Policy Preferences and the Formation of International Arrangements After the Asian Financial Crisis," *The Pacific Review* 16, no. 3 (September 2003): 331–359.

84. For Japan's effort to create the AMF, see Jennifer A. Amyx, "Japan and the Evolution of Regional Financial Arrangements in East Asia," in *Beyond Bilateralism: U.S.-Japan Relations in the New Asia-Pacific,* ed. Ellis S. Krauss and T. J. Pempel (Stanford: Stanford University Press, 2004), 198–218.

85. Yung Chul Park and Yunjong Wang, "The Chiang Mai Initiative and Beyond," *The World Economy* 28, no. 1 (January 2005): 91–101.

86. Guonan Ma and Eli M. Remolona, "Opening Markets Through a Regional Bond Fund: Lessons from ABF2," *BIS Quarterly Review* (June 2005): 81–92.

87. Takatoshio Ito and Yung Chui Park, eds., *Developing Asian Bond Markets* (Canberra: Asia Pacific Press, 2004).

88. Yonghyup Oh, Jongkyou Jeon, and Doo Yong Yang, "Financial Market Integration in East Asia: A Stock Market Perspective," in *Financial Interdependence and Exchange Rate Regimes in East Asia,* ed. Masahiro Kawai, conference proceedings, Korea Institute for International Economic Policy and Policy Research Institute of Japan Ministry of Finance, December 2–3, 2004, Tokyo, 87–102, www.mof.go.jp/english/soken/kiep2005/kiep2005_03.pdf.

89. Eichengreen and Park, "Financial Liberalization and Capital Market Integration in East Asia."

90. Paul Bowles, "Asia's Post-Crisis Regionalism: Bringing the State Back In, Keeping the (United) States Out," *Review of International Political Economy* 9, no. 2 (May 2002): 244–270.

91. Robert N. McCauley, San-Sau Fung, and Blaise Gadanesz, "Integrating the Finances of East Asia," *BIS Quarterly Review* (December 2002): 83–95.

92. For a broader discussion of the political consequences of bank-based versus securities-based financial systems, see John Zysman, *Governments, Markets, and Growth* (Ithaca, N.Y.: Cornell University Press, 1983).

93. Yasheng Huang, *Selling China: Foreign Direct Investment During the Reform Era* (New York: Cambridge University Press, 2003).

94. Kellee S. Tsai, *Back Alley Banking: Private Entrepreneurs in China* (Ithaca, N.Y.: Cornell University Press, 2002).

95. Jennifer A. Amyx, *Japan's Financial Crisis: Institutional Rigidity and Reluctant Change* (Princeton: Princeton University Press, 2004).

96. Jomo and Hamilton-Hart, "Financial Regulation, Crisis, and Policy Response," 78–79.

97. Fay and Jomo, "Financial Liberalization and System Vulnerability," 100–108.

98. *Diyicaijing ribao* [First finance and economics daily], May 31, 2005, http://finance.sina.com.cn/g/20060531/01252610670.shtml.

99. Paulette Kurzer, *Business and Banking: Political Change and Economic Integration in Western Europe* (Ithaca, N.Y.: Cornell University Press, 1993); Natasha Hamilton-Hart, *Asian States, Asian Bankers: Central Banking in Southeast Asia* (Ithaca, N.Y.: Cornell University Press, 2002).

100. Richard Werner, *Princes of the Yen: Japan's Central Bankers and the Transformation of the Japanese Economic Structure* (Armonk, N.Y.: M. E. Sharpe, 2002).

101. Helleiner, "Free Money." Two other reasons cited are pressure from the United States and Britain and the possibility that a country may not maintain financial and trade liberalization at the same time.

102. Hiwatari, "Embedded Policy Preferences."

CHAPTER **10**

The Political Economy of East Asian Monetary Relations

International monetary affairs, which are mainly about exchange rates, are conceptually different from international finance, which is about the flow of money across national borders. Exchange rates and international finance influence each other, particularly for an open economy with free flow of capital across national borders. For example, as shown in Chapter 6, a pegged exchange rate regime that reduced foreign exchange risks encouraged increased inflow of foreign capital, but the fear of an expected local currency depreciation led to a sudden exodus of capital, which forced the government to depreciate in a self-fulfilling effect.

This chapter discusses East Asian monetary relations on both the domestic and international level. On the domestic level, the chapter describes and explains the evolution and nature of East Asian exchange rate policies, which is narrower than a country's monetary policy that also covers issues such as money supply and interest rates. While being influenced by the international monetary system, individual countries' exchange rate policies constitute the international monetary system. For the international monetary system, the chapter addresses where East Asia is situated in the global monetary system and how the East Asian regional monetary system has evolved. The East Asian economies have been largely operating under the dollar standard since the end of World War II. The nonsocialist countries were part of the Bretton Woods system, which provided a stable monetary environment for these economies to flourish when they turned to export promotion. They virtually all maintained undervalued exchange rates that gave them significant export advantages. They maintained a soft peg to the U.S. dollar after the collapse of the Bretton Woods system in the early 1970s. Asian regionalism is taking place slowly.

EAST ASIAN EXCHANGE RATE POLICIES

Money is a standardized medium of transaction. Money includes coins, paper currency, and bank deposits. Money serves as a medium of exchange to replace barter trade, as a unit of account to measure value, and as a store of wealth. Money is a promise that the money one possesses will maintain its value in the future. Otherwise, a currency would not be that valuable. Money is an important issue for international political economy because the evolution of national currencies has been at the core of state building.[1] Domestic monetary policy covers also interest rates and inflation targeting, but this chapter focuses on exchange rates and foreign reserves.

Exchange Rate Policies

International money is needed for the international market. However, unlike in the domestic context, the international system is anarchical; that is, there is not an overarching political authority that can issue a global currency to facilitate international transactions. Transnational barter trade is too complicated to facilitate trade. The international community may also use precious metals such as gold as liquidity. However, a limited supply of gold means that we will not have sufficient liquidity to support expanding trade and will suffer a deflation as a result. Exchange rates thus become the international currency.

A government has to make at least four key decisions regarding exchange rates. First, should the country peg its currency to another one such as the U.S. dollar or allow the value of its currency to float? Like any commodity, the value of a national currency is fundamentally determined by supply and demand. If supply of a currency exceeds demand for it, the price of the currency goes down and vice versa. If the government wants to maintain the peg, it has to intervene in the currency market. The government may purchase its currency with foreign reserves, which increases the demand for its currency, when the value of its currency is pressed down by excessive supply. Conversely, the government may sell its currency in exchange for hard currencies such as the dollar, which increases the supply of its currency, when the value of its currency is pushed up by too much demand. A float exchange rate policy means that the government lets the currency market determine the value of its currency.

In practice, governments often choose to let their currencies float between certain limits to ensure stability in international transactions. A government's choice of exchange rate policy reflects its basic policy objectives at a given moment and is informed by the prevailing ideas about exchange rates. Economists tended to think in the early 1990s that a high-inflation country could introduce a soft peg (a target rate and a band around it) of its currency against the currency of a low-inflation country or a group of currencies without generating much loss in employment and growth. But with a subsequent explosion of cross-border capital flows, financial crises caused by reversal of capital flows, and contagion of crises between pegged exchange regimes, economists now tend to think that it is no longer possible to maintain a middle ground between a floating regime and monetary union.[2]

Second, governments need to make a choice about how strong they want their currencies to be relative to another currency or a group of foreign currencies. This choice is related to the first choice; the issue would be moot if a government adopted a free float policy. The relative strength of a currency is different in that the said currency may peg to another currency at different levels. Unlike arguments about free trade, there is not a clear-cut efficiency argument for a particular level of exchange rates.[3] The reasons for keeping a currency weak or strong vary. In recent decades a government keeps its currency weak to seek advantage in exports. For example, the Chinese yuan was pegged to the U.S. dollar at 8.28 yuan per U.S. dollar until recently. That means that a China-made product that sells for 828 yuan should be sold in the United States for $100 if we disregard transportation and other costs. However, if the Chinese currency appreciates by 30 percent to 5.80, as some would like to see, the same product would now cost $143 in the U.S. market, which would obviously make the China-made product far less competitive.

It is real exchange rate (net) rather than nominal exchange rate (gross) that is important. Real exchange rate determines how much one pays for foreign currency. Effective exchange rates are nominal rates plus other additional charges. A large nominal devaluation may be small in real terms, thus having little impact on trade.[4]

How do we know what is a fair exchange rate? One basic measurement to use is purchasing power parity (PPP); that is, a correct level of exchange between two currencies should equalize the prices of the same basket of goods and services in the two countries. In a creative way, the *Economist* proposed a Big Mac index in 1986. The basic idea is that the same hamburger should cost about the same in different countries, thus creating a Big Mac PPP. The difference between the Big Mac PPP and the actual exchange rate would show whether a currency is overvalued or undervalued. The Big Mac index for 1999, for example, shows China and Malaysia 51 percent undervalued against the U.S. dollar.[5]

Third, a government has to decide on the size of its foreign reserves. This is particularly important for pegged exchange rates. Foreign reserves may serve as a war chest to fend off future attacks. How much reserve does a country need? It is generally believed that a country needs sufficient reserves to cover three months of imports or pay for short-term debt. By that standard, most East Asian economies have excessive foreign reserves. As an example, as of October 2006, China's foreign reserves are sufficient for 15 months of import and six times more than its short-term debt.[6]

Foreign reserves may take several forms: (a) gold holdings; (b) international money created by international bodies, such as Special Drawing Rights (SDRs); or (c) widely accepted and valuable foreign currencies, which is the most common component of reserves. What currency one holds as reserves is affected by a number of factors. It makes sense to hold the currency of the country to which one owes money, so as to minimize exchange risks, or the currencies of one's major trading partners. Another consideration is the value of the currency one holds. A currency that is expected to lose its value would not be a good currency. One then tries to reduce the share of that currency in one's reserves.

Fourth, a country has to decide whether it should allow its currency to be freely convertible. This is about how open or closed a country's capital market is. This decision matters for the international monetary system because it affects financing of trade and other economic transactions. During the Bretton Woods period, International Monetary Fund (IMF) Article 8 requested currencies to be made freely convertible, but Article 9 gave exemption for a transition period, which essentially meant indefinitely for developing nation members. The IMF was mainly concerned about elimination of multiple exchange rates.[7] Whether or not the IMF puts pressure on this issue, a government has to make a choice about the currency convertibility of its currency.

East Asian Exchange Rate Policies Through the Early 1970s

East Asia was divided into two parts during the cold war. The nonsocialist world was part of the Bretton Woods system, with currencies pegged to the U.S. dollar. As shown in Table 10.1, the exchange rate between the yen and the dollar was ¥360 to $1 between 1953 and 1970 (¥361.1 in 1950 and 1951). Similarly, Singapore and Malaysia pegged their currencies to the dollar from 1950 to 1970. Thailand's baht and Hong Kong's dollar were pegged to the dollar as well, with slight variations. The Philippines' peso saw greater depreciation against the dollar. Taiwan depreciated its New Taiwan Dollar (NT$) in the 1950s and then maintained a rate of NT$40 per U.S. dollar in the 1960s. What is most noticeable in the table is how South Korea's nominal exchange rates depreciated continuously against the dollar from 1950 to 1970. Most of these currencies did not become fully convertible until the 1960s. Moreover, many nonsocialist countries adopted multiple exchange rate systems to advance their policy objectives.

Nonsocialist East Asian economies benefited from the Bretton Woods system. The Bretton Woods system ensured a stable international monetary system, which facilitated trade. Japan, for example, benefited from cheap yen and cheap oil for its economic miracle. The United States did not object to this unfair arrangement because of its dominant economic position and its hegemonic interests. This changed in 1971 when President Richard Nixon ended the Bretton Woods system.

The Bretton Woods system was a U.S.-dollar-dominated currency region writ large. It was a hegemonic system in which the United States dominated. The unique position of the dollar gave the United States advantages in terms of macroeconomic stability and microeconomic efficiency. Put simply, the United States

TABLE 10.1
East Asian Exchange Rates (per U.S. dollar, period average)

Year	Japanese Yen	Taiwan New Dollar	South Korea Won	Hong Kong Dollar	Singapore Dollar	Malaysian Ringgit	Thai Baht	Indonesian Rupiah	Philippine Peso	Chinese Yuan
1950	361.10	10.29	2.50	—	3.06	3.06	22.34	—	2.00	—
1951	361.10	15.63	6.00	—	3.06	3.06	21.56	—	2.00	—
1952	361.10	15.63	6.00	—	3.06	3.06	18.87	—	2.00	2.46
1953	360.00	18.76	18.00	—	3.06	3.06	18.23	—	2.00	2.46
1954	360.00	18.76	18.00	—	3.06	3.06	21.13	—	2.00	2.46
1955	360.00	32.24	50.00	—	3.06	3.06	20.46	—	2.00	2.46
1956	360.00	32.24	50.00	—	3.06	3.06	20.72	—	2.00	2.46
1957	360.00	30.84	50.00	—	3.06	3.06	20.71	—	2.00	2.46
1958	360.00	35.08	50.00	—	3.06	3.06	20.91	—	2.00	2.46
1959	360.00	39.47	50.00	—	3.06	3.06	21.10	—	2.00	2.46
1960	360.00	39.73	63.75	5.71	3.06	3.06	21.10	—	2.02	2.46
1961	360.00	40.00	127.50	5.71	3.06	3.06	20.98	—	2.02	2.46
1962	360.00	40.00	130.00	5.71	3.06	3.06	20.80	—	3.83	2.46
1963	360.00	40.00	130.00	5.71	3.06	3.06	20.78	—	3.91	2.46
1964	360.00	40.00	213.67	5.71	3.06	3.06	20.80	—	3.91	2.46
1965	360.00	40.00	266.74	5.71	3.06	3.06	20.80	235.00	3.91	2.46
1966	360.00	40.00	271.02	5.71	3.06	3.06	20.80	235.00	3.90	2.46
1967	360.00	40.00	269.48	5.74	3.06	3.06	20.80	153.67	3.90	2.46
1968	360.00	40.00	276.88	6.06	3.06	3.06	20.80	300.08	3.90	2.46
1969	360.00	40.00	288.72	6.06	3.06	3.06	20.80	326.00	3.90	2.46
1970	360.00	40.00	311.13	6.06	3.06	3.06	20.80	365.00	6.07	2.46
1971	349.83	40.00	350.80	5.98	3.05	3.05	20.80	393.42	6.43	2.46
1972	303.11	40.03	393.97	5.64	2.81	2.82	20.80	415.00	6.70	2.25
1973	271.22	38.26	398.32	5.15	2.44	2.44	20.62	415.00	6.76	1.99
1974	291.51	38.00	405.97	5.03	2.44	2.41	20.38	415.00	6.79	1.96

(Table continues on next page)

TABLE 10.1 (continued)
East Asian Exchange Rates (per U.S. dollar, period average)

Year	Japanese Yen	Taiwan New Dollar	South Korea Won	Hong Kong Dollar	Singapore Dollar	Malaysian Ringgit	Thai Baht	Indonesian Rupiah	Philippine Peso	Chinese Yuan
1975	296.80	38.00	484.00	4.94	2.37	2.40	20.38	415.00	7.27	1.86
1976	296.55	38.00	484.00	4.90	2.47	2.54	20.40	415.00	7.45	1.94
1977	268.51	38.00	484.00	4.66	2.44	2.46	20.40	415.00	7.41	1.86
1978	210.47	37.05	484.00	4.68	2.27	2.32	20.34	442.05	7.38	1.68
1979	219.14	36.03	484.00	5.00	2.17	2.19	20.42	623.06	7.38	1.55
1980	226.74	36.01	607.43	4.98	2.14	2.18	20.48	626.99	7.51	1.50
1981	220.54	36.85	681.03	5.59	2.11	2.30	21.82	631.76	7.90	1.70
1982	249.08	39.12	731.08	6.07	2.14	2.34	23.00	661.42	8.54	1.89
1983	237.51	40.07	775.75	7.27	2.11	2.32	23.00	909.26	11.11	1.98
1984	237.52	39.60	805.98	7.82	2.13	2.34	23.64	1,025.94	16.70	2.32
1985	238.54	39.85	870.02	7.79	2.20	2.48	27.16	1,110.58	18.61	2.94
1986	168.52	37.84	881.45	7.80	2.18	2.58	26.30	1,282.56	20.39	3.45
1987	144.64	31.74	822.57	7.80	2.11	2.52	25.72	1,643.85	20.57	3.72
1988	128.15	28.59	731.47	7.81	2.01	2.62	25.29	1,685.70	21.09	3.72
1989	137.96	26.41	671.46	7.80	1.95	2.71	25.70	1,770.06	21.74	3.77
1990	144.79	26.89	707.76	7.79	1.81	2.70	25.59	1,842.81	24.31	4.78
1991	134.71	26.82	733.35	7.77	1.73	2.75	25.52	1,950.32	27.48	5.32
1992	126.65	25.16	780.65	7.74	1.63	2.55	25.40	2,029.92	25.51	5.51
1993	111.20	26.39	802.67	7.74	1.62	2.57	25.32	2,087.10	27.12	5.76
1994	102.21	26.46	803.45	7.73	1.53	2.62	25.15	2,160.75	26.42	8.62
1995	94.06	26.49	771.27	7.74	1.42	2.50	24.92	2,248.61	25.71	8.35
1996	108.78	27.46	804.45	7.73	1.41	2.52	25.34	2,342.30	26.22	8.31
1997	120.99	28.70	951.29	7.74	1.48	2.81	31.36	2,909.38	29.47	8.29

Year										
1998	130.91	33.46	1,401.44	7.75	1.67	3.92	41.36	10,013.62	40.89	8.28
1999	113.91	32.27	1,188.82	7.76	1.69	3.80	37.81	7,855.15	39.09	8.28
2000	107.77	31.23	1,130.96	7.79	1.72	3.80	40.11	8,421.78	44.19	8.28
2001	121.53	33.80	1,290.99	7.80	1.79	3.80	44.43	10,260.85	50.99	8.28
2002	125.39	34.58	1,251.09	7.80	1.79	3.80	42.96	9,311.19	51.60	8.28
2003	115.93	34.42	1,191.61	7.79	1.74	3.80	41.48	8,577.13	54.20	8.28
2004	108.19	33.42	1,145.32	7.79	1.69	3.80	40.22	8,938.85	56.04	8.28
2005	110.22	32.17	1,024.12	7.78	1.66	3.79	40.22	9,704.74	55.09	8.19
2006	116.30	32.53	954.85	7.77	1.59	—	37.88	9,159.32	51.31	7.97

Source: International Monetary Fund, *International Financial Statistics Yearbook*, various years, for the data 1950–1978 (period average of market exchange rates) for the economies listed in the table except for Hong Kong. The data for Hong Kong in 1960–2006 are from the World Bank, World Development Indicators Database. Data for 1979–2006 for every economy except Taiwan are from the World Bank, World Development Indicators Database. The data for Taiwan in 1979–1980 are from the Council for Economic Planning and Development, *Taiwan Statistical Databook*, 1996, 4. The data for Taiwan in 1981–2004 are from the Asian Development Bank Statistical Database System. The data for 2005–2006 are from the Central Bank of the Republic of China (Taiwan), www.cbc.gov.tw/total_index.asp.

alone did not have foreign exchange risks. In the early stage, the United States also gained real resource benefits because it could simply pay for foreign purchases. However, as time went by, the fact that there were a large amount of dollars offshore also restricted U.S. ability to adopt interest rate polices at home and its ability to address its balance of payments deficits, which were needed to provide liquidity for expanding global trade. If the United States wants to raise interest rates to cool down the U.S. economy, dollars will flow back into the country, thus increasing money supply that heats up the economy. If the United States enjoys current account surpluses, the supply of international liquidity will decrease, thus hurting expanding global trade.

The American Occupation authority formulated Japan's initial exchange rate policy. Under the advice of Joseph Dodge, the dollar-yen exchange was set at ¥360 to the dollar in April 1949, which was lower than the ¥330 considered to be appropriate at the time. With slight variation in the early 1950s, that rate remained unchanged until 1971 when the Bretton Woods system collapsed. The ¥360 rate facilitated Japan's goal of achieving international competitiveness, which grew vis-à-vis other advanced countries over the years and helped secure balance of payment surpluses in the second half of the 1960s.[8] Japan did not allow currency convertibility until 1964, about six years later than Western European countries.

The Hong Kong dollar was pegged to the British sterling (1 pound = HK$16.00), which was the IMF parity, in December 1946. In November 1967, the Hong Kong dollar revalued to 14.55 but remained pegged to the sterling. In December 1971, the Hong Kong dollar pegged to SDR. The Hong Kong dollar was pegged to the U.S. dollar for the first time in July 1972 at 5.65 with a band of 2.25 percent, after the floating of the sterling.

The Kuomintang government in Taiwan introduced currency reform in June 1949, which was a key to controlling high inflation to ensure its political survival. Some Taiwanese economists saw the import substitution strategy as impractical since the small economy in Taiwan could not achieve economies of scale or allow Taiwan to take advantage of its comparative advantage. They pushed for devaluation and trade liberalization. In August 1959, the government set the exchange rate at NT$38.08 per U.S. dollar buying and NT$38.38 selling. The New Taiwan Dollar's exchange rate depreciated further to 40 in 1960 and became the pegged exchange within the IMF until 1973.[9] Taiwan's major currency depreciation gave its exports an edge in the global market.

South Korea had a multiple exchange rate system in the 1950s and the early 1960s. In the multiple exchange rate system, the official rate was overvalued but trade and other commercial transactions were conducted with different exchange rates cheaper than the official one. The South Korean government sharply devalued the won and then failed in an attempt to unify exchange rates. After the military coup, South Korea devalued the official rate from 103 won to 256 won per U.S. dollar and shifted to a unitary exchange rate in May 1964. In March 1965 the government allowed the floating of the won in the exchange market. But the Korean Monetary Authority promptly reverted to a pegged exchange rate regime. From 1968 to 1971, the government gradually depreciated the won to be consistent with the inflation rates of South Korea and its major trading partners.[10]

Singapore was part of the Sterling Area before 1972, which meant a peg of the Singapore dollar to the pound sterling within a band of 1 percent. Most of Singapore's foreign reserves were the sterling pound. Singapore left the sterling zone in June 1972 because the pound was now floated. Singapore's capital account was gradually liberalized. Singapore also switched to a peg to the U.S. dollar at S$2.8196 per U.S. dollar. Singapore was mainly interested in price stability and chose a strong Singapore dollar to prevent increases in import prices and cost of living, which were considered more important than export advantages. Singapore turned to a managed float in 1973 to fight imported inflation and inflow of hot money. The exchange rate was stable until 1970 and appreciated in 1971–1974, but with falling relative prices the real term exchange rate was the same in 1979 as in 1970.[11]

The Philippines initially did not possess the sovereign right over exchange rates due to the independence agreement with the United States in 1946. With the United States in control, the Philippines had an overvalued exchange rate of 2 pesos to a U.S. dollar. The government adopted a foreign exchange control regime in 1949 to ration foreign exchange for essential imports. The Philippines regained sovereignty in monetary affairs in 1954 but maintained the overvalued exchange rate to protect import substitution industries. The government began to depreciate the peso in 1960 in a framework of multiple exchange rates. The government removed exchange controls and adopted a uniform exchange rate regime except for exports in 1962. Exchange controls were reintroduced in 1967 due to balance of payments difficulties. The peso floated in February 1970 after a foreign exchange crisis but was eventually fixed at 6.4 pesos per dollar by December. The Philippine exchange rate regime was designed to promote import substitution and exports. The PPP-adjusted effective exchange rates grew by 5.2 times for imports of nonessential consumer goods and 3.2 times for imports of nonessential producer goods from 1949 to 1971, but only 1.2 times for traditional exports from 1950 to 1971.[12]

Similar to some of the nonsocialist economies at this time, China allowed its yuan currency to be overvalued to allow cheaper imports of foreign capital goods. Like other socialist countries China adopted the exchange control regime, which means that the state sets the exchange rate and no individuals or firms are allowed to hold foreign currencies. They need to apply for foreign currencies and trade foreign currencies earned in exports for the yuan. Violators would be punished severely. The advantage of this system was to ensure smooth adjustments, but these states had liquidity problems in that they needed hard currencies to purchase things they needed from abroad. For China, Hong Kong was left as a British colony partly because it served a useful purpose for Beijing to acquire hard currencies. The market forces worked in socialist countries as well. Despite severe punishments, black markets for hard currencies gradually developed, which undermined the exchange control regime.

North Vietnam essentially adopted a barter trade arrangement with the socialist countries and used the Soviet convertible ruble (equals five domestic rubles) as the unit of account. As a result, Vietnam had little foreign currency holding prior to 1985.[13]

From the Early 1970s to the 1997 Financial Crisis

Prior to the Asian financial crisis, East Asian countries chose to describe their currency policy as a managed float, but most East Asian economies in practice adopted an adjustable pegged exchange rate regime; that is, the authorities intervened in the currency market to peg their currencies to the dollar.[14] It is common that a government's actual exchange rate policy differs from its declaration.[15]

President Nixon's New Economic Program announced in August 1971 essentially ended the Bretton Woods system because a key component of the plan was to end the dollar's convertibility to gold, a pillar of the system. Japan was part of the reason for Nixon's drastic measures, which were designed to depreciate the dollar against major currencies such as the yen to reduce trade deficits. After some effort to maintain the ¥360 rate, the Japanese government set a new rate at ¥308 and then moved to a managed float. Japan was an outlier in East Asia in that virtually everyone else maintained a managed peg to the U.S. dollar or a basket of currencies heavily weighted toward the dollar.

Japan's ascendancy and its chronic current account surpluses led to increasing international pressure, particularly from the United States. Intended to help divert growing protectionist sentiment in the U.S. Congress, the finance ministers and central bankers of the Group of Five (G5)—the United States, Japan, Germany, Great Britain, and France—reached a landmark agreement to depreciate the dollar against the yen and the European currencies at Plaza Hotel in New York on September 22, 1985. The agreement, known as the Plaza Accord, was a success. The G5 countries sold $2.7 billion to intervene in the currency market in the following week, with $1.25 billion from Japan, $635 million from France, and $408 million from the United States. The Japanese yen appreciated by 11.8 percent against the dollar, the German mark by 7.8 percent, the French franc by 7.6 percent, and the British pound by 2.9 percent. By January 1986, the dollar had depreciated by 25 percent over the previous year.[16] Figure 10.1 for annual average official yen-

FIGURE 10.1
Dollar-Yen Exchange Rates, 1950–2006 (yearly average)

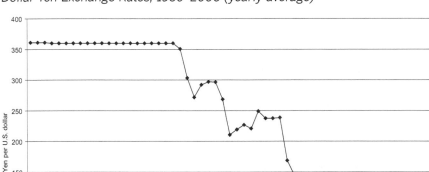

Source: Data for 1950–1959 are from IMF, *International Financial Statistics Yearbook,* various years; data for 1960–2006 are from World Bank, World Development Indicators Database.

dollar exchange rates in 1950–2006 shows a sharp appreciation between 1985 and 1988. The sharp yen appreciation, large current account surpluses, and insufficient domestic consumption led to a property bubble, the burst of which led to a decade-long economic stagnation. The Chinese government would later draw from the Plaza Accord what it considers to be a lesson not to appreciate its currency against the dollar too quickly.

From 1992 to 1998, the yen-dollar exchange rate varied between 100 and 135, but with a period of appreciation to 80 in the spring and summer of 1995. The Japan Ministry of Finance considered the appreciation to be detrimental to exports and intervened to push the rate back to the 100 level.[17] As explained in Chapter 6, Japan's depreciation after mid-1995 put pressure on export-dependent East Asian economies.

Hong Kong adjusted the exchange rate to HK$5.085 per U.S. dollar in February 1973 and floated its currency in November 1974. Hot money attacked Hong Kong in September 1983. In October 1983, the Hong Kong government adopted a currency board exchange rate policy in response to a sharp fall of the Hong Kong dollar due to market nervousness about the Sino-British talks on Hong Kong's future status. The currency board choice stabilized Hong Kong's financial system.[18] Currency board is a type of fixed exchange rate designed to withstand speculative attacks. Hong Kong is and has been the only East Asian economy to adopt a currency board. In a currency board regime, a government holds reserves of hard currency, gold, or IMF position that at least equal the quantity of domestic base money at the fixed exchange rate. Put differently, the government cannot issue additional domestic currency unless it has additional reserves to back it up. Because the government sets an exchange rate but does not set monetary policy, a currency board offers a stable and predictable exchange rate regime but deprives the government of the ability to affect domestic economy with interest rates.

Until 1980, South Korea adopted a de facto dollar-peg system. In February 1980, South Korea adopted the Multiple Currency Basket Peg System, aimed at real effective exchange rate (REER) depreciation, an objective achieved in the 1980s. South Korea managed to reduce current account deficits and its huge foreign debt. South Korea adopted the Market Average Exchange Rate System in March 1990 to allow the exchange rates to reflect the market fundamentals.

Indonesia allowed an open capital account and adopted a managed float against a basket of currencies until the Asian financial crisis. Malaysia also had a managed float, and its capital account gradually liberalized after the early 1970s. From November 1984 to July 1997, Thailand maintained a managed peg.[19] Thailand pegged with the U.S. dollar in the 1960s and 1970s. When the dollar appreciated sharply, Thailand shifted to a peg to a basket of currencies in the mid-1980s.

Once the Chinese reform began, the Chinese government was concerned about balance of payments crisis and shortage of foreign reserves, learning a lesson from the Latin American debt crisis. Beijing therefore maintained capital controls that included restriction of short-term foreign debt. Beijing also gradually depreciated the yuan to promote exports. As Table 10.1 shows, the value of yuan to the dollar decreased from 1.68 in 1978 to 8.62 in 1994, and the exchange rate appreciated slightly afterward and became essentially pegged at 8.28. Another feature of the Chinese exchange rate system was the existence of an official exchange rate and an unofficial exchange rate prior to 1994. Until the Asian financial crisis China did not face any external pressure for depreciation or appreciation.[20]

Vietnam's exchange rate policy began to change in 1986. The government unified the multiple exchange rate regime in 1989 and introduced a dramatic depreciation to bring the official rate close to the black market rate. Vietnam's foreign currency holding increased drastically from $2.4 million in 1986 to $2.2 billion in 1989 and $7.9 billion in 1993. Measured as U.S. dollars in operation in the country as a ratio of the domestic currency and as the propensity of domestic residents to turn to the dollar in response to changes in macroeconomic conditions such as the inflation rate, Vietnam had a higher degree of dollarization than East Asian countries such as Indonesia. Vietnam's dollarization since the mid-1980s was due to a shift of trade to the U.S. dollar for international transactions, wide use of the dollar in illegal trade, and remittance and investment of overseas Vietnamese. The government tried to limit the dollarization with tighter exchange controls in 1994, to no avail.[21]

Postcrisis East Asian Exchange Rate Regimes

The Asian financial crisis, for many observers, revealed a fundamental problem with the pegged exchange rate regime. The theory of "impossible trinity" discussed by Robert Mundell in the 1960s became popular again.[22] The impossible trinity refers to the hypothesis that it is impossible to have the following three goals simultaneously, namely a fixed exchange rate, free capital flow, and an autonomous monetary policy. If we want to regulate markets and maintain sovereignty, the goal of integrating with global financial markets will be compromised. If we want to maintain sovereignty but allow capital markets to integrate, we must accept an entirely free global financial market. If we want capital market integration and global regulation, national sovereignty will be compromised.

A dominant trend in recent years is that the Asian governments have intervened in the currency market to prevent appreciation of their currencies. Official declarations aside, the East Asian economies, except for Japan, have largely maintained a soft peg to the dollar.[23] After the crisis, the governments tend to overstate the flexibility and the degree of floating. However, East Asian monies have remained on a de facto dollar standard.[24] The dollar standard issue will be discussed in the next section.

After the Asian financial crisis, China's exchange rate policy became a focal point for critics of the country's enlarging trade surpluses. As Table 10.1 shows, after a major depreciation in 1994, China essentially maintained a peg around 8.3 yuan per U.S. dollar from 1995 to 2004. There has been much international pressure on the Chinese government to appreciate the yuan. The assessment of how undervalued the yuan is varies, but some long-term China observers believe that the yuan is undervalued by 15–20 percent.[25] It is in China's own interest to appreciate its currency. When the currency is off its real value, it creates efficiency loss. One important benefit from appreciation is to decrease the inflationary pressure. With rapidly increasing foreign capital flow into China, the Chinese government has to increase the supply of yuan to purchase the dollars. Much of the additional money has gone into real estate, which has led to increased demands for materials. A stronger yuan could also reduce the payment of foreign debt and force industrial upgrading. But the Chinese government is concerned that a stronger yuan will hurt exports of labor-intensive products and will thus worsen the unemployment situation.

The Chinese government officially adopted a managed float against a basket of currencies in July 2005, along with a 2 percent appreciation against the dollar and the introduction of a 0.3 percent daily fluctuation band against the dollar. Thanks to the April dry run and other advance preparations, the financial market reacted to the Chinese decision mildly.[26] With continuous pressure, the yuan appreciated to 7.70 yuan to the dollar on May 8, 2007. On May 18, 2007, the People's Bank of China announced that the daily fluctuation band against the dollar would expand from 0.3 to 0.5 effective May 21, the day before high-level economic talks between China and the United States were to be held in Washington, D.C. The yuan appreciated to 7.65 yuan to the dollar on May 24, 2007.

While China has attracted the most international criticism for its currency policy, the Japanese yen has weakened against the dollar. This means that the yen has weakened against the East Asian currencies pegged to the dollar as well, which gives its exports an advantage and may provoke international criticism accordingly. The Japanese government was interested in preventing premature appreciation to maintain export competitiveness and in expanding the money base through purchase of dollars to counter deflation. Figure 10.2 shows that Japan's REER index has decreased from 108.2 in 1995 to 79.4 in 2005, with the REER rate in 2000 as 100.

FIGURE 10.2

Real Effective Exchange Rate Index for Japan, China, and the United States, 1975–2005

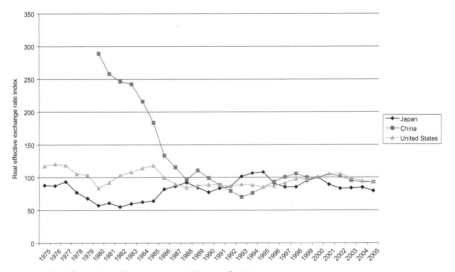

Source: World Bank, World Development Indicators Database.

Japan intervened heavily in the currency market starting in January 2003 to keep the yen low against the dollar. The Japanese government stopped doing that in March 2004. In a period of five quarters, the Ministry of Finance and Bank of Japan (MOF-BOJ) sold ¥35 trillion (about $317 billion), with 42 percent done in the first quarter of 2004. By contrast, the MOF-BOJ purchased less than ¥34 trillion from April 1991 to December 2002. The Japanese government did not publicize the intervention, which was meant to prevent yen appreciation.[27] This development has much to do with Asian purchases of the higher-yield dollar and the euro-denominated overseas assets. In fact, Japan's real trade-weighted value fell to the lowest point in September 2006 since 1982.[28] There has been support in Japan for depreciating the yen to reverse a devastating deflation in the Japanese economy through import inflation. But some empirical analysis suggests that the yen's depreciation is not as effective in creating an inflationary pressure as previously.[29]

Since 2001, the East Asian governments have dramatically increased their foreign reserves, partly due to intervention in the exchange market. The main reason for such intervention is to maintain stability, which suits domestic firms that find it difficult to hedge against foreign exchange risks because of weak domestic financial markets. There is also much concern about future international financial crises. As an exception, China's increase in foreign reserves reflects the fact that foreign capital flows heavily into China while capital outflows are subject to greater restrictions. The government has been intervening in the exchange market to alleviate upward pressure on the yuan.[30] China assumed the number one position in foreign reserves in the world by the end of February 2006. By March 1, 2007, China had $1,202.0 billion in foreign exchange reserves excluding gold.[31] As Table 10.2 shows, the eleven East Asian economies listed in the table had combined official reserves of $2.55 trillion at the end of 2005. Their combined foreign reserves accounted for 55.5 percent of the world total in 2004. Some analysts have pointed out that the recent increase in the East Asian reserves can be explained more by the inflow of capital than by deliberate government intervention to keep exchange rates undervalued.[32]

EAST ASIA IN THE GLOBAL MONETARY SYSTEM

International Monetary Regime

International monetary regime is in essence exchange rate regime, but it also relates to the nature of reserves and the flow of capital.[33] I have previously discussed the different exchange rate policies East Asian economies have adopted over the years. Similarly, an international monetary system may be dominated by fixed exchange rate regime, a free-floating regime, or a hybrid of both.

TABLE 10.2
East Asian Foreign Reserves, Including Gold (current U.S. $ billion)

	1965	1970	1975	1980	1985	1990	1995	2000	2004	2005
Japan	2.15	4.88	14.91	38.92	34.64	87.83	192.62	361.64	844.67	846.90
China	—	—	—	10.09	16.88	34.48	80.29	171.76	622.95	831.41
South Korea	0.15	0.61	0.80	3.10	2.97	14.92	32.80	96.25	199.20	210.55
Taiwan	—	—	—	—	23.52	78.06	95.91	111.37	246.56	253.29
Singapore	0.43	1.01	3.01	6.57	12.85	27.75	68.70	80.13	112.23	115.79
Hong Kong	—	—	—	—	—	24.66	55.42	107.56	123.57	124.28
Indonesia	0.02	0.16	0.59	6.80	5.99	8.66	14.91	29.35	36.31	34.58
Malaysia	0.47	0.67	1.69	5.75	5.68	10.66	24.70	28.65	66.39	70.45
Philippines	0.19	0.25	1.46	3.98	1.10	2.04	7.78	15.07	16.23	18.47
Thailand	0.74	0.91	2.01	3.03	3.00	14.26	36.94	32.67	49.85	52.08
Vietnam	—	—	—	—	—	—	1.32	3.42	7.04	9.05
World	—	—	—	—	743.06	1,276.97	1,814.80	2,230.17	4,193.56	4,623.55

Source: World Bank, World Development Indicators Database. The data for Taiwan are from the Asian Development Bank Statistical Database System.

An international monetary regime serves three basic functions: liquidity, adjustment, and confidence.[34] Liquidity and adjustment are closely linked. Liquidity refers to money as the facility of exchange of goods and services; volatile exchange rates weaken the liquidity function. Adjustment refers to the use of exchange rates to address imbalance of payments. Because an important source of payment imbalance is trade imbalance, the trading partners may resort to change in exchange rates to adjust the imbalances. The surplus country appreciates its currency whereas the deficit country depreciates its currency, a mechanism that decreases the exports of the surplus country by making its products and services more expensive and increases the exports of the deficit country by making its products and services less expensive. The other ways to address balance of payments deficits are to finance deficits or make painful domestic adjustments such as cutting expenditure. Politicians have incentives to avoid domestic adjustment and resort to manipulation of exchange rates to resolve their problems, which are in a crucial way caused domestically. This "dirty float" may cause an economic warfare, hurting the international community. A good international monetary system tries to facilitate settlement of payments through financing, exchange rate changes, exchange control, and adaptation of national policies.

Besides liquidity and adjustment, countries or individuals that hold a foreign currency must have confidence in the ability of that currency to maintain its value. Erosion of confidence often leads to instability of the monetary system. As a case in point, if East Asian economies lose their confidence in the dollar and start selling their dollar holdings massively, the whole international monetary system would be shaken, with a strong negative impact on the global economy.

East Asia and the Bretton Woods System

As discussed above, most East Asian economies were part of the Bretton Woods system. There is no question that the Bretton Woods system was a U.S.-led hegemonic system, only the second global monetary hegemony in human history, the other being the Gold Standard-British Sterling hegemony in the nineteenth century. The IMF has remained an important institution despite the collapse of the Bretton Woods system. As shown in Chapter 6, the IMF took a lead in dealing with the Asian financial crisis.

For East Asia, an important issue is its representation in the IMF, which has been dominated traditionally by the United States and Europe. East Asia's economic power has grown. In addition, Asian nations have been building up foreign reserves after the Asian financial crisis to avoid bailout packages from the IMF. This development makes some concerned that the IMF might become irrelevant. It thus makes sense to get Asian nations more involved. In particular, China's voting share in the IMF does not reflect its economic power. China has an economy twice that of Belgium and Holland combined, but the two European countries have 1.5 times as much voting power. The U.S. Treasury Department officials argued that adjustment of voting power will make adjustment of exchange rates easier.[35] The challenge was whether the Europeans would be willing to give up some share of voting power. At the IMF-World Bank meeting in April 2006, the IMF agreed on a plan to reshape the fund. The IMF decided to start a process to reapportion voting power to countries like China and South Korea. The shares of China, South Korea, Mexico, and Turkey increased modestly at the IMF-World Bank meeting in September 2006. China's voting share increased from 2.98 percent to 3.72 percent.

The Dollar Standard

The breakdown of the Bretton Woods system in the early 1970s did not end the dominant position of the dollar in international monetary affairs. In fact, the dollar standard was extended in East Asia when China joined the system with reforms that began in 1978 and Vietnam followed in the mid-1980s. However, a major difference in the post–Bretton Woods system is that while virtually all East Asian economies followed a dollar standard, the Japanese yen largely floated against the dollar.

A dollar standard means that the U.S. dollar is a store of value (foreign reserves), unit of accounting (trade invoicing), and means of exchange for trade and investment. It also serves as the preferred intervention in foreign exchange markets. In fact, there is some degree of dollarization in some countries in that the dollar partially or completely substitutes domestic currencies legally or de facto. Another important way to see the dominance of the U.S. dollar is that most East Asian nations peg their currencies to the U.S. dollar. I have already discussed the role of pegs to the U.S. dollar in the Asian financial crisis.

The dollar did not dominate just in East Asia but in the whole international economic system. In 1996, the dollar was 75 percent of external bond issues, 64 percent of official holdings of foreign exchange, and 45 percent of Eurocurrency deposits. The dollar accounts for between 40 and 80 percent of the various categories of international currency use.[36] It is also the currency of choice in foreign exchange markets (in organizing foreign exchange markets, large commercial banks can reduce transaction costs if they quote against only one vehicle). The dollar now accounts for almost 90 percent of interbank transactions. It also dominates in commodity trading, which is centralized and located largely in American cities such as Chicago and New York. This is important because about 70 percent of Japanese imports are denominated in the dollar because it imports many commodities and manufactured goods from the United States. Invoicing (statement of charges) for export is different. Countries with strong currencies tend to invoice exports in home currencies, as in the case of Germany and now the European Union. By contrast, Japan typically invoices only about 36 percent of its exports in the yen, mainly to maintain market shares. This is a good arrangement for the United States but not for Japan, since the United States is shielded from foreign exchange risk but Japan is not.[37]

After the Asian financial crisis, some East Asian economies officially gave up on the peg, but the dollar remains dominant because some Asian countries like China still peg to the U.S. dollar and because of other monetary functions the dollar continues to serve in East Asia. By 2004, most East Asian currencies were back to a soft peg to the U.S. dollar, measured by stable day-to-day exchange rates against the dollar, a stability backed by growing foreign reserves.[38]

The dominance of the dollar has a profound impact on East Asian economy. To start with, the exchange rate between the dollar and the yen, the currency of the strongest Asian economy, can be highly volatile. Figure 10.3 shows a drastic appreciation of the yen from ¥237.10 to the dollar in August 1985 to ¥122.00 in December 1987. Then the yen depreciated from ¥83.19 in May 1995 to ¥126.92 in April 1997 and ¥143.79 in July 1998. It has been argued that the yen was pushing upward continuously due to the expectation that it would appreciate in the long run because of U.S. pressure on Japan to appreciate the yen to reduce its trade surpluses with the United States. At the same time, the depreciation of the yen against the dollar in 1995–1998 had a negative impact on the East Asian economies that pegged their currencies to the dollar.[39] The yen's depreciation against the dollar in 1995 meant the appreciation of the East Asian currencies pegged to the dollar.

As discussed by Ronald McKinnon, it makes sense for the East Asian economies to peg their currencies to the dollar because the dollar is used for invoicing of East Asian trade. However, because of the inability of East Asian economies to raise debt in their own currencies, East Asian companies cannot hedge against exchange rate volatility, and the government has to maintain stable exchange rates against the dollar. For debtor economies (the situation of some East Asian economies before the 1997–1998 crisis), they experience a vicious cycle when companies seek to borrow dollar assets because of their lower risk premiums than domestic assets. For creditor nations (the case for most East Asian economies after the crisis), they lend in the dollar rather than in their own currencies. This creates a "conflicted virtue," virtue being high savings. When a country's dollar assets increase, the holders become worried that their dollar assets would take a loss if the domestic currency appreciates. Because of trade surplus, the country is under pressure to appreciate the currency, which may lead to deflation. This was a situation Japan faced in the 1980s and a situation China is facing now.[40]

Since the Asian financial crisis, Asian governments have been willing to finance America's current account deficits by purchasing U.S. Treasury bills because they

FIGURE 10.3

Yen-Dollar Exchange Rates, 1981–1998 (¥ per $ Tokyo market, end of month)

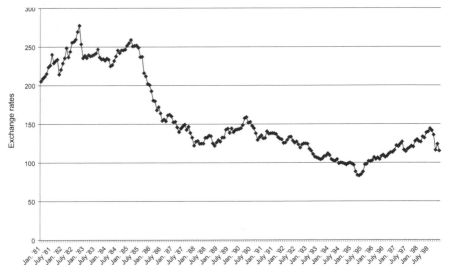

Source: Bank of Japan, www.boj.or.jp/en/type/stat/dlong/fin_stat/rate/cdab0780.csv.

want to keep their currencies relatively cheap to give their exports an edge. East Asian purchase of American debt instruments keeps U.S. bond yields low and overspending behavior unchanged. As discussed previously, a global imbalance exists. East Asia's foreign reserves have increased dramatically partly as a result of market intervention.

By the end of 2004, there was much concern about the declining U.S. dollar. The major problem is America's growing budget deficit and current account deficits, which put downward pressure on the U.S. dollar. The value of the dollar has dropped against the euro and the yen. This should be a serious concern for those who hold the dollar as foreign reserves. A depreciated dollar would reduce the value of their foreign reserves. The share of the dollar in the global foreign exchange reserve has decreased from 80 percent in the mid-1970s to around 65 percent in 2004.[41]

On February 22, 2005, out of concern over a sliding dollar, the Bank of Korea, South Korea's central bank, announced that it was planning to diversify its foreign reserves to more currencies.[42] Japanese Prime Minister Koizumi said on March 10, 2005, that the Japanese Central Bank should diversify the foreign currencies held by the bank. These remarks caused a stir in the global currency market. The value of the dollar dropped against the euro.

A depreciation of the U.S. dollar essentially taxes the holders of American securities to continue subsidizing American spending deficits. But East Asian countries like Japan and China are in a bind. If they start selling holdings of American securities, their action would move the market and decrease the values of their remaining holdings. They are already in too deep. All parties involved in the global imbalance need to participate to prevent a sharp adjustment that may lead to a global recession, tightening of U.S. monetary policy, relaxing of European monetary policy relative to the United States, and managed appreciation of East Asian currencies.[43]

EAST ASIAN REGIONAL MONETARY SYSTEM

My discussion above about the East Asian dilemma in monetary affairs points to the importance of a regional solution. East Asian economies need regional cooperation also because they need to avoid competitive depreciation. They watch, and often complain about, each other's foreign exchange.

Interstate monetary relations are characterized by cooperation, competition, and coercion. Whether a country's monetary policy will be considered cooperative is based on the objectives and interests of other players. This can be reflected in different ways. A principal area of cooperation and conflict is exchange rate. During the Asian financial crisis and afterward, China received high praise in East Asia and the United States for pledging not to depreciate the yuan. Beijing's action was meant to be cooperative and was seen as such. China meant to be cooperative because it said so. Others saw Beijing's pledge as cooperative because a cheaper yuan would put further pressure on the crisis countries in East Asia. Of course, China had self-interests in not depreciating the yuan, but that is not the point. To be cooperative, one does not have to deny one's own interests.

More than monetary cooperation, people have been discussing regional integration. One way for that to happen is to create currency regionalism whereby a currency is used beyond the sovereign jurisdiction of its issuing government. Another possibility is currency union, which may come about based on a strong anchor currency or based on regional cooperation.

Monetary Union

Currency union is not necessarily the same as creation of a common currency. Typically, currency union takes place before a common currency is created. Currency union means that the member states peg their currencies to each other and may or may not float against a third currency. Robert Mundell formulated the optimal currency area (OCA) theory in a seminal paper dated back to 1961.[44] Mundell defined a currency area as "a domain within which exchange rates are fixed." A zone in which factors of production, particularly labor, are mobile should have a common currency. This theory is now popular because of the experience of the European Monetary Union and other groupings. The idea was to figure out what is the most appropriate domain for a currency irrespective of national borders. More specifically, OCA theory studies the advantages and disadvantages for a country to abandon monetary autonomy to participate in a common currency or in a fixed exchange rate regime. Factors important for considerations of a common currency or fixed exchange rate include the following: wage and price flexibility, factor mobility, geographic trade patterns, the degree of commodity diversification, size and openness of economies, inflation trends, and the nature, source, and timing of potential payments disturbances.

Reasons for a common currency or fixed exchange rate are a more useful currency as a medium of exchange (reduced transaction costs), store of value (reduced exchange risk as number of currencies is reduced), and unit of account (reduced number of price quotations). Moreover, as part of a larger exchange rate market, one experiences decreasing currency volatility. Also, as part of the internationalization of a shared currency, participating countries enhance their purchasing power.

Conversely, one reason against forming a currency union is the loss of monetary authority to use macroeconomic measures such as interest rate and exchange rate to adjust to domestic disturbances or balance of payment problems. Moreover, some recent empirical research suggests that membership in the European Monetary Union has not brought as much benefit in trade and growth as widely thought.[45]

A government needs to consider all the factors mentioned above. The higher the potential gains and lower the potential loss, the more incentives a government has to join a currency area.

The 1997–1998 Asian financial crisis and the launch of the European Monetary Union in January 1999 were important reasons for growing discussion and initiatives in monetary integration in East Asia. It became accepted wisdom after the crisis that a government faces difficult choices of capital controls that discourage foreign direct investment and flexible exchange rates that remain volatile. In such a situation, regional monetary union is one solution to prevent future crises. Put differently, since the crisis was viewed as resulting from dependence on the dollar, some East Asians naturally yearned for independence from the dollar, and an Asian currency was viewed as a solution.[46] The European Monetary Union showed that regional monetary integration could work. Top East Asian leaders such as Malaysian Prime Minister Mahathir Mohamad and Philippine President

Joseph Estrada talked about creating a common currency, and there have been studies and meetings about East Asian monetary integration.

There are debates whether East Asia is ready to launch monetary integration. On the one hand, the conditions for a pegged East Asian exchange rate regime are not met because of weak economic convergence in terms of inflation between East Asian economies.[47] On the other hand, the economic conditions in East Asia are no less suitable than those in Europe for monetary integration. The barriers to integration are mainly political, namely China-Japan tensions, Japan's unwillingness to shoulder costs, and America's strong influence.[48] Recognizing the absence of political will for monetary integration, Robert McKinnon suggested a less politically demanding solution of creating a common monetary standard based on an anchor currency, which he proposed should continue to be the U.S. dollar.[49]

Some empirical studies suggest that a currency basket system would help stabilize trade and capital flows in East Asia. The challenge to create a currency basket is that a country's decision to shift exchange rate policy depends on what its neighbors do. The solution is for East Asian economies to make coordinated moves.[50]

East Asia has made progress with the creation of an Asian Currency Unit (ACU), modeled after the European Currency Unit. Note that the ACU is not meant to be a common currency. Rather, ACU is meant as an accounting unit for economic transactions. It would be calculated based on a basket of the thirteen regional currencies. The Asian Development Bank has taken a lead on this. On May 4, 2006, the finance ministers of China, Japan, and South Korea agreed to consider the creation of ACU for the first time.[51]

A Yen Bloc

East Asia is generally seen as one of three possible currency regions, the dollar, the euro, and the yen. With Japan emerging as the world's largest creditor nation in the late 1980s, it made sense then to believe that the yen should be a central international currency. However, it became clear under scrutiny that, while gaining more international use, the yen was far behind the dollar and the deutsche mark as an international currency. In fact, Japanese exports and imports were largely invoiced in a currency other than the yen, mainly the dollar. The share of Japanese exports invoiced in yen increased from 17.5 percent in 1975 to about 35 percent in the late 1980s, and the share of imports increased from less than 1 percent in 1975 to 14 percent in 1989. By contrast, the shares of exports and imports invoiced in their own currencies were about 96 percent and 85 percent for the United States and 40–80 percent and 27–52 percent for major Western European countries during the same period.[52] This situation has not changed much. In 2002, 48 percent of Japan's total exports and 68.7 percent of imports were invoiced in dollars and only 38.4 percent of exports and 24.6 percent of imports were invoiced in yen.[53]

Even in Asia, the yen accounted for 11.5 percent of official reserves in 1992, compared with 61.4 percent for the U.S. dollar, 13.1 percent for the German mark, and 8.0 percent for the British pound.[54]

Several reasons explain Japan's problems in this area. First, the Japanese financial sector remained more regulated and less developed than the financial markets in the United States and Europe. Second, Japanese firms prefer to use the dollar to maintain market shares in the North American market. Third, the share of imports invoiced in the dollar is high because Japan imports most of the primary resources it needs and because homogeneous primary products tend to be invoiced in the dollar. Fourth, there is inertia and economies of scale in use of an international currency, which favors the existing hegemonic currency, the dollar.[55]

Until the early 1990s, the Bank of Japan did not want the internationalization of the yen out of concern that this would compromise its ability to conduct monetary affairs at home. This attitude changed in the 1990s when the Japanese monetary authority became less concerned about maintaining a tight monetary policy.[56] The Japanese government began promoting the internationalization of the yen, particularly after the Asian financial crisis. Some analysts in Japan argued that the crisis revealed the limitation of pegging to the U.S. dollar. Furthermore, Japan had recently adopted the Big Bang for financial reform. Moreover, to avoid dollar-yen volatility, it was reasoned that East Asian economies should peg to the yen or give more weight to the yen in a currency basket. East Asia would benefit in macroeconomic stability and in microeconomic efficiency.[57] Internationalization of the yen would reduce exchange risks for the Japanese and would also enhance Japan's international status. The October 1998 Miyazawa Initiative to provide $30 billion aid to the crisis countries was also designed to encourage use of the yen by East Asian economies.

It is not clear whether a shift from the dollar to the yen would resolve the problem of dollar-yen volatility. Such a shift would clearly serve Japan's interest. But if the U.S. dollar and the yen are about the same, shifting pegs would shift costs of fluctuation to the United States without clear benefits to the rest of East Asia. Moreover, if there is volatility in the dollar-yen exchange, which currency should one choose? The dollar remains a better choice than the yen, particularly when the Japanese economy is not doing well. At the government level, East Asia largely depends on the United States for political and military support. The market still prefers the dollar, which makes transactions with the whole world easier, and the United States has a stronger and healthier economy than Japan. It will be difficult for the yen even under better circumstances. Japanese exporters choose non-Japanese currencies themselves. Only about 35–40 percent of Japanese exports (different estimates) and only 20 percent of Japanese imports are on a yen basis.[58]

The Japanese capital outflows have also been largely denominated in currencies other than the yen, and borrowing in foreign currencies has some advantages over yen-denominated borrowing because of factors such as reserve requirements. In the scheme of things, the U.S. economy is expanding while the Japanese economy is shrinking. The market size matters. One important reason that East Asia chooses the dollar for trade invoicing is that they are more dependent on the U.S. market than the Japanese market.

The Big Bang was supposed to create a fair and open financial center by the end of 2001. That has not happened. To internationalize currencies, one needs to have strong, open, deep, and broad financial markets. For example, the U.S. dollar dominates in commodity trade because of well-developed commodity markets in Chicago and New York. As recognized by Japanese analysts, the Tokyo financial market has declined in both quantitative and qualitative terms in recent years, compared with London and New York financial centers.[59] Hong Kong and Singapore are competing financial centers in East Asia, followed by rising financial centers such as Shanghai.

The Yuan's Arrival

The yuan is a new kid in the block. Some suggest that the yuan will replace the yen as the dominant East Asian currency. The yuan's growing influence reflects China's growing economic strength and financial and political stability. Now that China has joined the World Trade Organization, foreign banks are allowed to operate in China. An additional plus is that the Chinese government has put inflation under control since the mid-1990s.

The yuan has already become popular in countries neighboring China, partly because of a growing number of tourists from China. Another reason is increasing border trade. Also, the yuan has been stable, even during the Asian financial crisis, and the currency is based on a growing economy. With expanding ties and tourism, the yuan is also being used as a currency in Hong Kong.

As an indicator of things to come, trading on the yuan has increased dramatically. The traditional foreign exchange market turnover daily average over yuan grew by 530 percent from 2001 to 2004. At the same time, however, the absolute volume of yuan trading was still small, merely $1.8 billion in April 2004, compared with $1,573.1 billion for the U.S. dollar, $659.4 billion for the euro, and $359.2 billion for the yen.[60] In addition, a weak Chinese banking system and a nontransparent political and financial system remain serious problems for internationalization of the yuan. Last but not least, the yuan cannot be an anchor currency until it becomes fully convertible. As a result, it is unwise even for the Hong Kong dollar to be pegged to the yuan, let alone other currencies.

EAST ASIAN POLITICAL ECONOMY OF MONEY

East Asian monetary practices both result from and affect East Asian domestic political economy. Logically, the exchange rate policy has a distributional effect on domestic politics, and the sectoral preferences would in turn fight to shape the country's exchange rate policy. I have discussed above that a government considers the degree of flexibility (floating vs. fixed) and the level of exchange rate (appreciation vs. depreciation) when thinking about exchange rates. In general, companies that engage in international trade prefer stable exchange rates. It matters to them less whether the state maintains its capacity to formulate macroeconomic policies at home. By contrast, domestic firms of nontradable goods and import-competing products prefer floating exchange rates because of their high stake in a country's macroeconomic policies. On a different dimension, producers of tradable goods prefer currency depreciation to increase their competitiveness whereas producers of nontradable goods or importers prefer a stronger currency.[61] We do not have as much empirical evidence on exchange rate policy in the domestic context as on trade policy.[62] More needs to be done empirically about the domestic politics of East Asian exchange rates, but there is some evidence that the distributional logic discussed above applies to East Asia.

Whatever foreign exchange rate policies one adopts creates further developments. With an overvalued currency, one has incentives to invest in nontradable domestic industries rather than export or import substitution industries. Overvaluation leads to balance of payments difficulties, which leads to foreign exchange controls that have obvious impact on allocation of resources. Entrenched domestic interests make it difficult to shift gear. For example, in the Philippines, there was a heated policy debate between traditional exporters in sugar and import substitution industries. The overvalued exchange rate the Philippines had at the time was disadvantageous to exporters. In the end, with pressure from Congress and from public backlash against corruption within the import substitution sector, the Philippines depreciated the peso.[63]

Conversely, with an undervalued currency, one has incentives to invest in export industries. A cheap currency leads to balance of payments surpluses, resulting in greater foreign pressure. However, entrenched domestic interests make it difficult to change the course. China's resistance to a sharp currency appreciation is a case in point. The Bush administration has been asking the Chinese government to delink the yuan with the dollar in an effort to reduce growing U.S. trade deficits. A cheap yuan also has a negative impact on domestic political economy by encouraging speculative capital to rush in. The increasing foreign reserve adds to the money supply, which creates inflationary pressure. Many in the Chinese policy community now understand that the yuan has to appreciate to avoid an overheating of the Chinese economy, excessive demand for resources, and growing trade frictions. However, it is difficult to adjust exchange rates politically. The Chinese Central Bank wants to appreciate the yuan to avoid an overheated economy, its main responsibility, but cabinet ministries want to stay the course. In particular, the Ministry of Commerce wants to minimize adjustment. Chinese exporters predictably oppose appreciation. Consequently, the State Council is taking a middle road, trying to appreciate a few percentage points a year.

The global financial market also affects domestic political economy profoundly. East Asian governments all want financial stability and flow of capital into their economies, and they jealously guard their national independence. However, as the impossible trinity discussed earlier shows, governments cannot meet the policy objectives of stable exchange rates, integration with the global economy, and national autonomy simultaneously. This is particularly the case for small countries that are particularly vulnerable to the volatility of the global market. Moreover, as discussed in Chapter 6, the Asian financial crisis that resulted partly from pegged exchange rates led to economic and political reform measures in various East Asian economies.

CONCLUSION

East Asian economies have sought stable and advantageous exchange rate policies to facilitate their main objective of rapid industrialization. Most chose overvalued currencies in the early 1950s based on the idea that such an approach would reduce the cost of imports and would not overly impact exports since it was difficult to export in any case. Nonsocialist economies were part of the Bretton Woods system dominated by the United States and pegged their currencies to the U.S. dollar (a few pegged to the British pound at some point, but the British pound itself was pegged to the dollar). The socialist countries largely maintained overvalued currencies pegged to the dollar and adopted the exchange control regime necessary to handle a situation of excessive demand for "cheap" dollars. With a break from the Soviet Union and rapprochement with the United States, China became part of the mainstream international monetary system.

After the Bretton Woods system collapsed in the early 1970s, East Asian monetary affairs were characterized by a managed float between the U.S. dollar and the Japanese yen, whereas virtually every East Asian economy pegged its currency to the dollar. The sharp appreciation of the yen after the 1985 Plaza Accord had a profound impact on East Asian political economy as Japanese investment poured into East Asia and elsewhere. The subsequent appreciation of the New Taiwan Dollar and the South Korean won furthered the diffusion of industries and strengthened regional production networks. The depreciation of the Chinese yuan in 1994 and the depreciation of the yen after the mid-1990s put competitive pressure on Southeast Asia, contributing to the outbreak of the Asian financial crisis. Most East Asian economies returned to a de facto dollar standard a few years after the crisis ended.

It makes sense for East Asian economies to peg to the dollar, because the dollar is used for invoicing for their trade and the United States is the most important final market for their exports. However, since East Asian economies cannot raise debt in their own currencies, they cannot hedge against exchange rate fluctuations. The dollar assets East Asian economies have accumulated would suffer large losses if East Asian currencies appreciate against the dollar. Because of this well-understood problem, East Asian economies are now eager to increase regional monetary cooperation. East Asia has made some progress in this regard, creating an Asian Currency Unit, which is based on a basket of thirteen regional currencies, as an accounting unit for financial transactions. However, considerable obstacles to East Asian monetary regional integration exist.

Exchange rate policies have a significant distributional effect on domestic political economy, namely creating winners and losers. Consistent with East Asia's focus on production and exports, East Asian governments prefer stable but low exchange rates against the dollar. Like any other economic policies, exchange rate regimes also create vested interests, making adjustment politically difficult. Although East Asian governments want financial stability, gains from the global financial market, and national autonomy, they cannot simultaneously achieve all three.

SUGGESTED READINGS

Bergsten, C. Fred, and John Williamson, eds. *Dollar Adjustment: How Far? Against What?* (Washington, D.C.: Institute for International Economies, 2004).

Broz, J. Lawrence, and Jeffry A. Frieden. "The Political Economy of International Monetary Relations." *Annual Review of Political Science* 4 (June 2001): 317–343.

Calvo, Guillermo A., and Carmen M. Reinhart. "Fear of Floating." *Quarterly Journal of Economics* 117, no. 2 (May 2002): 379–408.

Cohen, Benjamin J. *Organizing the World's Money: The Political Economy of International Monetary Relations* (New York: Basic Books, 1977).

Cohen, Benjamin J. "The Political Economy of Currency Regions." In *The Political Economy of Regionalism*, ed. Edward D. Mansfield and Helen V. Milner (New York: Columbia University Press, 1997), 56–76.

Cooper, Richard N. "Prolegomena to the Choice of an International Monetary System." *International Organization* 29, no. 1 (Winter 1975): 63–97.

Corden, W. Max. "Exchange Rate Regimes for Emerging Market Economies: Lessons from Asia." *The Annals of the American Academy of Political and Social Science* 579 (January 2002): 26–37.

Frieden, Jeffrey A. "Invested Interests: The Politics of National Economies' Policies in a World of Global Finance." *International Organization* 45, no. 4 (Autumn 1991): 444–450.

Genberg, Hans, Robert McCauley, Yung Chul Park, and Avinash Persaud. *Official Reserves and Currency Management in Asia: Myth, Reality, and the Future,* Geneva Reports on the World Economy 7 (Geneva: International Center for Monetary and Banking Studies, 2005).

Hanke, Steve H. "Currency Boards." *The Annals of the American Academy of Political and Social Science* 579 (January 2002): 87–105.

Helleiner, Eric. *The Making of National Money: Territorial Currencies in Historical Perspective* (Ithaca, N.Y.: Cornell University Press, 2003).

Ho, Corrinne, Guonan Ma, and Robert McCauley. "Trading Asian Currencies." *BIS Quarterly Review* (March 2005): 49–58.

Iwami, Toru, and Kiyotaka Sato. "The Internationalization of the Yen: With an Emphasis on East Asia." *International Journal of Social Economics* 23, no. 10–11 (October–November 1996): 192–208.

Kwan, Chi Hung. *Yen Bloc: Toward Economic Integration in Asia* (Washington, D.C.: Brookings Institution, 2001).

Ma, Guonan, Corrinne Ho, Robert McCauley, and Eli Remolona. "Managing the Renminbi Regime Shift." *BIS Quarterly Review* (September 2005): 7–8.

McKinnon, Ronald I. *Exchange Rates Under the East Asian Dollar Standard: Living with Conflicted Virtue* (Cambridge: MIT Press, 2005).

McKinnon, Ronald I., and Kenichi Ohno. *Dollar and Yen: Resolving Economic Conflict Between the United States and Japan* (Cambridge: MIT Press, 1997).

Mundell, Robert A. *International Economics* (New York: Macmillan, 1968).

Ogawa, Eiji, and Kentaro Kawasaki. "Creating a Common Currency Basket for East Asia: Prospects and Key Issues." In *New East Asian Regionalism: Causes, Progress, and Country Perspectives,* ed. Charles Harvie, Fukunari Kimura, and Hyun-Hoon Lee (Northampton, Mass.: Edward Elgar, 2005), 283–305.

Tavlas, George S., and Yuzuru Ozeki. "The Internationalization of the Yen." *Finance and Development* 28, no. 2 (June 1991): 2–5.

Volcker, Paul, and Toyoo Gyohten. *Changing Fortunes: The World's Money and the Threat to American Leadership* (New York: Random House, 1992).

Williamson, John. "The Evolution of Thought on Intermediate Exchange Rate Regimes." *The Annals of the American Academy of Political and Social Science* 579 (January 2002): 73–86.

NOTES

1. Eric Helleiner, *The Making of National Money: Territorial Currencies in Historical Perspective* (Ithaca, N.Y.: Cornell University Press, 2003).
2. George S. Tavlas, "The Economics of Exchange-Rate Regimes: A Review Essay," *World Economy* 26, no. 8 (August 2003): 1215–1216; John Williamson, "The Evolution of Thought on Intermediate Exchange Rate Regimes," *The Annals of the American Academy of Political and Social Science* 579 (January 2002): 73–86.
3. J. Lawrence Broz and Jeffry A. Frieden, "The Political Economy of International Monetary Relations," *Annual Review of Political Science* 4 (June 2001): 319.
4. Anne O. Krueger, *Foreign Trade Regimes and Economic Development: Liberalization Attempts and Consequences* (New York: National Bureau of Economic Research, 1978), 69–78.
5. "Big MacCurrencies," *The Economist*, April 3, 1999, 66.
6. "China's Foreign Reserves," *The Economist*, October 28, 2006, 85.
7. Ian M. D. Little, *Economic Development: Theory, Policy, and International Relations* (New York: Basic Books, 1982), 306–307.
8. Nakamura, *Postwar Japanese Economy*, 38–39, 56–58.
9. S. C. Tsiang, "Foreign Trade and Investment as Boosters for Take-Off: The Experience of Taiwan," in *Export-Oriented Development Strategies: The Success of Five Newly Industrializing Countries*, ed. Vittorio Corbo, Anne O. Krueger, and Fernando Ossa (Boulder: Westview Press, 1985), 35–37.
10. Kim, "Korea," 22–27; Frank, Kim, and Westphal, *South Korea*.
11. Aw, "Singapore," 347–349.
12. Robert E. Baldwin, *The Philippines* (New York: National Bureau of Economic Research, distributed by Columbia University Press, 1975).
13. Suiwah Leung and Ngo Huy Duc, "Dollarization and Financial Sector Developments in Vietnam," in *Vietnam and the East Asian Crisis*, ed. Suiwah Leung (Northampton, Mass.: Edward Elgar, 1999), 84.
14. W. Max Corden, "Exchange Rate Regimes for Emerging Market Economies: Lessons from Asia," *The Annals of the American Academy of Political and Social Science* 579 (January 2002): 26–37.
15. Carmen M. Reinhart and Kenneth S. Rogoff, "The Modern History of Exchange Rate Arrangements: A Reinterpretation," Working Paper No. 8963 (Cambridge, Mass.: National Bureau of Economic Research, June 2002).
16. Paul Volcker and Toyoo Gyohten, *Changing Fortunes: The World's Money and the Threat to American Leadership* (New York: Random House, 1992), 228–258.

17. Takatoshi Ito, "The Yen and the Japanese Economy, 2004," in *Dollar Adjustment: How Far? Against What?* ed. C. Fred Bergsten and John Williamson (Washington, D.C.: Institute for International Economies, 2004), 184.

18. For currency board, see Steve H. Hanke, "Currency Boards," *The Annals of the American Academy of Political and Social Science* 579 (January 2002): 87–105.

19. Gordon de Brouwer, *Financial Integration in East Asia* (Cambridge: Cambridge University Press, 1999), 45–46.

20. Yu Yongding, "China's Capital Flow Liberalization and Reform of Exchange Rate Regime," in *Financial Interdependence and Exchange Rate Regimes in East Asia,* ed. Masahiro Kawai, conference proceedings, Korea Institute for International Economic Policy and Policy Research Institute of Japan Ministry of Finance, December 2–3, 2004, Tokyo, 130–154, www.mof.go.jp/english/soken/kiep2005/kiep2005_03.pdf.

21. Leung and Duc, "Dollarization and Financial Sector Developments in Vietnam."

22. Robert Mundell, "Capital Mobility and Stabilization Policy Under Fixed and Flexible Exchange Rates," *Canadian Journal of Economics and Political Science* 29, no. 4 (November 1963): 475–485 and Robert A. Mundell, *International Economics* (New York: Macmillan, 1968).

23. Guillermo A. Calvo and Carmen M. Reinhart, "Fear of Floating," *Quarterly Journal of Economics* 117, no. 2 (May 2002): 379–408.

24. Ronald I. McKinnon with Gunther Schnabl, "The East Asian Dollar Standard, Fear of Floating, and Original Sin," in *Exchange Rates Under the East Asian Dollar Standard: Living with Conflicted Virtue,* ed. Ronald I. McKinnon (Cambridge: MIT Press, 2005), 13–52.

25. Morris Goldstein, "China and the Renminbi Exchange Rate," in *Dollar Adjustment* (see note 17), 197–230.

26. Guonan Ma, Corrinne Ho, Robert McCauley, and Eli Remolona, "Managing the Renminbi Regime Shift," *BIS Quarterly Review* (September 2005): 7–8.

27. Ito, "Yen and the Japanese Economy."

28. "Yen and Yang," *The Economist,* September 30, 2006, 81.

29. Eiji Fujii, "Exchange Rate Pass-Through in Deflationary Japan: How Effective Is the Yen's Depreciation for Fighting Deflation," in *Japan's Great Stagnation: Financial and Monetary Policy Lessons for Advanced Economies,* ed. Michael M. Hutchison and Frank Westermann (Cambridge: MIT Press, 2006), 211–237.

30. Taniuchi, "Global Imbalances and Asian Economies," 18–23.

31. The People's Bank of China, www.pbc.gov.cn/diaochatongji/tongjishuju/gofile.asp?file=2007S09.htm (accessed on May 5, 2007).

32. Hans Genberg, Robert McCauley, Yung Chul Park, and Avinash Persaud, *Official Reserves and Currency Management in Asia: Myth, Reality, and the Future,*

Geneva Reports on the World Economy 7 (Geneva: International Center for Monetary and Banking Studies, 2005).

33. Richard N. Cooper, "Prolegomena to the Choice of an International Monetary System," *International Organization* 29, no. 1 (Winter 1975): 63–97.

34. Benjamin J. Cohen, *Organizing the World's Money: The Political Economy of International Monetary Relations* (New York: Basic Books, 1977).

35. Paul Blustein, "U.S. to Support More IMF Votes for China," *The Washington Post,* August 24, 2006, D5.

36. George S. Tavlas, "The International Use of Currencies: The U.S. Dollar and the Euro," *Finance and Development* 35, no. 2 (June 1998): 46–49.

37. Ronald I. McKinnon, "Euroland and East Asia in a Dollar-Based System: The Future of International Monetary Policy," *The International Economy* 13, no. 5 (September–October 1999): 40–45, 67.

38. McKinnon and Schnabl, "East Asian Dollar Standard," 13.

39. Ronald I. McKinnon with Kenichi Ohno, "Japan's Deflation and the Syndrome of the Ever-Higher Yen, 1971–1995," in *Exchange Rates Under the East Asian Dollar Standard* (see note 24), 77–102. Also see Ronald I. McKinnon and Kenichi Ohno, *Dollar and Yen: Resolving Economic Conflict Between the United States and Japan* (Cambridge: MIT Press, 1997).

40. Ronald I. McKinnon, "Introduction: The East Asian Exchange Rate Dilemma," in *Exchange Rates Under the East Asian Dollar Standard* (see note 24), 1–12.

41. "The Passing of the Buck?" *The Economist,* December 4, 2004, 71. This is an important article on the declining dollar.

42. Paul Blustein, "Korea to Limit Its Dollar Holdings," *The Washington Post,* February 23, 2005, E1.

43. World Bank, *Global Development Finance: Mobilizing Finance and Managing Vulnerability* (Washington, D.C.: World Bank, 2005), 3–4.

44. Robert A. Mundell, "A Theory of Optimum Currency Area," *American Economic Review* 51, no. 3 (September 1961): 657–665. Also see Paul R. Masson and Mark P. Taylor, "Currency Unions: A Survey of the Issues," in *Policy Issues in the Operation of Currency Unions,* ed. Paul R. Masson and Mark P. Taylor (Cambridge: Cambridge University Press, 1993), 3–51; George S. Tavlas, "The 'New' Theory of Optimum Currency Areas," *The World Economy* 16, no. 6 (November 1993): 663–685; Benjamin J. Cohen, "The Political Economy of Currency Regions," in *The Political Economy of Regionalism,* ed. Edward D. Mansfield and Helen V. Milner (New York: Columbia University Press, 1997), 56–76.

45. Richard E. Baldwin, "In or Out: Does It Matter? An Evidence-Based Analysis of the Trade Effects of the Euro," Center for Economic Policy Research, May 2006.

46. Group 21, "Japan Must Introduce an Asian Currency," *Japan Echo* (June 1999): 24.

47. Jung Sik Kim, "Is the Pegged Regime a Feasible Alternative in East Asia," in *Financial Interdependence and Exchange Rate Regimes in East Asia,* ed. Masahiro Kawai, conference proceedings, Korea Institute for International Economic Policy and Policy Research Institute of Japan Ministry of Finance, December 2–3, 2004, Tokyo, 204–229, www.mof.go.jp/english/soken/kiep 2005/kiep2005_04.pdf.

48. Yeongseop Rhee, "East Asian Monetary Integration: Destined to Fail?" *Social Science Japan Journal* 7, no. 1 (April 2004): 83–102.

49. Robert I. McKinnon, "Optimum Currency Areas and Key Currencies: Mundell I versus Mundell II," in *Exchange Rates Under the East Asian Dollar Standard* (see note 24), 224–225.

50. Eiji Ogawa and Kentaro Kawasaki, "Creating a Common Currency Basket for East Asia: Prospects and Key Issues," in *New East Asian Regionalism: Causes, Progress, and Country Perspectives,* ed. Charles Harvie, Fukunari Kimura, and Hyun-Hoon Lee (Northampton, Mass.: Edward Elgar, 2005), 283–305.

51. *Yomiuri Shimbun,* May 4, 2006, www.yomiuri.co.jp/atmoney/news/20060504it14 .htm?from=top.

52. George S. Tavlas and Yuzuru Ozeki, "The Internationalization of the Yen," *Finance and Development* 28, no. 2 (June 1991): 2–5.

53. McKinnon and Schnabl, "East Asian Dollar Standard," 20.

54. Toru Iwami and Kiyotaka Sato, "The Internationalization of the Yen: With an Emphasis on East Asia," *International Journal of Social Economics* 23, no. 10–11 (October–November 1996): 192–208.

55. Tavlas and Ozeki, "Internationalization of the Yen"; Iwami and Sato, "Internationalization of the Yen."

56. Iwami and Sato, "Internationalization of the Yen."

57. Chi Hung Kwan, *Yen Bloc: Toward Economic Integration in Asia* (Washington, D.C.: Brookings Institution, 2001).

58. Group 21, "Japan Must Introduce an Asian Currency," *Japan Echo* (June 1999): 24.

59. Ogawa, "Tokyo Financial Market as a Financial Center in East Asia."

60. Corrinne Ho, Guonan Ma, and Robert McCauley, "Trading Asian Currencies," *BIS Quarterly Review* (March 2005): 49–58.

61. Jeffrey A. Frieden, "Invested Interests: The Politics of National Economies' Policies in a World of Global Finance," *International Organization* 45, no. 4 (Autumn 1991): 444–450.

62. Broz and Frieden, "Political Economy of International Monetary Relations."

63. Shepherd and Alburo, "The Philippines," 178–193.

CHAPTER **11**

The Political Economy
of East Asian Regionalism

The origin, nature, and consequences of regionalism are important issues in East Asian political economy. If it succeeds, East Asian regionalism would usher in a new regional order. The previous chapters have demonstrated a strong regional dimension of East Asian political economy. Historically, East Asia was linked in a tribute system centered on China. While the Western powers created an imperialist order in East Asia after the mid-nineteenth century, an intra-Asia trade network expanded as well, with merchants and governments taking advantage of greater access to their neighboring countries and responding to competitive pressure from fellow Asians. The Japanese attempted unsuccessfully to create a Greater East Asian Co-Prosperity Sphere in the 1930s–1940s. The postwar East Asian economic miracle was a regional phenomenon. Most East Asian economies sank together in a regional contagion in the Asian financial crisis of 1997–1998. The chapters on production, trade, finance, and currencies have demonstrated extensive regional links in East Asia and have discussed some regional institutions in those areas. This chapter provides an overview of different, often competing approaches to East Asian regional integration.

The chapter addresses three sets of questions. First, how far has East Asian regionalization gone compared with other regions and from a historical perspective? Second, what are the basic features of East Asian regionalism? Why has East Asian regionalism evolved the way it has? What are some economic explanations for East Asian regionalism? What are some political economy explanations for East Asian regionalism? In particular, why did East Asians hesitate to develop formal and legalized institutions within Asia? Why did East Asians shift to a more formalistic approach after the Asian financial crisis? Third, how will East Asian regionalism affect the global and regional balance of power and the United States? How will East Asian regionalism affect the domestic economy of participating East Asian countries?

357

DEFINING REGIONALIZATION AND REGIONALISM

If we use geographical proximity as a key factor to define region or regionalism, regionalism may refer to a state of affairs, namely an unusually high concentration of economic transactions. Regionalism may also refer to the coordination of policy to promote economic transactions. One debate among analysts of regionalism is whether regionalism reflects natural forces such as proximity and comparative advantages or deliberate government efforts. Another way to define regionalism is to use nongeographical factors such as economic flows or cultural affinity. Benedict Anderson used "imagined community" to describe a nation.[1] In the same way, if some countries imagine themselves to be part of a community, then they are. In a survey of definitions, Andrew Hurrel pointed out five elements of regionalism: regionalization, regional awareness and identity, regional interstate cooperation, state-promoted regional integration, and regional cohesion.[2]

I adopt a geographical definition here. It is true that concentration of economic flows does not overlap with geographical location neatly, but it is better than the alternatives. Besides, this book has followed a geographic definition of East Asia, as discussed in Chapter 1. I differentiate regionalization from regionalism.[3] Regionalization here refers to a concentration of economic activities, whether caused by market forces or government policies. Regionalism refers to coordinated government policies to promote greater regional economic transactions.

EAST ASIAN REGIONALIZATION

There has been an increasing degree of regionalization in East Asia as reflected in trade and investment.[4] As discussed in Chapter 7, regionalization of production is a striking feature of contemporary East Asian political economy. Foreign direct investment (FDI), export promotion, and alliance and partnership among firms have helped to link production of East Asian economies to each other as well as to the West. The sharp appreciation of the yen and the currencies of the Asian tigers led to a major wave of direct investment to Southeast Asia, enhancing dramatically a regionalization of production. As Chapter 8 has shown, however we measure it, East Asia has experienced greater regional trade integration since the mid-1980s even if we factor in the region's increasing share in the global trade. While the United States remains the largest final export market for East Asian goods, East Asian economies have also become more dependent on each other for exports and capital investment. At the same time, the center of gravity in regional trade flows is shifting from Japan to China.

As Chapter 9 has shown, compared with trade, East Asian financial integration has progressed unevenly. Related to regionalization of production, flow of direct investment has shown greater regional interdependence. But judging by other measures of financial integration such as interest rate parities, shared regional bond issues, and flows of portfolio investments, East Asia has not experienced nearly as significant a regional financial integration as Europe. In fact, East Asia is tied closely with the financial centers of the West, particularly New York and London. Financial globalization rather than financial regionalization defines current East Asian finance. In terms of exchange rate regimes, as discussed in Chapter 10, East Asia is fundamentally fragmented in that the yen, the most powerful East Asian currency, floats against the U.S. dollar and the euro, while virtually every other East Asian currency remains pegged to the dollar, official declarations aside. Put simply, East Asia remains on the dollar standard, and the situation will not change much in the near future.

Closer economic ties mean that it is important for East Asian economies to cooperate to achieve greater economic efficiency. In addition, more than regional concentration, the fates of East Asian economies have become increasingly bound together. Since they are viewed as part of the same group, they go up (with inflow of capital) and down (with a sudden reversal of capital flows that led to the 1997–1998 financial crisis). Also, since the early 1980s, Hong Kong, Indonesia, South Korea, Malaysia, Taiwan, and Thailand had synchronized business cycles while the Philippines and Singapore also loosely correlated in growth rates.[5]

A growing share of trade among countries in the region does not necessarily indicate discriminatory action against others. As East Asian economies became bigger traders relative to other regions, their share of trade with each other should naturally increase as well. To be discriminatory, East Asian nations would have to adopt trade and investment policies that deliberately favor their neighbors, which is not the case in East Asia. Moreover, growing regionalization in other parts of the world, particularly in Europe and North America, means greater intraregional concentration in East Asia.

Much of East Asian integration is market based. Fundamentally, firms rather than governments have been driving regionalization of production. This was particularly the case before the Asian financial crisis.[6] There are three major groups of agents that drive the regional integration, namely Japanese, Western, and ethnic Chinese capital. Japanese firms are stakeholder capitalist, Western firms are shareholder capitalist, whereas ethnic Chinese capital is largely family based. But they all adopt transnational market strategies. One should also note that it is not necessarily Japanese competing against Chinese or Western firms. Alliances and rivalries go in all directions.

Government programs have been important, but firms will not do what is against their basic economic interests. As a case in point, Taiwanese businesses eagerly go to mainland China for investment despite government discouragement.

At the same time, the state has been involved in the integration process. Japan had to promote FDI, and its monetary and fiscal policy also had the implication for moving operations to the rest of East Asia. The rest of East Asia had to liberalize their economies and encourage inflow of FDI. The Chinese government was at the center of an emerging Greater China Circle. Moreover, the state has taken the center stage in regional cooperation since the Asian financial crisis.

EAST ASIAN REGIONALISM

Two features stand out in East Asian regionalism. First, despite great diversities in traditions, cultures, stages of economic development, and political systems, East Asians have actively engaged in building regionalism, spearheaded by the governments, business communities, academics, and nongovernmental organizations.[7] Second, East Asians practiced a so-called "open regionalism" before the 1997-1998 Asian financial crisis, turned to more exclusive and formal regionalism after the crisis, and are recently taking another turn to formal but less exclusive regionalism.

East Asian regionalism based on voluntary participation has been a phenomenon since the end of World War II, particularly in light of ongoing integration in Western Europe and elsewhere. Engaging in intergovernmental economic regionalism only in the 1980s, East Asia has fallen behind Europe and North America.[8] Western Europe began integration shortly after World War II. The United States, Canada, and Mexico launched the North American Free Trade Agreement (NAFTA) in January 1994.

Scholars and businesspeople dominated in the initial efforts for Asian regional integration. The Pacific Trade and Development Conference (PAFTAD) created in 1968 by academics evolved into a major network of economists and policy experts throughout the region. The Pacific Basin Economic Council (PBEC) created in Tokyo in 1967 by business representatives from Japan, Australia, and New Zealand now includes the United States, Canada, and some other countries outside the region. The Pacific Economic Cooperation Council (PECC) created in 1980 includes some leaders of PAFTAD and PBEC as well as government officials. There is a reason that the word Pacific was so prominent. The countries most interested in these ideas were the United States, Japan, and Australia. The governments became formally involved in regional integration with the creation of the Asia-Pacific Economic Cooperation forum (APEC) in 1989.

Open Regionalism

Before the 1997 Asian financial crisis, East Asia was known as practicing an "open regionalism," a notion closely associated with APEC. The 1993 APEC meeting announced the goal of open regionalism. The term *open regionalism* has never been officially defined, but most analysts view it as meaning that APEC member countries would adopt a Most Favored Nation standard that does not discriminate against nonmembers, that APEC membership is open to all Asian countries or the countries bordering on the Pacific Ocean, and that APEC members would continue to promote unilateral trade liberalization and participation in the global free trade negotiations.[9] Put simply, open regionalism means that East Asia wants to use regionalism to become more integrated into the global economy.

APEC is open, now with 18 members from East Asia, Oceania, North America, and Latin America. Since the APEC meeting in Seattle in 1993, APEC has become an occasion for summits of leaders, providing a platform for leaders to discuss global, regional, and bilateral issues.

East Asia's open regionalism principle was striking when other regions were institutionalizing regional integration. The European Union (EU) was formally established with the ratification of the Maastricht Treaty, and NAFTA was ratified by the U.S. Congress in November 1993, right before the APEC summit.

APEC follows a gradualist and consensual approach. When Australian Prime Minister Bob Hawke proposed the idea of APEC in early 1989, he envisioned the organization to be similar to the Organization for Economic Cooperation and Development (OECD) to promote technical and economic cooperation. Over time, however, the United States, Canada, Australia, and New Zealand wanted to put trade liberalization on the agenda. An Eminent Persons Group was formed in 1993, which recommended establishment of a free trade agreement (FTA) for developed countries by 2010 and for developing nations by 2020. That vision was adopted at the APEC meeting in Bogor, Indonesia, in 1994. However, that goal soon appeared unrealistic.

An important reason for the failure of the Bogor vision is that East Asian governments resisted pressure from the West and introduced the principles of "concerted unilateralism," namely voluntary unilateral actions and granting these concessions on a nonreciprocal basis to all World Trade Organization (WTO) members. The United States was not interested in unilateral trade liberalization. Japan did not want to use APEC as a forum for trade liberation because of domestic concern. When the United States succeeded in putting a sectoral-based trade liberalization plan, so-called Early Voluntary Sectoral Liberalization (EVSL), on the APEC agenda, Japan destroyed the proposal by opposing liberalization of the fisheries and forestry sectors at the 1998 Kuala Lumpur meeting.[10] The failed EVSL process and the Asian financial crisis weakened APEC so much that it is now simply a diplomatic forum. The best it can hope for is to be what Hawke had envisioned in the first place, namely a forum for technical and economic cooperation. The United States has shifted attention elsewhere. East Asians are building East Asian-only groups.

A strong institution such as the WTO has specified obligations, legally binding commitments, reciprocity, and nondiscrimination. APEC, by contrast, has only uncertain, unilaterally defined commitments.[11] In fact, East Asian regional groups have exhibited weak institutionalization in general.[12] There was certainly not an Asian version of Maastricht, a grand scheme for regional integration.

While APEC dominated on the diplomatic agenda in the early 1990s, there were alternative institutional schemes for economic regionalism. The importance of the Association of Southeast Asian Nations (ASEAN) cannot be overstated. Created in 1967, ASEAN had five original members—Indonesia, Malaysia, the Philippines, Singapore, and Thailand—and later admitted Brunei (1984), Vietnam (1995), Laos and Myanmar (1997), and Cambodia (1999). ASEAN took on regionalism in the early 1990s, formulating a plan for the ASEAN Free Trade Area (AFTA). AFTA followed the principle of open regionalism.[13] AFTA has made some progress, but free trade is defined loosely, which explains why countries like Singapore have been trying to establish bilateral FTAs with outside countries on their own.

In a direct challenge to the West, Malaysian Prime Minister Mahathir bin Mohamad proposed in December 1990 an East Asian Economic Group (renamed the East Asian Economic Caucus or EAEC in 1991 on Indonesia's initiative) that would include only East Asian economies. However, faced with Washington's strong opposition and Tokyo's unwillingness to challenge the United States at the time, the Mahathir proposal failed to materialize. The EAEC was integrated into the APEC framework at the ASEAN Foreign Ministers' Meeting in June 1993.[14] Ironically, while opposing an East Asian trading group, the United States negotiated with Canada and Mexico to form NAFTA, which came into effect in 1994. Washington's perceived double standard was one reason why East Asian economies continue to explore East Asian regional cooperation.

The New East Asian Regionalism

The 1997–1998 Asian financial crisis was a watershed in East Asian political economy. East Asian economies have embraced a new form of regionalism since the crisis. The new East Asian regionalism was essentially a type of regionalism more institutionalized and more exclusive in membership, diverging significantly from the open regionalism principle discussed above.[15]

Monetary cooperation took the lead in East Asia's postcrisis regionalism. This made sense. After all, the threat to regional economy revealed by the crisis was financial volatility.[16] By contrast, a typical process is for trade agreements to happen first. Besides the financial crisis, other motivating forces for East Asian cooperation include regionalization of trade and investment, ASEAN's difficulties after the crisis, Northeast Asia's interest in joining AFTA, and defensive measures in response to the growth of EU and NAFTA.[17]

Since 1997 the East Asian group envisioned by Mahathir has quietly taken shape in the framework of "ASEAN Plus Three" (China, Japan, and South Korea), which has a membership virtually identical to that of the EAEC (Taiwan is not included in the current structure). ASEAN Plus Three convened its first meeting in Malaysia in December 1997. The discussion centered on monetary issues. In November 1999 in Manila, the third meeting of East Asian leaders issued a joint statement on East Asian cooperation for the first time. The areas for cooperation include trade and investment, monetary and financial cooperation through policy dialogues, human resource development, and security dialogue. Philippine President Joseph Estrada declared that the goal of ASEAN Plus Three was to create a common market, monetary union, and an East Asian Community.

At ASEAN's initiation, ASEAN Plus Three countries set up a currency swap scheme in Chiang Mai, Thailand, in May 2000 after earlier agreements among financial and banking officials. Although there had been similar agreements to swap and repurchase reserves, the Chiang Mai Initiative established a framework for future discussion on regional monetary cooperation. The swap basically means that when a country is in a currency crisis, it can borrow from the reserves of other East Asian countries. The Chiang Mai Initiative was reaffirmed at the ASEAN Plus Three leaders' meeting in Singapore in November 2000. The East Asian Vision Group was established to consider an East Asian FTA, a regional monetary fund and exchange rate regime, and regional institutional building.

The swap agreements are more symbolic than real at this point. Japan pledged up to $3 billion to South Korea, up to $2 billion to Thailand, and up to $1 billion to Malaysia. However, only 10 percent of the pledged funds would be automatically available. The rest is subjected to International Monetary Fund (IMF) approval. Nevertheless, the Chiang Mai currency swap agreements indicated East Asia's desire for deeper regional integration.

When it comes to trade, bilateral FTAs rather than an ASEAN Plus Three FTA have made the most progress so far. All major trading powers engage in bilateral FTA negotiations with countries in and outside East Asia. For example, Singapore launched formal negotiations with Japan for an economic partnership agreement (EPA) in October 2000 and with the United States for an FTA in November 2000, reaching agreements with Japan in January 2002 and with the United States in May 2003. Singapore reached an FTA agreement with South Korea in November 2004.

Although a latecomer in free trade talks, China has moved fast, reflecting and reinforcing its rapid rise in the region.[18] China and ASEAN announced in November 2000 a plan to create an FTA within 10 years. The proposed ASEAN-China FTA is a first for both ASEAN and China. Significantly, the ASEAN-China pact bypassed Japan and the United States, the two largest economies in the Asia Pacific region. Even a partially realized ASEAN-China FTA, which has a combined market of $1.7 billion and a total GDP of $2 trillion, would enhance China's political and economic influence in East Asia relative to Japan and the United States, an important objective for Beijing in the first place. Besides expanding trade and securing a friendly environment for economic development, Beijing also wants to be a founding member of a trading arrangement. Fifteen years spent in negotiation over WTO membership showed China's leaders the influence rule makers wield. Now Japan or others that want to join the new FTA will have to abide by the rules established by China and ASEAN.

The fact that it took China and ASEAN only one year to reach an agreement reflects strong mutual economic interests and political resolve from the two sides. China had an "early harvest" agreement with ASEAN, according to which China and ASEAN would begin to reduce tariffs on 600 categories of agricultural products and remove tariffs by 2006. On October 1, 2003, China and Thailand removed tariffs on 188 categories of fruits and vegetables, leading to a sharp increase in bilateral trade volumes in fruits and vegetables, with Thailand enjoying a significant surplus. In January 2007 China and ASEAN signed a service trade FTA.

China is uniquely positioned to take a proactive stance in FTA initiatives. First, China has a long way to go in trade liberalization, thus it has more room for concessions and greater incentives for potential partners. Second, although the United States and Japan have larger economies, China has an expanding market. Third, China is partly developed and partly developing, thus a better fit with ASEAN. By contrast, Japan prefers free trade talks with countries of similar stages of development. Moreover, this is free trade's moment in China. China joined the WTO on November 10, 2000, and could ride on that momentum for further trade liberalization arrangements. Fights for trade liberalization have already been fought and won. In the context of WTO-related structural adjustments, a new trade deal with ASEAN is unlikely to cause new domestic fights.

Weakened by the Asian financial crisis and facing intense global competition, ASEAN is desperately reaching out to strong economic partners, be it the United States, Japan, China, Australia, South Korea, or India. ASEAN has been discussing free trade with Japan, India, Australia, and New Zealand. ASEAN and the United States signed a trade and investment framework agreement in August 2006, which laid the foundation for FTA negotiations.

Facing Chinese competition, Japan made a bigger push for EPAs with ASEAN countries. Japan signed an EPA with Singapore in January 2002, with Thailand in principle in September 2005, with Malaysia in December 2005, and with the Philippines in September 2006. Japan is also negotiating with South Korea. Japan began studies of EPA with Vietnam in September 2006. Japan began negotiations with ASEAN in April 2005 and reached an EPA in principle on May 4, 2007.

East Asian countries have also been creating bilateral FTAs with countries outside East Asia. Japan signed an EPA with Mexico in September 2004 and with Chile in March 2007. China reached an FTA with Chile in November 2005 and began FTA negotiations with New Zealand in December 2004 and with Australia in May 2005. The United States has an FTA with Singapore, signed an FTA with South Korea in April 2007, and is now talking with Thailand. The United States and ASEAN reached a trade and investment framework agreement in August 2006, which laid a good foundation for a U.S.-ASEAN FTA. Thailand has an FTA with Australia. Singapore also has an FTA with Mexico.

The real progress in East Asian regionalism has been modest despite heavy activities in the diplomatic and academic realms.[19] Moreover, East Asian economies remain linked closely with outside powers like the United States. Nevertheless, the eagerness of the East Asian governments to pursue regionalism still needs to be explained. One should also not dismiss East Asian regionalism even if it is not as closed as the traditional regional blocs. In fact, it has been suggested that both Asia and Europe are "porous" regions because of globalization and American influence.[20]

"East Asia Plus" Versus "East Asia Minus" Regionalism

Former South Korean President Kim Dae Jung proposed the "East Asia Community." The East Asia Study Group explored the feasibility of the proposal in 2002. It had seventeen short-term objectives and nine medium- and long-term objectives to create an FTA zone, financial cooperation, and antiterrorism coordination. The special Japan-ASEAN Summit held in December 2003 passed the Tokyo Declaration, which treated the creation of the East Asian Community as an objective. At the ASEAN Plus Three Summit held in Laos in November 2004, a basic agreement on the East Asian Community was reached. Malaysia was selected to host the first East Asian Summit in December 2005, including ASEAN Plus Three countries as well as Australia, New Zealand, and India. Russia and Pakistan also want to join the East Asian Summit. Now the East Asian Summit members are considering the possibility of creating an FTA within 10 years.

Japan wanted to include Australia, New Zealand, and India in the East Asian Summit, a position supported by the United States. Both countries are concerned about China's growing influence in Asia and worry that an East Asian regional club would necessarily mean Chinese domination in the group. Mixing in outside powers like Australia and India in the East Asian Summit necessarily balances China's influence.

Japan proposed an East Asian EPA, starting in early 2006, that includes Japan, China, South Korea, ASEAN states, India, Australia, and New Zealand. Nikai

Toshihiro, from Japan's Ministry of Economy, Trade, and Industry (METI), told journalists on August 24, 2006, that ASEAN had accepted the proposal to discuss the East Asian EPA at the East Asian Summit to be held in the Philippines in December 2006.[21] The Japanese government is hoping to create an East Asian version of OECD, based on Japanese funding. METI is thus pushing for an East Asia plus regionalism. As Naoko Munakata put it simply, "the East Asia summit could accelerate cooperation between East Asian countries and the three new participants—Australia, India, and New Zealand—and thus might lead to the redefinition of an appropriate geographical scope of regional integration and community-building for the countries in East Asia."[22] Japan's EPA is broader than FTA and is often accompanied by discussion of values and other software issues. Not surprisingly, the Chinese government viewed the Japanese proposal as a ploy to win leadership in East Asia.

By contrast, China has been involved in studies of a Northeast Asia FTA as well as the ASEAN Plus Three FTA. Beijing made a proposal in 2004 for an East Asian FTA. It is too early to see whether the Japanese or the Chinese vision will prevail. It is harder for China because it cannot openly oppose inclusion of major powers like Australia and India, whose friendship Beijing is also seeking. However, what is likely to happen will be China's greater energy devoted to its FTA with ASEAN, which is really an East Asia minus regionalism. The Chinese government now frequently expresses its strong desire to open its growing market for Southeast Asian exports.

THEORIES OF REGIONALISM

Economic Theories of Regionalism

Economists who study trade regionalism focus on two questions. First, will trade regionalism increase or decrease welfare (i.e., material requisites of well-being)? Second, how does regionalism affect global trade negotiations? Their empirical research has yielded mixed results.[23]

Regional integration both creates and distorts trade. Some scholars have argued that regional cooperation is particularly beneficial for developing nations. First, regional cooperation contributes to peace and stability, which are necessary conditions for economic growth. Second, regional cooperation contributes to sound macroeconomic policies that are often required for the purpose. Third, regional cooperation facilitates greater technology transfers. Fourth, regional cooperation increases economies of scale. Fifth, regional cooperation improves production standards. Sixth, regional cooperation facilitates liberalization of national economy policies. Last, regional integration leads to greater participation in multilateral economic integration.[24]

For Asia, some empirical research has suggested that larger FTAs such as a would-be APEC FTA would bring great benefits to member states with little effect on nonmembers. By contrast, an ASEAN FTA would mean few benefits for members.[25]

Economists also debate the impact of regional trade agreements on the global trade regime.[26] Some see regional trade agreements as a stumbling block to global trade liberalization, using the trade diversion theory developed by Jacob Viner or the argument that regional agreements erode political support for global free trade negotiations.[27] The opposite view is that FTAs may be stepping stones or building blocks in that the member countries of FTAs have to adopt policy reforms.[28]

As discussed in Chapter 10, there are also economic theories such as the optimal currency area (OCA) theory about monetary integration. Similar to economic theories of trade regionalism, the focus of OCA theory is on costs and benefits.

As some scholars have pointed out, the economic theories of regional integration are wanting. For instance, why do states sometimes enter into trading arrangements that are not welfare maximizing?[29] This is particularly the case for East Asian regionalism. There are political economy reasons why East Asian governments have been so eager to build regional institutions even when economic rationale is not always convincing.

Political Economy Theories of Regionalism

Political scientists have developed a number of approaches to study regionalism. In their edited book on regionalism, Edward Mansfield and Helen Milner discussed four approaches, namely functional/institutionalist, realist, constructivist, and domestic approaches.[30] I will not address the domestic politics approach here since the domestic political economy of regionalism will be covered in the next section. Instead, I will discuss a strategic approach toward regionalism, which I think is the most useful for understanding East Asian regionalism.

Functional/institutionalist explanations. Studies of regional institutions were popular in the late 1950s and the early 1960s because a large number of regional groups were being created. In particular, several Western European countries were creating a European Economic Community. Integration thus became an important research topic. Integration is understood as a process that is multidimensional, political, economic, social, and cultural. Integration scholars see integration as a process that leads to the creation of a political community. Ernst Haas defined integration as a "process whereby political actors in several distinct national settings are persuaded to shift their loyalties, expectations, and political activities toward a new center, whose institutions possess or demand jurisdiction over the pre-existing national states."[31] Integration scholars share a common concern about how loyalty is being shifted from nations to a larger grouping, and they study communication and transactions within units of an integrating body. They also argue that there is a spillover effect; nations that have learned to cooperate in one area may also cooperate in other areas.

The integration school adopted a functionalist or neo-functionalist approach to regional integration. It is functional in that regional integrations were created to meet certain functional needs. David Mitrany laid the functionalist foundation for later works on integration and cooperation. In his 1943 book, *A Working Peace System*, he argued that in the twentieth century countries needed to cooperate to resolve many functional problems that go across national borders, accomplished by technicians outside the political context. Successes in one functional area set examples for cooperation in other functional areas (he called this ramification).[32]

Neo-functionalism built on the functionalist school and modified and tested hypotheses about integration. Ernst Haas, for example, is considered a neo-functionalist. Others include Philippe Schmitter, Leon Lindberg, Joseph S. Nye, Robert O. Keohane, and Lawrence Scheineman. In particular, Nye highlighted seven process mechanisms, namely functionalist linkage of tasks or spillover, rising transactions, deliberate linkages and coalition formation, elite socialization, regional group formation, ideological-identitive appeal, and involvement of external actors. He also used integrative potential for the conditions for integration, namely symmetry of unity, elite value complementarity, existence of pluralism, and capacity to adapt and respond.[33]

We can also use the theory of international regime to explain regionalism. International regimes refer to principles, norms, rules, and decision-making procedures. International regimes can be both formal and informal. International regimes overcome collective action problems by reducing transaction costs and encouraging reciprocity because of repeated interactions.[34] Basically, international regime theorists see regionalism as resulting from the incentives institutions may provide for countries in the region to cooperate for a common good.

Does functionalism/institutionalism apply to East Asia? Superficially, like regionalism everywhere else, East Asian regionalism is meant to serve functional purposes. That is why much focus was put on financial regionalism after the Asian financial crisis, because of the perceived needs. Trade regionalism is meant to increase intraregional trade, and monetary regionalism is meant to create stability in the regional monetary system. However, we do not see a process of regional integration as is seen in European integration. There is simply not an accepted process of shifting loyalties from national to regional institutions. Thus, functional arguments may explain the creation of the EU and NAFTA but not developments in East Asia and Latin America.[35] As discussed above, East Asian economies have made greater efforts at institutionalization since the Asian financial crisis, but we still see a weak institutionalized East Asia. Using institutionalist arguments, we can explain the weak regional institutionalization by failure to overcome the collective action problem in achieving regional cooperation.

Realist explanations. For neo-realists, domestic and transnational politics are not important in an anarchical world. As sovereign states need to fend for their survival, interstate cooperation is limited. Realism is a big tent, however, and some scholars who consider themselves realists have discussed international political economy issues.

First, security alliances shape the pattern of international trade.[36] Second, some scholars are interested in relative gains in international economic transactions, meaning that countries are supposed to be more concerned about whether other countries will gain relatively more than they should be about their own absolute gains from the interaction. Third, the presence of hegemony is important for the creation and maintenance of regional groups.[37]

East Asia does not have hegemony, which partly explains its difficulty in achieving economic cooperation. If we consider the United States to be the real hegemon in East Asia, that would create a serious problem for East Asian regionalism, since the United States would be suspicious of such a move. Moreover, dependence of some East Asian nations such as Japan on the United States weakens the resolve for regional integration. Last but not the least, tensions between major powers in the region such as China and Japan are problems for regionalism. In fact, narrow nationalisms have impeded regional integration in Northeast Asia.[38]

On the other hand, competition with other regions in the world is a major driving force for East Asian regionalism. In fact, the IMF handling of the Asian financial crisis has led to much resentment in the region toward the IMF and the United States. East Asians feel that they should unite to have a collective voice in global political economy.[39]

East Asian economies do exhibit some relative gains concerns. This is particularly the case for Japan worrying about China's rise. However, virtually all governments want to push for more rather than less regional integration. Moreover, smaller economies in the region often choose to bandwagon onto major powers, on Japan in the late 1980s and on China at present. As for the correlation between alliances and trade flows, the United States does trade heavily with its Asian allies, namely Japan, South Korea, and the Philippines. At the same time, it is absence of hostility rather than alliances per se that has had the greatest impact on trade distribution. After all, China, which does not have any formal alliance with any country, has become a major trading partner for all East Asian economies.

Constructivist explanations. The basic constructivist argument is that the world is what we make of it.[40] Put simply, it is not just material interests that shape developments in the world. To operationalize this approach, we examine issues like ideas, norms, and identity.

One impetus for East Asian regionalism is the familiarity with some of the ideas for regional integration that have been tested elsewhere in the world, particularly in Western Europe and North America. More broadly, the idea of East Asian regionalism matters in that proponents continue to promote regionalism against apparent odds.

If we look at norms and identity, we see formidable obstacles to East Asian regionalism. Norms of rules of law and democracy are not universally shared in the region. A rising China is not democratic. Compared with Europe and Latin America, East Asian awareness and identity are relatively weak, which is a major hindrance to regional integration.[41]

However, things are beginning to change in East Asia. First, on the political level, there has always been much rhetoric of an East Asian community. Although this has been largely reactive to Western pressure and criticism, over time, there has been more substance to it. Second, a significant development in East Asia is the emergence of a young generation of businesspeople who travel extensively in the region. Third, with advances in telecommunications, there has been a greater degree of Asian fusion movement: Hong Kong martial arts movies, Japanese cartoons and fashion, Taiwanese and South Korean pop music, and so on.[42] Note, however, that while regional awareness is growing in East Asia, it has largely grown along with global awareness. A stronger East Asian identity does not have to mean us against them.[43]

Last but not least, there are competing regionalist projects by the United States, Japan, China, and, to a lesser extent, other regional countries. These projects are related to the identities of these countries, namely a U.S.-dominated market economy, a Japan-led flying geese formation, a China-centered regional economy.[44]

Strategic explanations. Why does East Asia have weak institutionalization? Some have argued that Asian values and cultures explain weak institutionalization in the region.[45] However, the cultural argument does not make sense since East Asian nations have resorted to global legalized institutions. An alternative argument is that East Asia's weak institutionalization has resulted from state strategies.[46]

From a strategic perspective, the way to examine regionalism is to see the pros and cons for decision makers facing both the domestic and international arenas. Regionalism can be seen as a flexible policy instrument to meet a variety of objectives.

Why did East Asian nations insist on treating APEC as an open regionalism? The answer is straightforward: East Asians did not want to turn APEC into another trade forum in which the West dominates.[47] Why did East Asians turn to a more exclusive form of regionalism after the Asian financial crisis? Again, they did not want the West to dominate in these groups. Why do many East Asians reach out to players like India and Australia? The answer is that they do not want to see China dominate too much in regional groups.

One challenge East Asia faces in institutionalization is the very different national preferences and national strategies. For example, ASEAN nations have followed a noninterference approach since 1967. Non-Asians tend to be critical of this practice and believe that ASEAN cannot truly become an effective institution until it adopts a more assertive approach. ASEAN wants regional integration, but it has also been afraid that its role will be diluted in a larger grouping. ASEAN began the first preferential trade agreement in East Asia, forming the ASEAN Free Trade Area (AFTA) in 1992. While a similar effort was rejected after the mid-1980s due to concerns that regionalism would reduce the members' ties with the global economic system, regionalism came to be viewed as furthering their integration into the global market. ASEAN hoped regional integration would make it more attractive for FDI and more competitive in the global marketplace.[48] Before the Asian financial crisis, it insisted that APEC exercised an open regionalism. The crisis has significantly weakened the prestige and effectiveness of ASEAN. There is a growing sense that ASEAN needs to hook up with bigger players outside, be it China or Japan or the United States. There is a growing division within ASEAN. Indonesia is weakened. Impatient with the pace of the ASEAN Free Trade Area, Singapore is striking its own bilateral FTAs.

Japan did not see many benefits in linking up with its Asian neighbors if it meant losing access to North America and Western Europe. That is why Japan was interested in open regionalism.[49] Makoto Kuroda, a former Ministry of International Trade and Industry (MITI) vice minister, commented in 1989 that although East Asia would integrate naturally, it should not seek to build its own economic bloc to counter the creation of blocs in other parts of the world because Asia would lose more by confronting the other groups. Rather, it should promote a global free trade regime.[50]

Japan shifted its strategy in favor of regionalism in the late 1990s. The policy shift was reflected in the 1999 white paper on trade by MITI. The report concluded that Japan was an anomaly in the international trade system as most WTO members are involved in regional trade arrangements and that regional FTAs can contribute to the global free trade regime. While Japan had been active in the global financial system, it paid more attention to regional financial initiatives in East Asia after 2000. Japan did not see this shift as choosing between globalism and regionalism. Rather, Japan saw a stronger regional financial structure as complementary to a strong global financial structure.[51] This shift reflected Japan's greater interdependence on East Asia around the same time. Take Japan's electronics industry, for example. Although Japan experienced a significant decline in the 1990s, its electronics industry experienced a comeback after 2000 because of greater trade and investment in East Asia. Unlike in the previous periods, Japanese electronics firms now are more dependent on East Asia and increasingly play an equal role or even secondary role in some areas to other East Asian firms.[52]

In yet another turn, Japan now does not really want to promote East Asia–only regionalism. Rather, Japan wants to include Australia, New Zealand, and India in East Asian economic regionalism. The main reason is that Japan sees its relations with the United States as the most important and is increasingly concerned about being in a group where China might dominate.

South Korea shifted in favor of East Asian regionalism around the same time as Japan did. South Korea began its FTA negotiation with Chile in 1998 and concluded the trade deal in 2002. South Korea then launched negotiations with various other partners, partly to keep up with China and Japan.[53] South Korea is interested in regional integration because it serves its economic and political interests. Some South Koreans also feel that South Korea is in a unique position to take the lead because it will not arouse suspicion of other Asian nations, unlike China and Japan. Some non-Korean analysts endorse such a view of Korean centrality in Northeast Asian integration.[54]

China is a relative latecomer in initiating regionalist projects. But the Chinese increasingly feel that China should act as a great power and take the lead in regional integration. Once China made the policy choice, it acted quickly. On November 25, 2000, at the ASEAN Plus China Summit, Premier Zhu Rongji indicated interest in an FTA between China and ASEAN. At the meeting, Zhu also expressed China's wish for ASEAN Plus Three to be the main channel for East Asian regional cooperation.[55] China has a comparative advantage compared with countries like the United States. U.S. negotiators need to include the environment and labor conditions to win congressional approval, and they also need to protect sensitive sectors at home. By contrast, China adopts a simpler strategy of lowering tariffs without qualifying conditions.

Much of the drive for regionalism is defensive in nature. East Asia feels the pressure from other regions' regionalism as well as competitive pressure from within the region. With China taking a lead in forming an FTA with ASEAN, Japan and South Korea also feel they have to do something.[56]

POLITICAL ECONOMY OF REGIONALISM

There are political reasons for regionalism and regionalism has political consequences. How does domestic politics explain regionalism? Obviously, domestic politics may get in the way of regional cooperation if citizens in the countries involved
do not trust each other and if politicians utilize narrow-minded nationalism to
advance their own political agenda. It has been pointed out how East Asian domestic politics have hindered regional cooperation, particularly in Northeast Asia.[57]

From a political economy perspective, like any other policy shift in foreign economic policy, a country's decision on regionalism has a distributive effect on
domestic groups by generating losers and winners. Losers will oppose the policy
while winners will endorse it. Thus, a country's policy regarding regionalism is
often consistent with the most powerful and organized social groups. For example, South Korea's politically sensitive sectors of agriculture, forestry, and fishery
worried about an FTA with Chile while the manufacturing sector supported it.
The reason was Chile's perceived comparative advantage in agriculture, forestry,
and fisheries.[58] By contrast, winners lobby for forming FTAs. As a case in point,
Japan's leading business group Japan Business Federation (*Keidanren*) promoted
and was heavily involved in the negotiations over EPAs both to advance Japanese
companies' business interests overseas and to force structural adjustment of
uncompetitive firms at home.[59]

Politicians select liberalization in certain areas to advance regionalism to balance their needs to be reelected and to accommodate special interest groups.[60]
This dynamic is seen more clearly in more democratic regimes, such as Japan and
South Korea. Although it might not be obvious to outsiders, the same dynamic
works in less transparent governments such as China as well. At the same time,
consistent with earlier discussions of the developmental state, East Asian governments also play an important role in shaping national interests, including those
regarding regionalism.

Domestic politics can be used to explain the rapid spread of regionalism. From
a domestic politics perspective, once a regional group is formed, the firms that
export to the group become more energized to lobby for entry into the arrangement, often tipping the political balance in the country. The more countries join,
the greater energies the exporting firms in nonmember countries will try to per-
suade their governments to join. We thus see a domino effect.[61]

More broadly, the expanding middle class in East Asia, created by rapid economic growth, provides a social basis for regionalism. With similar professional
background and lifestyle, the middle class throughout the region constitutes an
expanding regional consumer market.[62]

At the same time, the need to form FTAs has had a strong impact on domestic politics in East Asia. Competitive regionalist projects have forced the countries to do more to open up trade. As a case in point, Japan now has political and strategic interests not to accommodate its protectionist agricultural sector as much as it would otherwise. FTA negotiations have transformed the Japanese policy debate and weakened public support for agricultural protection. The Japanese business community has become more vocal against agricultural protection policy. FTAs also expand Japanese agricultural exports even though they do not nearly match agricultural imports at this point.[63]

Besides competition with Japan and other major trading powers, Chinese advocates for regional integration openly see one benefit of regionalism as using "external power" to further domestic reform.[64] In the early 1990s, China had the highest level of tariffs among the APEC countries, which meant that it had to make greater adjustment. China was willing to do so because it was trying to join the WTO, which also required it to reduce tariffs.

CONCLUSION

Building on discussion in the previous chapters, this chapter suggests that regionalization has increased in recent decades, but East Asian companies have not been trading more with each other against their best interests just to promote regionalization. The United States and the European Union remain active participants in East Asian economy. At the same time, although there is little bias embedded in growing regional integration, the fact that East Asian nations have become more interdependent with each other provides an important rationale for them to institutionalize regional cooperation.

East Asian regionalism is characterized by East Asian enthusiasm and limited institutionalization. East Asian regional integration began as open regionalism and is now moving toward formal institutions. Economically, it makes sense to have a regional grouping because strong regional links already exist, because other regions have already built regional groups, and because a regional group does not necessarily impede a global free trade regime. Politically, it has been difficult to establish East Asian regionalism because of strong domestic resistance, particularly in leading countries like Japan, because the United States does not want to be excluded, and because China and Japan have a tense political relationship. At the same time, competition between major powers like China and Japan also serves to push forward trade liberalization as they need to present better terms to trading partners than they would have otherwise.

If successful, East Asian regionalism would help create a three-pillar world economy. It would give East Asia greater negotiating power, although that might also mean greater difficulties in global coordination. Regionalism would necessarily affect regional distribution of power. China might be the initial winner, but Japan and other countries would also have their shot in this ongoing game. A more compelling regionalism might help to further reform domestic political economy, but a weaker version of regional institution in place of a stronger global institution would delay the process of reform.

SUGGESTED READINGS

Armstrong, Charles K., Gilbert Rozman, Samuel S. Kim, and Stephen Kotkin, eds. *Korea at the Center: Dynamics of Regionalism in Northeast Asia* (Armonk, N.Y.: M. E. Sharpe, 2006).

Bergsten, C. Fred, ed. *Whither APEC? The Progress to Date and Agenda for the Future* (Washington, D.C.: Institute for International Economics, 1999).

Bowles, Paul. "Asia's Post-Crisis Regionalism: Bringing the State Back In, Keeping the (United) States Out." *Review of International Political Economy* 9, no. 2 (May 2002): 244–270.

Dieter, Heribert, and Richard Higgott. "Exploring Alternative Theories of Economic Regionalism: From Trade to Finance in Asian Co-operation?" *Review of International Political Economy* 10, no. 3 (August 2003): 430–454.

Friedman, Edward, and Sung Chull Kim, eds. *Regional Cooperation and Its Enemies in Northeast Asia: The Impact of Domestic Forces* (London: Routlege, 2006).

Haas, Ernst B. *The Uniting of Europe: Political, Social, and Economic Forces 1950–1957* (Stanford: Stanford University Press, 1958).

Higgott, Richard, and Richard Stubbs. "Competing Conceptions of Economic Regionalism: APEC Versus EAEC in the Asia Pacific." *Review of International Political Economy* 2, no. 3 (Summer 1995): 516–535.

Kahler, Miles. "Legalization as Strategy: The Asia-Pacific Case." In *Legalization and World Politics*, ed. Judith L. Goldstein, Miles Kahler, Robert O. Keohane, and Anne-Marie Slaughter (Cambridge: MIT Press, 2001), 165–187.

Katzenstein, Peter J. *A World of Regions: Asia and Europe in the American Imperium* (Ithaca, N.Y.: Cornell University Press, 2005).

Katzenstein, Peter J., and Takashi Shiraishi, eds. *Beyond Japan: The Dynamics of East Asian Regionalism* (Ithaca, N.Y.: Cornell University Press, 2006).

Kim, Samuel S. "Regionalization and Regionalism in East Asia." *Journal of East Asian Studies* 4, no. 1 (January–April 2004): 39–67.

Krueger, Anne O. "Are Preferential Trading Arrangements Trade Liberalizing or Protectionist?" *Journal of Economic Perspectives* 13, no. 4 (Autumn 1999): 105–124.

Levy, Philip I. "A Political-Economic Analysis of Free Trade Agreements." *American Economic Review* 87, no. 4 (September 1997): 506–519.

Lincoln, Edward J. *East Asian Economic Regionalism* (Brookings Institution Press, 2004).

Mansfield, Edward D., and Helen V. Milner, eds. *The Political Economy of Regionalism* (New York: Columbia University Press, 1997).

Munakata, Naoko. *Transforming East Asia: The Evolution of Regional Economic Integration* (Washington, D.C.: Brookings Institution Press and Tokyo: Research Institute of Economy, Trade and Industry, 2006).

Panagariya, Arvind. "Preferential Trade Liberalization: The Traditional Theory and New Developments." *Journal of Economic Literature* 38, no. 2 (June 2000): 287–331.

Pempel, T. J., ed. *Remapping East Asia: The Construction of a Region* (Ithaca, N.Y.: Cornell University Press, 2005).

Ravenhill, John. "APEC Adrift: Implications for Economic Regionalism in Asia and the Pacific." *Pacific Review* 13, no. 2 (2000): 319–333.

Rozman, Gilbert. *Northeast Asia's Stunted Regionalism: Bilateral Distrust in the Shadow of Globalization* (Cambridge: Cambridge University Press, 2004).

Shambaugh, David, ed. *Power Shift: China and Asia's New Dynamic* (Berkeley: University of California Press, 2006).

Yoshimatsu, Hidetaka. "Japan's Keidanren and Free Trade Agreements: Societal Interests and Trade Policy." *Asian Survey* 45, no. 2 (March/April 2005): 258–278.

NOTES

1. Benedict Anderson, *Imagined Communities: Reflections on the Origins and Spread of Nationalism* (London: Verso, 1983).

2. Andrew Hurrell, "Regionalism in Theoretical Perspective," in *Regionalism in World Politics: Regional Organization and International Order,* ed. Louise Fawcett and Andrew Hurrell (New York: Oxford University Press, 1995), 37–73.

3. For discussion of regionalism and regionalization, see Edward D. Mansfield and Helen V. Milner, "The Political Economy of Regionalism: An Overview," in *The Political Economy of Regionalism,* ed. Edward D. Mansfield and Helen V. Milner (New York: Columbia University Press, 1997), 3–4; Samuel S. Kim, "Regionalization and Regionalism in East Asia," *Journal of East Asian Studies* 4, no. 1 (January–April 2004): 40–41.

4. Naoko Munakata, *Transforming East Asia: The Evolution of Regional Economic Integration* (Washington, D.C.: Brookings Institution Press and Tokyo: Research Institute of Economy, Trade and Industry, 2006), 37–61.

5. Ronald I. McKinnon with Gunther Schnabl, "Synchronized Business Cycles in East Asia and Fluctuation in the Yen/Dollar Exchange Rate," in *Exchange Rates Under the East Asian Dollar Standard: Living with Conflicted Virtue,* ed. Ronald I. McKinnon (Cambridge: MIT Press, 2005), 53–76.

6. Richard Stubbs, "Asia-Pacific Regionalization and the Global Economy: A Third Form of Capitalism," *Asian Survey* 35, no. 9 (September 1995): 785–797.

7. T. J. Pempel, "Introduction: Emerging Webs of Regional Connectedness," in *Remapping East Asia: The Construction of a Region,* ed. T. J. Pempel (Ithaca, N.Y.: Cornell University Press, 2005), 1–28; Paul Evans, "Between Regionalism and Regionalization: Policy Networks and the Nascent East Asian Institutional Identity," in *Remapping East Asia,* 195–215.

8. For comparative studies of regionalism, see Jamie De Melo and Arvind Pana-gariya, eds., *New Dimensions in Regional Integration* (Cambridge: Cambridge University Press, 1993); Mansfield and Milner, eds., *The Political Economy of Regionalism* (New York: Columbia University Press, 1997).

9. C. Fred Bergsten, "Open Regionalism," *World Economy* 20, no. 5 (1997): 545–565; and C. Fred Bergsten, ed., *Whither APEC? The Progress to Date and Agenda for the Future* (Washington, D.C.: Institute for International Econom-ics, 1997).

10. John Ravenhill, "APEC Adrift: Implications for Economic Regionalism in Asia and the Pacific," *Pacific Review* 13, no. 2 (2000): 319–333. For a discussion of broader criticism of several countries, see Okamoto, *Trade Liberalization and APEC.*

11. Ravenhill, "APEC and the WTO."

12. Miles Kahler, "Legalization as Strategy: The Asia-Pacific Case," in *Legalization and World Politics,* ed. Judith L. Goldstein, Miles Kahler, Robert O. Keohane, and Anne-Marie Slaughter (Cambridge: MIT Press, 2001), 165–187.

13. Paul Bowles and Brian MacLean, "Understanding Trade Bloc Formation: The Case of the ASEAN Free Trade Area," *Review of International Political Economy* 3, no. 2 (Summer 1996): 319–348.

14. Richard Higgott and Richard Stubbs, "Competing Conceptions of Economic Regionalism: APEC Versus EAEC in the Asia Pacific," *Review of International Political Economy* 2, no. 3 (Summer 1995): 516–535.

15. Paul Bowles, "Asia's Post-Crisis Regionalism: Bringing the State Back In, Keeping the (United) States Out," *Review of International Political Economy* 9, no. 2 (May 2002): 244–270.

16. Heribert Dieter and Richard Higgott, "Exploring Alternative Theories of Eco-nomic Regionalism: From Trade to Finance in Asian Co-operation?" *Review of International Political Economy* 10, no. 3 (August 2003): 430–454.

17. Kim, "Regionalization and Regionalism in East Asia."

18. David Shambaugh, ed., *Power Shift: China and Asia's New Dynamic* (Berkeley: University of California Press, 2006).

19. Lincoln, *East Asian Economic Regionalism.*

20. Peter J. Katzenstein, *A World of Regions: Asia and Europe in the American Imperium* (Ithaca, N.Y.: Cornell University Press, 2005).

21. *Yomiuri shimbun,* August 24, 2006, www.yomiuri.co.jp/atmoney/news/ 20060824ib25.htm.

22. Munakata, *Transforming East Asia,* 15.

23. Wilfred J. Ethier, "The New Regionalism," *The Economic Journal* 108, no. 449 (July 1998): 1149.

24. Naya, *Asian Development Experience,* 97–101.

25. Jeffrey D. Lewis and Sherman Robinson, "Partners or Predators? The Impact of Regional Trade Liberalization on Indonesia," Policy Research Working Paper No. 1626, Country Operations Division, World Bank, Washington, D.C., July 1996.

26. Anne O. Krueger, "Are Preferential Trading Arrangements Trade Liberalizing or Protectionist?" *Journal of Economic Perspectives* 13, no. 4 (Autumn 1999): 105–124; Arvind Panagariya, "Preferential Trade Liberalization: The Traditional Theory and New Developments," *Journal of Economic Literature* 38, no. 2 (June 2000): 287–331.

27. Jacob Viner, *The Customs Union Issue* (New York: Carnegie Endowment for International Peace, 1950); Bela Balassa, *The Theory of Economic Integration* (Homewood, Ill.: Richard Irwin, 1961); Jagdish Bhagwati, "Regionalism and Multilateralism: An Overview," in *New Dimensions in Regional Integration* (see note 8), 22–51; Philip I. Levy, "A Political-Economic Analysis of Free Trade Agreements," *American Economic Review* 87, no. 4 (September 1997): 506–519.

28. Wilfred J. Ethier, "Regionalism in a Multilateral World," *Journal of Political Economy* 106, no. 6 (December 1998), 1214–1245.

29. Bowles and MacLean, "Understanding Trade Bloc Formation," 324.

30. Mansfield and Milner, "Political Economy of Regionalism," 1–19.

31. Ernst B. Haas, *The Uniting of Europe: Political, Social, and Economic Forces 1950–1957* (Stanford: Stanford University Press, 1958), 16.

32. David Mitrany, *A Working Peace System* (Chicago: Quadrangle Books, 1966).

33. Joseph Nye, *Peace in Parts: Integration and Conflict in Regional Organization* (Boston: Little, Brown, 1971).

34. Stephen D. Krasner, ed., *International Regimes* (Ithaca, N.Y.: Cornell University Press, 1983); Robert O. Keohane, *After Hegemony: Cooperation and Discord in the World Political Economy* (Princeton: Princeton University Press, 1984) and *International Institutions and State Power: Essays in International Relations Theory* (Boulder: Westview Press, 1989).

35. Joseph M. Grieco, "Systemic Sources of Variation in Regional Institutionalization in Western Europe, East Asia, and the Americas," in *The Political Economy of Regionalism* (see note 3), 164–187.
36. Joanne Gowa, *Allies, Adversaries, and International Trade* (Princeton: Princeton University Press, 1994).
37. Grieco, "Systemic Sources of Variation in Regional Institutionalization."
38. Gilbert Rozman, *Northeast Asia's Stunted Regionalism: Bilateral Distrust in the Shadow of Globalization* (Cambridge: Cambridge University Press, 2004).
39. Bowles, "Asia's Post-Crisis Regionalism."
40. Alexander Wendt, *Social Theory of International Politics* (New York: Cambridge University Press, 1999).
41. Kim, "Regionalization and Regionalism in East Asia," 44–47.
42. David Leheny, "A Narrow Place to Cross Swords: Soft Power and the Politics of Japanese Popular Culture in East Asia," in *Beyond Japan: The Dynamics of East Asian Regionalism,* ed. Peter J. Katzenstein and Takashi Shiraishi (Ithaca, N.Y.: Cornell University Press, 2006), 211–233.
43. For a broad discussion of how globalization has affected East Asia, see Samuel S. Kim, ed., *East Asia and Globalization* (Lanham, Md.: Rowman and Littlefield, 2000).
44. Ngai-Ling Sum, "The NICs and Competing Strategies of East Asian Regionalism," in *Regionalism and World Order,* ed. Andrew Gamble and Anthony Payne (New York: St. Martin's Press, 1996), 207–245.
45. Carl J. Green, "APEC and Trans-Pacific Dispute Management," *Law and Policy in International Business* 26, no. 3 (1995): 719–734.
46. Kahler, "Legalization as Strategy."
47. Ravenhill, "APEC Adrift."
48. Suthiphand Chirathivat, "The ASEAN Perspective on East Asian-Wide Regionalism," in *New East Asian Regionalism: Causes, Progress, and Country Perspectives,* ed. Charles Harvie, Fukunari Kimura, and Hyun-Hoon Lee (Northampton, Mass.: Edward Elgar, 2005), 151.
49. For Japan's interest in open regionalism, see Kozo Kato's chapter in Peter Katzenstein, Natasha Hamilton-Hart, Kozo Kato, and Ming Yue, *Asian Regionalism* (Ithaca, N.Y.: Cornell University East Asia Program, 2000).
50. Cited in Charles Smith, "Protectionist Fear Over Trade Blocs," *Far Eastern Economic Review,* June 8, 1989, 68.
51. Natasha Hamilton-Hart, "Creating a Regional Arena: Financial Sector Reconstruction, Globalization, and Region-Making," in *Beyond Japan* (see note 42), 108–129.
52. Dieter Ernst, "Searching for a New Role in East Asian Regionalization—Japanese Production Networks in the Electronics Industry," in *Beyond Japan* (see note 42), 161–187.

53. Chan-Hyun Sohn and Hyun-Hoon Lee, "Korea's Perspectives on East Asian Regionalism," in *New East Asian Regionalism* (see note 48), 171–212.

54. Charles K. Armstrong, Gilbert Rozman, Samuel S. Kim, and Stephen Kotkin, eds., *Korea at the Center: Dynamics of Regionalism in Northeast Asia* (Armonk, N.Y.: M. E. Sharpe, 2006).

55. Hu Zhaoliang, "Dongya hezuo de xianzhuang yu weilai" [The present and future of East Asian cooperation], *Guoji wenti yanjiu* [Journal of International Studies] 1 (2002): 21–25. Hu is a senior Chinese diplomat.

56. Stephan Haggard, "The Balance of Power, Globalization, and Democracy: International Relations Theory in Northeast Asia," *Journal of East Asian Studies* 4, no. 1 (January–April 2004): 1–38.

57. Rozman, *Northeast Asia's Stunted Regionalism*; Edward Friedman and Sung Chull Kim, eds., *Regional Cooperation and Its Enemies in Northeast Asia: The Impact of Domestic Forces* (London: Routlege, 2006).

58. Sohn and Lee, "Korea's Perspectives on East Asian Regionalism," 181.

59. Hidetaka Yoshimatsu, "Japan's Keidanren and Free Trade Agreements: Societal Interests and Trade Policy," *Asian Survey* 45, no. 2 (March/April 2005): 258–278.

60. Helen Milner, "Industries, Governments, and Regional Trade Blocs," in *The Political Economy of Regionalism* (see note 3), 77–106.

61. Richard E. Baldwin, "A Domino Theory of Regionalism," in *Trading Blocs: Alternative Approaches to Analyzing Preferential Trade Agreements,* ed. Jagdish Bhagwati, Pravin Krishna, and Arvind Panagariya (Cambridge: MIT Press, 1999), 479–502.

62. Takashi Shiraishi, "The Third Wave: Southeast Asia and Middle-Class Formation in the Making of a Region," in *Beyond Japan* (see note 42), 237–271.

63. Munakata, *Transforming East Asia,* 143–144.

64. Feng Zhaokui, "Zouxiang dongya ziyou maoyiqu zhi lu" [The path to East Asian free trade area], *Shijie jingji yu zhengzhi* [World Economics and International Politics] 3 (2002): 21–26.

INDEX

Note: *f* refers to figures and *t* to tables.